Economics and Morality

SOCIETY FOR ECONOMIC ANTHROPOLOGY (SEA) MONOGRAPHS

Dolores Koenig, American University
General Editor, Society for Economic Anthropology

Monographs for the Society for Economic Anthropology contain original essays that explore the connections between economics and social life. Each year's volume focuses on a different theme in economic anthropology. Earlier volumes were published with the University Press of America, Inc. (#1–15, 17), Rowman & Littlefield Publishers, Inc. (#16). The monographs are now published jointly by AltaMira Press and the Society for Economic Anthropology (http://sea.org.ohio-state.edu).

No. 18 Jean Ensminger, ed., *Theory in Economic Anthropology*
No. 19 Jeffrey H. Cohen and Norbert Dannhaeuser, eds., *Economic Development: An Anthropological Approach*
No. 20 Gracia Clark, ed., *Gender at Work in Economic Life*
No. 21 Cynthia Werner and Duran Bell, eds., *Values and Valuables: From the Sacred to the Symbolic*
No. 22 Lillian Trager, ed., *Migration and Economy: Global and Local Dynamics*
No. 23 E. Paul Durrenberger and Judith Martí, eds., *Labor in Cross-Cultural Perspective*
No. 24 Richard Wilk, ed., *Fast Food/Slow Food*
No. 25 Lisa Cliggett and Christopher A. Pool, eds., *Economies and the Transformation of Landscape*
No. 26 Katherine E. Browne and B. Lynne Milgram, eds., *Economics and Morality: Anthropological Approaches*

To find more books in this series, go to www.altamirapress.com/series.

Economics and Morality

Anthropological Approaches

Edited by
Katherine E. Browne
and B. Lynne Milgram

ALTAMIRA
PRESS
A division of
ROWMAN & LITTLEFIELD PUBLISHERS, INC.
Lanham • New York • Toronto • Plymouth, UK

ALTAMIRA PRESS
A division of Rowman & Littlefield Publishers, Inc.
A wholly owned subsidiary of The Rowman & Littlefield Publishing Group, Inc.
4501 Forbes Boulevard, Suite 200, Lanham, MD 20706
www.altamirapress.com

Estover Road, Plymouth PL6 7PY, United Kingdom

British Library Cataloguing in Publication Information Available

Library of Congress Cataloging-in-Publication Data

Economics and morality : anthropological approaches / edited by Katherine E. Browne and B. Lynne Milgram.
p. cm.—(Society for Economic Anthropology (SEA) monographs)
Includes bibliographical references and index.
ISBN-13: 978-0-7591-1201-8 (hardcover : alk. paper)
ISBN-10: 0-7591-1201-0 (hardcover)
eISBN-13: 978-0-7591-1226-1
eISBN-10: 0-7591-1226-6
1. Economic anthropology—Case studies. 2. Economics—Moral and ethical aspects—Case studies. I. Browne, Katherine E., 1953- II. Milgram, B. Lynne (Barbara Lynne), 1948- III. Society for Economic Anthropology (U.S.)

GN448.E275 2009
306.3—dc22 2008019350

Printed in the United States of America

∞™ The paper used in this publication meets the minimum requirements of American National Standard for Information Sciences—Permanence of Paper for Printed Library Materials, ANSI/NISO Z39.48-1992.

Contents

List of Figures and Tables

FIGURES

TABLE

Acknowledgments

Producing *Economics and Morality* has been a work of pleasure from start to finish. From the beginning, we believed the topic was timely and promising for anthropological consideration. We are grateful to the Society for Economic Anthropology (SEA) for selecting our theme for its 2006 annual meeting. In the process of organizing the conference, from which come the papers for this volume, we had the good fortune of help from Paul Rivera of California State University, Channel Islands, who deftly handled all the local arrangements. Thanks to him the Ventura, California, site provided a beautiful ocean setting and facilities that encouraged a genial exchange of ideas. We were fortunate to have drawn a distinguished group of international scholars whose provocative papers kept collective discussions animated and productive. Now, with this book, we aim to build on the energy and insights from this conference and encourage an explicit research agenda devoted to an anthropology of economics and morality.

We are sincerely grateful to all our contributors for sharing their work, enduring multiple rounds of revisions, and making the job of editing this volume a smooth one. We would also like to thank Bill Maurer for generously agreeing to write the afterword for the volume. We wish to thank the three external reviewers of the volume, who provided thorough and incisive comments to each author and contributed to helping all of us achieve a better piece of scholarship. We also thank Dolores Koenig who, as SEA series editor, has been a most supportive coach, shepherding us well through the hoops of preparing an edited volume. We also extend our special thanks to Jack Meinhardt and to all of the production team at AltaMira Press, who have been wonderful to work with.

As coeditors, we feel most fortunate to have had the opportunity to work with each other to bring this volume to fruition. We have enjoyed every phase of the work—thinking about the topic, organizing the conference, working with contributors, and putting the book together. Good collaborative projects require a special kind of collegiality, one based on trust, generosity, and reciprocity. The spirit of these gifts have served us well and, we believe, helped us produce a strong and useful book.

—Kate Browne and Lynne Milgram

Economics and Morality: Introduction

Katherine E. Browne

> Morality represents the way people would like the world to work—whereas economics represents how it actually *does* work.
>
> —Stephen Levitt (2005)

> Thinking of the market system as morally neutral is dangerous.
>
> —Daniel Hausman and Michael McPherson (2006)

> Anthropologists are not very happy in the marketplace and this gives many of them a jaundiced perspective on money.
>
> —Keith Hart (2005)

> Why is the world today so very different from that of our ancestors? I think we're unlikely to make progress in answering [the] question if we insist at the outset that "capitalism" just *means* modern greed.
>
> —Deirdre McCloskey (2006)

Some of us doubt that there is any such thing as morality in the realm of economic life. Some say moral commitments in an economy characterize only precapitalist societies where systems of reciprocity bind people to each other and to the social good. Others point out that capitalist systems are inherently moral because they enshrine the rights of individuals. Today, as capitalism spreads its logic to remote parts of the world, many economists and economic thinkers such as Thomas Friedman (2005) argue that the morality of individual choice is winning the day as globalization and technology work to flatten historic inequalities of opportunity. At the same time, a tiny but growing minority of economists, such as Nobel Prize–winning economist Amartya Sen, argue that moral principles will remain absent from neoliberal economies unless we deliberately shift the focus from measures of income growth to measures of human capabilities and different kinds of freedoms. With such wildly disparate assertions about morality and economics, how can we properly evaluate all these competing claims? How do we reckon with the contradictions and confusion of so many different ideas?[1]

The variability in how people view what constitutes morality requires us to ask: What exactly is morality? Sociologist Andrew Sayer, who has written at length about the "moral economy," offers a robust set of parameters:

> The moral concerns lay norms (informal and formal), conventions, values, dispositions and commitments regarding what is just and what constitutes good behavior in relation to others, and implies certain broader conceptions of the good or well-being. (2005)

This definition is useful precisely because it allows us to include religious values and proscriptions, as well as individual and cultural-level views about what is good and right. And, as Sayer (2005) explains, an inclusive view of morality makes possible a consideration not only of how moral ideas are expressed in our economic choices, but also of how the organization of the economy affects social well-being. To think about the relationship of morality and economics is to connect the most abstract and perhaps meaningful realm of human life with the most banal—to consider how the everyday matter of living gets infused with our deepest beliefs of what we live for and how we live well. These fascinating intersections are at the heart of this volume.

AIMS AND SCOPE OF THE VOLUME

In *Economics and Morality*, we seek to illuminate multiple kinds of analyses relating morality and economic behavior in particular kinds of economic systems. The chapters included here represent fieldwork in indigenous societies of variable scales and degrees of integration with capitalist systems, as well as fieldwork from a variety of capitalist societies, including those organized around welfare-state economies, economies shaped by an Islamic state, and neoliberal Western states. The papers intersect in interesting and numerous ways, but to capture the thrust of their arguments, we have grouped the papers into three sets. In the first set, we include work focused on moral challenges in non-Western economic systems undergoing profound change (Robbins, Walsh, and Little). The second set of papers focuses on grassroots movements and moral claims generated from the ground up in the context of capitalism (Halperin, Prentice, Werner, and Dolan). The third set focuses on new movements taking place within corporate and state institutions to forward a more explicit, moral basis for enacting the terms of capitalist economic behavior (Garsten and Hernes, Rajak, and Pitluck). An afterword by Bill Maurer offers a hopeful perspective to conclude the volume.

The anthropological approach of this volume presents two distinct contributions to the larger discussion of economics and morality in the social sciences. First, anthropological insights draw their value and endurance from on-the-ground, ethnographic investigation. Each of the chapters here presents original analyses anchored to data from firsthand fieldwork. Recognizing and engaging with concrete realities often complicates theory and, in the course of this volume, authors suggest a number of ways that theoretical arguments about the gift and about morality in market systems must be reconsidered to accommodate data on the ground. Second, the anthropological tradition of studying non-Western as well as Western societies brings critical perspectives to both the congruities and discontinuities between very different kinds of societies. In this volume, ethnographic work reveals the relevance of moral systems in contemporary non-Western societies to the understanding of moralities and economies in Western societies.[2]

The concerns of morality and economics seem intuitively to belong to the fields of philosophy and economics. At one time, during the Enlightenment period in Europe and after the church no longer held sway as the exclusive keeper of knowledge and arbiter of moral principles, moral and economic philosophy constituted a unified area of study. Adam Smith's own writings during this era of classical political economy reflected the integrated study of morality and economics. But in the late eighteenth century, the holistic approach of Western classical studies to the analysis of human life became parsed out into discrete disciplines, and philosophy became separated from economics. Since that time, Western philosophers have tended to study moral meanings and systems of thought, but not how these esoteric values get exercised in the course of everyday economic life. For their part, Western economists have focused on the workings and outcomes of market systems—how things get produced, distributed, and exchanged, as well as the effects of regulation and deregulation on these processes. Rarely have they considered whether and how moral meanings may be implicated in economic choices, much less how these meanings are significant or how they might derive from influences beyond individual tastes and preferences.[3]

Anthropologists are in a privileged position to document the local upheavals or continuities in moral systems of meaning once capitalist influences appear in indigenous societies, and some have done so.[4] However, a variety of factors may have discouraged anthropological scholarship focused on these issues. To begin with, there are no models to react to in disciplines like economics and philosophy. Second, anthropologists tend to work with economic data or with cognitive data, but not often both. Third, we often hold romantic attachments to gift-based societies where systems of reciprocity are seen to contribute to a more humane "moral economy." And finally, related to these attachments, many scholars hold convictions about the morally vacuous nature of capitalism. For a combination of reasons, anthropologists have a long way to go to mine the relationship of morality and economics across societies in a systematic way.

Economics and Morality brings together the work of scholars concerned to respond to this research lacuna and to the morally charged moment of our consumption-oriented, rapidly globalizing and unsustainable world.[5] Because the moral challenges in a given capitalist society can no longer be effectively addressed without considering the interaction and influences of different societies in the global system, ethnographic research from around the world can help document and make sense of the changes sweeping our planet. Our contributors are American, Norwegian, Canadian, British, and Swedish. The data for the work presented here draws on their fieldwork from a broad range of societies, including Papua New Guinea, Malaysia, Norway, Madagascar, Guatemala, Trinidad, South Africa, North America, and Kenya.

ORGANIZATION

The questions behind contributors' studies are wide ranging. These concerns fall naturally into three primary areas that organize the volume.

Part 1 of *Economics and Morality* focuses on the challenges and adaptations related to the movement of capitalism into societies that have, until recently, remained outside the reach of Western economic logic and exchange. The chapters by Robbins, Walsh, and Little bring ethnographic research to bear on the way in which moral norms embedded in a given system are thrown into sharp relief through the economic interactions across systems with profoundly different histories.

Part 2 shifts the focus to market economies and how moral conflict and struggle in the economic realm variously operate. Multiple, coexisting moralities provide the source of this conflict and, in some cases, lead to new adaptations. The chapters by Halperin, Prentice, Werner, and Dolan speak to these themes.

Part 3 of the volume offers top-down ethnographic research that conveys the moral assertions and practices emerging in many societies among corporations and state governments. Such movements promote identifiable standards of economic behavior regarded as "ethical" as discussed in chapters by Garsten and Hernes, Rajak, and Pitluck.

Before discussing in more depth the ideas grounding each section of the volume, it is useful to back up and consider a question that is so basic it is commonly neglected: is morality an inherent part of all economies or only some? I make the argument here that, in fact, all economies possess a moral center. The path toward this conclusion begins with anthropological work in non-Western societies and ends in neoliberal economies where it is most difficult for many to detect how morality is functioning. Understanding how much and what kinds of moral norms are built into an economy will clarify how some kinds of efforts to increase moral accountability in the economy get traction while others do not.

FINDING THE RELEVANCE OF MORALITY TO ECONOMIES

Studies of non-Western societies are a good place to begin a search for the systematic interweaving of morality with economic life. In the late 1800s, after the field of sociology had been established, French scholars Emile Durkheim and his nephew, Marcel Mauss, offered early models for the social glue of small-scale, non-Western societies. Their studies foreshadow the importance of these societies to the understanding of those based on advanced capitalism. Durkheim proposed that "primitive" societies hold together because members share a great deal in common, especially the kinds of work needed to survive. These commonalities foster a collective consciousness reinforced by social norms that regulate conformity and serve as the basis of social solidarity. Thirty years later, Mauss drew on ethnographic research from various societies to develop his influential ideas about how gifts are the currency exchanged between members of such societies. That is, gifts fulfill a society's social and economic needs. In his seminal essay, *The Gift* (1990 [1925]), Mauss argued that when someone gives yams, shell bracelets, or some other resource to another person, it is not merely the thing that is given, but also a part of the giver's spirit. Because such gifts are "inalienable," (inseparable from the giver) they compel people to both accept them and, in turn, give back something vested with their own spirit. Building on his uncle's work, Mauss claimed that the entire system of self-provisioning is built on social relationships of "*moral persons* who carry on exchanges" (Parry 1986: 456), binding them to each other and, thus, to the good of the group. These models have since inspired the work of generations of sociologists and anthropologists and established a baseline definition for economic morality.

Mauss developed his ideas in part by using findings from Bronislaw Malinowski's long-term fieldwork with the Trobriand Islanders near Papua New Guinea (1961 [1922]). There, Malinowski studied the curious inter-island trade known as the kula ring, in which men traded shell armbands and necklaces in prestigious, ritual voyages to other islands. What struck Malinowski was that the economic behavior of Trobrianders could not be described in terms that neoclassical economists had suggested motivated human beings everywhere: material self-interest. Instead, he argued, islanders were motivated to exchange shell jewelry for all kinds of social reasons, from traditional duties to beliefs in magic, to potential for prestige. The work of Malinowski, Mauss, Durkheim, and others inspired economic historian, Karl Polanyi (1957). Polanyi used anthropological insights as he considered how different kinds of societies organize their economies: by reciprocity, as in the small-scale societies Mauss had described; by redistribution, as in chiefdoms and tributary systems; or by market exchange, as in capitalism. One of these systems dominates every society, Polanyi said, so it makes no sense to use the tools of Western economic science to describe nonmarket societies. The associated assumptions about rational individuals making economic choices based on self-interest and personal gain simply do not apply in these contexts, he said, echoing the claims of Malinowski (Wilk and Cliggett 2007: 8).

By the 1960s, anthropologists had accumulated fieldwork experience in a broad range of societies. Many, who had also found that social life was deeply embedded in economic acts, came to wage an intellectual battle with neoclassical "formalists" over this idea. These "substantivist" anthropologists, like Bohannon and Dalton (1965), used the ideas of Polanyi to contest the claims of formalists. Not all humans were motivated by self-interest, they argued, and thus the market model could not be applied universally. Scott Cook's classic denunciation helped formalists strike back. Substantivists, he argued, were just "romanticists" who harbored an "anti-market" ideology and were guilty of "gross oversimplification of the history of Western economic thought" (1966: 336).[6]

The intellectual legacies of twentieth-century anthropology thus fostered a strong anthropological conviction about the inseparability of social norms and economic life in precapitalist societies. The work of E. P. Thompson carried this pattern of thinking to a new moral frontier by applying the idea of a "moral economy" to a peasant context.[7] In 1971, Thompson published work that drew on Mauss's argument about the implicit obligations in gift-based economies to explain the conflict when different economic logics are at work in the same society. Thompson noted that in eighteenth-century England, peasants' expectations of food security were violated by market sellers. These vendors were selling bread at higher prices than normal to make up for grain shortages, leaving a basic staple unaffordable for many. The outrage of peasants and the working class led to massive riots. Thompson explained that there had been an unwritten "moral economy" that acted as a normative contract between peasants and landlords, one that peasants trusted they could count on. To peasants, the price hikes on grain constituted an immoral breach of an understood contract.[8] James C. Scott (1976) drew similar conclusions to Thompson's to describe the peasant struggles against the state in Southeast Asia during the late nineteenth and early twentieth centuries. Scott asserted that peasants had organized themselves in rational ways to share resources through reciprocity. The "risk-averse" moral economy that characterized these peasants, said Scott, involved their "safety first" orientation to food security and to concern for protecting control over their lives in the face of colonialism (1976: 4–5).

It may be relevant to note as well that Mauss's work detailing the social logic of gift-based societies was in large measure inspired by his own anticapitalist convictions and socialist political activism (Hart 2007). Thus, even though Mauss rejected the idea that "primitive" societies were built on altruism, perhaps it is no surprise that anthropologists have leveraged his work along with Polanyi's and others in this vein to suggest evidence of the inherent moral value and social complexity of such societies. With both Scott and Thompson's description of subsistence-based peasant systems as "moral economies," the rhetorical inference of moral superiority was reinforced. Morality in economics for some has thus become synonymous with the particular set of principles inscribed in reciprocity-based, noncapitalist societies. In this view, the advent of capitalism caused a rupture that pushed treasured moral norms to the sidelines and stripped the economy of its true moral foundation. The most trenchant critiques of capitalism point to its betrayal of these moral values, values that had once bound groups of people to each other and to the common good (Hart 2005; Wilk and Cliggett 2007: 160).[9]

The subtle and sometimes not so subtle binary idea of moral, precapitalist societies and amoral or immoral capitalist societies draws on anthropological insights about the historical shifts that accompany profound economic transformations, that is, from concern for the social good to a concern for individual choices. Enlightenment commitments to rationality, progress, and private property all shaped the logic of capitalism, but the premise of the free market system is grounded on a concept of individuals as autonomous actors, deciding for themselves what is best. Anthropologists and social theorists compare the wants, desires, choices, and identities of individuals who become the source of meaning in market economies to the interdependence of social actors and socially led motivations in precapitalist societies. The result is a nostalgia-based critique of capitalist economies that are seen to have no moral center. But as Foucault warned, "There is in this hatred of the present or the immediate past a dangerous tendency to invoke a completely mythical past" (1993: 165).

Anthropological depictions of the individualistic, economistic, and amoral behaviors fostered by market economies also owe much to the work of Max Weber. Following his visit to the United States in 1904, Weber wrote his seminal argument about how a new Protestant ethic had spurred the rise of capitalist society (1992 [1930]). Since Calvinists and Puritans believed in predestination, they needed a sign of God's grace in order to identify who would be chosen for salvation. In the context of early American society, Weber said, that "sign" came to be reflected in an individual's economic success. The conviction that material wealth signaled an individual's selection for salvation thus became folded into a distinctly Protestant cultural attitude spurring a fierce work ethic. Moreover, because it was considered unseemly to show off one's wealth, members of these religious groups effectively "hid" their accumulations by investing in their own enterprises. As Weber indicates, investing in this way had the amazing, "unintended consequence" of creating new forms of capital that spurred the development of capitalism itself! Ultimately, investing one's earnings made possible an unapologetic goal of wealth accumulation.

Weber's story of the moral shift that permitted the rise of capitalism is only one of many accounts. Albert Hirschman, economic historian, proposes an alternative view in *The Passions and the Interests* (1997 [1977]). According to Hirschman, European political philosophers of the seventeenth and eighteenth century believed that the expanding role of commerce and industry offered hope as a harmless distraction from dangerous human "passions" such as ambition and the lust for power and sex. Reason was not strong enough to rein in such passions, but relatively "innocuous" passions such as greed and avarice (known as "interests") could be used to "tame" the more destructive passions. Hirschman argues that the political encouragement to act on one's "interests" was seen to save European society from its base human nature. It was in this context, he states, that moral philosopher Adam Smith interpreted self-interest in economic terms.[10] By the late 1700s, a bourgeois ethos of accumulation had developed and economic self-interest had become firm ground for the defense of a capitalist economy.[11]

Mauss too weighed in on the moral transitions required of capitalist economies. During the seventeenth and eighteenth centuries, he said, it became increasingly common "to hold that the self springs from individual consciousness as an irreducible being" and that the result of this was that "the only valid source of motivation was the individual" rather than a self identified in terms of social relationships (Carrier 1997: 138). With the shifts in land tenure and the commodification of labor associated with capitalism, changes in the autonomy of the individual impacted understandings about social obligations and what represented the "moral good" (Carrier 1997: 139).[12]

Each of these views emphasizes the extraordinary shifts required in moral consciousness that accompanied the rise of capitalist logic, but it is Weber's account that continues to dominate the imagination of anthropologists and sociologists about the moral origins of market economies. Sociologist Ronald Glassman, for example, holds that in the transition from a logic of self-provisioning to a logic of competition for wealth, capitalism in Protestant societies was never intended to serve the interests of morality, at least not the moral concerns of social groups (2000: 195–96). Mark Banks adds that a capitalist society "only provides a new kind of individuated tyranny in which economic relations continue to devolve into increasingly amoral and immoral territory" (2006: 56). Because noncapitalist societies are our frame of reference for what morality looks like in an economy, it is no wonder that many see capitalism as the road to moral ruin. Recent scholarship has begun to crack some of these long-held assumptions by documenting a degree of fluidity between market and nonmarket systems, and gift and commodity exchange, as we will see. Yet oppositional portrayals persist.

As anthropologists with at least a generation of practice at exploding false dichotomies, we are surprisingly complicit with our binary regard of morality in the economy. Perhaps this implicit polarization occurs because our personal moral commitments are at stake, commitments that may run deeper than our professional identities. If we do not see moral principles we believe in embraced by the economic system we are part of, it is hard to know how morality plays a role. Moreover, in our professional lives as fieldworkers, many of us witness the worst of capitalist sprawl. We see firsthand how free-market products and media increasingly capture and then betray the hopes of remote indigenous peoples, as new ideologies about individualism, competition, and Christian salvation undermine long-standing kinship relations, systems of reciprocity, and beliefs about the supernatural. Can it be prudent to argue that market economies have a discernable morality?

While the views of anthropologists and sociologists on these questions often reflect dichotomous thinking, economists are likely to deflect the question of morality in the economy altogether. Among mainstream economists today, the starting point for analyzing capitalist economies is a utilitarian model of economic behavior known as "preference theory" or "rational choice theory." The model assumes that people make choices based on what will best serve their individual interests. Until recently, most economists still argued that material self-interest was the utility that rational individuals sought. Today, many recognize that individual choices can maximize anything—status, reputation, opportunities for children, feelings of altruism. Yet because the model collapses every economic choice down to a function of the utility that choice serves, moral influences are of little matter to most economists.

In stark contrast to both the economic models that ignore the role of morality and the nostalgia-based critiques of capitalism that decry the loss of the moral, social good, there are ideological advocates of market systems who argue that the moral good is fully woven into the fabric of capitalism.

Western conceptualizations of the market system as it was emerging in eighteenth-century Europe have profoundly shaped these ideas. Foremost among these early intellectuals was Adam Smith (1723–1790), whose seminal work, *The Wealth of Nations* (1976 [1776]), became the rootstock of "classical" economic science. Smith argued that when markets are unimpeded by government controls, individuals act in their own self-interest, and ultimately serve the good of the society at large (note the slant that Hirschman's thesis provides on this idea). According to Smith, the "invisible hand" of the market efficiently induces competition, which in turn keeps prices low and monopolies out. The "greater good" made possible by unfettered markets is compromised, he said, when controls (wrought by a "visible hand") are imposed on the freedom of the market. However, it is worth remembering that the context of European political economies during Smith's era were strongly interventionist, hardly resembling the neoliberal incarnation of contemporary Anglo-Saxon economic systems (Wilk and Cliggett 2007: 53).

A hundred years after Smith, the details of a "neo" classical economic model emerged, clarifying both the market mechanisms of supply and demand, as well as the central assumptions that individuals make rational choices to maximize their utility based on their knowledge of the relevant choices. Alfred Marshall's *Principles of Economics* (1948 [1890]) articulated a foundation of the theory that became known as neoclassical economics. Since then, new textbooks have modified certain portions of the model, but the overarching principles of minimal government interference, free markets, and the invisible hand have remained central tenets of the contemporary neoclassical credo.

Since the early 1990s, a number of scholars have published fresh considerations of Smith's work, eager to point out some of his neglected ideas in contrast to those that came to dominate modern readings of his work. Many of these analyses point to Smith's prior work, *The Theory of Moral Sentiments* (1976 [1759]), as a testament to the moral framework that Smith had assumed would characterize "self-interest" in capitalist exchanges. Perhaps the reinterpretations of Smith correspond to an increasing urgency among market proponents and academic scholars to locate new moral insights from an intellectual ancestor who can speak to the concerns of extreme neoliberal expansion, unseemly market abuses and betrayals of public trust.[13]

Advocates of laissez-faire markets continue to regard capitalism as the ultimate moral achievement of our human history. These supporters of a "liberal" economy—that is, markets that are free from government interference, not to be confused with left-wing political sensibilities in the United States today—argue that capitalism is the only system to uphold the freedom of the individual. Individuals are freed from systems that allow little space for autonomy or individual empowerment, from tyrannical governments, oppressive feudal systems, or morally corrupt alternatives of socialism (Gagnier 1997: 446). The very fact that individuals have choices like never before is seen to constitute a "moral good" (Carrier 1997: 3).

In other words, the freedom granted individuals in a capitalist society carries its own kind of morality. Heterodox economists Hausman and McPherson elaborate on this understanding by explaining the values that inhere in "neo" liberal thought, politically closest to libertarian philosophy[14] (2006: 168). The overall emphasis of neoliberal policy is on freeing the movement of goods, services, and capital by dismantling restrictions on investments and capital flows, shrinking the size of the public sector, deregulating markets, lifting the burden of too many taxes from individuals and businesses, and giving room to market forces to work out the costs and benefits of everyday life. Neoliberal philosophy is explicit in stating that the central moral force of a just society revolves around individual property rights—including the rights of individuals to pass on property to whomever they choose—and to legal protection of these rights.[15] These ideas about "rights and liberties" intrinsic to capitalist systems are naturalized, in part, because they appear to derive seamlessly from the larger evolution of moral and political democratization in Europe and the United States (2006: 172).

Ultimately, what separates the market-as-morality fundamentalists from the nostalgia-based critics who see no morality in the market can be usefully rendered in terms of a contemporary debate in political philosophy. Modern political theory suggests that liberal market advocates tend to emphasize "negative" kinds of morality, that is, the right to be free *from* interference and the moral duty *not to interfere* with the rights of others. In other words, the force of moral commitments in neoliberal models of capitalism is tied strictly to the rights of individuals to remain free from control except when the rights of others have been jeopardized (Christman 2005). Some taxes are required to support legitimate, state-level activities such as national defense, police, and the courts, but, in theory, there are few *positive* moral requirements demanded by a neoliberal market system. Thus there are no rights *to* basic welfare, such as state-provisioning of food or shelter or health care for the poor.[16] From this vantage point, the "right to life is a right not to be killed, not a right to be given subsistence" (Hausman and McPherson 2006: 169). Not all capitalist systems are neoliberal, however, and we will return to this variation later.

Thus, in the search for an answer to whether moral commitments organize some part of all economic systems, we encounter an interesting set of narratives. Among many anthropologists and sociologists, "moral" economies are those organized around reciprocal exchange because social obligations bind people to each other and support the needs of communities. From this perspective, societies organized around commodity exchange excessively indulge the individual's self-interest, undermining social values that benefit all.

Pro-market advocates, on the other hand, rehearse a different narrative. Capitalist economies represent a moral breakthrough for individual freedom, an Enlightenment-led release from overdetermined and oppressive precapitalist regimes. Both groups are steeped in their own romanticized depictions; however, the claims of both also point to partial truths about the moral dimensions of different kinds of economies, even if the emphasis of those dimensions can be debated. A third group, representing mainstream neoclassical economists, has taken morality off the table altogether by funneling all curiosity about culture and economy into a science-framed narrative of utility and maximization.

We will take up the implications of these arguments in the sections to come, premised on the idea that all economies—not merely pre- or noncapitalist ones—are moral economies. The authors in this volume offer groundbreaking, ethnographic testimony of this argument. It is to their work we turn next.

PART 1: THE STAKES OF MORALITY, RECIPROCITY, AND CHANGE

In part 1 of *Economics and Morality*, each author presents a case study that advances our theoretical and ethnographic understanding of gift-based societies in transition. Until recently, few scholars have attempted to probe the theoretical limits of the applicability of Mauss's argument.[17] Chapters by Robbins, Walsh, and Little (part 1), as well as those by Halperin (part 2) and Rajak (part 3), all contribute to a reconsideration of Maussian ideas and assert in different ways how the intersection of market and gift economies is often a seamless one.

This work comes at a good time. For although Mauss's theory of the gift and the reciprocity it obligates has provided anthropologists with critical tools to think with and to teach with, it has also contributed to misinterpretations of smaller scale, noncapitalist societies as static and morally superior (Booth 1994: 658). The inevitable contrast with capitalist societies leads many to demonize those economies based on commodities that are impersonal and driven by self-interest and material gain.[18] These ideas have been reinscribed by a long line of major social theorists, including Marx, Weber, Horkheimer and Adorno, Bourdieu, Bauman, Giddens, Beck, and Putnam,[19] all of whom have pointed in varying degrees to the loss of morality and conscience and the collapse of the social bond of community in economies built on capitalism.

However detailed and nuanced and partially true these depictions may be, they have fostered an anthropological skepticism about morality in capitalist systems that "tend by antithesis to treat the world of gift exchange as non-exploitative, innocent and even transparent" (Bloch and Parry 1989: 9). Work such as Chris Gregory's *Gifts and Commodities* (1982) offered detailed accounts of the separate logics of each system, but in so doing contributed to this boundary-building pattern. This work had a profound impact on Melanesianists as well as other anthropologists studying gift societies.

More recent work has clarified the fact that only by letting go of ideas about morality and economics built on oversimplified juxtapositions can we hope to realize that all economies emerge from a social context in which a key set of moral principles operates. A number of authors have contributed to complicating the rigid boundaries Gregory portrayed as separating societies based on gift or commodity exchange. In his 1986 book, *The Social Life of Things*, Arjun Appadurai shows how both commodities and gifts may circulate across different contexts, thus making the case that things exchanged in one sphere do not necessarily "belong" to that realm of exchange alone. In 1989, Bloch and Parry's seminal volume appeared, *Money and the Morality of Exchange* (1989), showcasing numerous examples that further contribute to this effort. In that volume, Jonathan Parry, for example, documents how it is gifts rather than commodities that are seen to carry moral danger in India; C. J. Fuller shows how monetary exchange has long coexisted within the prevailing system of gift exchange in rural Indian communities; and M. J. Sallnow and Bloch both show how gift exchanges are "far from being politically innocent" (1989: 9). Moreover, say Bloch and Parry, the appearance of money, though sometimes regarded as a threat to social relations, may also be seen as helping to maintain relations, or offering positive benefits to the community (1989: 22). In another volume, van Binsbergen (2005: 23) introduces the multisited fieldwork of contributor Rijk Van Dijk who researches Ghanians in and out of Ghana and shows how gifts are potentially polluting and thus morally problematic. As Dinah Rajak notes in chapter 9 of this volume, even Charles Dickens understood that gifts can "pauperize" (1854: 158). In a more recent book (1997), Gregory has modified his earlier argument to accommodate more fluid boundaries between systems.

Work in this complicating vein carries an important implication for our discussion. If gift and commodity exchange (or precapitalist and capitalist economies) are not so wholly discrete as assumed, then continuities connecting them suggest that morality in a capitalist economy does not simply get shunted out of the picture. Instead, morality gets reworked to match up with the reworked terms of the economy. A corollary implication of this connectedness, then, is that in order to appreciate how morality works in different kinds of economies, we must examine the moral premises of *that* system and avoid judgment from the frame of reference of a system with a different social context and different sets of needs.[20]

Chapters in part 1 build on these insights and expose further complexities in the terrain of morality and economics. The authors here draw on data from non-Western societies that, to different degrees, are becoming integrated with outside market economies.[21] The presence of such "outside" influences from the West thrusts the moral premises of the "insider" system into sharp relief. It is in this space of vulnerability where the local moralities vested in routine economic expectations become clearly tested. As in the encounters of strangers, the crossroads that link people coming from different directions present more danger, but also more opportunity, than travels along a single road. Some groups ignore the hazards of such encounters and explicitly assert their faith in the moral continuity of the inside system. Andrew Walsh's study about the Malagasy (chapter 2) speaks eloquently to the surprises and costs of such choices. Similarly, Joel Robbins points out how a local act of generosity leaves no trace on the outsider who did not recognize his violation of a morally binding, "insider" expectation (chapter 1). The cost to the Urapmin of Papua New Guinea was their time, but more importantly as in Walsh's case, the real cost was to their faith in a shared moral order. Like Laura Bohannan's "Shakespeare in the Bush," (1966) the common presumption that mutually intelligible moral codes guide economic life and transcend people with vastly different histories only reveals the ethnocentrism of everyone who believed it so.[22] The cautionary tale reminds us that presuming the validity of a single set of moral principles as one travels across different social contexts may well lead to confusion, disappointment, or other unintended consequences!

If we recognize that every economic system draws on its own moral resources, we can begin to locate the moral logic that animates various economic choices. As this first set of papers demonstrates, when people participate in different economic systems at the same time, when profound economic change is occurring, there are unusual opportunities to glimpse how those moral convictions that are anchored to economic habits get drawn into question. This line of anthropological inquiry exposes some of the deepest difficulties associated with change.

Robbins applies his understanding of a Papua New Guinea people to propose an innovative, emotion-centered bridge to link the logics of gift and commodity systems. Robbins's research draws on many years of fieldwork with the Urapmin. What if, he asks, Western economists have altogether missed a critical factor that underlies capitalist logic? What if, in analyzing the motivational content of gift exchange in precapitalist societies, we discover a force that is socially defined yet intimately individual? Robbins argues that exchanges carry emotional weight and that anthropologists and economists, concerned with the thing exchanged and the system it is built upon more than the underlying motivation, have neglected the force of this emotional reality. Sociologist Amitai Etzioni and a number of heterodox economists have criticized the neoclassical model of capitalism for subsuming all motivations under a single aggregate concept of "preferences," thus denying any influence from moral commitments (Etzioni 1988; Hausman and McPherson 2006).[23] Robbins suggests that if we understand that the morally binding motivation in any exchange, noncapitalist or capitalist, is powered by the need for mutual recognition, then we can begin to see new potential connections between gift and commodity economies in ways that challenge assumptions about their analytically discrete nature. By linking the two types of economies with such a theoretical bridge, we have a fresh way to jostle static depictions and move the discussion forward.

Another kind of fluidity connects societies dominated by practices of gift exchange and those dominated by commodity exchange: the search for self-gain. In many noncapitalist societies, Weber argued, the search for personal gain is not morally constrained so long as any advantages to oneself originate outside the functioning unit of kin or community (Roseberry 1997: 255). Walter Little's work with indigenous Maya (chapter 3) presents ethnographic witness to this pattern. We learn how encounters with outsiders may present benefits for insiders who are positioned to leverage their mysterious powers and benefit from new economic opportunities, all the while avoiding disruption to the moral universe of the local society. Little explains that traditional Maya healers have become sought after for their insights and healing power by individuals from the United States and Europe. These new, prosperous Western clients can be morally accommodated within the rules of the inside system because the system has no taboos forbidding cash gifts taken from outside one's own community.[24]

Another way of realizing the difficulty of walling off gifts from commodity societies is by seeing how people may slip imperceptibly from one group into another. Andrew Walsh discusses his research with a local community in Malagasy where the sudden rise of outside trade in sapphires has blurred the understanding of who is who and what rules of reciprocity apply. The profitable trade of gems implicates some, but not all, insiders and complicates Thompson's juxtaposition of clearly discernable groups—the moral economy of peasants versus the profit orientation of shopkeepers. Walsh's case clarifies the latitude that is always available in the context of moral behavior. By pointing out how habits of exchange may get interrupted or go wrong in the context of change, he exposes the underbelly of Mauss's notion of gift-based societies. The Maussian idea that obligations compel an individual to give, receive, and reciprocate, Walsh argues, must be understood as only "potential" obligations. In effect, the choices one makes can reproduce the system or challenge its relevance. Walsh shows how individual agency exposes the limits of the structure of exchange in a context of change. Like Robbins who looks at gift-giving systems as templates that can be challenged, shifted, or ignored, Walsh's insights reveal how new choices bearing moral weight expose the ragged, uncharted interaction of capitalist and indigenous logics of exchange.

The moral latitude that inheres in any ethic of exchange can thus clarify the adaptability of certain choices in the context of change. Little's work also demonstrates how people can negotiate between the structure of exchange (that imposes limits inside the system) and the freedom of agency (to negotiate different terms outside this community structure). Clearly, depictions of the gift economies as "moral" and the market economies as "immoral" block the kind of insights that might help us grasp our complex moral and economic worlds.

PART 2: MORAL AGENCY INSIDE MARKET LOGIC

Recognizing that precapitalist systems built around reciprocity and capitalist systems built around commodities are less discrete than we might have imagined can help us think about how morality fits into capitalism. As anthropologists trained to step inside the logic of other systems and analyze them from within, taking the view from the inside should not be so hard. Yet very few have attempted to work out an emic comprehension of the system to which we ourselves belong. One notable exception is the work of James Carrier and his contributors in the 1997 volume, *The Meaning of the Market: The Free Market in Western Culture*. Carrier points out that too often we do not distinguish between the neoclassical *model* of the economy and the economy itself. Thus, he argues, assumptions that underlie economic theory have led many to assume that capitalism necessarily involves impersonal exchanges made by autonomous individuals based on their rational choices among the known universe of alternatives. The problem, Carrier says, is that such assumptions do not in fact describe what actually takes place in a market economy. Instead, firms develop personal ties with other firms, employees with each other, and practices of gift giving and network building routinely create certain obligations among and across individuals and firms alike. In fact, one might argue, only a system with some degree of porosity would allow ordinary individuals to push their own agendas and sometimes effect an integration of moral positions into the functioning of a market economy.[25]

Before we consider the case studies that explore moral claims of ordinary people in part 2 of the volume, we need to identify the nature of morality that operates in the system itself. Just how is capitalism a moral system? And if morality is indeed a constituent part of a capitalist system, how do we explain the fact that market forces have led to massive deforestation, global warming, pharmaceutical dumping, illegal trade in human beings, organs, and endangered animal parts? What morality constrains those companies that rush to export production to countries with the cheapest labor and weakest environmental laws? The easiest solution is to regard the system as simply amoral, maybe even immoral.

Earlier we considered how different theorists have explained the moral transformations leading to the embrace of the autonomous self and self-interest that accompanied the rise of capitalism. These transitions establish the context for how morality operates in capitalist economies. Before the rise of capitalism, the church represented the primary institutional force regulating moral behavior. The material changes that fostered capitalist exchange[26] led to the commodification of land, labor, tools, and machinery, and for this reason, the need to protect one's property emerged.[27] Protecting property in turn created a new form of contract that bound the parties involved to legal enforcement of property rights. Thus, with the rise of capitalist economic arrangements, the moral concerns of the economy became located in the state and in laws of the state designed to enforce the new, moral rights of ownership.

At this point in our discussion, it is useful to consider how an image may help us think about the complexity and variations in moral understandings that arise in different kinds of economies. I propose it advisedly, for heuristic value. If we were to imagine a sphere indicating the space that moral expectations occupy in the exchanges between people in reciprocity-based societies, we might well imagine one large enough to encompass the entire society—exchanges enforce that wholeness and solidarity of the system. But as Durkheim made clear, such societies demand a group consciousness in which all members comply with a single set of norms.[28] When any piece of such a system is injured or made vulnerable by violations of these norms, the entire moral order of society is threatened. By contrast, the moral force of exchange in capitalist societies occupies much less real estate relative to the society at large. Here, we might more appropriately imagine the morality of the economy as a small sphere inside a much larger one. Two key points clarify the meaning of a moral sphere in capitalist societies: (1) it is clearly interior to the larger social context, and (2) the sphere's relative size and contents reflect not the degree to which the economy is moral but rather the degree to which certain mandates (as expressed in law or custom) organize the moral concerns of the economy. In capitalist societies generally, market economies make fewer moral demands on economic actors than precapitalist economies, where all economic exchange carries a moral mandate. Yet because moral behavior in capitalist societies results not only from the mandates of a moral sphere, but also from the voluntary initiatives of individuals and firms, the ultimate "morality" of a capitalist economy cannot be presumed.

In a capitalist society, the constituent parts of a moral sphere include assumptions about the economic rights of individuals: to own property, to accumulate wealth, to create firms, to buy and sell with little encumbrance. Some of these rights, such as the protection of one's property, are codified in law; others rise only to the level of common expectation based on customary practice. However, the fact that these rights carry the power of law or customary practice does not necessarily mean they are shared ideas. In fact, the constituent elements of a moral sphere vary over time and across capitalist societies and, as we will explore, are as likely as not to be contested.

The moral spheres of capitalist societies are neither static nor hard edged. They are instead elastic and permeable—capable of change in size and content. In a system that is not bound by group dictates, individuals have a great deal of autonomy. Irrespective of the socioeconomic inequalities or social norms that constrain the autonomy of some much more than others, the fact remains that there are far more choices than exist in other kinds of systems. All this latitude creates a lot of variability in what people choose to do, possess, and believe, differences that reinforce the system's need for adaptability to survive, a capacity for accommodation and change that Marx neither witnessed nor predicted would occur. This same variability is also the source for the many points of view about what constitutes morality in an economic realm.

With its nonencompassing moral sphere, a capitalist system generally makes no attempt to accommodate concerns about moral economic activity that lie outside the sphere *unless* these concerns either threaten to undermine an enterprise or present an opportunity to profit by integrating the concern. So, for example, when public pressure to clean up the environment leads to legislative proposals to regulate polluting industries, those industries complain and attempt to leverage the moral center of capitalism—arguing that controls on the free market reduce their ability to compete and thus survive. But if public pressure is great enough, the legislation will pass, forcing the permeable moral sphere of capitalism to expand to accommodate a larger set of moral concerns than it did before. Similarly, when there is profit potential in responding to public sensibilities about moral concerns, this incentive, too, may act to enlarge the moral sphere.

Many companies today, for example, are finding ways to capitalize on the growing public concern about global warming, unsustainable consumption, and inhumane labor practices. Hotels market their competitive "ethical" edge by promoting earth-friendly laundering and recycling, beer companies market their all-sustainable production facilities, restaurants develop menus according to what is available from local, sustainable farms, and clothing manufacturers offer "sweatshop-free" labor guarantees. Modern churches are also attempting to promote moral behavior as good for business. In a kind of inversion of Adam Smith's logic, new research suggests that firms that do good by society often end up also doing well by themselves (Hausman and McPherson 2006; McCloskey 2006).

The relative size of a capitalist moral sphere varies according to the sociopolitical context in which it is situated. A relatively smaller sphere imposes fewer moral constraints on market actors and leaves more choices to individuals or businesses. For example, in the 1980s the Reagan administration took certain kinds of initiative that effectively shrank the moral sphere of U.S. capitalism from its post–World War II, Keynesian-influenced character. Government deregulated industries, privatized public utilities, and allowed more mergers and acquisitions than ever before, effectively turning over to markets a greater share of decisions, moral and otherwise. Currently, the smallest moral sphere of a capitalist system is the neoliberal economy. By contrast, in welfare-state economies, the moral sphere organized by states occupies a more dominant space in the society.

It is worth noting that beyond the issue of relative size, not all of the constituent moral elements of Western capitalism translate into other market economies, as increasing numbers of anthropological studies suggest. For example, Alan Smart (1997) identifies two other models: one, associated with Japan and South Korea and the need to identify one's interests with a larger group. The other is associated with Hong Kong, Taiwan, and the overseas Chinese in Southeast Asia, where the practice of *guanxi* emphasizes obligations of trust, reciprocity, and cooperation between networks of business partners. Thus, although Western-style, growth-oriented market economies are taking root elsewhere, there is not necessarily a concomitant transfer of associated moral premises (Ferguson 2006; Hefner 1998; Ong 2006). The thrust of moral expectations in different contexts of capitalism may effectively decouple economic growth from individual choice, hands-off government, or even the sacred idea of efficiency, replacing these Western moralities with alternative principles that are locally meaningful and perhaps equally or more effective.

Irrespective of their size or content in a given economy, all moral spheres can be made smaller in a variety of ways: (1) through the power of political leaders in government who enact policies in line with market liberalism, (2) through the leverage of muscular global institutions such as the World Bank and IMF that are empowered to withhold foreign aid unless a country agrees to neoliberal reforms, and (3) through powerful lobbies such as the pharmaceutical or tobacco industries that "contribute" to political parties in exchange for legislators' willingness to squelch potential bills that might cost billions of dollars in regulation compliance every year.[29]

Earlier in the chapter, I identified negative and positive types of morality. Negative moralities are associated with convictions that people should be free from interference by state or institutional controls. Policies to eradicate poverty would, in this view, impose unfair and undue tax burdens on those with more income (itself a form of property). Thus, neoliberal versions of capitalist models theoretically embrace few of the "positive" types of morality that characterize reciprocity-based societies. There are no built-in moral mandates to foster or sustain communities; to nurture social bonds; to protect the quality of air, water, or land; to help the poor; develop the arts; or support quality education—mandates that do exist to varying degrees in other kinds of capitalist systems. The point is not that liberal market advocates do not see some problems with the distribution of rewards in a capitalist system. Many do. They simply do not believe that there is any alternative system that is more equitable or more just. For them, the weight of a high tax burden to support these goals, however virtuous, is too steep a moral trade off when one considers the lost entrepreneurial energy and workforce productivity at stake (Berliner 1999: 294).

We all know many exceptions to the characterization of capitalist relations as lacking soul or heart because, as Carrier cautions us, the neoclassical model and the actual economy are not the same thing. Without nudging from government and without direct pressure, some businesses will take it upon themselves to do more to uphold certain moral norms than what is required by the moral sphere of the system. However, these exceptions are not reliable and, thus, raise the value of identifying more systematic routes for expanding the moral accountability of the market.

How then does a moral sphere extend its influence? As was true for strategies to contract the scope of the sphere, there are several ways: (1) regulation at any level of government can force the market to accommodate a moral norm in the larger society—assuring safety in workplaces, protecting endangered wildlife, or prohibiting the use of lead in products and toxins in rivers; (2) businesses can voluntarily adopt standards that are effectively enforced through the power of reputation (as with the beverage industry's decision in 2006 to withdraw full-calorie sodas from vending machines in schools[30]); and (3) activist volunteer organizations and nonprofit groups can attempt to promote their values and thereby apply direct pressure to firms and industries to adapt (as with "morality-driven," religion-based business alliances, organizations that sell offsets to carbon footprints, and watchdog groups for income inequality).[31]

In part 2 of the volume, we present four cases involving market and nonmarket activities that operate at the individual and community level, activities of ordinary people who make claims about what is economically moral. These cases can help us think about what kinds of pressures permeate the moral sphere, pressing it to expand, and what kinds do not achieve that degree of influence.

Catherine Dolan (chapter 7) focuses on the increasing cachet of moral consumption among British consumers eager to feel that they are contributing to a better world through the fair-trade flowers they purchase. She suggests that careful consumption is part of a growing social movement in the West designed to fulfill a sense of individual efficacy in choosing to consume "ethically." Dolan's study demonstrates how British consumers of Kenyan fair-trade flowers intend by their choices to participate in solving the well-publicized problems of inhumane working conditions and endemic poverty of cash crop producers in poor countries. For the slight premium in cost, consumers are able to re-create themselves as "moral selves," who are helping poor producers in poor countries. In effect, Dolan argues, the British consumers she interviewed are able to mediate the tensions of greed and generosity—tensions born of capitalist morality and anchored to the market economy. The fair-trade phenomenon has spread rapidly from handicrafts to agricultural commodities, such as coffee, tea, sugar, honey, and bananas, to cotton and other textiles, effectively expanding the moral sphere of Western capitalist systems.[32] In part, fair trade as a "moral" alternative owes its success to the system's place inside the market, thus providing consumers with everyday convenience and market legitimacy. In addition, the fair-trade surcharge to consumers is small, making it an affordable practice to exercise a moral stand. As more and more mainstream companies like Starbucks fold fair-trade practices into their product line, this moral "alternative" may come to reconfigure capitalism's moral sphere.

Rebecca Prentice presents a case that highlights the critical need to understand a society's own social history in order to see how some moral claims gain currency in certain contexts that would be unlikely to occur in other contexts. Using her fieldwork in a Trinidadian garment factory, Prentice documents female workers who produce a line of high-fashion garments, but who may also participate in a clandestine parallel activity in which they cut and stitch garments for themselves during their normal workdays. Prentice's methodological approach is innovative, and she makes clear that it is only after she risks involving herself in these side activities that she is allowed to learn the extent of the practice. Her analysis is important because it points out how this kind of "within the system" tactic is not an oppositional stance directed against the boss or the constraints of the capitalist system. Rather, Prentice shows that these women view "thiefing a chance" as a morally defensible act because, unlike outright stealing, it requires their own labor. The practice thus fulfills cultural values that derive from Caribbean work histories in which moral rights to self-reliance and autonomy, even if exercised in illicit ways, are widely accepted and highly prized achievements, my central argument in *Creole Economics* (Browne 2004). In Prentice's case, the formal understanding of the moral sphere of the Trinidadian economy would not condone illegal activity. As in many other Caribbean societies, however, local custom may turn a blind eye on petty theft when it involves the respect of self-labor and entrepreneurial skill. These cultural phenomena, in which some people systematically perform economic acts that they regard as moral despite their illegality, are certainly not limited to the Caribbean (Milgram 2008).

Different kinds of grassroots efforts to put pressure on the moral sphere occur when nonprofit or volunteer-based groups attempt to compensate for the inadequacy of capitalist markets to supply "public goods." Rhoda Halperin's case of "extreme gifting" in Cincinnati presents an excellent example of the heroic grassroots effort required to make a charter school work (chapter 4). Within market economies, argues Halperin, hidden or unrecognized "moral" economies may also thrive. Ultimately, she points out, Mauss's idea of the gift economy must be reformulated to accommodate gift-based microeconomies that emerge in the context of neoliberal capitalism. Halperin suggests that sustaining a vital and personal ethic of exchange among community members effectively rewrites the logic of impersonal, commodified exchange at a time when survival itself is at stake. "Doing what it takes" is code for "making choices that go outside normal economic relations," giving individuals the implicit moral authority to pursue creative economic acts in order to help save the group. At the same time, however, these economic activities that benefit the community rather than the self do not lie entirely outside the realm of the market economy; to some degree, in fact, they depend on it. Like Walsh and Little, Halperin thus shows how gift and commodity economies are bound up together. Her chapter also clarifies how morally led economic claims and activities that operate outside the moral sphere are at a disadvantage in gaining ground within it. Without the pressure produced from greater numbers of people, or the opportunities for market players to somehow profit from the moral commitment of gifters to keep their school alive, the needs of the school will continue to require heroic volunteer efforts like extreme gifting.

The moral quandary of negotiating whose morality matters is at the center of Cynthia Werner's work (chapter 6) on radioactive waste disposal in Texas. In this instance, Werner recounts how members of a small West Texas community attempt to press their rights with regulatory agencies to have a private company bury the waste near their town. The moral position they take is unusual, but by arguing that they should be permitted to decide for themselves whether the waste site should be allowed near their community, the townspeople are clearly relying on energy from the moral sphere of capitalism: the logic of freedom of choice and unfettered markets. Werner's own role as a consultant with the state regulatory agency that reviews license applications for waste disposal positions her to understand the stakes of all parties involved and to collect detailed ethnographic data from multiple perspectives. As an insider, she had access to the variety of moral views held: the company wanting the right to pursue a dump site with a willing town; the town residents and leaders who want the freedom to contract with the company without interference; the environmental activist groups who object to the lack of moral accountability by the company; and the state authorities who want to control the process.

Werner points out that because residents are strongly concerned about the viability of their town's future, what they believe about the small risks associated with waste disposal are well worth the economic benefits they would most certainly accrue. She points out that some in the town have worked to frame the choice as a patriotic one while outsiders like the Sierra Club voice strong opposition to the prospect, also on moral grounds. The case demonstrates how a grassroots effort can reinscribe the legitimacy of the moral sphere and, at the same time, demonstrate that what is regarded as moral or immoral economically varies in relation to where one is situated in the system. Unlike the case of fair trade, the costs of the moral position of townspeople seem potentially high, yet given the alternatives of a town that has no basis for survival, the risks are perceived as relatively small.

Many would argue that in the United States and in Britain, where neoliberal policies have their greatest foothold, there are serious problems with significant and growing income inequalities, among them the fact that tens of millions of people live without health insurance and millions are homeless. The world looks at post-Katrina New Orleans and wonders how the richest nation on earth could tolerate the chronic suffering of hundreds of thousands of American citizens.[33] These unseemly realities might appear to call into question the moral character of the economic system. And yet, with a system that recognizes few "positive" types of moral claims, accountability for these problems would take a legal breach in which someone could be found guilty and assigned blame. But has any company or group of people actively violated the law or even the principles of the market? As Milton Friedman argued, the corporation is not like an individual (1990 [1970]). There is no "person" to hold accountable when gross inequities occur, precisely the problem that Ulrich Beck notes about the character of global capitalism today (Beck and Cronin 2006). Glassman too recognizes this problem, noting that "the market system has no mechanism within its own rules for dealing with or caring for the less fortunate" (2000: 198). Economist Duncan Foley echoes this view, arguing that "we cannot depend on the spread of capitalism by itself to solve the problems of poverty and inequality. Capital accumulation will increase material wealth, but will distribute it unevenly" (Foley 2006: 224).

If a moral cause extends beyond the fundamental promises and mandates of the moral sphere of an economic system, there is necessarily a struggle between those who do not believe its influence should expand and those who believe it must. But it is also the case that the very nature of capitalism requires it to be flexible and adapt to market forces. When individuals, firms, or the state itself applies adequate pressure, the sphere can and will grow or contract accordingly.

PART 3: FRONTIERS OF SOCIAL RESPONSIBILITY

Doing good can come with a cost, even if there are obvious benefits to oneself or one's group or company. The cost of making a moral choice can be especially high when there is wide latitude to make different choices. When choice is directed, by contrast, either by group norms or legal regulations, the costs of moral action are, in a sense, neutralized because they are shared by all. When we are free to choose between different options and it costs no more to make a moral economic choice, most of us will likely opt for that choice. But it is almost invariably more expensive to produce a commodity using well-paid, well-treated employees than to produce that same commodity using techniques that simply ensure the lowest cost and most efficient way to profit. The point is that to appreciate the patterned ways in which moral principles are most likely to get absorbed into the moral sphere of capitalist economies, we need to consider the costs as well as benefits of doing something we believe is the right thing.

In the two previous sections of this introduction, we encountered some examples in which the "cost" of what is seen to be a moral good is high. Walsh's chapter details how local villagers in Madagascar stood to lose their stock of sapphires to strangers if they acted with moral assumptions that were out of sync with the changing economic realities. Halperin's chapter about the Cincinnati charter school offers another example of the high cost of moral choices when "doing what it takes" requires immense energy and resource contributions of school staff and parents just to keep the school alive and functioning in the context of an underfunded school system. Generally, in cases like these where a moral choice comes at a high price, either the choice is unsustainable in the long run or those making such choices simply continue to pay the cost. For the cost to come down, many more people will have to decide to make the same moral choice.

On the other hand, there are some moral choices that cost relatively little. Dolan's example of fair-trade flower consumption offers a good example of the slight premium required to buy the satisfaction of a moral conscience.[34] When it does not cost too much to make an economic choice that seems morally good, the choice resonates easily with the economic rationality of capitalism. Those moral actions that seem to make good economic sense also stand a better chance of becoming absorbed into the moral sphere of capitalism, either on the strength of widespread customary practice, or because such choices become the political will of legislators who get them inscribed into law.

Before we consider the material in part 3 of the volume, let us review some of the key ways that moral principles can be incorporated into the moral sphere of a capitalist economy:

1. Private individuals and groups can take charge of pushing for change (the focus of part 2).
2. Businesses and corporations can choose to enact moral standards of their own.
3. Governments can create regulations or a strong "environment" to encourage businesses to adopt certain moral principles.

The chapters comprising part 3 of the volume consider the second and third types of pressures that can impact the moral sphere. Here, I will draw attention where possible to the cost of moral choices, adding another dimension to my initial argument that all economies have a moral sphere, and to the subsequent discussion of the variable content and flexible nature of capitalist moral spheres. Chapters by Garsten and Hernes and Rajak suggest how transnational companies may be compelled to adopt standards of corporate social responsibility that ensure certain benefits. The different cases reveal two patterns: first, that the adoption of these principles is a strategic business decision, and second, that depending on the degree to which such standards are internalized, the associated costs can vary a great deal. By contrast, Pitluck's chapter offers a view of how an Asian state has embraced standards of socially responsible investing in ways that promise benefits to investors at a reasonably low cost. Together, these three cases offer ethnographic material that helps explain the variability of top-down choices and moral behavior across firms and states.

Moral Branding

There is mounting global pressure on capitalist enterprises to be seen as moral economic actors. In part, this pressure derives from a breathtaking number of moral breaches in recent years. On occasion, these cases—such as Tyco, Enron, and WorldCom—end up in ugly courtroom dramas where astonishing greed and corruption are exposed to a shocked public. Alongside these criminal violations of public trust stand the morally questionable tactics employed by many corporations that prey on society's vulnerability in the interests of profit at any cost. They target teens for cigarette sales; sell expired drugs and unload toxic waste in poor countries; sell arms to totalitarian governments; and price-gouge victims of disaster circumstances. They sell subprime real estate loans to people who have no financial capacity to repay the loan and market credit cards to college students and people already in debt. Even the lives of children are not exempt from exploitation by corporations seeking new markets. Fast food corporations that have secured school lunch contracts serve fried, fatty foods and sugary drinks, recklessly nurturing unhealthy cravings. In the transnational context, Stiglitz calls the phenomenon of global corporations scouring the world over for the cheapest workers and the weakest laws protecting labor and the environment a "race to the bottom" (2006: 199). In all these cases, the cost of doing the right thing is presumably too high given the potential profits to be made by ignoring such moral concerns.

How does any economic system with a true morality allow such moral collapses? How is the sense of social good maintained when private interests abuse public faith in the system? In neoliberal capitalism, as discussed earlier, morality is written into a set of rights that assures the widest possible latitude for individuals and the smallest possible space for control by government. Having the right to make choices, however, also means bearing the burden of moral economic decisions. If people and firms do not bear this burden, if they make poor moral choices, society suffers.

When a moral breach is considered reprehensible, like marketing cigarettes to teens or selling expired drugs to developing nations, public outrage can sometimes bring about legislation to make such activities illegal. In these cases, the new laws add fresh content to the moral sphere. When an economic activity becomes strictly proscribed by law or custom, the permeable cells of the sphere absorb the new mandate. Once a principle or economic act becomes a constituent part of the moral sphere, such as antidiscrimination law, for example, it is better positioned to endure changing political tides, social backlashes, and the volatility of economic markets. Chances are better, but as George W. Bush's eight-year administration has reminded us, there are no guarantees.[35] If there are no prohibitions against morally problematic schemes that companies invent to extend their markets or improve their bottom line, they may well carry on with impunity and without censure (as tobacco companies do when they continue to heavily promote lethal products in developing countries).

Tracking moral accountability is not the business of a free market system, but in this moment of rapid, simultaneous communication around the globe, when problems of morality in business become apparent, the market can be called to account. Between traditional media coverage, Internet blogs, and activist monitoring in recent years, public awareness has dramatically increased, tagging the companies that risk public health and safety, abuse employees, breach contracts with consumers, or betray consumer trust. The convergence of such pressures has contributed to the institutionalizing of voluntary moralities within capitalist systems such as fair trade, where standards of certification are meant to ensure better treatment of producers, CSR (corporate social responsibility) sometimes called business social responsibility (BSR), and SRI (socially responsible investing).

CSR is a rapidly growing philosophy that asserts an ethical commitment to do business according to certain guidelines.[36] SRI represents a similar commitment that is growing in the world of financial markets. Because both of these systems are voluntary, the extent to which they may enlarge the moral sphere of capitalism in an evolutionary way depends on market factors. That is, can these companies remain competitive in the market, and are these behaviors important enough to consumers that they will selectively choose those companies they understand to be acting morally?

Christina Garsten and Tor Hernes (chapter 8) lay out a detailed review of the historical emergence of CSR and the new standards associated with it. Their research with dozens of CSR leaders helped them create a typology that describes the range of variation characterizing this emerging phenomenon. The benefits of becoming recognized as a CSR company are significant, particularly for publicly traded companies that depend on a corporate reputation to attract stockholders and capital. In their study, Garsten and Hernes profile the rise, fall, and struggle to rise again of a Norwegian dairy cooperative faced with dramatic changes in the public understanding of milk. After seventy years in business with the nutritious qualities of milk underscoring the company's success, the post–World War II era brought about new research that began to link milk fat to health problems. The authors show how the company adapted to the shifting views of milk through a variety of strategies including a stronger marketing orientation and the adoption of CSR standards. However, as Garsten and Hernes point out, intense market pressures and demands of shareholders and stakeholders ultimately led company leaders to make some unethical choices that were not preempted by their CSR commitments. The critical insight of this work reveals that a company's embrace of ethical "standards" may be partial, and whether intentional or not, a partial commitment can mask problem areas that violate commonly accepted standards of moral conduct (as was the case with Enron, beloved benefactor of Houston, Texas). In effect, if CSR is just one strategy among many, rather than the prevailing company ethic, there is plenty of room for doublethink and internal contradiction.

It is useful to remember that being good in a commercial universe *is* likely to be part of a conscious business strategy because, after all, for-profit companies are in business to make a profit. Every community is home to some businesses that are known for their "people-first" policies. These companies certainly want to survive even if they are not organized around making the most money in the shortest time possible. But if the cost of being a moral player means your company could go broke, then you are obligated to find ways either to compromise profits or to set aside certain moral standards. It is no surprise that companies practicing CSR make every attempt to leverage a competitive "moral" edge by marketing their reputation. For them, whatever cost is involved in adopting these standards must be offset, either by reducing other costs, increasing productivity, or attracting enough consumers who will agree to subsidize the added cost. When the moral commitment of a company is only partial, however, or relegated to a marketing principle alone, the limitations of CSR or any other attempt to promote good behavior become evident.

Dinah Rajak (chapter 9) presents an ethnographic look at a company's commitment to CSR that goes deeper, permeating the organizational culture of the company. Her case points out how traditional corporate philanthropy is increasingly rebranded as morally led partnerships with the local community to promote sustainable development, enhancing the moral merit provided by the company's very presence. Rajak's fieldwork takes place in a South African mining operation run by the world's largest platinum-producing company, based in London. Her study ties together several themes of the volume. She shows how the claims to moral purpose by company management suggest a near-spiritual mission to bring morality back into the workplace. Enacting this mission through the terms of CSR principles, company managers are quick to communicate their financial and emotional commitment to workers and to the community through the various projects the company supports. Rajak describes how Mauss's ideas about the gift in "primitive" societies are relevant in thinking about how this version of CSR works. She explores how the categories of benefactor and recipient in this context function as they did in nonmarket societies to create a "logic of the gift." Here, she argues, the gift of support to workers and their community acts to naturalize the authority of management on the one hand, while compelling a "return" gift of employee loyalty on the other. In effect, she says, the moral terms of CSR reassert asymmetrical, dependent relations.

In this South African context, the investment in employees and the community may represent a straightforward case of enlightened self-interest. By keeping the flow of gifts from the company in constant view, managers are able to maintain a positive public profile, keep the peace, and retain workers who remain in their debt. Rajak's case reinforces the idea that when public goodwill can determine a company's viability, investing in visibly moral conduct may be the necessary cost of doing business. In this sense, the cost to the company of doing good in order to remain viable is a worthwhile trade-off.

In line with the critical analyses of CSR practices by Garsten and Hernes and Rajak, Joseph Stiglitz notes the contradictions of many companies that claim to respect moral standards:

> Today, all companies, even the worst polluters and those with the worst labor records, have hired public relations firms to laud their sense of corporate responsibility and their concern for the environment and workers' rights. Corporations are becoming adept at image manipulation, and have learned to speak in favor of social responsibility even while they continue to evade it. (2006: 199)

According to Stiglitz, the solution to such problems will require more than a campaign of social responsibility. In his view, the only solution is to enact regulations (e.g., positive moral principles) to mandate the terms of moral citizenship among market players. However, even if the realities of CSR standards are not matched by the appearances of do-good companies, the increasing cachet of claiming moral conscience works to raise the bar. If only out of enlightened self-interest, companies need to do well by their workers and by the needs of their communities. But they must also stay in business. Today, in business schools all over the world, there are new programs emerging in business ethics, sustainable business, and social entrepreneurship, all of which signal the increasing energy and investment in generating new models of capitalist moral economies. This profusion of efforts is aimed at carving out a new paradigm, one that may help level the costs of moral action by spreading the desire for higher standards across a majority of businesses. We may be tempted to call this window dressing or ideological manipulation, but because it is not yet clear where these new movements may lead, they merit our anthropological curiosity and scholarly attention.

Aaron Pitluck (chapter 10) demonstrates how moral choices by businesses can sometimes be very affordable when a state creates a set of incentives for moral accountability that are compatible with the local values. By comparing the world of high finance in two market economies—Malaysia and the United States, Pitluck argues that the different structure of incentives in these systems makes a real difference in the outcome of moral choices. The author introduces the concept of SRI that emerged in the West in the 1980s in association with social movements attempting to end investments in South African firms keeping the apartheid system alive. In other parts of the world, pan-Islamic social movements and oil wealth helped spur a system of "Islamic finance" conceived in the 1970s.

Pitluck describes how U.S. investors who communicate SRI preferences to money managers often exert little to no impact on redirecting corporate behavior toward such standards. The bottom-up system in which clients indicate their interest in making certain morally led investments ends up having little effect because the money managers that select the funds maintain a great deal of legal control in interpreting client preferences. Pitluck contrasts this situation with Malaysia where top-down government initiatives provide clear encouragement for companies to meet standards of business that explicitly reflect Islamic principles.

This comparative case study suggests the potential benefits of adhering to state-level incentives that reflect the moral values of a given cultural environment. As Pitluck shows, the coordinating initiative of the Malaysian government to collect and report data on publicly held companies in terms of their Shariah compliance puts significantly more pressure on companies to comply, and the majority of businesses do. The cost of compliance to a given company depends on the nature of its business, but all companies share the cost of reporting and the cost of refraining from interest-bearing financial instruments. In such a case, compliance presents more benefits than costs. The potential profitability of Shariah-compliant companies is underscored by the fact that there are large investable funds controlled by Muslim individuals, organizations, and governments worldwide. A conservative estimate by Moody's Investors Service, a credit rating agency, indicates that there is approximately $550 billion in Islamic mutual funds and Islamic banks alone (see Pitluck chapter, note 9).

CONCLUDING THOUGHTS

Market economies function according to moral spheres that differ in scope and content depending on the local political and social context in which they operate. Unlike societies organized around gift exchange that impose strict norms on the behavior of individuals, capitalist economies privilege the choices of individuals and, therefore, allow for a wide range of moral outcomes. But across capitalist economies, fundamental differences in philosophy and policy exist. In welfare-state economies as in France or Sweden, for example, the rights of individuals share political space with the rights of everyone in society to access certain public goods. Thus, the moral sphere of these societies assumes the cost of minimal provisioning for all by imposing significant tax burdens on income earners and employers.[37] It is no coincidence that in welfare-state economies, there are much smaller gaps between rich and poor[38] than in neoliberal societies where the rights of individuals dominate. In the United States or Britain, the economic system honors few rights of society; instead, individuals and businesses enjoy a system with far fewer rules, regulations, and taxes.

It is also important to remember that the moral spheres of market economies in non-Western societies reflect their own models of capitalist logic. In the Asian Tiger economies of South Korea and Singapore, for example, there is a strong, interventionist role for the state. Variable forms of capitalism and the moral spheres distinguishing them also exist in Latin American and African countries, differentiated often by the political leadership of the moment. In the Malaysian instance discussed by Pitluck, the state initiated top-down incentives for businesses to act ethically according to Islamic laws of finance. If these same attempts at pressuring moral conduct were tried in many other contexts, they would doubtless be rejected.

But a relativistic position about differences in capitalist moral spheres misses the political power of those systems that presume to dominate the global economic field. Today, the American version of capitalist logic is sweeping other parts of Europe and most areas of the developing world. In the last twenty-five years since neoliberal policy came to shape the U.S. economy, the tenets of free choice embodied in this style of Western capitalism have been forced on many societies that, ironically, had no choice but to accept them. Through IMF and World Bank requirements for aid and debt relief, the market fundamentalism of neoliberal government has been grafted onto societies irrespective of compatibility with the local rootstock, their preparation, or their desire for such transformations. These grafts require local economies to make "structural adjustments" to shrink the public sector, privatize industry, and downsize social benefits.

Many anthropologists and sociologists who work on the ground in developing societies and bear firsthand witness to the ravages of imposed neoliberal policies point out that the "freedoms" anticipated by liberal market advocates are often less apparent than the grave problems these policies have fostered—massive-scale poverty, unemployment, and increasing inequalities in health and education as well as income (Elyachar 2005: 214; Escobar 1995; Ferguson 1999, 2006: 11, 35). These failures relate in part to the misguided assumptions in the West about the legitimacy of "scientific capitalism" without regard for its need to be translated and made to work in moral as well as technical terms. In Africa, says Ferguson, "The morality of the market thus denies its own status as a morality, presenting itself as mere technique" and so the move to neoliberal policies "will eventually have to be taken up in a moral key in a way that recognizes the inevitable connection of social, economic and cosmological orders" (2006: 80–81). Julia Elyachar echoes the point that if free markets are to become successfully rooted in Egypt, policy makers must realize that "markets are social and political worlds with their own cosmologies" and that, in addition to translating a set of foreign processes in order to make them work in local soil, "ethical attitudes" associated with these processes must also be explicitly identified and translated (2005: 214). These recent studies suggest that moral understandings and accountability reside at the center of the contested terrain of economic change.[39]

The work comprising *Economics and Morality* presents a clear indication that a new anthropological scholarship is emerging. It is no coincidence that this fertile research landscape is opening up at a critical time in our history, a time of profound economic change in the world and urgency to comprehend how we can grasp and make good this uncharted future. As Bill Maurer states in his eloquent afterword to this volume, in a post-foundational world, we are compelled by the need for moral and ethical grounding, however tentative these stances may be.

Our economic lives are full of choices, and our choices are full of mysteries. Studying moral frameworks, however tentative, can help us see into the power, fear, and commitment woven into many of these choices. Anthropologists and ethnographers of all disciplines have much to offer this discussion. We learn from the authors here how attention to moral worldviews can help explain the local meaning and cost of moral action. We learn how muscular economic forces and logics can compel moral change or adaptation. We learn most of all how the care of ethnographic work continues to provide insights into the deepest questions of humanity and how methodological ingenuity and courage are required to study ourselves without the baggage of our traditional sympathies.

NOTES

Acknowledgments. I wish to thank my generous and thoughtful colleague Lynne Milgram for her unflinching support of my work on this introduction. I also offer heartfelt thanks to the readers whose contributions have helped me greatly: Rhoda Halperin, Bill Maurer, Joel Robbins, Alan Smart, and Rick Wilk. I also wish to thank the Series Editor, Dolores Koenig, and the three outside reviewers, all of whom offered substantive, valuable comments about this work. Most of all, I owe thanks to my partner Jane DeHart Albritton who keeps me laughing and thinking and doing better work.

1. Arguments about the place of morality in economic life go back a very long time and have appeared in many societies outside Europe and the United States. As Wilk and Cliggett note, "moral issues are never far from economic life, and the two are often hard to separate" (2007: 121–22).

2. As Eric Wolf (1982) and others have shown, it is increasingly problematic, given the flows of labor, ideas, goods, and so on, to assume a conceptual chasm between non-Western and Western societies. I use these terms advisedly, in part to expose these very limitations.

3. There are exceptions. In philosophy, there are "applied" moral philosophers, such as Jeffrey Reiman (2007), who consider the moral dimensions of capitalist economies. In economics, there are "heterodox" and "institutional" schools of thought that attempt to challenge the dominant model of welfare economics based on its claims of moral concern for social welfare. As Hausman and McPherson point out, because the measure of social welfare is calculated from the sum of individual utilities, moral values have little role in economic analysis (2006: 92). Deirdre McCloskey is less restrained in her analysis of the claims of welfare economics, arguing that the "faint stirrings of complexity in ethical thought" are in fact better described as a "Victorian, utilitarian parrot, stuffed and mounted and fitted with remarkable eyes" (2006: 195).

4. Marshall Sahlins took up the issue in *Stone Age Economics* (1972) as did structural Marxists like Godelier (1986) and formalist and substantivist anthropologists. More recent anthropological treatments of morality and economics can be seen in Bloch (2006); Bloch and Parry (1989); Austin-Broos (1996); Parry (1986); Smart (1997); Carrier (1997); Robbins (2004); and Laidlaw (2002).

5. Many new books have appeared in recent years decrying the scope of ethical problems that have come to plague capitalism. One best-selling example is David

Callahan's *The Cheating Culture: Why More Americans Are Doing Wrong to Get Ahead* (2004), in which the author points to the increasingly competitive global environment that has nurtured a startling devolution in the moral standards of business. Along this line, anthropologists have become more concerned to investigate corruption in various forms, as evidenced by books like *Corruption and the Secret of Law: A Legal Anthropological Perspective* (Nuijten 2007); *Global Outlaws: Crime, Money, and Power in the Contemporary World* (Nordstrom 2007); and *Illicit Flows and Criminal Things: States, Borders and the Other Side of Globalization* (van Schendel and Abraham 2005).

6. Frank Cancian's insightful analysis (1966) showed how the great divide might have been reconciled if both sides had realized that they were simply debating the definition of maximization. Cancian's argument did not, however, help the sides see eye to eye, and the debate fizzled out without a winner. Still today, these points of view are commonly seen to divide economic anthropologists from economists (Wilk and Cliggett 2007: 13).

7. Thompson (1991: 336–37) borrowed the term from late eighteenth-century critics of capitalism who had drawn comparisons between economic action for the good of all and "the laissez-faire 'political economy' espoused by 'quacks,'" a history Edelman details (2005: 33). However, William James Booth points out that the idea of a "moral economy" had its origins in the Aristotelian notion of how to best fulfill a "good life." Following this line of thinking, Booth asserts that the moral economy was not a reference at all to the marketplace but, rather, to a life of leisure and freedom to participate in the life of the city. The "oikos" or household in Aristotle's time, was thus organized around the "moral economy" of ensuring the master's freedom so that he could pursue his greatest potential for active citizenship (Booth 1994).

8. In his famous 1965 article, George Foster drew on fieldwork with Mexican peasants to propose the idea that the moral universe of peasants is different from capitalist morality because peasants act in accordance with an "image of limited good." For them, he said, all good things are in limited supply, so that any attempt to maximize gains in one area necessarily depleted resources in another. Eric Wolf subsequently (1966) showed that these "cognitive" orientations could more easily be explained by structural realities.

9. Marxist critiques, in particular, are primarily concerned with the fact of the capitalist's control over the labor of others, rendering the majority of people "alienated" from their own work and self.

10. Thanks to Bill Maurer for pointing me to these ideas.

11. Hirschman notes that the moral critiques of capitalism that have since arisen suggest a twist on Weber's formulation: rather than a case of "unintended consequences," Hirschman's story reveals how the "intended consequence" of building a moral society through the promotion of self interest *was not realized*. Instead, "capitalism was supposed to accomplish exactly what was soon to be denounced as its worst feature" (Hirschman 1997 [1977]: 132).

12. Georg Simmel (1978) argued that as early as the advent of money and the concomitant possibility of exchange between distant parties, a new cognitive orientation had developed, one focused on rational calculation. This new way of thinking loosened the grip of bonds to kin and community, and in its place, fostered connections of trust to a much larger social universe (Bloch and Parry 1989: 4–5).

13. One of the most eloquent and forceful displays of such an effort is Deirdre McCloskey's recent work *The Bourgeois Virtues* (2006). McCloskey argues that Smith's command and embrace of virtue ethics is the template we need to return to now in order to fully enact the terms of a morally led capitalism in Smith's vision. For other examples of this trend, see Foley (2006), Sen (1999), Levitt (2005).

14. Neoliberal ideas arose in the 1970s in the United States and Britain as opposition to the dominant Keynesian model of economic policy that allowed for a strong state. However, advocates of neoliberal ideas tend to accept a greater role for the state than do libertarian thinkers who typically argue that the state should be limited to the absolute minimum required to protect citizenry and their property from foreign or domestic harm.

15. Peruvian economist Hernando de Soto (2000) argues that secure property rights are the key to the success of capitalist economies and to relieving poverty in the developing world. DeSoto's ideas have taken root in international development circles. For a useful discussion of new forms of global, "accelerated" property rights, see Bill Maurer and Gabriele Schwab (2006).

16. However, the idea of rights to certain public goods is not absent in all or even most capitalist societies.

17. *The Question of the Gift* (Osteen 2002) is an excellent recent volume focused on revisiting Mauss's work using contributors from across several disciplines. Keith Hart has also revisited the Maussian legacy in interesting ways (2005, 2007).

18. This divide suggests a striking continuity with the century-old *Gemeinschaft* versus *Gesellschaft* concept separating rural from town life and the moral propriety in the former as compared to the moral wasteland of the latter, articulated by Tönnies in 1887.

19. Marx (1977); Weber (1992 [1930]); Horkheimer and Adorno (1972 [1947]); Bourdieu (1998); Bauman (1995); Giddens (1990); Beck (1992); and Putnam (2000).

20. See William James Booth for an extensive treatment of the arguments about embedded, "moral" economies and "disembedded" capitalist economies (Booth 1994).

21. Many "non-Western" societies have been interacting with market economies for a very long time. What distinguishes these interactions is the nature and degree of integration with capitalist economies. For treatments of these issues see Wolf (1982); Wilk and Cliggett (2007); McCloskey (2006).

22. "Shakespeare in the Bush" (1966) presents a wonderful lesson based on Bohannan's bet that a story as basic in its moral structure as Hamlet, would translate easily among the Tiv in West Africa with whom she had worked for many years. To her surprise, however, almost immediately upon recounting the story to a group of Tiv, questions began popping up, interrupting her tale and forcing her to defend the story line in spite of their efforts to rewrite it in ways that made sense. Ultimately, the Tiv chiefs reinterpreted the story to fit the moral universe of the Tiv, reassuring Bohannan that she now understood the true tale.

23. A small but growing number of economists, economic historians, and economic sociologists have attempted to propose revisions to this utilitarian model of capitalist economies specifying the importance of moral influences to economic decision making. Some of the prominent critics represented by these alternative approaches include for example, Amartya Sen (1999), Joseph Stiglitz (2006), Ha-Joon Chang (2007), and Daniel Hausman and Michael McPherson (2006).

24. For another ethnographic example of this pattern, see Carsten (1989).

25. Mark Granovetter has contributed valuable insights about how social relations shape individual action in market economies (1985).

26. Economic historians and anthropologists now recognize that markets in land and labor existed well before European mercantilism, in the European Middle ages when "more was for sale, arguably, than is now: husbands, wives, slaves, serfs, kingdoms, market days, and eternal salvation" (Hejeebu and McCloskey [2004: 13]; see also Wilk and Cliggett [2007: 11]). For a thorough account of the rise of capitalism, see Wolf (1982).

27. Bill Roseberry makes the point that in the process of commodification, wherever resources were held by families for the use of all, these resources had to be withdrawn from group access, their socially-vested character purged, and inside/outside boundaries dictating access dissolved (1997: 256).

28. Durkheim's "social facts" (1938 [1895]) represented the collective consciousness of group-based norms such that anyone found to violate one would feel the scorn of the others and be brought into line.

29. Nobel Prize economist Joseph Stiglitz (2006: 191) notes that lobbyists for forty-one U.S. companies "contributed" $150 million to federal political campaigns between 1991 and 2001, and in three years alone, benefited from $55 billion in tax breaks. The lobbying success of pharmaceutical companies is even more astonishing, as Stiglitz demonstrates.

30. Still, as a recent *New York Times* article points out, beverage companies continue to stock school vending machines with sugared waters, teas, and juices (Martin 2007).

31. According to the nonprofit organization United for a Fair Economy, in 2006, CEOs of large U.S. corporations averaged compensation packages of $10.8 million, more than 364 times the pay of the average U.S. worker. The top twenty private equity and hedge fund managers earned an average of $657.5 million, a stunning 22,255 times the pay of the average U.S. worker (www.faireconomy.org).

32. The economic logic of fair trade involves cutting out middlemen marketing groups and ensuring a fair return to producers. Fair trade also requires some financial commitment to local communities of producers. For a critical assessment of the problems and potential of the fair-trade movement, see Raynolds et al. (2007).

33. I learned firsthand about the indignities and economic hardships faced by Katrina survivors during my research and film collaboration with Ginny Martin, filmmaker. We followed a large African-American family of 155 people over eighteen months and witnessed their hope and optimism slowly degrade over time as a result of unresponsive and mysterious bureaucracies they were made to depend on. *Still Waiting: Life after Katrina* (2007) was broadcast on PBS in 2007 and 2008.

34. As Dolan points out, the perception by consumers that they are participating in relieving poverty and unequal relations with outsiders is not necessarily the reality. Fair-trade arrangements help the community and ensure the continuity of work, but laborers on these plantations still work for very modest wages.

35. The Bush administration has successfully dismantled large chunks of longstanding environmental regulations and civil rights of citizens (McKibben 2007).

36. According to a Lexis Nexus search, between 1978 and 2007, there were a total of 3,720 articles in "major world publications," with the term "corporate social responsibility" appearing in the headline or lead paragraph. More telling is the fact that 95 percent of these articles (3,530) have appeared since 2001.

37. In France, at least until recently, when transportation workers demanded better pay, their cause was routinely taken up by workers in other sectors who strike "in solidarity." Welfare-state economies condition citizens to tolerate fewer choices and higher costs for the benefits of an economic structure that builds in prescriptive moral behavior. Today, in France, however, the Sarkozy government is stepping up the neoliberal reforms begun by Chirac, forcing a contraction of the moral sphere of French society.

38. Many welfare-state societies are facing unprecedented fiscal crises impacting their capacity to support the publicly funded salaries and numbers of programs dedicated to benefiting society. The unsustainable budgets relate to the costs of aging populations, rising health care costs, and swelling numbers of new residents from formerly colonized areas who are accessing their share of benefits.

39. The World Resources Institute, an environmental policy think tank founded in 1982, has recently issued a report entitled, *Development without Conflict: The Business Case for Community Consent* in which they recommend that "informed consent of a community affected by development projects . . . makes good business sense" (www.wri.org/publication/content/7800).

REFERENCES

Appadurai, Arjun, ed. 1986. *The Social Life of Things: Commodities in Cultural Perspective*. Cambridge: Cambridge University Press.

Austin-Broos, Diane. 1996. Morality and Culture of the Market. In *Economics and Ethics?* ed. P. Groenewegen, 173–183. London: Routledge.

Banks, Mark. 2006. Moral Economy and Cultural Work. *Sociology* 40:455.

Bauman, Zygmunt. 1995. *Life in Fragments: Essays in Postmodern Morality*. Oxford: Blackwell.

Beck, Ulrich. 1992. *Risk Society: Towards a New Modernity*. Thousand Oaks, CA: Sage.

Beck, Ulrich, and Ciaran Cronin. 2006. *Cosmopolitan Vision*. Queensland, Australia: Polity.

Berliner, Joseph S. 1999. *The Economics of the Good Society*. Oxford: Blackwell.

Bloch, Maurice. 1989. The Symbolism of Money in Imerina. In *Money and the Morality of Exchange*, ed. J. Parry and M. Bloch, 165–90. Cambridge: Cambridge University Press.

Bloch, Maurice, and Jonathan Parry. 1989. Introduction: Money and the Morality of Exchange. In *Money and the Morality of Exchange*, ed. J. Parry and M. Bloch, 1–32. Cambridge: Cambridge University Press.

Block, Fred. 2006. A Moral Economy. *The Nation*, March 20.

Bohannan, Laura. 1966. Shakespeare in the Bush. *Natural History*, August/September.

Bohannan, Paul, and George Dalton, eds. 1965. *Markets in Africa: Eight Subsistence Economies in Transition*. Garden City, NY: Anchor Books.

Booth, William James. 1994. On the Idea of the Moral Economy. *American Political Science Review* 88: 653–67.

Bourdieu, Pierre. 1998. The Essence of Neoliberalism: Utopia of Endless Exploitation. Trans. Jeremy Shapiro. *Le Monde Diplomatique*, December 12.

Browne, Katherine E. 2004. *Creole Economics: Caribbean Cunning under the French Flag*. Austin: University of Texas Press.

Browne, Kate, and Ginny Martin. 2007. *Still Waiting: Life after Katrina*. www.still-waiting.colostate.edu. Documentary film, broadcast multiple times on PBS stations from August 2007 through 2008.

Callahan, David. 2004. *The Cheating Culture: Why More Americans Are Doing Wrong to Get Ahead*. New York: Harcourt Brace.

Cancian, Frank. 1966. Maximization as Norm, Strategy, and Theory: A Comment on Programmatic Statements in Economic Anthropology. *American Anthropologist* 68(2): 465–70.

Carrier, James G. 1997. Introduction. In *Meanings of the Market: The Free Market in Western Culture*, ed. J. G. Carrier, 1–68. Oxford: Berg.

Carsten, Janet. 1989. Cooking Money: Gender and the Symbolic Transformation of Means of Exchange in a Malay Fishing Community. In *Money and the Morality of Exchange*, ed. J. Parry and M. Bloch, 117–41. Cambridge: Cambridge University Press.

Chang, Ha-Joon. 2007. *Bad Samaritans: The Myth of Free Trade and the Secret History of Capitalism*. New York: Bloomsbury Press.

Christman, John. 2005. Saving Positive Freedom. *Political Theory* 33(1): 79–88.

Cook, Scott. 1966. The Obsolete "Anti-Market" Mentality: A Critique of the Substantive Approach to Economic Anthropology. *American Anthropologist* 68(2): 323–43.

Dickens, Charles. 1854. *Hard Times*. New York: Harper & Brothers Publishers.

Durkheim, Emile. 1938 [1895]. *The Rules of the Sociological Method*. Trans. Sarah Solvay and John Mueller. Chicago: University of Chicago Press.

Edelman, Mark. 2005. Bringing the Moral Economy Back in . . . to the Study of 21st-Century Transnational Peasant Movements. *American Anthropologist* 107(3): 331–45.

Elyachar, Julia. 2005. *Markets of Dispossession: NGOs, Economic Development, and the State in Cairo*. Durham, NC: Duke University Press.

Escobar, Arturo. 1995. *Encountering Development: The Making and Unmaking of the Third World*. Princeton, NJ: Princeton University Press.

Etzioni, Amitai. 1988. *The Moral Dimension: Toward a New Economics*. New York: Free Press.

Ferguson, James. 1999. *Expectations of Modernity: Myths and Meanings of Urban Life on the Zambian Copperbelt*. Berkeley: University of California Press.

———. 2006. *Global Shadows: Africa in the Neoliberal World Order*. Durham, NC: Duke University Press.

Foley, Duncan K. 2006. *Adam's Fallacy*. Cambridge, MA: Belknap Press of Harvard University Press.

Foster, George. 1965. Peasant Society and the Image of Limited Good. *American Anthropologist* 67(2): 293–315.

Foucault, Michel. 1993. Space, Power, and Knowledge. In *The Cultural Studies Reader*, ed. S. During, 161–69. London: Routledge.

Friedman, Milton. 1990 [1970]. The Social Responsibility of Business Is to Increase Its Profits. In *Business Ethics: Readings and Cases in Corporate Morality*, ed. W. M. Hoffman, and J. Moore, 153–57. New York. McGraw-Hill.

Friedman, Thomas. 2005. *The World Is Flat: A Brief History of the Twenty-first Century*. New York: Farrar, Strauss and Giroux.
Fuller, C. J. 1989. Misconceiving the Grain Heap: A Critique of the Concept of the Indian Jajmani System. In *Money and the Morality of Exchange*, ed. J. Parry and M. Bloch, 33–63. Cambridge: Cambridge University Press.
Gagnier, Regenia. 1997. Neoliberalism and the Political Theory of the Market. *Political Theory* 25(3): 434–54.
Giddens, Anthony.1990. *The Consequences of Modernity*. Stanford: Stanford University Press.
Glassman, Ronald M. 2000. *Caring Capitalism*. New York: St. Martin's Press.
Godelier, Maurice. 1986. *The Making of Great Men*. Cambridge: Cambridge University Press.
Granovetter, Mark. 1985. Economic Action and Social Structure: The Problem of Embededness. *American Journal of Sociology* 91(3): 481–510.
Gregory, Chris. 1982. *Gifts and Commodities*. London: Academic Press.
——.1997. *Savage Money*. London: Routledge.
Hart, Keith. 2005. Notes Towards an Anthropology of Money. *Kritikos* 2 http://intertheory.org/kritikos.
——.2007. Marcel Mauss: Our Guide to the Future. Posted 20 March 2007. www.thememorybank.co.uk (accessed January 9, 2008).
Hausman, Daniel M., and Michael S. McPherson. 2006. *Economic Analysis, Moral Philosophy, and Public Policy*. 2nd edition. Cambridge: Cambridge University Press.
Hefner, Robert, ed. 1998. *Market Cultures: Society and Morality in the New Asian Capitalisms*. Boulder, CO: Westview Press.
Hejeebu, Santhi, and Deirdre McCloskey. 2004. Polanyi and the History of Capitalism: Rejoinder to Blyth. *Critical Review* 16(1): 135–42.
Hirschman, Albert O. 1997 [1977]. *The Passions and the Interests: Political Arguments for Capitalism before Its Triumph*. Princeton, NJ: Princeton University Press.
Horkheimer, Max, and Theodor W. Adorno. 1972 [1947]. *Dialectic of Enlightenment*. Trans. John Cumming. New York: Herder and Herder.
Laidlaw, James. 2002. A Free Gift Makes No Friends. In *The Question of the Gift*, ed. M. Osteen, 45–66. London: Routledge.
Levitt, Steven D. 2005. *Freakonomics: A Rogue Economist Explores the Hidden Side of Everything*. New York: William Morrow.
McCloskey, Deirdre N. 2006. *The Bourgeois Virtues: Ethics for an Age of Capitalism*. Chicago: University of Chicago Press.
McKibben, Bill. 2007. Undoing Bush: How to Repair Eight Years of Sabotage, Bungling, and Neglect. *Harper's Magazine*, June.
Malinowski, Bronislaw. 1961 [1922]. *Argonauts of the Western Pacific*. New York: Dutton.
Marshall, Alfred. 1948 [1890]. *Principles of Economics*. New York: Macmillan.
Martin, Andrew. 2007. Sugar Finds Its Way Back to the School Cafeteria. *New York Times*, September 16.
Marx, Karl. 1977. *Capital*. New York: Vintage Books.
Mauss, Marcel. 1990 [1925]. *The Gift: The Form and Reasons for Exchange in Archaic Societies*. Trans., W. D. Halls. London: Routledge.
Maurer, Bill, and Gabriele Schwab. 2006. Introduction: The Political and Psychic Economies of Accelerating Possession. In *Accelerating Possession: Global Futures of*

Property and Personhood, ed. B. Maurer and G. Schwab, 1–20. New York: Columbia University Press.

Milgram, B. Lynne. 2008. Activating Frontier Livelihoods: Women and the Transnational Secondhand Clothing Trade between Hong Kong and the Philippines. *Urban Anthropology and Studies of Cultural Systems and World Economic Development* 37(1): 5–47.

Nordstrom, Carolyn. 2007. *Global Outlaws: Crime, Money, and Power in the Contemporary World*. Berkeley: University of California Press.

Nuijten, Monique, ed. 2007. Corruption and the Secret of Law: A Legal Anthropological Perspective. Abingdon, UK: Ashgate Publishers.

Ong, Aihwa. 2006. Corporate Players, New Cosmopolitans, and Guanxi in Shanghai. In *Frontiers of Capital: Ethnographic Reflections on the New Economy*, ed. M. Fisher and G. Downey, 163–90. Durham, NC: Duke University Press.

Osteen, Mark, ed. 2002. *The Question of the Gift*. London: Routledge.

Parry, Jonathan. 1986. On the Moral Perils of Exchange. In *Money and the Morality of Exchange*, ed. J. Parry and M. Bloch, 64–93. Cambridge: Cambridge University Press.

Polanyi, Karl. 1957. The Economy as Instituted Process. In *Trade and Market in the Early Empires*, ed. K. Polanyi, C. Arensberg, and H. Pearson, 243–70. New York: Free Press.

Putnam, Robert D. 2000. *Bowling Alone: The Collapse and Revival of American Community*. New York: Simon & Schuster.

Raynolds, Laura, Douglas Murray, and John Wilkinson. 2007. *Fair Trade: The Challenges of Transforming Globalization*. New York: Routledge.

Reiman, Jeffrey. 2007. *The Rich Get Richer and the Poor Get Prison: Ideology, Class, and Criminal Justice*, 8th edition [originally published, 2003]. Boston: Allyn & Bacon

Robbins, Joel. 2004. *Becoming Sinners: Christianity and Moral Torment in a Papua New Guinea Society*. Berkeley: University of California Press.

Roseberry, William. 1997. Afterword. In *Meanings of the Market: The Free Market in Western Culture*, ed. J. G. Carrier, 251–60. Oxford: Berg.

Sahlins, Marshall. 1972. *Stone Age Economics*. Chicago: Aldine.

Sallnow, M. J. 1989. Precious Metals in the Andean Moral Economy. In *Money and the Morality of Exchange*, ed. J. Parry and M. Bloch, 209–31. Cambridge: Cambridge University Press.

Sayer, Andrew. 2005. Perspectives on Moral Economy. Unpublished manuscript prepared for conference on Moral Economy at Lancaster University, UK, in August 2005.

Scott, James C. 1976. *The Moral Economy of the Peasant*. New Haven, CT: Yale University Press.

Sen, Amartya. 1999. *Development as Freedom*. New York: Alfred A. Knopf.

Simmel, Georg. 1978. *The Philosophy of Money*. London: Routledge and Kegan Paul.

Smart, Alan. 1997. Oriental Despotism and Sugar-Coated Bullets: Representations of the Market in China. In *Meanings of the Market: The Free Market in Western Culture*, ed. J. G. Carrier, 159–94. Oxford: Berg.

Smith, Adam. 1976 [1759]. *The Theory of Moral Sentiments*, ed. D. D. Raphael and A. L. Macfie. Oxford: Clarendon Press.

———. 1976 [1776]. *An Inquiry into the Nature and Causes of the Wealth of Nations*, ed. R. H. Campbell and A. S. Skinner. Oxford: Clarendon Press.

Soto, Hernando de. 2000. *The Mystery of Capital: Why Capitalism Triumphs in the West and Fails Everywhere Else.* Basic Books.
Stiglitz, Joseph E. 2006. *Making Globalization Work.* London: W. W. Norton & Co.
Thompson, E. P. 1991. *Customs in Common.* New York: New Press.
———. 1971. The Moral Economy of the English Crowd in the Eighteenth Century. *Past and Present* 50: 76–136.
Tönnies, Ferdinand. 1957 [1887]. *Community and Society (Gemeinschaft und Gesellschaft).* Ed. and trans. C. P. Loomis. East Lansing: Michigan State University Press.
United for a Fair Economy. 2007. Americans Pay a Staggering Cost for Corporate Leadership. www.faireconomy.org/press/2007 (accessed December 10, 2007).
van Binsbergen, Wim. 2005. Commodification: Things, Agency, and Identities: Introduction. In *Commodification: Things, Agency, and Identities: The Social Life of Things Revisited,* ed. W. van Binsbergen and P. Geschiere. Berlin/Munster: LIT.
van Schendel, Willem, and Itty Abraham, eds. 2005. *Illicit Flows and Criminal Things: States, Borders, and the Other Side of Globalization.* Bloomington: Indiana University Press.
Weber, Max. 1992 [1930]. *The Protestant Ethic and the Spirit of Capitalism.* London: Routledge.
Wilk, Richard R., and Lisa C. Cliggett. 2007. *Economies and Cultures: Foundations of Economic Anthropology,* 2nd edition. Boulder, CO: Westview Press.
Wolf, Eric. 1966. *Peasants.* Englewood Cliffs, NJ: Prentice Hall.
———.1982. *Europe and the People without History.* Berkeley: University of California Press.
World Resources Institute. 2007. Development without Conflict: The Business Case for Community Consent. www.wri.org/publication/content/7800 (accessed February 27, 2008).

1

THE STAKES OF MORALITY, RECIPROCITY, AND CHANGE

1

Rethinking Gifts and Commodities

Reciprocity, Recognition, and the Morality of Exchange

Joel Robbins

To talk about finding the moral in the economic is in many circles to invite a cynical response. For those who are sure they know what people want out of economic transactions, and who define what people want as the maximum benefit for themselves with the least expenditure of resources, any moral pieties that might surround the conduct of economic relations are at best expressions of false consciousness and at worst just one more strategic element in a kind of interaction that is already dominated by them. To be sure, there is a kind of utilitarian moral punch to the invisible-hand arguments that in various forms still underwrite claims for the value of the free market, but they are arguments made over the heads of ordinary economic actors who are deemed to have their eyes, not on the greatest good for the greatest number of their fellows, nor on the reproduction of the social system, but on the main chance for themselves. Indeed, such arguments are famously designed to make individual morality, except in the narrow sense in which it is defined by the liberal legal order, all but irrelevant to the way market-oriented economic action achieves its moral goals.

It was the great promise of classical Marxism that, contra this widely accepted picture of the moral emptiness of the economic domain in modern societies, some resources for a moral critique of the capitalist system could in fact be found within economic interaction. In Marxist understanding, an elemental sense of alienation and unfair treatment in the economic realm would provide the working class with the grounds to criticize and eventually overthrow the capitalist system. Such Marxist claims about the moral potential of the economic domain have, however, been severely tested in light of the historical failure of the working class to emerge en bloc as the primary agent of historical change. For prominent heirs of the Marxist tradition, at least within academia, this failure has led to a sharp turn to looking for the moral grounds of critical thought and action in domains other than that of the economy. Thus Habermas, to take perhaps the single most influential living representative of this tradition, rests his critical theory on the moral bedrock of what he takes to be universally valid norms of communication, rather than on the way the subject is formed through labor. Similarly, for a whole generation of cultural studies scholars, generally younger than Habermas, it is not communication so much as the domains of culture, identity, and the psyche that are taken to supply people with the basic needs which, when they go unmet, trigger moral resistance or revolt.

I've just gone through this somewhat potted history of modern Western ways of thinking about the relationship of economy and morality in order to indicate that even from the side of various forms of critical theory, their conjunction is not now taken to be a natural one; the strongest sources of morality seem to almost everyone to lie elsewhere than in the economic domain (Cannon 2001). This makes the task of talking about economy and morality together a challenging one. Yet it is also the case that it is perhaps less challenging for anthropologists to talk about the relationship between economy and morality than it would be for other kinds of scholars. Anthropologists are long practiced, after all, at arguing that many nonmodern economies do not constitute separate cultural domains, governed by their own rules. Economies are instead, as Polanyi (1944) long ago taught us, embedded in their societies understood as wholes, and they answer to the overarching moral rules and values of those societies. Furthermore, anthropologists have often shown the way people who have continued to live in such embedded economies, or have grown up within them before migrating from home, react to being confronted with disembedded capitalist economic forms and the demand those forms make that moral concerns be kept separate from economic ones. From Bohannan's (1959) early piece on how traditional economies react to the coming of state monies, to Taussig's (1980) classic book *The Devil and Commodity Fetishism in South America*, and continuing in literally hundreds of works produced in the last twenty years or so, anthropologists have demonstrated that those who are new to capitalism are adept at drawing on their traditional values to offer sharp moral critiques of its focus on individual self-interest at the expense of all other motivations and individual gain at the expense of more socially defined goals. On the basis of cross-cultural research then, anthropologists have not had a hard time showing that (1) morality and economy do not always and everywhere have to be separate and (2) that people who come from economies that do not separate them are often inclined to bring their traditional moral concerns to bear on the capitalist economy when they confront it.

I take these anthropological points to be in essence settled science by now, and for this very reason I'm not inclined simply to rehearse them here by presenting another case analyzed in their familiar terms. What I would like to do instead is ask if the ideas and observations that have come out of this anthropological literature concerning the moral impulses that are important constituents of many noncapitalist economies can teach us anything that might be useful for that other project I've been discussing—the now largely abandoned critical theoretical one that aimed at determining whether or not it might be possible to find a set of moral concerns at the heart of capitalist economic activity that could suggest internal resources that might be useful in its critique. In order to bring anthropological materials to bear on this problem, I want to shift the terms in which anthropologists generally discuss noncapitalist criticisms of the capitalist order: rather than talk about problems of alienation, exploitation, domination, or individualism, all important in their own right but also by now all fairly well understood, I want to talk about problems of mutual recognition. And I want to situate problems of recognition ethnographically by reviving a somewhat unfashionable distinction between gift economies and commodity economies. As I hope to show on the basis of my research in Papua New Guinea, this rethinking of one aspect of what might be at stake in the confrontation between noncapitalists and the global capitalist market can both help us discover new things ethnographically and open a door for us to contribute to currently important debates about economic morality in the West.

ON RECIPROCITY AND RECOGNITION

The modern form of the idea that recognition is central to social life comes originally from Hegel. In Hegel's (1979a) account, laid out most famously in his discussion of the master-slave dialectic in the *Phenomenology of Spirit*, the person's coming into being as a self-conscious subject requires that he/she recognize another person and be recognized by him/her in return. Key to this scheme is a three-part structure whereby in order to be a subject you must recognize the other, the other must acknowledge your recognition, and the other must recognize you in return. It is true that the master-slave story as it is told in the *Phenomenology of Spirit* is not a happy one, for it is designed to illustrate how the ability of recognition to create subjects is defeated if any of the three parts of this structure are not realized.[1] Yet a broader reading of Hegel's argument, particularly one that takes into account both the works written before *The Phenomenology of Spirit* and the later discussion of stable forms of recognition in the *Philosophy of Right* (Hegel 1991), has to acknowledge that Hegel made mutual recognition the basis of self-conscious selfhood and therefore described the drive to recognize others and be recognized in return as the most fundamental source of people's motivations for action (Hegel 1979b, 1983, 1991; my discussion here also draws extensively on Honneth [1996, 2000], whose work is discussed further below).

At the core of the present paper lies the hypothesis that the anthropological theory of reciprocity as a foundational social form first developed by Mauss (1990 [1925]) and then widely elaborated in several different literatures can in important respects be said to cover ground similar to Hegel's theory of recognition, and to enrich it in certain ways. Important support for this claim comes from that fact that both reciprocity and recognition have a similar three-part rhythm: in both, something (the gift/recognition) must be given to the other, must be received by the other (who thereby acknowledges his/her worthiness as a subject), and must be matched by a return from the other (who thereby recognizes the worthiness of the giver as a subject). Furthermore, in both schemes, each partner must play all three roles (giver, receiver, reciprocator) in order for things to end on a satisfactory note—if there is any asymmetry in roles, things fall apart for both parties involved (see Walsh, this volume). Finally, as I have documented in detail elsewhere, in *The Philosophy of Right*, Hegel (1991) sees the exchange of property as the most basic way in which mutual recognition is accomplished (Robbins 2003a). Here he comes very close to Mauss, for he gives the exchange of material goods a fundamental role to play in shaping human personhood and social life through mutual recognition.

All of the above arguments in favor of seeing Hegel's theory of recognition and Mauss's theory of reciprocity as compatible with one another are based on similarities in the models of human social process they lay out. A second kind of support for reading both theories together comes from their being pitched against a similar foe: the portrait of humans as selfishly struggling for their individual survival and aggrandizement that constitutes Hobbes's model of human beings in the state of nature and that continues to be the dominant image of human nature in capitalist culture today. Hegel was explicitly aiming at Hobbes when he developed his theory of recognition, arguing that social relations of mutuality precede selfhood and that therefore the drive for sociality is the primary human drive (on Hegel's relationship to Hobbes, see Honneth [1996], Ricoeur [2005]; Robbins [2003a] provides an extensive set of references on this topic). Moreover, Hegel made his argument in terms not so distant from those Durkheim (1984) would use in his famous argument about the noncontractual basis of contract, an argument that in turn laid important parts of the groundwork for Mauss's approach to social life. Hence both Hegel's and Mauss's theories have in common the goal of displacing the widespread assumption that the search for individual security and power comes first among human motivations.

Against the background of these common features of Hegel's theory of recognition and Mauss's theory of gift exchange, several scholars, most notably Hénaff (2002), followed by Ricoeur (2005), have recently argued that it would be fruitful to read Mauss's ideas as a contribution to a more general theory of the role of mutual recognition in human life (see also Robbins 2003a). Ricoeur (2005: 227) provides a cogent account of why this link, which can seem almost obvious once it has been pointed out, has so rarely been noticed in the past. Lévi-Strauss's (1987) famous critique of Mauss's theory of the gift took Mauss to task for using the indigenous Maori idea of the *hau* as an explanation for why there is an obligation to return, rather than grounding the obligation to return in the universal unconscious structures that construct society as a system of exchange. In the wake of this criticism, and of Lévi-Strauss's construction of a major theoretical edifice designed to allow for the analysis of societies as interlinked systems of exchange, anthropologists have paid almost exclusive attention to the structure of systems of reciprocity, rather than to the phenomenology of exchange as a form of mutuality (see also Robbins [2003b]). Once we attend to what reciprocity means for actors and not only for the systems in which they live, Ricoeur suggests, the importance of mutual recognition as a key goal and product of reciprocal exchange becomes clear. In light of Ricoeur's claim, which strikes me as correct, I want to take up this recent line of thought about the relationship between reciprocal exchange and recognition and develop it by way of the anthropological contrast between gift and commodity economies.

My resort to this latter contrast perhaps requires some explanation. The distinction between gift economies and commodity economies was central to Melanesian anthropology—economic and otherwise—in the 1980s. Based in important respects on Mauss and also on the extensive elaboration of his ideas about reciprocity in the Melanesianist literature, the distinction between gift and commodity economies found its clearest articulation in Gregory's (1982) book *Gifts and Commodities*. Drawing on Gregory (1982: 10–28), an economist turned anthropologist, the distinction between the two economies can be summed up as follows: in gift economies people come together to exchange inalienable goods in order to make or reaffirm relationships; in commodity economies people come together without forming enduring relationships to exchange alienable goods in order to acquire things. Marilyn Strathern (1988) picked up the distinction in roughly these terms from Gregory and made it one of the cornerstones of her widely influential book, *The Gender of the Gift*, thus ensuring that it would have some currency in anthropological thinking well beyond Melanesianist circles and for some time beyond its 1980s heyday. Yet, as always happens to ideal-typical distinctions framed in binary terms, criticisms that pointed to the lack of pure types of either economy in reality soon began to crowd the field. There were, as it turned out, profit-seeking commodity exchanges in gift economies (sometimes glossed in the literature as "trade") and relationship-seeking gift exchanges in commodity economies (holiday presents being the clearest case). Under the force of this critique, by the middle of the 1990s, the use of the distinction in its original spirit to point to two distinct kinds of economies came to seem naive to many anthropologists, and having faded to gray it has largely dropped out of the literature—although it experiences a small revival in this volume, as both Walsh's and Little's chapters do draw on it to some extent.

But even as such opposed ideal types always do a lot of their work by inviting people to dissolve them in the acid bath of empirical observation, it is also true that they often prove worthy of periodic renewal—of being once again given an opportunity to remind people of the major outlines of difference they captured so productively at the start. In the context of my effort to make recognition a key term in our understanding of the motivations for and moral bases of exchange, just such a renewal of the gift economy–commodity economy distinction is in order. The reason for this is that if we look at the role social relationships play in the two economies, it is clear that in gift economies, where the creation and affirmation of relationships is the key goal of interaction, exchange is carried out precisely in order to foster mutual recognition, whereas that is not in any respect a conscious goal of actors in a commodity economy, for whom enhancement of the self and its enterprises without regard for the other is what ideally motivates economic action. Everything lines up, then, as if there is a real contrast here, and it is one between economies of mutual recognition, on the one hand, and those that are set to maximize individual acquisition, on the other.

In what follows, I unpack and in some respects modify this claim in two steps. First, in the next section, I present the economy of the Urapmin as a gift economy of mutual recognition. Second, in a final section, I look at the current moral and political debate over the place of recognition in Western societies in order to ask what an analysis of gift economies such as that of the Urapmin might be able to teach us about both the real and the morally ideal role of recognition in capitalist societies.

RECIPROCITY AND RECOGNITION AMONG THE URAPMIN OF PAPUA NEW GUINEA

The Urapmin are a group of 390 people living in the remote West Sepik Province of Papua New Guinea. Only contacted to any significant extent in the late 1940s, the Urapmin still live their economic lives largely in traditional terms. Everyone in the community is a subsistence gardener, with men supplementing their garden work by hunting, and women supplementing theirs by raising pigs that are killed on ceremonially marked occasions. There are no regular opportunities for wage labor in Urapmin itself. Many men have experiences of working for wages for short stints, rarely more than two years, at a large gold and copper mine located about four days' walk to the south. And many men and women will on occasion work for wages clearing roads or will earn cash selling vegetables in the area around the government station of Telefomin, about a half-day's walk to the east across the Sepik River. But no one living in the community depends on wage labor for their livelihood, and despite people's interest in acquiring cash both to buy small goods like soap and to funnel into the ceremonial economy, wage work is not a regular or predictable feature of anyone's life. In economic terms, then, it makes sense to describe Urapmin as a traditional community. And this holds true even in spite of the very thorough experience of Christian conversion that has radically transformed Urapmin religious life. While Urapmin Christian morality has challenged some of the people's traditional ideas about the moral basis of exchange that underlie their gift economy, it has not removed those ideas from the center of their lives (Robbins 2004).

Urapmin families, consisting minimally of a man and a woman (these need not be husband and wife, as father and teenage or adult daughter or mother and teenage or adult son will suffice) are largely self-sufficient in terms of providing for their own subsistence. While they need the help of others to put thatch roofs on their houses (since the roofs must be completed quickly and then cured with smoke before the leaves rot) and to build pig fences (which are more of a luxury than a necessity), families can otherwise make it on their own. Indeed, many families do live on their own in bush houses near their gardens for most of the week, returning to their villages only on the weekends for Christian ritual activities, and at any given time a few families choose to maintain no house in a village and live completely on their own.

Against the background of this ability of families to live autonomously, one is struck by the constant flow of gifts and counter-gifts that mark all interaction between households whenever people meet. Rarely a day goes by during which people do not give food to others and receive food from them, and while black palms bows, string bags, and other exchange goods do not circulate in the quantity or at the velocity of garden crops, they routinely pass between people as well. This kind of give-and-take, organized in the familiar terms of informal generalized reciprocity, constitutes the dominant form of everyday interaction in Urapmin.

The key transitions of Urapmin life are also marked by reciprocal giving, in this case of the formal, ceremonial kind. Deaths are marked by simultaneous exchanges of exactly equivalent goods (a bow of a certain length for an identical one, etc.) (*tisol dalamin*). The creation of new friendships either with people from outside Urapmin or from socially distant quarters within the community is also affected by the exchange of equivalent goods, though this time in delayed rather than simultaneous fashion. Marriages, for their part, are marked by the exchange of unlike goods (most notably a bride and pigs for durable goods, including shell money, given as bridewealth [*unang kun*]). In the long run, however, even this exchange of unlike goods is expected to become an exchange of like goods, as participants in a bridewealth exchange are expected to line up on opposite sides when daughters produced by a marriage themselves become brides in turn. Urapmin social life is thus marked by a series of major exchanges in which equivalence either in the moment or over time is the ideal.

To this point, the description I have given of the Urapmin economy is similar to one that would hold for many societies in Papua New Guinea, at least for those of the great man type (Godelier 1986). In purely material terms, there is little need for exchange. People rarely receive from others things they do not already have, and they rarely give to others things those others can be said to need. As a few Urapmin who now have some familiarity with the market put it, using an English loan word, there is no "profit" in their traditional exchanges. Yet in one respect, the Urapmin case strikingly differs from what one generally expects of people living in a gift economy. This has to do with the way the Urapmin talk about their motives for engaging in exchange and what they expect exchange to accomplish.

As suggested above, descriptions of gift economies based on Lévi-Strauss's injunction to study them as systems have left questions of people's motivations and their own notions of what exchange accomplishes largely out of account. Hence, anthropologists have come to write as if people living in gift economies engage in exchange primarily in order to instantiate such systems, or to bring their actions into accordance with them. It is impossible to provide such an account for the Urapmin. People in Urapmin never talk about their exchanges in terms of the larger structures they construct or affirm. They do not, for example, ever say they are exchanging something with someone because that person stands in a particular relationship of kinship or affinity to them. Rather, they explain their exchange behavior by referring to the ways emotions of anger (*aget atul*) and shame (*fitom*) in relation to other people lead them to want to give to and receive from them. These emotions, which are products of relational absence or failure, point to the centrality of the problem of mutual recognition in Urapmin understandings of exchange.

The role of emotions that signal an absence or failure of mutual recognition in motivating exchange is most easily documented in the case of formal exchanges, for people talk about their involvement in such exchanges explicitly in these terms. When a visitor with whom one is not already engaged in a relationship of generalized reciprocity comes and stays at one's house, Urapmin say one feels shame (*fitom*)—a shame that is based on the combination of physical intimacy and relational nonrecognition. As the visitor prepares to leave, one addresses this feeling of shame by giving him (or occasionally her) a gift of a bow or other durable good. He/she is expected to return a similar item when the original giver makes a return visit to his/her home. Once this has been accomplished, once the two parties have mutually recognized one another with gifts, the two parties call one another "trade friend" (*tisol dup*) and their relationship becomes regularized.

Other important kinds of exchange are also motivated by emotional responses to failures or potential failures of recognition, but in these cases the emotion involved is anger (*aget atul*) rather than shame. Death exchanges are one example. When a person dies, those of deceased's relatives who have not been living with the deceased come and challenge the surviving spouse and the relatives who have been living near the deceased to buy the anger they feel over the negligence that has led to the loss of their relative. This leads to a large-scale exchange of exactly equivalent items that settles the anger and puts the two groups into a relationship of mutual recognition again. Similarly, people talk about bridewealth in terms of anger. Rather than refer to it as a ritual form that must be met, relatives of a recently betrothed young woman always speak of the need for the prospective husband's side to pay bridewealth in terms of how angry they are at the prospect of losing her to another family, one that has not yet recognized the need for a relationship with them. So central is anger to people's understanding of the reasons for bridewealth exchange that they adjust the amount they demand on the basis of the level of anger they feel. Negotiations over the amount to be paid often take a year or more, and it is only as the initial flush of anger on the wife-givers' side cools that her relatives begin to make demands that are at all reasonable. At the heart of the final exchange, as in the other cases we have discussed, is a mutual recognition by both wife-givers and wife-takers of the humanity and right to respect of their opposite number.

In the case of everyday exchanges, the stakes in terms of recognition are less evident on the surface of things, since people rarely talk much about such exchanges or about their motives for carrying them out. It is about these kinds of exchanges that the inquiring anthropologist is most likely to hear that the Urapmin do them because being generous is their custom. Yet two kinds of data argue that recognition is in fact central to everyday exchanges as well. One is that it turns out that the Urapmin do note and monitor quite closely these kinds of exchanges, and they remember each one of them for a good deal of time. They attend carefully to who usually gives them what and what they usually give to others, and they have a very keen sense that they are constantly using things that were originally the property of others and that others are using things that were once theirs (Robbins 2003a). In other words, as casual as everyday exchange appears, Urapmin do not think about it casually, and instead consider it a key barometer of the regard in which others hold them and in which they hold others. As with ceremonial exchange, but perhaps even more so, it is crucial to their sense of personhood and the social relatedness upon which that sense of personhood is based.

The second kind of data that bears on the role of recognition in everyday exchange involves how the Urapmin handle it when everyday relationships break down. When people become angry with or are shamed by one another in the course of daily life, they quickly move to avoid one another. That is to say, they cease to recognize one another socially. This is relatively easy to do in Urapmin, since people can withdraw to their garden houses and do not need to engage with each other to meet their subsistence needs. Yet there is a strong push from the community for members to address their differences and return to a state of mutual recognition, and this they do by "buying" one another's shame (*fitom sanin*) or anger (*aget atul sanin*). In practice, this is usually done by a formal exchange of exactly equivalent goods (*tisol dalamin*, as in death exchanges). Dispute resolution thus climaxes with a ritual of reciprocal exchange that is explicitly about putting people back on a footing of mutual recognition. In my experience, such dispute resolving exchanges are always effective—people who before the exchange had been furious with one another, and/or so ashamed in each others' presence that no relationship was possible, carry on after the exchange as if the relationship had never been disturbed. For the purposes of my argument, therefore, these dispute resolving exchanges amount to a dramatization of the sufficiency of exchange by itself to construct such mutual recognition, since it creates or re-creates recognition in a relationship in which it had before the exchange been completely lacking.[2]

The material I have presented so far has been aimed at demonstrating that the Urapmin gift economy is an economy of recognition; what is at stake in the constant exchanges that mark Urapmin life is the ability of people to construct one another as human subjects through mutual recognition. In considering why an entire economy should be dedicated to the task of allowing people to construct themselves through mutual recognition, it is helpful to consider what Honneth (2001), the key contemporary theorist of recognition (see below), has recently called "the epistemology of recognition." He uses this phrase to raise the question of how it is that human beings communicate that they recognize one another. It is fair to assume that this is accomplished differently in different cultures. In Urapmin, it is gifts given and received that communicate recognition. As I have discussed in detail elsewhere, Urapmin do not believe that speech can ever communicate what another person is thinking or feeling (Robbins 2001). For this reason, verbal recognition carries no weight in Urapmin. The task of communicating recognition falls wholly onto things, and the reciprocal gift economy is the domain in which things are able to carry out this task. The intensity with which the Urapmin engage that economy—one which is materially without profit—is a testament to how important the constant give-and-take of mutual recognition is to them, and to how profoundly it serves to motivate their behavior.

Before turning to a consideration of arguments about the place of recognition in capitalist economies, I want to point out two corollaries of our understanding of the Urapmin gift economy as an economy of recognition. First, what counts as "economic" progress from the Urapmin point of view is an expansion of relations of mutual recognition. They are always seeking new reciprocal exchange relationships. Second, what counts as "economic" failure for them is the inability to initiate or sustain such relations. Most humiliating in this regard is when one cannot make a relationship with someone because one has nothing to give that the other will recognize as an acceptable gift. Precisely this approach to progress and this kind of failure have marked the Urapmin encounter with the West, and the desire to address their failure to achieve progress in this encounter motivates a strong interest among the Urapmin in the possibility of attaining what they call "development"—which would be the ability to make on their own or buy with money they can obtain at home the kinds of goods that would allow them to enter relations of recognition with all of the kinds of people they now know to exist in the world.

The closest the Urapmin have come to what they think of as development has been some mineral prospecting that the Kennecott mining company has carried out on their land. This has provided some sporadic wage labor, for a week or so at a time, within the community. It has also raised tremendous hopes that a mine might be built. My interest here, however, is not in the prospecting experience in general, but in a specific incident that happened at a meeting that took place when Kennecott's representatives, along with a representative of the Papua New Guinea government, came to Urapmin to renew the company's prospecting license. At the end of this meeting, after the Urapmin agreed that the license should be renewed, the main Kennecott representative, someone whom the Urapmin knew fairly well by this point, approached the local councilor, an official the Urapmin elect to represent them to the wider Papua New Guinea government and other outsiders. The Kennecott representative tried to pay the councilor the mandatory compensation that Kennecott owed the Urapmin for the trees and ground that had been disturbed during the prospecting that had gone on under the expired lease. The amount he tried to give the councilor was a large one in local terms, but the councilor refused to take it. He told the Kennecott representative, "Keep that money, just come back and continue prospecting until you find enough gold to build a mine." The Kennecott representative, intent on meeting his company's legal obligations, persisted in offering the money, but the councilor stood firm in his refusal to take it. Eventually, since it was getting dark and rain was threatening, the man offering the money and the other outsiders who had come to the meeting got in their helicopter and left. Kennecott later sold the Urapmin prospect and to my knowledge never returned to the community. The money, as far as I know, was never paid and no mine has been built.

The councilor who refused the money is, because of his personal history, the person in the Urapmin community with the most experience of how people operate in a market economy. At the heart of his refusal to take the cash was his belief that such an outright swap of soil and trees for money would at least potentially end the relationship between the Kennecott corporation and the Urapmin people, rather than signal a moment of mutual recognition in a developing history of such recognition that would eventually lead Kennecott to give the Urapmin a mine. The payment would mark an end to obligations between the two parties, as purchases in the capitalist market tend to do, rather than the kind of deepening of them such a return gift would signal in a gift economy. The councilor, and other Urapmin, hoped for something more by way of recognition and relationship building from Kennecott than market transactions generally deliver, and thus they were wary of engaging in such a transaction with the company. Their wariness raises a general comparative question about whether this kind of hope for recognition through exchange, a hope fostered by long experience of the gift economy, is completely misplaced when it comes to the commodity economy. Is there, or should there be, a place for recognition within the economic sphere in capitalist cultures?

IS GIFT TO COMMODITY AS RECOGNITION IS TO REDISTRIBUTION?

As it happens, this question of whether recognition plays a role in the economic sphere in capitalist societies has been a crucial issue of contention in one of the most prominent debates in contemporary critical theory. Nancy Fraser (1997a; Fraser and Honneth 2003), whose work is at the origin of the debate, has argued that in the late twentieth and early twenty-first centuries political struggle in Western democracies ceased to a great extent to center on economic issues of redistribution organized along class lines and came instead to focus on issues of recognition organized along lines of shared cultural identity. For her, this shift raised the dangerous possibility that the problems of the economic realm might be forgotten altogether. To counteract this possibility, she has suggested that analysts adopt a "perspectival dualist" approach in which they look at all situations in terms of both the economic injuries and the cultural insults that might be occurring within them (Fraser and Honneth 2003: 217–18). Injustices in both the economic and cultural spheres require understanding in their own terms, Fraser argues. Both kinds of injustices can morally ground demands for change, but the two kinds of injustice nonetheless remain distinct and we need to understand them as such in order not to lose sight of the specificity of the economic domain. In her view, to put it most simply, the economy is about distribution—recognition happens elsewhere.

In response to Fraser's arguments, Axel Honneth has further developed the "recognition-theoretic" approach to critical theory that he first laid out in his book *The Struggle for Recognition: The Moral Grammar of Social Conflicts* (1996). Although the argument that has ensued between Honneth and Fraser has a number of facets, the primary one that concerns us here is Honneth's claim that issues of recognition are primary for people in all spheres of action, and that they underlie issues of economic distribution in a way that Fraser's dualist model elides (Fraser and Honneth 2003). In support of this claim, he argues that one's wages reflect social recognition of one's work. To be undercompensated, or unemployed because your skills are not valued, is to be unrecognized in the economic sphere. What those who are subject to these injustices thus militate to change is the recognition order that governs the economy of their society, and it is changes in this order that will produce a redistribution of wealth. Struggles to have one's economic worth recognized are thus different in focus but not absolutely different in kind from struggles to have other aspects of one's self socially acknowledged.[3]

Neither Fraser nor Honneth look in any serious way at data from noncapitalist societies, or even from non-Western capitalist societies. On my analysis of gift economies as economies of recognition, I would argue that such data would support Honneth's nondualist position. For people who, like the Urapmin, live in such economies, recognition is a key part of what is at issue in every material transaction. Given this, Honneth might use the probable fact of the precedence of gift economies in human history to suggest that to the extent that capitalist social relations cover over or disregard the issues of recognition that are always at stake in human exchanges, they routinely lend themselves to the perpetration of injustices of recognition.[4] Such an argument could bolster Honneth's claim that knowledge of the human drive for recognition constitutes a major opening in the critical theoretical project of finding moral grounds internal to society from which to critique its institutions.

Of course, Fraser's argument that the economy is not a sphere of recognition—that in essence gifts are to commodities as recognition is to redistribution—is in ethnographic terms a fine rendering of Western ideology; the same ideology that represents the economic sphere as essentially a moral void. Honneth's bet, though, is that Western ideology does not tell the whole story about what people look for from their economic lives, and that material distribution is thus not the only or even primary issue that can fire people's, even Western people's, moral imaginations. Data on how those who live in gift economies respond to their experience of nonrecognition in the capitalist market—often with versions of what the Urapmin call anger and shame—suggest that in human terms this is quite plausible. It remains for further work on economic experience in the West to see if vestiges of the drive for recognition and the moral valuation of its achievement can still be found in robust form within it. If it can, then perhaps questions of the relation between economy and morality can return to the center of critical theoretical debate, and the gift economy/commodity economy distinction can once again find a place for itself in contemporary scholarly discussion.

NOTES

1. Stern (2002: 25) provides a helpful reading of the *Phenomenology* as a whole as a record of these kinds of failures in all of the areas it discusses. It is important to take account of the context of Hegel's discussion of the master-slave dialectic in order to avoid taking only a dark view of recognition. Macey (1995), in a discussion of Kojève's highly influential reading of the master-slave dialectic as it is presented in the *Phenomenology*, a reading that has shaped almost all twentieth-century discussions of the dialectic outside of technical philosophical works, has nicely captured what an undue focus on the account of recognition in the *Phenomenology* has done to our common understandings of its role in social life. As he writes, "theories of relationship with the other that take as their paradigm Kojève's reading of the master-slave dialectic . . . rarely transcend hostility or outline any concept of mutuality or reciprocity" (Macey 1995: 38–39).

2. The case of dispute resolution exchanges raises an issue that is also relevant to the cases of ceremonial exchange I have discussed. In all of these cases, a good deal of work goes on before the exchange by way of discussions and negotiations that set it up. One might be inclined to see this period of mutual talk as when the real work of mutual recognition is accomplished. The final exchange would then serve merely as an ornamental symbol of this accomplished recognition, not as the mechanism that creates it. This is not, however, how the Urapmin see it. As I discuss later in the text, they do not trust speech to carry recognition between people, and more generally, it is only ritual that makes things socially real, and this includes making mutual recognition socially real (for a detailed argument concerning this, see Robbins [2001]).

3. Several scholars have also extended Honneth's understanding of the role of recognition in the economic sphere. Cannon (2001) argues that many labor movements aim to increase the sphere of recognition in which workers participate by limiting the extent to which their relations with employers and other workers can be constituted solely in market terms. Sayer (2005) suggests that struggles over the dis-

tribution of material goods are not best understood as narrowly economic in motivation, but rather seek a fairer distribution of those goods people need to constitute themselves as worthy of recognition. These are early contributions to what one hopes will become a growing literature on the forms demands for recognition take or can take in the economic sphere in capitalist societies.

4. In an article critical of Fraser's initial formulations of the recognition-redistribution contrast, Butler (1997) does draw on anthropological data and arrives at a nondualist position. In doing so, she makes a point that echoes my own here: "Although Fraser distinguishes between matters of cultural recognition and political economy, it is important to remember that only by entering into exchange does one become 'recognizable' and that recognition itself is a form of exchange." What I am adding to this is the claim that if we consider the importance of recognition to exchange in gift economies, we should also consider whether all exchanges, even economic ones in capitalist economies, might be fruitfully seen as involving issues of recognition, along with whatever other issues they involve. In her response to Butler, Fraser (1997b) explicitly denies the relevance of anthropological materials to debates about the contemporary economy (though she suggests that they can be useful in considering historical questions), arguing that part of what makes modernity distinct is that it has separated out the cultural and economic spheres in a way prior social formations did not. This begs the key question: whether in doing so, modernity has disregarded moral demands for recognition that are properly at home in the economic domain.

REFERENCES

Bohannan, Paul. 1959. The Impact of Money on an African Subsistence Economy. *Journal of Economic History* 19(4): 491–527.

Butler, Judith. 1997. Merely Cultural. *Social Text* 15(3-4): 265–77.

Cannon, Bob. 2001. *Rethinking the Normative Grounds of Critical Theory: Marx, Habermas and Beyond*. Hampshire, UK: Palgrave.

Durkheim, Emile. 1984. *The Division of Labor in Society*, trans. W. D. Halls. New York: Free Press.

Fraser, Nancy. 1997a. *Justice Interruptus: Critical Reflections on the "Postsocialist" Condition*. New York: Routledge.

———. 1997b. Heterosexism, Misrecognition, and Capitalism. *Social Text* 15(3-4): 279–89.

Fraser, Nancy, and Axel Honneth. 2003. *Redistribution or Recognition: A Political-Philosophical Exchange*. London: Verso.

Godelier, Maurice. 1986. *The Making of Great Men: Male Domination and Power among the New Guinea Baruya*. New York: Cambridge University Press.

Gregory, C. A. 1982. *Gifts and Commodities*. London: Academic Press.

Hegel, G. W. F. 1979a. *Phenomenology of Spirit*, trans. A. V. Miller. Oxford: Clarendon Press.

———. 1979b. *System of Ethical Life and First Philosophy of Spirit*, trans. H. S. Harris and T. M. Knox. Albany: State University of New York Press.

———. 1983. *Hegel and the Human Spirit: A Translation of the Jena Lectures on the Philosophy of Spirit (1805–1806) with Commentary*, trans. L. Rauch. Detroit, MI: Wayne State University Press.
———. 1991. *Elements of the Philosophy of Right*, trans. H. B. Nisbet. Cambridge: Cambridge University Press.
Hénaff, Marcel. 2002. *Le Prix de las Vérité: Le Don, L'Argent, La Philosophie*. Paris: Seuil.
Honneth, Axel. 1996. *The Struggle for Recognition: The Moral Grammar of Social Conflicts*, trans. J. Anderson. Cambridge, MA: MIT Press.
———. 2000. *Suffering from Indeterminacy: An Attempt at a Reactualization of Hegel's Philosophy of Right*, trans. J. Ben-Levi. Assen: Van Gorcum.
———. 2001. Invisibility: On the Epistemology of "Recognition." *Aristotelian Society* LXXV: 111–26.
Lévi-Strauss, Claude. 1987. *Introduction to the Work of Marcel Mauss*, trans. F. Baker. London: Routledge and Kegan Paul.
Macey, David. 1995. Bataille the Impossible: Review of Georges Bataille, *The Absence of Myth* and Michael Richardson, *Georges Bataille*: *Radical Philosophy* 73: 38–39.
Mauss, Marcel. 1990 [1925]. *The Gift: The Form and Reason for Exchange in Archaic Societies*, trans. W. D. Halls. London: Routledge.
Polanyi, Karl. 1944. *The Great Transformation: The Political and Economic Origins of Our Times*. Boston: Beacon Press.
Ricoeur, Paul. 2005. *The Course of Recognition*, trans. D. Pellauer. Cambridge, MA: Harvard University Press.
Robbins, Joel. 2001. God Is Nothing But Talk: Modernity, Language and Prayer in a Papua New Guinea Society. *American Anthropologist* 103(4): 901–12.
———. 2003a. Properties of Nature, Properties of Culture: Possession, Recognition, and the Substance of Politics in a Papua New Guinea Society. *Journal of the Finnish Anthropological Society* (Suomen Antropologi) 28(1): 9–28.
———. 2003b. Given to Anger, Given to Shame: The Psychology of the Gift among the Urapmin of Papua New Guinea. *Paideuma* 49: 249–61.
———. 2004. *Becoming Sinners: Christianity and Moral Torment in a Papua New Guinea Society*. Berkeley: University of California Press.
Sayer, Andrew. 2005. *The Moral Significance of Class*. Cambridge: Cambridge University Press.
Stern, Robert. 2002. *Hegel and the Phenomenology of Spirit*. London: Routledge.
Strathern, Marilyn. 1988. *The Gender of the Gift: Problems with Women and Problems with Society in Melanesia*. Berkeley: University of California Press.
Taussig, Michael T. 1980. *The Devil and Commodity Fetishism in South America*. Chapel Hill: University of North Carolina Press.

2

The Grift

Getting Burned in the Northern Malagasy Sapphire Trade

Andrew Walsh

> The grift has a gentle touch.
>
> —Maurer (1974: 3)

This chapter focuses on how people in the northern Malagasy sapphire mining town of Ambondromifehy are sometimes "burned" through participation in reciprocal exchange relationships that are, to borrow Mauss's words, "permeated with the atmosphere of the gift" (1990 [1925]: 65). In addition to highlighting the difficulties of navigating a social context in which the most needed relationships are the ones that have the potential to do the most harm, it discusses the inherent fragility of all systems of moral and economic exchange in which reciprocity and confidence play key roles. By way of introduction, I offer three stories of just what getting burned in Ambondromifehy can look like. The first is almost a success story.

> Mme Fernand has done well from sapphires. She owns the biggest most popular bar in Ambondromifehy, operates a fleet of bush taxis that serve the town, and has enough operating capital to buy large quantities of stones every week. The story of her success is a revealing one. Using money left to her by her late French husband, she made the most of her considerable negotiating skills and bought up as many sapphires as she could in the opening months of Ambondromifehy's first boom in 1996. In those early days few involved in the local trade knew the true value of sapphires, meaning that people like her with the necessary means and knowledge were able to amass large stocks of stones with ridiculously little investment. Rumor has it that Mme Fernand was among those who bought stones by the standard market measure of a condensed milk can, paying not much more for sapphires than she would for the same quantity of

beans. Of course, over the years more local traders have learned more about the value of sapphires on the global market, and Mme Fernand's knowledge advantage has lessened. Still, she continues to do very well for herself, thanks in large part to the very profitable relationships she has developed over the years with several West African buyers—men who transport the stones they buy from her and other Malagasy traders to Thailand where they sell them to their own connections in the Thai trade.

Madame Fernand's relationship with the buyers to whom she sells is, as people in Ambondromifehy might say, strictly *biznesy*; in the same way that she profits from the connections and knowledge that her fellow Malagasy traders do not have, she understands that the foreigners to whom she sells profit from their own advantages, and she does not resent them for this, or at least, she didn't, until recently. In 2003, Madame Fernand consented to advance a stock of stones to an African trader with whom she had had a particularly profitable relationship in the past; they agreed that he would sell the stones for her in Thailand and then pay her for them upon his return. He took the stones, left . . . and never returned. None of the other African traders could tell Mme Fernand what had happened to him, and she had no way of knowing whether or not they were telling the truth. All that was certain was that he was gone, and with him about $20,000 worth of her sapphires. In local terms, Mme Fernand had been "burned."

Given how often I have heard slight variations on the second story related here, it makes sense to tell a generic version of it. This one is almost a love story.

Jao, a man, and Soa, a woman, meet in Ambondromifehy. Like most people here, both are from other parts of Madagascar, drawn to this place by the promise of the fortunes to be made here (stories about people like Madame Fernand circulated all throughout Madagascar in the late 1990s); they are people who, as the saying goes here, have "met when grown," having no past locality or family connections. Still, they develop a stable, trusting relationship, and decide to combine their efforts in the sapphire trade, working together toward the goal of a shared fortune. Jao does the mining, Soa helps with the sieving, keeps house, and often deals with traders. Although no rituals have been performed to mark their union, they live as a married couple calling one another *vady*, or "spouse," and sharing a bed, a house, and, as their efforts begin to pay off, earnings and the goods they buy. And then one day, out of the blue, everything changes. After Jao goes out to dig in his pit, Soa packs up everything of value in the house, piles it into and on top of one of the hundreds of bush-taxis that pass through Ambondromifehy every day, and skips town. Upon returning from his pit Jao is shocked to find his spouse gone, and with her all of the savings and furnishings they had accumulated together. Everything "down to the last spoon," it is often said. It dawns on Jao that he has been "burned," "struck" by what some refer to as a "red suitcase [woman]" (*voa valise mena*)—a woman of now mythical status in Ambondromifehy who, sometimes with the help of traditional medicines, draws a man into a relationship only to take him for everything he has. Joa knows better than to hop in a bush taxi himself and go after Soa. Not only can't he be sure that she is from anywhere near her professed region of origin, he can't even be sure that he ever knew her real name.

For the last of my three stories, I refer to field notes written in 2003 following a conversation I had with Zama, a seventy-year-old longtime resident of Ambondromifehy. Like the previous two, this is ultimately a story of abandonment.

> Sitting here now, Zama says, is like watching *cinema,* nothing like what it was a decade ago before the discovery of sapphires. People going to and from the marketplace take shortcuts through his yard, right in front of us. Most ignore us completely, others remark my presence and nod to me but say nothing to Zama; still others offer an unthinking "*mbolatsara,*" or "hello," some even calling Zama "*papa*" or "*dadilahy*" ("father" or "grandfather") as they pass. Over an hour, only two do what Zama would say they are meant to do. Only two stop, sit down with us, and offer a respectful "*Akory aro*" ("How are you?") to which we respond, as convention has it, "*Meva, akory aro*" ("Well, and how are you?").
>
> Zama is quick to concede that in the early days of the sapphire rush, he and other longtime residents of Ambondromifehy were quite happy to welcome the many young prospectors who descended on their community. After all, such newcomers brought the promise of vitality and new and supportive relationships to a small community that had been losing its youth to nearby towns and cities for years. Before long, though, any hopes for the sort of positive and orderly growth that Zama and others had envisioned were dashed. Dozens of new arrivals per week became hundreds per day, and within a couple months, new newcomers could scarcely have imagined the small, sleepy community that Ambondromifehy had once been. To hear Zama tell it now, the "visitors" who now dominate this place are nothing like the people that longtime residents had once expected they would be. These are not migrants intent on a little land and a community in which they and their families might settle and prosper over the long term. Time and experience have revealed them to be taboo-transgressing, crop-stealing, irrigation-trench-destroying, water-polluting visitors—people who are far more interested in short-term gains than in long-term commitments. These people aren't here to settle, Zama tells me pointing to a young couple flirting shamelessly only a few meters in front of us, they're here to "burn our community."

While much could be made of the significant differences among the protagonists involved in these stories or about how their different experiences reveal some of what makes Ambondromifehy such an interesting place, for the purposes of this paper, I would like to focus on what Madame Fernand, Jao, and Zama have in common, namely, the fact that they have all been "burned"—Madame Fernand by a trusted African buyer, Jao by a "red suitcase" woman, and Zama (and by extension his community) by just about everyone who enters his field of vision. As the stories just related suggest, getting "burned" in Ambondromifehy involves a particular sort of victimization, one that can only be appreciated through the careful consideration of the basis of the relationships that allow it to happen. Madame Fernand's relationship with the buyer who cheated her was long in the making, built through years of successful trades and much mutual flirting and flattery. Similarly, up until the fateful afternoon just described, Jao's relationship with Soa was not so different from countless other give-and-take relationships among men and women throughout Madagascar. And then there is the case of Zama, a man who gave all that a Malagasy host is expected to give visitors with the conviction that doing so would ultimately benefit his community. As far as the people involved are concerned, then, these are not just stories of victimization; they are stories of exchange gone wrong, or, more precisely, exchange stopped short. All stories of people getting burned tend to end in the same surprising way, with the failure of expected returns to materialize. Put another way, then, these might all be described as stories of people victimized by grifts of one sort or another—that is, stories of people who have been done in not just by the clever predations of devious others, but by their own self-interested giving and misplaced confidence.

In wording the title of this paper as I have, I intend to recall Mauss's influential *Essay on the Gift*, commonly referred to simply as *The Gift* (1990 [1925]). Simply put, I would here like to discuss what links might be drawn between grifting—the work of grifters or confidence artists, broadly conceived—and the processes of gift exchange analyzed by Mauss. While some might think these phenomena fundamentally different, in Ambondromifehy the processes involved in grifting and gifting are hard to pry apart. Not only is this place a haven for people who might be characterized as grifters or confidence artists, it is also a place in which reciprocal relationships among people are forged and perpetuated through gift-like exchanges of knowledge, goods, services, and support. And to put the central point of this paper quite simply, this coexistence of grifting and gifting is no coincidence. In Ambondromifehy, grifting (or the semblance thereof) is made possible by the prevalence of gifting, and gifting is always tempered with concerns over the perceived prevalence of grifting. Shortly I will discuss how this is so with reference to some specific features of life in this town. First, however, I offer some general thoughts on gifting, grifting, and what they have in common.

GIFTING AND GRIFTING

While the most commonly cited element of Mauss's (1990 [1925]) argument in *The Gift* is that collectively acknowledged obligations to give, receive, and reciprocate can be essential to the functioning and reproduction of social and economic networks, by no means is this the only insight to be drawn from his work. Of particular interest to me here are points that might be extrapolated from Mauss's consideration of these three obligations in light of the always immanent possible consequences of human liberty. Obligations do not just indicate the means by which individuals unthinkingly reproduce the systems in which they participate. In fact, by their very nature, obligations can indicate the opposite just as effectively, namely, the ever-present possibility that individuals might act in ways that threaten such systems. The fact is that obligations would neither be apparent nor conceived in the way that they are if the actors they seemed to oblige weren't actually only ever *potentially* obliged, always free to neglect the obligatory. In a sense, then, obligations might be understood as having the same sort of social force as taboos; while they can certainly indicate in very powerful ways how people should behave, they have no agency in and of themselves and thus no intrinsic power to actually force such behavior (Walsh 2002). What compels people to fulfill obligations *must* have another source, and it is the search for this compelling force that motivates Mauss through a good part of *The Gift*. Just what is it, Mauss famously asks, that "*compels the gift that has been received to be obligatorily reciprocated? What power resides in the object given that causes its recipient to pay it back?*" (1990 [1925]: 3, emphasis in original).

Rather than weigh in here on the complex arguments surrounding "the spirit of the thing given" (Mauss 1990 [1925]: 10) or on what Mauss, his sources, or his sources' translators might have meant by this phrase, I would rather nudge things in the direction of my own interests by suggesting a simple and obvious, albeit incomplete, response to Mauss's research questions—a response that may well be applicable in just about any context permeated with the atmosphere of the gift (Mauss 1990 [1925]: 65). Based on my understanding of the systems of social and economic exchange that I have come to know through my research in northern Madagascar over the years—systems in which, as Mauss might put it, "obligation and liberty intermingle" (1990: 65)—it seems clear to me that at least one of the things that compels people to act in ways that keep such systems going is confidence, and more specifically, their confidence in the integrity of these systems. In the Malagasy communities in which I have lived, people do not simply give to others with a sense that doing so is the proper thing to do, but also with the unspoken understanding that those to whom they give have the same sense of what is proper. And when those to whom they give then receive and reciprocate in appropriate ways, they too are compelled by the same sort of confidence. In a sense, then, confidence both compels and becomes more compelling as it circulates; it is yet another part of the giver that goes with what is given, compelling receivers to reciprocate and, ultimately, returning to its source, more compelling than ever.

Given that the sort of confidence I have in mind here is not something that people tend to talk about much—it is implicit more often than explicit, assumed more often than described—some might reasonably ask how I can be so sure that it exists, let alone that it has the compelling force that I suggest it does. Simply put, we can know that people's confidence in the integrity of systems of social and economic exchange exists because we can observe it being shaken, and we can discern how such confidence is compelling from the regrets it inspires among those who feel as though they have heeded it carelessly. Just as the power of taboos is never more apparent than in the aftermath of transgressions, the compelling force of confidence is never more discernable than when confidence is betrayed. And, just as the study of taboo transgressions can offer insights into the social orders that such transgressions seem to undermine, so can the study of betrayals of confidence provide food for thought on the systems of social and economic exchange that make such betrayals possible. In both cases, juxtaposing seemingly timeless models of moral behavior with the always immanent possibilities of human freedom reveals the tenuousness of systems of social and economic exchange in which "obligation and liberty intermingle" (Mauss 1990 [1925]: 65). As Joel Robbins notes (this volume), however, focusing only on such idealized systems is limiting. Going a step further and examining the reflections and responses of people in particular real-world contexts who feel as though they have experienced the worst effects of moral transgressions reveals that it is much more than just systems that are at stake when people break the rules. As the cases with which I began this chapter attest, and as I will discuss further in the following three sections, in Ambondromifehy, moral transgressions do more than just upset people, they can quite easily *ruin* them. Before proceeding to how this is so, however, let me turn briefly to the practitioners of the sort of transgression on which I will focus most—people who make an art of attracting misplaced confidence.

In the opening sentence of *The American Confidence Man* (1974: 3), the linguist David Maurer hints at what makes grifting such a unique art: "The grift," he writes, "has a gentle touch." Unlike common thieves, grifters don't take from others, but rather, convince others to give to them, willingly and with confidence that a return of one sort or another is forthcoming; unlike thugs, they don't deal in violence or intimidation, but rather, in the genteel art of seduction, charismatically drawing their victims or "marks" in first with the provision of mutually beneficial transactions and then, deeper still, with the promise of more to come. Grifters strike only after having inspired sufficient confidence in their marks, meaning that, if they are good, they are always found out too late. Not that they are so different from those on whom they prey. It is quite the opposite, in fact. As Maurer puts it:

> There is nothing superhuman about confidence men. . . . They are neither violent, blood-thirsty, nor thieving in the ordinary sense of that word. They are not antisocial. . . . If confidence men operate outside the law, it must be remembered that they are not much further outside than many of our pillars of society who go under names less sinister. They only carry to an ultimate and very logical conclusion certain trends which are often inherent in various forms of legitimate business. (1974: 152)

While Maurer was writing here of American grifters or confidence men of the 1920s and 1930s, for the purposes of this paper I would like to channel his insights into the definition of a more broadly relevant archetype. In the most general terms possible, we might consider grifters to be those who "carry to an ultimate and very logical conclusion certain trends inherent" (Maurer 1974: 152) in any systems of exchange in which participation is compelled by confidence, including those in which Mauss took such an interest. As noted earlier, the gift and the grift aren't so far apart as some might assume. Where the rhythm of the gift is ideally regular and continuous—give, receive, reciprocate; give, receive, reciprocate; give, receive, reciprocate—the rhythm of the grift differs only by one beat—give, receive, reciprocate; give, receive, reciprocate; give, receive, . . . nothing. Grifting only works when those who are victimized by it don't see the end coming, lulled as they are into the familiar give-and-take of relationships that they expect to be beneficial.

In the following sections I illustrate some of the points I have made here about gifting and grifting by returning to the cases from Ambondromifehy with which I began, showing how the features of life and work that necessitate gifting in this place are, in fact, the same features that make grifting a constant possibility.

THE RISK OF TRUST IN THE SAPPHIRE BUSINESS

When asked to comment on what is most distinctive about their work in the local sapphire trade, miners and traders in Ambondromifehy are often quick to highlight the significant role played by various sorts of deception in what they do; in a context in which knowledge withheld can be worth considerably more than knowledge shared, there is little incentive for anyone to tell all and great incentive for all to tell lies (Walsh 2004). That noted, the northern Malagasy sapphire trade is also, and not coincidentally, a context in which people rely heavily on mutually beneficial reciprocal relationships based on trust. In this section I discuss this paradoxical state of affairs by returning to the case of Madame Fernand.

Of all the things I observed over the days I spent with Madame Fernand in 2003, nothing struck me more than the complexity of her relationships with the miners and traders from whom she bought sapphires. Although she professed a certain detachment regarding these people—at one point, she drew my attention to the fact that she only ever looks closely at the stones people bring her, and never at the faces of those offering them—her exchanges with her transaction partners was anything but impersonal. Oftentimes, she called them "father," "sister," or "brother," speaking to them in terms and in a style generally reserved for close friends or kin; she often joked with and cajoled them, at times recalling past exchanges with them from which she claimed to have taken a loss. She also kept a bottle of water at the ready, offering it whenever asked by parched miners passing by her table, assuring them as she did so that, after all, they were "all one family." On several occasions, she responded to requests for help from miners by handing over significant sums of money to them, money that she stressed was not a loan but a "*cadeau*," or gift, for which she expected nothing in return. All the while, of course, she was profiting considerably from these same people, offering them only a fraction of what they wanted for the stones they put before her, knowing both that they needed the money more than she needed the stones and that she would in all likelihood be able to sell what she bought from them to her own buyers for much more in a few days. Although the days of buying sapphires by the measure of a condensed milk can may have been over, having the knowledge and wealth necessary for effective speculating in the trade were no less advantageous in 2003 than they had been in the early years of the boom. Still, Madame Fernand always seemed to know enough to never go too far, aware that her success depended on keeping the miners and traders with whom she had developed profitable relationships happy, loyal, and willing to go on selling to her. Whatever obligations these sellers may have felt toward her, they were always free to sell to whomever they pleased.

Although Madame Fernand is a particularly privileged player in Ambondromifehy's sapphire trade, the way in which she does *biznesy* is really no different from how others, at all levels of the trade, operate. To borrow a phrase from Geertz's classic description of the Moroccan bazaar, the northern Malagasy sapphire trade is well described as the domain of "intimate antagonists" (1979: 225, 299), where agonistic bargaining reinforces, rather than threatens, reciprocal relationships among familiars. Relationships among buyers and sellers develop in such a way as to offer all parties a degree of order and certainty in a context in which disorder and uncertainty seem to reign. And key to the development of such relationships is trust, or at least the closest thing to trust that the setting allows. As Geertz (1979: 203) puts it: "Keeping your feet in the bazaar mob is mainly a matter of deciding whom, what, and how much to believe and, believing (or half-believing), what and how much—and to whom—to confide." The sapphire trade is no different. Here too "mistrust is an adaptive attitude" (Geertz 1979: 208) and yet one that must ultimately be overcome in certain situations. Paradoxically, the only way to succeed in a trade built on various sorts of deception is to seek out and foster relationships in which one can have confidence.

With these points in mind, let us return to the case of Madame Fernand, or, more specifically, to the question that I couldn't help but ask when I first heard of how she had been burned: why was she willing to entrust another buyer with a valuable stock of stones without an up-front payment? First, it should be noted that credit arrangements among buyers and sellers are common in the sapphire trade. In fact, provided that both parties come to an agreeable end, such arrangements are among the means by which players in the trade build confidence in the relationships on which their work depends. Obviously, such trust-testing arrangements start out with minimal risk involved—with stationary traders entrusting mobile protégés (called *demarchers*) with single stones to show around town, for example. Over time, though, and as confidence in relationships builds, the stakes tend to get higher. Thus, when an African buyer with whom Madame Fernand had had years of successful exchanges informed her that she should buy up as much of a particular sort of sapphire as she could, she understood this to mean that he would eventually buy this stock from her. And when he then informed her prior to his departure for Thailand that he would not be able to pay her for these stones until his return, she took his word for it, aware that withholding her stones from him could well jeopardize what had until then been a profitable relationship. In our conversation on this matter, Madame Fernand was adamant that she would not have done what she did with just anyone. She entrusted her stones to the buyer in question only because she had good reason to trust him; past transactions had transpired without a hitch, ending just as such cycles are meant to end—with the promise of never ending. Ultimately, it was her confidence in this promise of continuing returns that left her open to being burned.

While I do not mean to argue that the sapphire trade operates entirely like a gift economy, the case of Madame Fernand suggests that there are enough parallels between the two to make a comparison interesting. Indeed, reading *The Gift* alongside Geertz's description of the bazaar, one can't but note the commonalities between Mauss's (1990 [1925]) account of gift giving, receiving, and reciprocating and Geertz's (1979) account of bargaining. Both authors describe how ongoing relationships among transaction partners can be deepened, rather than threatened, by agonistic interchange. What is more, in both gift economies and the bazaar, the deeper the relationships among exchange partners get, the more mutual confidence seems to grow; and the more mutual confidence seems to grow, the less inclination there is for any party to pay much attention to the fragile foundation on which such relationships are actually based. This, despite the fact that, as the story of Madame Fernand illustrates, even the seemingly deepest reciprocal relationships can fall apart quite easily when one or another partner unexpectedly exercises the freedom that is always their prerogative.

THE BENEFITS AND DANGERS OF "MEETING WHEN GROWN"

As in any boomtown, "meeting [people] when grown"—namely, having no past connection with the people one meets—is an unavoidable feature of life in Ambondromifehy. Not surprisingly, then, the people who have come and stayed here over the years tend to be adept both at finding new social networks into which they might fit and at including others into existing networks of their own. While conducting interviews with miners and traders in 1999, I was particularly struck by people's accounts of how quickly they were able to establish the relationships on which they had come to depend in this place. On one occasion, a young woman told of learning the ropes of life in Ambondromifehy from a group of women, soon to become "sisters," she had met on her first day in town. In another interview, a young man told of how he disembarked from a bush taxi one evening at dusk, got himself caught up in the whirlwind celebration of an unacquainted miner's recent windfall, and then, less than twenty-four hours later, found himself working in a pit as part of that miner's team. Others told similar tales of rapid incorporation, recounting how they were first drawn into existing social networks characterized by relations of reciprocal exchange among members, and then into related social, domestic, and working milieus. There were not only happy stories to be told, however. In Ambondromifehy, relationships are as quick to dissolve as they are to appear, and thus many informants also described relationships that didn't work out. In this section, I discuss how the qualities that make Ambondromifehy such an easy place in which to settle are the same ones that make it a place in which settlers are especially prone to falling prey to the people on whom they come to most rely.

However quickly relationships develop amidst the chaos of life in a boomtown like Ambondromifehy, personal connections here are by no means randomly made. Opportunities for reckoning relatedness despite "meeting when grown" are many and variable. For some, religious affiliation is a key factor. At the height of the sapphire boom in 1998, Ambondromifehy was home to at least five Christian churches and two mosques, all of which welcomed brethren with open arms, providing them with connections, support and, often, a place to stay. One evangelical Christian church even distributed membership cards so that congregants might move more easily from one community to another. For other newcomers, mutual aid associations comprised of people from the same home region are important. Generally speaking, people join and contribute money to such associations as a form of death insurance, with the understanding that the association will cover the cost of transporting their bodies back home should they happen to die in Ambondromifehy. But these associations do more than just that. In that they bring together people from a single region, they tend to be rich sources of contacts for new arrivals hailing from these regions. That association members are as likely as not to have no previous connections with one another isn't such an obstacle; in a place like Ambondromifehy, being from the same general region is tantamount to being kin. In fact, for many newcomers, first meetings with others, especially those from the same home regions, are often occasions for determining just how they might be related *as* kin. Since descent is traced bilaterally throughout Madagascar, anyone coming into Ambondromifehy has a wide range of descent-group affiliations from which to draw in seeking to establish relatedness with others they meet. Add to this the various long-standing alliances that exist among particular descent groups, and the web of possible connections grows even wider. What all of this means is that when people in Ambondromifehy use kin terms to refer to others they have only recently met, they are not necessarily doing so simply for the sake of convenience. Malagasy norms of relatedness and sociality both encourage and enable the rapid development of such connections and, by extension, of the reciprocal relationships that tend to spring from them.

Given that Ambondromifehy's boom-time population growth was fueled largely by the influx of young men and women, it shouldn't be surprising that another common means by which people developed sustaining connections and entered existing social networks was through relations with the opposite sex. The earlier related story of Jao and Soa, strangers who quickly became "spouses," was not at all uncommon in this town, nor were accounts of other, more fleeting, relationships between young men and women. Significantly, people tended to describe the longer lasting of these relationships as reciprocal in nature, with men doing the mining and sharing a portion of the money earned from their finds with "spouses" while women reciprocated in various ways: having sex with their partners, cooking for them, doing their washing, and, in some cases, selling their stones. Where circumstances allowed it, men and women sometimes worked together in shared pits, splitting their finds in much the way that all-male mining teams would. In other cases, unattached women simply brought empty rice sacks with them to a mining pit or cave with the expectation that the men mining there would fill them with sapphire rich earth. Men who gave up earth in this way could expect any number of things in return, the most obvious being sex.

I am certainly not the first to suggest that relationships between men and women of the sort described here bear a resemblance to the reciprocal gift-giving relationships with which Mauss was concerned. Indeed, it bears mentioning that Mauss himself was critical of Malinowski's (1922) assessment of the Trobriand husband-wife relationship as one in which husbands provided pure gifts to their wives and received nothing in return. In Mauss's view, such support is better viewed as "a kind of salary for sexual services rendered" (1990 [1925]: 73) or, more generally, "total counter services not only made with a view to paying for services or things, but also to maintaining a profitable alliance." However crude all this might sound to some ears, I should note that Mauss's remarks are not so far from the assessments of several of the young men and women I interviewed in Ambondromifehy. No different than any other relationships established here, they described how their relationships with their spouses were intended from the start to be productive, reciprocal, and even "profitable." What this means, of course, is that if one partner involved in such a relationship decides to neglect his or her obligations by exercising his or her freedom and leaving, the other partner is likely to be left with much less than just a broken heart. Nowhere is concern over the ever-present possibility of being burned in such a relationship better represented than in stories of "red suitcase" women and the men they leave behind.

It is important not to take any one telling of the story of a "red suitcase" woman too literally. The generic way in which I presented the story earlier is precisely how it was most commonly presented to me, usually by third parties talking either about something that had happened to someone they knew or something they had heard rumor of having happened. This is not to say that these stories are nothing but rumors, or that women don't ever leave men high and dry in Ambondromifehy—they do, just not always so dramatically or in keeping with the standard script. Nor is it the case that men never leave women the same way. In fact, this latter fate was by all accounts much more common than the former. Other, newer, mining boomtowns in Madagascar are constant draws for young men on the lookout for new opportunities, meaning that Ambondromifehy is now home to a good number of women, some with young children, waiting to hear back from spouses who have left for other parts of the island. For such women, as for Jao, it would seem that the reciprocity and confidence that had drawn them deep into promising relationships has, in the end, left them all alone.

DEALING WITH VISITORS

In the previous two sections, I examined how the features of work and life in Ambondromifehy that seem to encourage reciprocal relations among people also leave these people particularly susceptible to being burned in one way or another. In this section, I revisit the last of the three stories with which I began. By recounting some of what happened in the years leading up to my conversation with Zama in 2003, I illustrate how and why it is that he and other preboom residents of the community came to feel abandoned and burned by people from whom they had initially expected so much.

Zama was one of about 400 people already living in Ambondromifehy at the time of the discovery of sapphires in the region. In fact, he was the son of one of the brothers who had first established this community back in the 1930s. As a young man, he had traveled to different regions of Madagascar, but he always came back—after all, this was the place where he retained a house and rice fields, and where he hoped eventually to be buried. After his father died, he settled in Ambondromifehy permanently, taking over his father's house and many of the responsibilities that came with being a senior "parent" (*reyamandreny*) of the community. Among other things, he became the *mpijoro*, or "invoker," associated with a sacred site established by his father, a tree only a few meters from his house. More generally, he became a senior "person responsible for the community" (*tompontanana*), a community authority that newcomers intending to settle here were advised to see first.

Unsurprisingly, Zama was a very busy man during the first weeks of the sapphire rush. In response to the first prospecting visitors who sought him out, he did as was expected of him and offered them reassuring words about the community they were entering and all that could be expected from those already living here. He also informed them of the local taboos that must be respected if they and everyone around them were to go on prospering in this place. In return, at least some of these visitors responded correctly to this welcome, living responsibly by respecting local taboos against digging in the ground on Tuesdays and avoiding inappropriate contact with local sacred sites, for example. Some even sought to deepen their relationships with longtime residents by asking to perform the rites necessary for securing the blessing of local ancestors and spirits. At first, Zama took such requests seriously, leading these visitors to the sacred invocation site for which he was responsible and taking them through a rite (called *tsakafara*) in which they requested blessing for their mining efforts. As part of this rite, they promised to return to this place with a sacrifice should the blessing requested prove to be efficacious. Predictably, and to Zama's initial delight, several of those who requested blessing here made extravagant promises, assuring Zama and his ancestors that they would return with barrels of rum, steers, and other large offerings as sacrifice once they had earned enough to do so. Unfortunately, however, and to Zama's great dismay, few were ever inclined to actually live up to these promises, even despite their successes and Zama's frequent reminders. As Zama described it, these were the worst sort of shirkers—people who had so obviously benefited from the blessings that he had made available to them, but who refused to acknowledge this by fulfilling the obligations incurred by what they had received. Their irresponsibility was more than just insulting, however. By failing to reciprocate in appropriate ways, these visitors threatened the integrity of the site at which their invocations had been made, as well as Zama's own relationship with the forces invoked there.

To hear Zama tell it, after the first few months of the boom, almost no newcomers bothered to even inquire after the community's longtime residents upon arrival; they were better served by connections of the sort described in the previous section. And they didn't concern themselves with local taboos either, although many certainly knew about them. To young men mining illegally within dangerous caves or pits in a local conservation area, chancing run-ins with the police, cave-ins, and falling into crevices, breaking local taboos was just another risk entailed by their work (Walsh 2003).

Some did listen to Zama and others who linked the dwindling supply of easily accessed sapphires to the disrespect that had been shown to longtime residents, local ancestors, spirits, and sacred sites. About a year into the boom, a group of visitors approached Zama offering to atone for their transgressions in the hopes of improving their luck. Under his instructions, they bought and sacrificed a steer in order to cleanse Ambondromifehy's most significant sacred site, an invocation site on the banks of a lake to the west of town. Within months, however, this site had once again been "broken" (*robaka*) by disrespectful visitors. One day in 1999 Zama reported to anyone who would listen that he had had a dream in which a water spirit, in the guise of a crocodile, informed him of its intention to leave this site. And with this departure, he claimed, the promise of prosperity that the presence of this spirit had long guaranteed would go as well. This time, there was no response from his newest neighbors.

Here again we have a variation on a familiar story in Ambondromifehy: the tale of the dissolution of a relationship that was once, or was intended to be, reciprocal and mutually beneficial. Where longtime residents of Ambondromifehy had once encouraged newcomers to settle and enter committed long-term relationships with them, by the time I met him in 1999, Zama had been burned once too often to ever be so giving again. In fact, only a few months prior to our first conversation, Zama had constructed a fence around the invocation tree next to his house blocking newcomers' access to what was once a site for creating and fostering reciprocal relationships with longtime residents (Walsh 2006). The damage had been done, however. Ambondromifehy would never, and never will, return to the community it had once been; the cycle of give-and-take whereby visitors might previously have become more deeply rooted in this place had stopped by 1999, leaving people like Zama with nothing to do but complain and try to protect what had yet to be broken.

AFTER THE GRIFT

In the previous three sections, I have illustrated how the features of social life that make gifting necessary and grifting possible are both found in abundance and are interconnected in Ambondromifehy. What remains to be discussed is just how unusual this state of affairs is. Is the intertwined coexistence of gifting and grifting that I have been discussing here a unique feature of communities like Ambondromifehy, or might we be able to conclude (as Mauss did at the end of *The Gift*) (1990 [1925]: 65) by extending the observations made here to other social contexts? Just what can a study of grifting tell us about gifting? Let me begin my answer to these questions by pointing out again that, despite their similar trajectories, the gift and the grift do differ in at least one very significant way, namely, in how they end. While the rhythm of the gift is ideally continuous, obliging givers to give and receivers to reciprocate, the grift always ends short and, for some at least, abruptly. What this means, of course, is that the gift and the grift tend to inspire different responses in those they involve: where gift transactions are likely to be followed by the anticipation of more of the same, a well executed grift is likely to be followed by reflections on what went wrong and on how things might have gone differently. Put another way, incidences of grifting are likely to inspire critical reflection on the inherent precariousness of reciprocal exchange relations in ways that run of the mill gift-giving is not.

In a well-known essay on the fragility of the self, Erving Goffman (1952: 452) lamented the sorry position of those victimized by confidence artists in American society, noting how their "expectations and self-conceptions [are] built up and shattered" through dealings that reveal, ultimately, just how far they are from being the shrewd operators they thought they were. Goffman notes how marks compromised by the combination of misplaced confidence and an inflated sense of self often require consolation—or "cooling out" in the argot of the grift—in order to deal with the many losses (psychological as much as financial) that come from being conned. Taking Goffman's argument as a product of theoretical and analytical inclinations consistent with the North American society that he claimed to be describing in his work, one can't help but wonder what other insights might be drawn from other sorts of "cooling out" in other sociocultural contexts. What sorts of consolation appeal to people, like those in Ambondromifehy, who are perhaps not so "self"-centered as Goffman's subjects; people for whom acts of grifting imply not just or so much the fragility of the self, but rather the fragility of the social networks through which complex selves and livelihoods are made?

For the people discussed in this paper, reasoning after the grift tended to lead them in a number of different directions. Some advocated a stricter sort of traditionalism than was being most commonly practiced here, one in which reciprocal and mutually beneficial relationships are rooted in long-standing kin relationships that are not so easily abandoned as those forged in this boomtown setting. Thus, several people who felt as though they had been let down by the fictive kin they had made after arriving in Ambondromifehy described how they had encouraged family from home communities to come and join them in the hopes that such kin would make for more reliable work partners. I also interviewed several young men who had given up hope on relationships with women they had met or might meet in Ambondromifehy, opting instead to have elder kin in home communities organize to have suitable partners sent to them. In both situations, the reasoning seems to have been the same: better to rely on relationships with people you know than with people you don't. Interestingly, however, not all agreed with this logic, noting how reciprocal relationships among long-standing kin are subject to the same problematic possibilities as are those newly created among people who have only "met when grown." In fact, some argued that reciprocal relations with long-standing kin are even more dangerous that those with relative strangers since they are so much harder to abandon if they do not work out. While there is no questioning the morality of those who give up on a stranger who burns them, dealing with kin who do the same is much more complicated. To some, it seems, getting burned by kin has become a recurring obligation that they would much rather live without.

A second common reaction among people who felt as though they had been "burned" was to idealize and advocate the sort of impersonal, alienating exchanges allowed for by the market. Madame Fernand was among those in this camp, as evidenced by her reflections on the business practices of the Thai buyers with whom she sometimes dealt. Where African buyers like the one who did her in were friendly and sought to create long-lasting reciprocal relationships with Malagasy traders, the Thais, she claimed, were much less social and were only interested in sapphires. They bought what they wanted from whoever was offering, doing sellers no particular favors, but not burdening them with obligations either. For obvious reasons, Madame Fernand imagined that all would be better off if everyone operated in this way—if everyone just looked at the stones regardless of the face of the person selling them. But then it is also worth mentioning that Madame Fernand would not have had the early successes she did were it not for the way of doing business to which she so adamantly objected.

However the people discussed above might have reacted to being burned, the key point that I would like to end on is that their reactions and reflections were an important realization; namely, that relationships "permeated with [the] . . . atmosphere of the gift, where obligation and liberty intermingle" (Mauss 1990 [1925]: 65) are inherently fragile. Based on their experiences, they understood how reciprocal relationships that can be so important and productive can also be so damaging. Put another way, they understood just how dangerously close gifting and grifting can appear until it is too late; all that is required for the former to be revealed as the latter is for one or another party to exercise freedom, a possibility that is always there. In appreciating this simple point, I expect that they are not alone in the world. While Goffman might be right in arguing that being victimized by a grift can lead people to reflect on themselves, those who suffer this fate are just as likely to reflect more broadly on the nature of the exchange relationships that led them to the confidence that would ultimately be betrayed. And as it does for them, so it might for those of us with an interest in making sense of such relationships and their place in the communities we study.

Rather than view incidences of grifting as nothing but glitches in otherwise stable systems of reciprocal exchange, we might better view them as impetuses for reflection on just how ambiguous such systems really are for those they involve. While I will admit to being among those who, like Mauss (1990 [1925]: 65), finds consolation in the knowledge that "everything is still not wholly categorized in terms of buying and selling" and that "there still remain people and classes that keep to the morality of former times," I am also wary of romanticizing or making a doctrine of *The Gift*. It is all well and good to do as Mauss (1990 [1925]: 71) counsels and "adopt as the principle of our life what has always been a principle of action . . . : to emerge from self, to give, freely and obligatorily" with the assurance that "we run no risk of disappointment," but let it never be forgotten that anyone who has fallen victim to a grift is likely to have heard that line at least one too many times before. For such people, consolation must be sought elsewhere.

Acknowledgments. The research on which this chapter is based was supported by a postdoctoral fellowship and a standard research grant from the Social Sciences and Humanities Research Council of Canada (SSHRC). My greatest thanks are due to the people of Ambondromifehy, without whose cooperation this research could not have been completed. I am grateful to Kate Browne and Lynne Milgram for inviting me to participate in the conference from which this volume has come, for their extensive comments on an earlier draft of this chapter, and for their commitment to seeing this project through. I am also very grateful to Dan Jorgensen for the conversations, insights, and suggestions that inspired much of what appears here. Thanks also to Tim Bisha, Jennifer Cole, and Karin Schwerdtner for commenting on earlier versions of this chapter.

REFERENCES

Geertz, Clifford. 1979. Suq: The Bazaar Economy in Sefrou. In *Meaning and Order in Moroccan Society: Three Essays in Cultural Analysis*, 123–314. Cambridge: Cambridge University Press.

Goffman, Erving. 1952. On Cooling the Mark Out: Some Aspects of Adaptation to Failure. *Psychiatry* 15(4): 451–63.

Malinowski, Bronislaw. 1922. *Argonauts of the Western Pacific*. New York: E. P. Dutton & Co., Inc.

Maurer, David W. 1974. *The American Confidence Man*. Springfield, IL: Charles C. Thomas Publisher.

Mauss, Marcel. 1990 [1925]. *The Gift: The Form and Reason for Exchange in Archaic Societies*, Trans. W. D. Halls. New York: W. W. Norton.

Walsh, Andrew. 2002. Responsibility, Taboos and the "Freedom to Do Otherwise" in Ankarana, Northern Madagascar. *Journal of the Royal Anthropological Institute* 8(3): 451–68.

———. 2003. "Hot money" and Daring Consumption in a Northern Malagasy Sapphire-Mining Town. *American Ethnologist* 30(2): 290–305.

———. 2004. In the Wake of Things: Speculating in and about Sapphires in Northern Madagascar. *American Anthropologist* 106(2): 225–37.

———. 2006. "Nobody Has a Money Taboo": Situating Ethics in the Northern Malagasy Sapphire Trade. *Anthropology Today* 22(4): 4–8.

3

Maya Daykeepers

New Spiritual Clients and the Morality of Making Money

Walter E. Little

> Maybe the trouble lies with the word "moral." . . . Nothing has made my critics angrier than the notion that a food rioter might have been more "moral" than a disciple of Dr. Adam Smith. But that was not my meaning.
>
> —E. P. Thompson (1993: 271)

As the opening quotation suggests, what is considered moral is difficult to apply universally across different class and cultural groups, as well as from the perspectives of producers and consumers.[1] This case study considers the moral economy of Maya spirituality and how it is changing due to globalization. Is it permissible for Maya daykeepers to enrich themselves through the spiritual work they perform for individuals and community? The genesis of this question relates to a common sentiment expressed by daykeepers (*ajq'ija'*[2]) that ajq'ija' should not profit from their clients, namely, people who seek spiritual guidance. Ajq'ija' explain that they are obligated to perform ceremonies and do so in the service of their clients, be they individuals or communities of people. Personal economic gain, they emphasize, should not motivate them to fulfill their spiritual duties. Over the twelve years that I have worked with them, ajq'ija' have seen significant material gains that are directly related to their spiritual work (Little 2004). This contradiction between obligatory service and market relations (ajq'ija' are paid) inspires this inquiry into the community norms that influence ajq'ij economic practices and notions of service. This case study also provides an example of how gift- and monetary-based systems can overlap within the contemporary neoliberal state in which the state contributes to the institutionalization of morality.

Looking at the socioeconomics of Maya spirituality offers a way to consider the relationship among production, exchange, and consumption in the configuration of contemporary Maya moral economy. In highland Guatemalan towns, ajq'ija' have performed (produced) particular services for primarily local clients (consumers) for centuries. What were considered appropriate practices and charges by ajq'ija', as worked out via the local community (market) through social sanctions on overcharging, are being reconfigured in the contemporary global context. Furthermore, the moral economy of the ceremonial practice of ajq'ija', when it moves from a local to global context and is performed for clients with different cultural and economic practices, raises new dilemmas about the relationship between economic and spiritual value.

Highland Guatemalan Mayas did not in the past, nor do they today, have an aversion to economic exchange—be it gift or money based. As members of agricultural communities already linked to a market system, ajq'ija' themselves often directly participate in both farm work and the marketplace. Whereas Thompson's (1993) and Scott's (1976) respective work teases out what happens in the market when prices are perceived as unfair and working conditions and wages are unjust, namely everyday resistance, protest, riots, and boycotts, the tension that they suggest is ultimately between persons of different social classes. In other words, their examples tend to hinge on economic relations that pit members of the same culture, but of different social classes, against each other.

In contrast to the moral expectation of a "fair" price in a market, the moral basis for economic behavior among Maya is delineated from within a community. Whereas Thompson and Scott use interclass relations to discuss moral economy, I am interested, first, in how and the extent to which, intracommunity socioeconomic relations of ajq'ija' and their clients reveal a community-based moral economy. Second, the contemporary spiritual-economic work of ajq'ija' also includes foreigners who bring very different cultural and moral values. The transactions that ajq'ija' have with these outsiders, however, are not framed primarily by class relations, but are rather the result of a tension between two opposing approaches to moral economies. I discuss these contrasting moral economies in terms of how serving and profiting from foreigner clients affects local notions of morality and income-generation to suggest that local moral economy is being reconstituted as a national moral economy by Maya ajq'ija'.

Mayas' complaints about ajq'ija' profiteering and ajq'ij discourses related to the inappropriateness of profiteering do not relate to the condemnation of economic exchange in relation to spiritual work. Instead, I argue that local Maya concerns relate more to the sets of constraints, obligations, norms, and imperatives in which ajq'ija' are enmeshed. This reality effectively illustrates Parry and Bloch's (1989) point that exchange, gift, or commodity, is not necessarily intrinsically moral or immoral. In fact, it would be misleading to claim that Mayas, ajq'ija', or their clients are mystified by capitalist relations of production or markets (physical places or metaphorical) any more than are people from Europe or the United States. Rather than interpret the market of Maya spirituality à la Michael Taussig (1980)—that successful ajq'ija' increase their wealth through pacts with the devil (or any other spiritual entity)—it is more productive to consider the discourses of the ajq'ija' and their clients, as well as community sanctions imposed on ceremonial practice. This helps avoid "making" the economic institutions "that actually shaped markets invisible as well as creating the appearance of a separate and autonomous economic domain disembodied from society" (Edelman 2005:332). In other words, with regard to spiritual practice, Mayas may be resisting the changing capitalist relations in which they are a part by not allowing the economic to become disarticulated from the social. They do not lose sight that ajq'ij spiritual work is, at once, economic, spiritual, and political. Both Robbins and Walsh (this volume) illustrate the similarly intertwined domains of economic and social relations, especially with respect to gift-based societies and their intersection with capitalist commodity-based systems.

In this case, Mayas participate in an economic exchange in which the gift-commodity distinction is effectively collapsed. However, the form of exchanges (commodity and gift) that occur between people belonging to the same community now includes exchanges with people unknown to each other. This can shed light on the differential practice of morality across sociocultural spheres as well as what is considered moral in economic spheres.

This chapter is divided into two main sections. The first outlines the traditional "moral economy" of Maya spirituality. It does not present an overview of the esoteric practices of ajq'ija', a topic that has been covered by Guatemalan (Barrios 2004; Kawoq 2005; León Chic 1999) and foreign (Colby and Colby 1981; Tedlock 1982) scholars. Rather, it draws on ethnographic research, largely conducted in the 1940s and uses this earlier data here as historical documents to help establish what was the intracommunity economic morality of Maya spirituality before ajq'ija' began serving foreigners. The second section discusses interactions ajq'ija' have with their new clients who are not members of their same community. This section also details the effect that this interaction has and the impacts in terms of moral economy that these outsiders have on Maya communities. I conclude with a discussion of whether the moral economy of Maya spirituality has indeed changed, to what extent ajq'ija' can use their profession to increase their personal wealth within the global economic conditions they now work, and what community and state sanctions exist to regulate ajq'ij practice.

MORAL ECONOMY OF TRADITIONAL MAYA SPIRITUALITY

> The business affairs of shamans remain pretty much a mystery.
>
> —Sol Tax (1953: 97)

Tax's comment still summarizes ajq'ij economics. My goal in this section is to locate traditional Maya spiritual practices within a local political economic context in order to outline the moral economy of highland Maya spirituality. This will establish a baseline from which to discuss how the work and earning potential of ajq'ija' have changed as a result of the new non-Maya clients they now serve.

In general, ajq'ija' throughout the Guatemalan highlands have served local community material and spiritual needs through rituals and divinations that honor and appease ancestors and *nawales*,[3] resolve community conflicts, and help mediate individual and community "life-cycle" events. The ritual and divinatory services that ajq'ija' provide are fundamentally rooted in the material world, as they deal with real life problems that are the result of conflicts between individuals within the community, potentially hostile outside forces (Ladinos, foreigners, mountain spirits), and insufficient veneration of the nawales, the saints, and the ancestors, which all reside within and are a living, active part of the community. Neglecting their obligations to these community internal and external entities, as well as conflicts with co-community members, can lead to poor crops and harvests, sickness, loss of wealth, and alienation from their respective communities and families. Similar to Robbins's discussion of reciprocity and recognition and Walsh's example of grift versus gift (this volume), the social relations of economic exchange and what is moral emerge in the case of transgressions and failures to live up to various social obligations.

The traditional economics of ajq'ij ritual can be interpreted from earlier ethnographies about Guatemalan Mayas. Ajq'ija' did not perform ceremonies without an economic transaction, either in the form of gifts or money or both. Maud Oakes (1951: 83–88), who conducted research in Todos Santos from 1945 to 1947, illuminates this economic relationship in her account of when she was accused of being a witch, particularly because she had been giving away medicine and medical services rather than receiving some form of payment. Despite the fact that she donated her services and was not expecting gifts or payment, some people she cured presented her with gifts.

How much an ajq'ij gets paid and how much profit he or she makes remains as much a mystery today as during the period of Sol Tax's fieldwork in the 1930s. Unlike vendors who work in a public place and whose economic transactions can be watched and calculated, ajq'ij economic exchanges take place in private and charges for services are ambiguous and scaled to the specific problem and wealth of the client. A Kaqchikel ajq'ij explained to me:

> I don't charge anything for my work, but my clients are expected to cover my expenses, pay for the ritual materials (*samajib'äl*), and, if they feel I've done a good job, give me a gift. For the ceremony to have any power, the client has to give enough that they feel it, that they suffer some.

On another occasion, however, the same ajq'ij revealed that he typically charges a minimum fee of 300 quetzales[4] for a ceremony. Many of his clients, however, are the non-Maya clients who are discussed in the next section. Ajq'ija' today, and probably in the past as well, are not forthcoming about what they make. They are wont to complain that they do not get enough compensation for their work. In the 1940s, according to one Todos Santos *chimán*, "God will pay you. The people of this pueblo give nothing. They give food, a drink, cigarettes, only such things, and for this reason we are poor" (Oakes 1951: 124).

Generally, the market for the services of ajq'ija' is constrained by how one is called to service, the obligation to serve community spiritual needs over individual economic gain, the obligation to repay the ancestors and nawales some or all of one's individual economic gain, the community political constraints, and local economic constraints. Maya cultural revitalization movements and the serving of non-Maya clients are challenging these sociocultural and economic constraints. The remainder of this section discusses the interplay of these constraints in order to consider: first, ajq'ij service to local-community spiritual needs, to resolve community conflicts, and to help mediate individual and community "life-cycle" events; second, what ajq'ija' are paid and how payment relates to the local economy; and third, community sanctions on profit-driven ajq'ija'.

The ceremonial practice of ajq'ija' must first be contextualized within community politics. In Tax's (1953) ethnography about Kaqchikel Maya in Panajachel, aq'ija' occupied an ambiguous place in politics. They appeared to be economic professionals, who are not as formally integrated into the political hierarchies of the community as those who enter the civil-religious hierarchy—the primary authority structure in traditional Mesoamerican communities. Instead, they served to resolve conflicts among individuals or mediate between the community and outside hostile forces. Tax's contemporaries, Bunzel (1952), Oakes (1951), and Wagley (1949), all similarly noted ajq'ija' performing these roles in the respective communities that they studied in the 1930s and 1940s. Of these studies, ajq'ija' in Panajachel appeared to have the least access to political power. In their research in the K'iche' Maya town of Chichicastenango and the Mam Maya town of Todos Santos, Bunzel (1952) and Oakes (1951), respectively, are more specific with regard to the important political roles the ajq'ija' performed. There was a dual sense of obligation and responsibility to perform ceremonies for the good of the community, regardless of economic remuneration. When community leaders called upon their services, they were obliged to comply. For example, Oakes (1951: 24) noted *chimánes* (the Todos Santos term for ajq'ija') were expected to learn why the *dueño de cerro* punished them by not providing rain to prevent epidemics, to determine the times of fiestas (1951: 56), and to protect the spirit of the *Caja Real*. One *chimán* explained: "But I and all of us here work for the *Caja Real*, and its spirit works for the pueblo. A grave responsibility is ours, for if we do not take proper care of the *Caja* harm will come to the pueblo, to our crops, our animals, all the people of the pueblo" (Oakes 1951: 68). Bunzel (1952:79) wrote that the *chuch qajaw* (literally "mother-father" but a top ajq'ij position among the K'iche') (see Tedlock [1982: 31–36] and Carmack [1995]) "is the most important professional man in Chichicastenango." She added, "The position of the layman in approaching the supernatural is very much like that of an average American citizen in a court of law. . . . [H]e may defend himself if he wishes, but the wise man hires a lawyer." Hence, the position in which ajq'ija' found themselves was as a specialized mediator who acts out of responsibility and obligation on community and individual levels to interpret the spiritual and ancestral forces that affect community and individual life. They held specialized knowledge that was part of local political domains, but they were not necessarily the most powerful political figure in their respective communities. For instance, the chuch qajaw's "authority was not questioned, but limited" (Carmack 1995: 37; Brintnall 1979: 97–98; Warren 1989: 66–67; Watanabe 1992: 208–9).[5]

Tedlock (1982) thoroughly described the process that one must go through to become an ajq'ij, but Tax (1953: 195) was succinct, "shamans and midwives are said to be 'called' to their professions (which they then practice, lest they sicken and die)." My traditionalist ajq'ij friends maintain this is true today.[6] Many of them endured numerous physical torments, afflictions, family disasters, and economic setbacks on the path to becoming an ajq'ij. I asked three ajq'ija' (July 26, 2006) from different towns in the Kaqchikel linguistic region of Guatemala if they could leave their spiritual work behind and do something else. The man from Santa María de Jésus refused to answer on the grounds it was too dangerous. The woman from Santa Catarina Palopó explained that my question did not make sense because an ajq'ij does not have a choice in the matter. The man from Santa Catarina Barahona replied that performing one's spiritual duties was paramount to living.

The important but politically ambiguous role that ajq'ija' play serving local community spiritual needs was sometimes exploited for economic gain. As holders of specialized knowledge who work between sacred-spiritual and profane domains, ajq'ija' appear to be in an ideal place to take economic advantage of their peers. In the cases of Todos Santos (Oakes 1951), Chichicastenango (Bunzel 1952), and Momostenango (Tedlock 1982; Carmack 1995) ajq'ija' were clearly powerful community figures, who placed economic demands on their clients. Ceremonies, when based in the community, then, as now, were expensive, but this did not necessarily allow for ajq'ija' to significantly increase their personal wealth.

The local economic context tended to limit the capabilities of ajq'ija' to make money. Poor farmers did not have much or any money to give. In ethnographic fieldwork that was conducted in the 1930s and 1940s, ceremonial costs for materials were exorbitant by local conditions, even before gifts and payments to ajq'ija' were made. Most of the economic descriptions of Maya ceremony and ritual were vague. Usually, just the items used in the ritual were listed. For example, Oakes (1951: 145) wrote that the materials used in one ceremony included sixteen beeswax candles, sixteen candles made from fat, four large beeswax candles, turkey eggs, copal (an incense made from resinous pine), other types of incense (most likely frankincense, myrrh, and various kinds of resinous pine incense), *aguardiente* (crude cane liquor), cigarettes, coffee, sugar, bread, two roosters, and four skyrockets. With the addition of Florida water and other herbal-infused liquids, chocolate, cigars, turkeys, flowers, and tortillas, the list of ritual items that are burned in the ceremonial fire had been consistently used from the 1920s through the present. Bunzel (1952: 84) commented, "The cost of incense and candles, roses and aguardiente that are sacrificed on the *quemadores* in the course of a year in the life of an average family head, runs into large sums, just how large it is impossible to estimate." She explained that when dealing with problems—sickness, loss of employment, conflicts, or special occasions—fiesta days and major life-cycle events like marriage—the K'iche' Maya residents of Chichicastenango spent great sums of money.

Aside from the cost of ritual items, all of which get consumed in the sacrificial fire, clients were also expected to pay the ajq'ij for her or his services. Bunzel (1952: 299) noted that for a basic divination or ceremony the ritual specialist was paid a fee of five cents, unless the ceremony was lengthy and complex, then the chuch qajaw "is given meals in addition to his fee, and usually some additional gift—a chicken, aguardiente or money." In comparison, Wagley (1949: 69) observed that chimánes in the Mam Maya town of Chimaltenango paid ten to fifteen cents for these services, adding that a portion of this money must in turn be offered in a ceremony. Oakes (1951: 106) noted that a fee of ten cents was expected in Todos Santos.

Tax (1953) provides the most comprehensive description of ajq'ij economics, but as implied in the quotation opening this section, he was probably suspicious of his calculations. He figured that ajq'ija' in Panajachel worked an average of 118 days per year, performing 234 rituals, from which one earned $210 (Tax 1953: 95). Of the eleven ajq'ija' he interviewed, he considered only seven to be full-time practitioners, although all of them also combined their ritual work with agricultural work (Tax 1953: 96; see also Carmack [1995: 187]). The two most active ajq'ija' averaged a ceremony per week, which typically lasted three to four hours and was performed at night (Tax 1953: 97). Ajq'ija' in Panajachel usually earned fifty cents per ceremony, plus food, which Tax calculated at forty cents, and liquor, which he calculated at sixty cents. He also observed that in the vicinity of Lake Atitlán, where Panajachel is located, the fees given to an ajq'ij for ceremonies could range from twenty-five cents to three dollars. Tax (1953: 98) was not sure if the larger amount was for "one visit or ritual or the entire cure."

To place these economic calculations in context, Tax estimated that the average agricultural laborer's daily wage was one dollar per week. This compares with other 1930s wage estimates (see also Bunzel [1952: 407–9]; McCreery [1994: 313]; Sieder [2000: 290]). By the time the typical agricultural worker paid for the average cost of a basic ceremony, a week's wages or more were spent, representing an incredible burden on the client. Compared to the contemporary ajq'ij mentioned earlier whose fees represented about 67 percent of a full-time agricultural worker's monthly income, fees in the past appear to be more in line with local economic conditions. The earlier mentioned ajq'ij did lower his fees when working within his community.

In Panajachel, the average earning of an ajq'ij outstripped the typical agricultural worker four to one, but Tax did not report how much of these earnings were, in turn, returned to the nawales or the ancestors in ritual fires. Interestingly, ethnographic descriptions of Maya communities and ajq'ij practices[7] do not describe significant differences in wealth between ajq'ija' and other community members. Bunzel (1952: 24) offered an example of one man in Chichicastenango who may have used his influence as an ajq'ij to enrich himself by exploiting others. In this case, the community turned against him, and conflicts within his family resulted. One reason that ajq'ija' do not appear to be relatively wealthier than others in their community may have to do with the local sanctions placed on ajq'ija', such as gossip and concepts of "limited good" (Foster 1965), as well as enculturated notions of obligation and responsibility that they have to the community. Given that the income of ajq'ija' tended to derive from service to individuals and groups from the same area, local economic and cultural constraints against profiteering were strong, especially in poorer, more rural communities.

Thompson (1993), Scott (1976, 1985), and even Edelman (2005), respectively, identify unequal market conditions where price gouging occurs between economically hierarchal social positions, power differentials within the relations of production between peasants and capitalists, and the impact of powerful global economic and political forces on peasants. They use differences in economic class to highlight the moral economy—teasing out just what is considered fair—and illustrate how the politically and economically weak resist grossly unequal relations of production and market conditions. By contrast, the notion of economic fairness, which as Edelman (2005: 332) notes is the continuing appeal of Scott's work, is used to discuss what are the locally defined constraints on the abilities of ajq'ija' to accrue wealth. As Thompson (1993: 344–45) posits about Scott's use of moral economy, "One benefit that has accrued from the term's transportation into peasant studies is that it can be viewed in operation within cultures whose moral premises are not identical with those of a Judeo-Christian inheritance." Indeed, the attendance to the ancestors, nawales, mountain spirits, and intercommunity social relations in relation to the economics of Maya spirituality reveals a moral economy that limits ajq'ija' from using their knowledge and ambiguous political power to their advantage. This is not to imply that ajq'ija' are immune to local political and religious struggles[8] or that Maya spirituality is not a means to resist the dominant Ladino society or global forces. Furthermore, in past and contemporary times, both ajq'ija' and community members agree that in the traditional local community context, ajq'ija' must sacrifice their profits, especially what are considered excesses, to the ceremonial fire. They are expected to repay the debt (*k'as*) they incur from receiving gifts by making payments (*toj*) to nawales. To not repay the k'as by paying toj offends the person's ancestors, the community saints, and the nawales, which leads to the weakening of the community against outside forces, contributes to intracommunity conflict, and even leads to the death of the ajq'ij (see also Fischer [2001: 244]). Hence, strong cultural beliefs about the causes and effects of Maya spiritual practice constrain ajq'ija' in their practices.

NEW SPIRITUAL CLIENTS

> [The] building of the Mayan Inn at Chichicastenango and the influx of tourists who invade homes and desecrate sacred places have increased the hostility to whites, and resulted in a withdrawal of the Indians comparable to that in the pueblos on the Rio Grande in New Mexico.
>
> —Ruth Bunzel (1952: 8)

The discussion about the moral economy of Maya spirituality and ajq'ij practices in the previous section is meant to show the importance of those practices in Maya history, but also to help emphasize that the new clients for whom the ajq'ija' perform ceremonies is a recent development. As the above quotation from Bunzel suggests, Mayas in the 1930s were not receptive to outsiders, despite the fact that they shared information with occasional anthropologists (Bunzel 1952; Oakes 1951; Tax 1953; Wagley 1949) and authors (Huxley 1934). Carmack (1995: 183) notes that with regard to Ladinos, both they and Mayas promoted religious segregation and that although outsiders could observe some public ceremonies, "rural clan ceremonies were undoubtedly even more strongly taboo for Ladinos."

The detailed research that Colby and Colby (1981) and Tedlock (1982) conducted on traditional Maya religious practice came just before the military's genocidal assault on Maya communities in which more than 200,000 people were killed or disappeared, more than 200,000 forced into foreign exile, and over a million internally displaced (Carmack 1988; Comisión para el Esclarecimiento Histórico 1999; REMHI 1998). Throughout the 1980s, the violence in the highlands against Mayas chilled ethnographic research of all kinds and Maya spiritual practices went underground as they had during repressions in the colonial period (Carmack 1995; Carmack et al. 1995).

In the early 1990s, Mayas were suspicious of outsiders observing, much less actually participating, in ceremonies. In the Oxlajuj Aj Maya Language and Culture program (Brown et al. 2006), sponsored by Tulane University to train linguists and ethnographers, as well as build collaborative scholarly relations among Mayas, foreigners, and Ladinos, an ajq'ij performed ceremonies for the class. The teachers and the ajq'ij warned the students about the potential danger of such ceremonies in Guatemala's then political climate, asking them to keep ceremonies secret. They were reluctant to invite students to ceremonies strictly conducted for other Mayas. Edward Fischer (2001) who is an alumnus of the Oxlajuj Aj class describes the reaction he received in 1993 when he attended a *Waqxaqi' B'atz* ceremony, which marks the day on the 260-day sacred calendar upon which ajq'ija' reaffirm their spiritual commitment and fortify their links to the nawales:

> An affluent Kaqchikel doctor from Tecpán, denounced the presence of voyeuristic gringos who hoped to capture a part of Maya sacredness, collect it as folkloric relic, and commercialize it in publications sold in the US; Don Tomás concurred with the doctor in questioning our presence and intentions. . . . After this, our many overtures were rebuffed during our first year of residence. (Fischer 2001: 111)

Questioning outsiders' motives to watch ceremonies was common among Mayas during this period in which the resurgence of Maya religion gained momentum and linked to the Pan-Maya cultural revitalization movement (Fischer 2001: 249–50). Today, in part because of the Peace Accords in 1996 between the military and guerrilla forces, Maya spirituality is conducted in public and is considerably more open to outsiders. Waqxaqi' B'atz is now attended by non-Mayas and ajq'ija' perform ceremonies for outsiders. Alvaro Colom (2008–2012) even announced that he practiced Maya religion and was an ajq'ij himself. Colom participated in the Council of Mayan Elders, an organization with the goal of improving indigenous and nonindigenous relations.

It is beyond the scope of this essay to explain why ajq'ija' are more open to non-Maya clients. Rather, I will describe these clients and outline the economic-oriented interactions in which they and ajq'ija' are engaged. There are three general types of clients with whom ajq'ija' work: Ladinos, New Age spiritualists, and academics. Although ajq'ija' do work with tourists, "tourist," as a type, is too broad a social category to have utility here. In addition, the work that ajq'ija' do with Ladinos, New Age spiritualists, and academics represents a less transitory relationship than that typified by tourists on vacation.

Ladinos

Historically, Mayas have been socially excluded, economically marginalized, and politically repressed by the Ladinos in control of the market and government. At best, Mayas and Ladinos ignored each other; at worst, Mayas were killed (Carmack 1988; Carmack et al. 1995; Comisión para el Esclarecimiento Histórico 1999; REMHI 1998; Smith 1990). In 2001 it came as a surprise when one of my ajq'ij friends invited me to participate in a ceremony he was conducting for a Ladino man. He had come from a town near Antigua because of heartbreak he had suffered and was seeking help for his "profound sadness" and inability to meet a new love.

I was introduced as an anthropologist who was interested in the content of the ceremony. The man agreed, and I observed the ceremony, which structurally followed typical conventions: The ajq'ij opened the ceremony by asking the nawales and ancestors for permission to conduct it, then the petition was made for the client, and finally, thanks and appreciation was given to have been permitted to make the petition. The petition, which was in a mixture of Spanish and Kaqchikel, lasted roughly 10 percent of the ceremony. The rest of it was in Kaqchikel, a language that the client did not know and had no interest in learning.

Since then, I witnessed many other ceremonies by the same ajq'ij who has (as of 2007) developed a large Ladino clientele, who employ him to help them mediate spiritual-based illnesses, including *susto* (fright), *envidia* (jealousy), and *mal de ojo* (evil eye), as well as problems with money, romance, and employment. What I did not notice in that first ceremony and has been present in all subsequent ones is that the ajq'ij's role was less as a mediator of the spiritual realm, skilled at communicating with ancestors and nawales. He is more a psychologist, listening carefully to their problems. He makes them feel at ease, asks pointed questions to get at what may be the cause of their problems, and then suggests causes of action, which invariably include a spiritual component, like burning incense and candles at specified times during the day.

These Ladino clients tend to be poor to middle class and disenfranchised from economic and political—even family and community—support systems.

They are the clients from whom the ajq'ij expects to collect the 300-quetzal fee. A surprising number of them are return customers, and they recommend him to family and friends, suggesting satisfaction with his counsel. Although economic relations between ajq'ija' and Ladino clients are typically capitalistic and based on market values of the services performed, gift and market exchanges, however, can blend into each other. When Ladinos, especially the wealthier businesspersons for whom he conducts spiritual work, receive positive results, they generally give gifts as well. Some of the more extravagant have included 18-carat gold jewelry and airplane trips. As long as these Ladino clients are willing to pay, he can demand whatever fee he can get for his services, but to demand gifts is regarded as improper. In the ajq'ij's own words,

> Doing a ceremony is work. I work for my clients and for that I am paid. Sometimes, they don't listen to the advice and their problems get worse. Sometimes, their problems are resolved. They don't owe me anymore. But sometimes, out of their own volition or because of what their heart tells them, they will give me a gift. It can be small—flowers for my altar—or large—a new watch, but I can't expect these gifts. It would be wrong and offend my ancestors and the nawales.

New Age Spiritualists

New Age spiritualists in Guatemala comprise a diverse group of well-traveled, transnational cosmopolitans who seek esoteric spiritual links from a wide range of culturally diverse religious forms of expression. Typically, they mix and match religious practices and ideologies, looking for, as one practitioner explained to me, common threads that indicate an "underlying spiritual unity that connects all the forces of the universe." This perspective, as one believer commented, allows "humankind to work toward peace and realize its humble place in the universe."

With regard to the spiritual-economic or economic-spiritual encounters of New Age spiritualists and Maya ajq'ija', there is less a "symbolic struggle" than two one-way discussions that sometimes converge around Maya calendar systems and vague notions of peace and equality. For example, in January 2005, I hiked to a cornfield on *Junapu'*, the sacred volcano Agua, outside Antigua, with a group of New Age spiritualists and two ajq'ija' with two assistants. One of the ajq'ija', a Tzutujil Maya, had been mentoring one of the New Age spiritualists, and the reason for the ceremony was to mark the completion of one cycle of his lessons. Walking through the brown, dry post-harvest cornfields in the early morning sun, the New Age spiritualists and I talked about what interested them about Maya spirituality. They explained that as it is an "original religion," it serves as "a way to spiritually connect to pure, positive cosmic forces" via the 260-day ritual calendar and divining with the *tz'ite'*, red ritual seeds (Tedlock 1982). I asked the person who the ceremony was being held for how he could afford to live in Guatemala for several months studying with an ajq'ij while covering the expenses for ritual materials? He paid his and the ajq'ij's travel expenses to sacred sites, as well as the fees normally collected by ajq'ija'. He and the others said that the money is not important, that my interest in the material is what has caused so much conflict in the world. One of them posited, "What things we have don't matter. You can't worry about that. What we need to do is to direct our spiritual energy to positive, helpful means to change the world for the better."

A couple of weeks later, some of the same New Age spiritualists had asked an ajq'ij to help "purify" them and fortify their "spiritual energy." For this ceremony, the ajq'ij asked me to help with the ceremony. We purchased the requisite ritual items in the market: candles, incense, aromatic herbs, Florida water, top-shelf rum, and chocolate—costing roughly 600 quetzales. They paid for the materials and gave the ajq'ij a gift of roughly the same amount of money. In this instance too, they rebuffed my attempts to learn how much they were spending on ceremonies. One explained that the rituals are a way to connect "to ancient power forces that help unify humankind." Another expanded on this:

> In the year 2012, the Maya calendar will end and there will be an opportunity to make real changes, to get beyond our differences. Some think the world will end, maybe it will, but it doesn't have to. That is one reason we do these ceremonies to spiritually unify humanity.

It is important to note that the New Age spiritualists I have met are university-educated persons of some economic means, who are successful in their work and part of supportive family and friend networks. They do not worry about their own and others' material conditions because they have not had to want for basic necessities. Instead, it is through discourses of (and practices related to bringing) peace, harmony, and unity to humankind that they hope to overcome strife in the world. Ajq'ija' working with them are sympathetic to these ideals, but they are not convinced that inattention to material concerns, which can be tied to the disrespecting or ignoring the ancestors and nawales, will help the New Age spiritualists attain their goals. The ceremony in which I assisted was conducted entirely in Kaqchikel. The ajq'ij followed the standard ceremonial structure previously noted. During the petition, the ajq'ij asked the nawales and the ancestors of the participants if they had any grievances. He then asked what could be done to help make them content. A participant asked him to direct the energy of the ceremonial fire to connect with "cosmic forces that will bring harmony to the earth." The ajq'ij, however, asked the nawales and the ancestors for advice on how to help people meet their material needs.

After the ceremony some of the New Age spiritualists remarked that they could feel the "strength of the fire" and that it "really helped rejuvenate them." One commented that by "focusing their positive energies" through ceremonies like this, "they will help prepare us and the world for 2012." Another added, "Yes, if we [speaking collectively for New Age spiritualists worldwide] all focus our energy on peace through the ceremonies of all the true religions, the changes in 2012 will be positive." I asked if they wanted to know what had been said in Kaqchikel, but they "got the message through the energy of the fire."

Later, when talking with the ajq'ij, I asked about the contradiction between what he said during the ceremony and how his clients interpreted the ceremony. "They are good people," he said. "They want the world to be better and that is good. But it is hard to read the fire, to listen to the nawales and the ancestors when the questions are vague, about making the world peaceful. You can see suffering. People suffer because they don't have food, a home, and the things they need. In the ceremony, I sometimes ask my clients to help them with this." A long-term client has done this by donating her money and time to charitable activities to help Maya communities.

Overall, both New Age spiritualists and ajq'ija' minimize the economic side of the encounter. New Age spiritualists downplay the economic exchange because it reminds them of the material world that they find problematic and a cause of suffering. Ajq'ija' know this discourse well enough to strategically avoid placing economic payment upfront, which they do with their Ladino and Maya clients. This has ultimately served them well, since these clients tend to be very generous. One Kaqchikel Maya ajq'ij was able to accrue enough money to purchase a car, and another Tzutujil Maya ajq'ij was able to remodel his home.

Foreign Academics

The third category of new clients with whom contemporary ajq'ija' work are foreign academics. My observations are based primarily on the ceremonies I have participated in as a member and director of the Oxlajuj Aj Kaqchikel Maya language and culture class for the past thirteen years and random invitations from other academics, who include professors and graduate students. Although we share overlapping interests in Maya spirituality and are concerned with Maya spiritual practice, our research interests are diverse—from learning about contemporary ritual in order to better understand the archaeological record to tracing Maya cultural continuities and practices through time to understanding the relationship of Maya spirituality to political economy in historic and contemporary times.

Apart from this research, we have a wide range of personal spiritual beliefs. For instance, I am not the most religious-minded individual, but after watching me struggle a number of years to get a tenure-track position, two ajq'ij friends took it upon themselves to conduct a ceremony for my benefit. They wanted to see if I had not made a transgression against the nawales or ancestors or if I was the object of some conflict or jealousy. I agreed to the ceremony, paid for the ritual items, about $300, but at their insistence contributed no additional fee or gifts. They identified the cause of my suffering as having to do with the jealousy of another who envied my director position in the Kaqchikel class. They asked my nawal, Kan, and my ancestors to mediate. Being the central figure in a private ceremony gave me a better understanding of ritual practice, and the following year I took a tenure-track position at the University at Albany. Neither eventuality made me a believer, but the latter was proof to the ajq'ija' and our Kaqchikel friends that they had repaired the problem in my life.

Interactions between ajq'ija' and academics make me question whether the relationship is symbiotic or exploitative. To be clear, academics pay for the ceremonies they participate in for research, covering the travel expenses of the ajq'ij, the costs of the ritual materials, and providing additional fees or gifts according to local norms. They treat ajq'ija' as professionals, paying them consulting fees for giving formal talks and interviews about Maya spirituality that match those of other Ladino and Maya professionals in Guatemala. The fact remains, however, as in the ceremony for my benefit, that they sometimes do not charge for their services and frequently allow academics to participate in Maya, Ladino, and New Age spiritualist ceremonies without paying them—only contributing a small gift to be consumed in the ceremonial fire.

Whether the relationship is symbiotic or exploitative depends on the relations of exchange. Do ajq'ija' get anything out of it: knowledge or money or favors? Ultimately, because the relationship between ajq'ija' and academics is an intensely personal intersubjective one, exchange is not based purely on monetary-based market relations or gift-oriented reciprocal relations, but it is a fusion of the two, which can embed both parties into long-term socioeconomic relations, of which the big economic and social payoffs can be delayed for years. For an example, academic connections can lead to guest lectures in the United States, Canada, Europe, or Japan, which contribute to an ajq'ij's prestige and can be converted to wealth through the increased demand for their services. Ajqija' limit academics with short-term research interests by contributing to research projects on their time not the academic's schedule, and sometimes subjecting the scholar to numerous delays and questions about the research, particularly what benefit it may have for Mayas.

As in the respective cases by Robbins and Walsh (this volume), gift and capitalist exchanges are not necessarily separate domains of exchange, but the one that predominates can indicate a particular social relationship with corresponding notions of fairness and morality embedded in the exchange. Maya ajq'ija' use particular types of economic exchanges to determine the social relations they will have with certain kinds of clients. They recognize that a purely capitalistic exchange of money for services will not necessarily result in an ongoing exchange relationship, like one that is based on gift exchanges (see Robbins, this volume).

MAYA SPIRITUAL ORGANIZATIONS AND THE STATE

> . . . develop the organization, coordination and participation of Ajq'ija' from the distinct linguistic communities of the Pueblo Maya at the local, regional, and national levels by strategic action means, through programs and projects oriented at the rescue, defense, and promotion of spirituality, Sacred Sites, ancestral knowledge, research, and training.
>
> —Oxlajuj Ajpop mission statement 2001

The rise of national-level organizations, such as Oxlajuj Ajpop, to regulate economic practices of ajq'ija' and standardize training for aspiring ajq'ija' indicates that ajq'ij leaders are attempting to establish norms of ritual protocol in changing economic and political times by imposing conditions that would place constraints at the level of the nation similar to those at the level of the local community. Oxlajuj Ajpop is at the forefront of this movement, publishing a number of books that delineate what is Maya religious and political authority (*Aj Awarem*, Oxlajuj Ajpop 2003) and writing on the history of Maya religion within the contexts of colonialism, resistance, and Maya political and religious autonomy (*Uxe'al Pixab' re K'iche' Amaq'*, Oxlajuj Ajpop 2001). In addition, it advocates the regulation of ritual and ceremonial practice, as well as the standardization of ajq'ij training and the establishment of an official ajq'ij identification card.

Other organizations, engaged in similar initiatives, include the Kaqchikel Cholchi' (Kaqchikel Linguistic Community) and Consejo Maya Jun Ajpu' Ixb'alamke. The former published the monolingual report, *Maya' Nimab'äl K'ux Pa Kaqchikel Tinamït*. It is a comprehensive study of spiritual practice, an explanation of appropriate spiritual protocol, and a list of sacred sites and names of ajq'ija'. The latter published a similar book, *Wajxaqib' B'aatz* (Consejo Maya Jun Ajpu' Ixb'alamke 1999). This monolingual K'iche' book goes beyond the description of an important ceremony. It explains appropriate protocol for ajq'ija', as well as their responsibilities and obligations.

I return to the question with which I began this case study—is it okay for ajq'ija' to enrich themselves through their spiritual work? Within the home community there are collective moral imperatives, which ajq'ija' commonly iterate in terms of obligations to the nawales, the ancestors, and to the other members of their community. In this context it is not appropriate to profiteer. The rise of regulatory and standard-setting Maya spiritual organizations at the national level suggests the formation of a new, larger community that emphasizes the same responsibilities and obligations as those as the local community, including the necessity of ajq'ija' and their clients to pay their debt (k'as) through sacrificial payments (toj). The state and state-level organizations indicate attempts to impose a type of morality on these spiritual exchanges, be they gift or market oriented, at national and transnational levels. It is unclear in this move to forge a larger community where the new clients fit in. I have no answer to this, but it is clear that ajq'ija' see no reason why they should not make money from such exchanges.

CONCLUSION: A NEW MORAL ORDER

Thompson's (1993) and Scott's (1976, 1985) respective theoretical perspectives relate to what are considered appropriately moral economic transactions that are defined through the social, economic, and political relations of a community of people. The economic value of the practices of Maya ajq'ija' is embedded in the moral economy of highland Maya communities. Local political struggles, economic limitations, and group membership constrain ajq'ija' from making significant profits. As members of the same class and cultural and community group as their clients, testing the market or even demonstrating minor conspicuous consumption can result in community sanctions and exclusion from social and public life.

In the exchanges between ajq'ija' and new clients, there are few community-based constraints that prevent ajq'ija' from profiting from the new clients described above. Indeed, ajq'ija' working within their respective communities are bound to the moral economic conventions that are shaped by local norms of fairness and that are established through ongoing social relations. What they earn from outsiders relates to their ability to exploit a more universal "market" of Maya spirituality. I intentionally provided examples of successful, from the ajq'ij perspective, transactions. Some ajq'ija' unsuccessfully exploit this market, failing to make connections with new clients or failing to be convincing or adequately skilled at their work. What makes economically successful ajq'ija' just that, successful, is their ability to converse with new clients, to communicate with culturally different others. In contrast to ceremonies based on locally defined interactions with ancestors and nawales and restricted by material conditions, economic interactions with new clients are ambiguous. For example, although they are significantly less transient than tourists, New Age clients are generally not regarded as community members and not linked to community-based nawales and ancestors who can impose sanctions or help. In this context, ajq'ij money earning is part of broader global trends in which money comes from outside the community and is not necessarily bound by local constraints.

The comparison of the traditional moral economy of ajq'ij economic practice with that of their economic transactions with new clients suggests what is problematic about Thompson's (1993), Scott's (1976), and Edelman's (2005) theories of moral economy. These hinge on conflict, if not outright exploitation of weaker groups by more powerful others. The moral economy of the weaker group comes to light through that group's resistance to the impositions and unjust economic conditions that they face. In the first section of this chapter, I outlined how cultural, social, political, and economic constraints come from within a group, a community of people. These place limits on ajq'ija', especially their ability to reap significant profits from members of their community. Within the community, capitalist and gift economies blend in ways that socially bind ajq'ija' to their peers and limit them from exploiting those same peers. In the second section, we see categorically different people—socially, culturally, materially, etc.—engage in economic transactions that likewise blend gift and capitalist economies. What distinguishes these examples from the cases discussed in Thompson, Scott, and Edelman is that the transaction—the production of the ceremony, the marketplace exchange between the ajq'ij and the client, the consumption of the ceremony by client—is not inherently one in which one party is trying to exploit the other. Why would it even be considered immoral for ajq'ija' to make as much money off of the new clients as they can? After all, the new clients are clearly not part of the ajq'ij's community and should they not get as much money for their work as this transnational market will support? The problem with the articulations between actors from different economic systems is that increases of wealth among ajq'ija' are not problem free and can lead to conflict within Maya communities, just as can the earnings of transnational migrant laborers coming into the community from outside sources. The articulations of different economies and influxes of wealth from outside the traditional and explainable domains of Maya communities have engendered responses that are not based on resistance. In fact, one response is an attempt to restore moral order and conduct at the level of the state.

Moral economic order is difficult to establish across transnational spaces because the context of market and consumptive relations between ajq'ija' and new clients are, at root, determined by culturally distinct norms. The economics of traditional Maya ajq'ij spiritual practice can be framed even today in understandable terms by Mayas for Mayas. However, although ajq'ija' and new clients seem to agree upon a fair market price for services, what each knows economically about the other is limited, and this can lead to disputes within communities. The articulation between Mayas' economic morals and transnational clients' economic morals is difficult to resolve for ajq'ija', since conflicts can result between them and members of their respective communities as a result of new material differences and access to the economic, political, and social benefits that non-Maya clients can potentially bring them. Added to this situation, national-level Maya spirituality organizations' attempts to standardize and regulate ceremonial practices of ajq'ija' can be seen as a reaction to these processes, which are differentiating Maya communities. As such, the changing conditions in which ajq'ija' work with traditional clients and with Ladino and new transnational clients indicate that moral economic order for them and for other Mayas is in reformation at both the community and the state level.

NOTES

1. This, according to Edelman (2005: 332), explains the difference between Scott's (1976) focus on peasants' culturally contextualized morals and values of production and Thompson's (1993) emphasis on consumers in the marketplace. Scott explains how peasants' sense of economic morality manifests as resistance to the unjust system of production in which they work, while Thompson contends that consumers react, sometimes by rioting, to unfair prices in the marketplace. An important point to take from Edelman's (2005) review of Scott's research is that economics is not unmoored from other types of social relations. Capitalism tends to obscure these relations.

2. *Ajq'ij* (singular; *ajq'ija'* plural) is the Kaqchikel Maya word for daykeeper. Tedlock's (1982: 2) definition of *ajq'ij* is appropriate, "person whose occupation is the days" since ajq'ija' manage sacred 260-day calendars, which are used to regulate material and spiritual problems.

3. *Nawal* (*nagual*) has various meanings: guardian spirit, shape-shifting witch, and companion spirit (Tedlock 1982: 221). Martín del Campo (2006) argues that its meanings are the result of hegemonic historical processes in relation to local power. Kawoq's (2005: 53) contemporary definition of *nawal* is "the energy, force, protective spirit that protects a person."

4. A 300-quetzal fee, plus the costs of materials and the travel expenses of the petitioner, possibly family members, and the ajq'ij and possibly an assistant, can add up to a sizeable amount of money for a full-time agricultural laborer making as little as 360 quetzales per month.

5. Only Wagley (1949: 95) places the chimán del pueblo unambiguously within the local political hierarchy. He is located just below the community's highest-ranking authority, serving as the town's public ritual specialist and spiritual advisor to the *principales*.

6. My ajq'ij and Kaqchikel Maya teacher friends explained that a woman we knew was killed in a tragic accident because she disregarded her true calling as a midwife, especially since two different ajq'ija' divined independently that she needed to undergo midwife training.

7. See Brintnall (1979); Bunzel (1952); Colby and Colby (1981); Oakes (1951); Tax (1953); Tedlock (1982); Wagley (1949); and Watanabe (1992) for detailed community studies, which describe ajq'ij practices and local politics.

8. Carmack (1995), Brintnall (1979), Warren (1989), and Watanabe (1992) illustrate how ajq'ija' can support others' political struggles. Furthermore, Maya spiritual practices did place economic burdens on communities, which was why community members turned against ajq'ija' and provided inroads for Protestant missionaries and Catholic reformists.

REFERENCES

Barrios, Carlos. 2004. *Ch'umilal Wuj: El libro del destino*. Guatemala City: Cholsamaj.

Brintnall, Douglas E. 1979. *Revolt against the Dead: The Modernization of a Mayan Community in the Highlands of Guatemala*. New York: Gordon and Breach.

Brown, R. McKenna, Judith M. Maxwell, and Walter E. Little. 2006. *¿La ütz awäch? Introduction to Kaqchikel Maya Language*. Austin: University of Texas Press.

Bunzel, Ruth. 1952. *Chichicastenango: A Guatemalan Village*. American Ethnological Society Publication 22. Seattle: University of Washington Press.

Carmack, Robert M., ed. 1988. *Harvest of Violence: The Maya Indians and the Guatemalan Crisis*. Norman: University of Oklahoma Press.

Carmack, Robert M. 1995. *Rebels of Highland Guatemala: The Quiché-Mayas of Momostenango*. Norman: University of Oklahoma Press.

Carmack, Robert M., Janine Gasco, and Gary H. Gossen, eds. 1995. *Legacy of Mesoamerica: The History and Culture of a Native American Civilization*. Upper Saddle River, NJ: Prentice Hall.

Colby, Benjamin, and Lore Colby. 1981. *The Daykeeper: The Life and Discourse of an Ixil Diviner*. Cambridge, MA: Harvard University Press.

Comsión para el Esclarecimiento Histórico. 1999. *Guatemala, memoria del silencio*. Guatemala City: UNOPS.

Consejo Maya Jun Ajpu' Ixb'alamke. 1999. *Wajxaqib' B'aatz*. Guatemala City: Editorial Serviprensa.

Edelman, Marc. 2005. Bringing the Moral Economy Back into the Study of 21st-Century Transnational Peasant Movements. *American Anthropologist* 107(3): 331–45.

Fischer, Edward F. 2001. *Cultural Logics and Global Economies: Maya Identity in Thought and Practice*. Austin: University of Texas Press.

Foster, George A. 1965. Peasant Society and the Image of Limited Good. *American Anthropologist* 67(2): 293–315.

Huxley, Aldous. 1934. *Beyond the Mexique Bay*. London: Chatto and Windus.

Kawoq (Cuma Chávez, Baldomero). 2005. *Pensamiento filosófico y espiritualidad maya*. Antigua, Guatemala City: Editorial Junajpu.

León Chic, Eduardo. 1999. *El corazón de la sabiduría del pueblo maya:Uk'u'xal ranima' ri qano'jib'al*. Iximulew, Guatemala: Fundación CEDIM.

Little, Walter E. 2004. *Mayas in the Marketplace: Tourism, Globalization, and Cultural Identity*. Austin: University of Texas Press.

McCreery, David. 1994. *Rural Guatemala: 1760–1940*. Stanford, CA: Stanford University Press.
Martín del Campo, Edgar. 2006. "The Nagual Hiding in Shadows: Metamorphic Supernaturals, Contested Discourse, and the Complications of Fieldwork in the Huasteca Veracruzana of Northeast Mexico." PhD dissertation. State University of New York at Albany.
Oakes, Maud. 1951. *The Two Crosses of Todos Santos: Survivals of Maya Religious Ritual*. Princeton, NJ: Princeton University Press.
Oxlajuj Ajpop. 2001. *Uxe'al Pixab' re K'iche' Amaq' (Fuentes y fundamentos del derecho de la nación Maya K'iche')*. Guatemala City: Editorial Serviprensa.
———. 2003. Aj Awarem: Las Autoridades responsables de Gobernarlos, Un análisis comparativo sobre la heterogeneidad de las Autoridades en el contexto del Sistema Jurídico Maya en Guatemala. Guatemala: Conferencia Nacional de Ministros de la Espiritualidad Maya "Oxlajuj Ajpop."
Parry, J., and M. Bloch, eds. 1989. *Money and the Morality of Exchange*. Cambridge: Cambridge University Press.
REMHI (Proyecto Interdiocesano de Recuperación de la Memoria Histórica). 1998. *Guatemala: Nunca más*. Guatemala City: Oficina de Derechos Humanos del Azobispado.
Scott, James. 1976. *The Moral Economy of the Peasant: Rebellion and Subsistence in Southeast Asia*. New Haven, CT: Yale University Press.
———. 1985. *Weapons of the Weak: Everyday Forms of Peasant Resistance*. New Haven, CT: Yale University Press.
Sieder, Rachel. 2000. Paz, progreso, justicia y honradez': Law and Citizenship in Alta Verapaz during the Regime of Jorge Ubico. *Bulletin of Latin American Research* 19: 283–302.
Smith, Carol. 1990. *Guatemala Indians and the State: 1540 to 1988*. Austin: University of Texas Press.
Taussig, Michael. 1980. *The Devil and Commodity Fetishism in South America*. Chapel Hill: University of North Carolina Press.
Tax, Sol. 1953. *Penny Capitalism: A Guatemalan Indian Economy*. Smithsonian Institute of Social Anthropology, No. 16. Washington, DC: Smithsonian Institute of Social Anthropology.
Tedlock, Barbara. 1982. *Time and the Highland Maya*. Albuquerque: University of New Mexico Press.
Thompson, E. P. 1993. *Customs in Common: Studies in Traditional Popular Culture*. New York: New Press.
Wagley, Charles. 1949. *The Social and Religious Life of a Guatemalan Village*. *American Anthropologist* 51, No. 4, Part 2. Memoir Number 71. Washington, DC: American Anthropological Association.
Warren, Kay B. 1989. *The Symbolism of Subordination: Indian Identity in a Guatemalan Town*. Austin: University of Texas Press.
Watanabe, John. 1992. *Maya Saints and Souls in a Changing World*. Austin: University of Texas Press.

2

MORAL AGENCY INSIDE MARKET LOGIC

4

Extreme Gifting

The Moral Economy of a Community School

Rhoda H. Halperin

> Each culture cuts its slices of moral reality in a different way and meets approval and disapproval to counterpoised virtues and vices according to the local views.
>
> —Douglas and Isherwood (1979: 26)

This chapter examines local moral economic practices in a public community charter school celebrating its eighth year in 2007–2008. Since its opening in September 2000, in a diverse working poor neighborhood in Cincinnati, Ohio, the East End Community Heritage School (EECHS) has been a space for generating and elaborating extraordinary economic practices that I call extreme gifting. These gifting practices extend well beyond the ordinary professional expectations of teachers and staff. EECHS serves a subaltern urban population for which extreme gifting is essential to the life of the school and its students.

EECHS is a nonprofit corporation chartered under Cincinnati Public Schools. It receives state per-capita dollars for students and other subsidies including free breakfast and lunch for all students. The school is a nonmarket (nonprofit) economic formation that has embedded in it deeper moral economic practices namely, extreme gifting. Such gifting uses the market economy creatively, but is itself a set of locally generated, unpriced (free) and highly valued resources that are distributed to children from adults, from other children, and from working-class youth in the greater community.

Extreme gifting is not gift exchange in any conventional anthropological usage (Bloch and Parry 1989; Carrier 1995, 1997; Godelier 1999; Mauss 1954 [1925]). Rather, it consists of voluntary, one-way flows of resources from one person to another without obligations or expectations for returns. Reciprocation would be inappropriate and border on insult. To reciprocate would violate the moral realities of working-class culture that construct gifts as necessities.

This analysis of local moral economic practices puts human agents and working-class culture at its core and recognizes that extreme gifting is embedded in structures of power: the state department of education that awarded EECHS a large planning grant, the city board of education, local developers, and trustees of the school. As the structures of power change, the agents respond accordingly, and in turn, affect the structures (Giddens 1979). By conceptualizing these extraordinary moral economic practices as extreme gifting, we can understand some of the limitations of exchange theory and begin to craft new concepts more fitting of a complex global political economy of late capitalism.

As neoliberal capitalism intensifies over time, extreme gifting attempts to make up for gaps in state and city provisioning. Examples of extreme gifting practices include teachers working for long periods without pay, staff providing food, clothing, housing, school supplies, and holiday gifts for children to give kin, and many other similar practices, small and large. All of these practices use many different economic arrangements, including the informal economy. In the long run, the gifts aggregate to considerable material resources. Over the school's life, gifting practices have become more elaborate as the school faces dire resource shortages caused by hegemonically (political and market) driven, dramatic (bordering on violent), and repeated school relocations in the city. Each time the school relocates, costs are incurred, staff members are cut, and gifting intensifies. Gifters must compensate for what families cannot provide (Halperin 1990) and for what the state takes away.

In the expanding moral economy of EECHS, extreme gifters are, with a few exceptions, individuals who can least afford gifting. That is, the lowest-paid and least job-secure school staffers and high-risk children expend resources beyond their means to insure the longevity of the school and the success of working-class children. Most gifters are women. Extreme gifting is driven by the strong "moral reality," to use Douglas and Isherwood's (1979: 26) term—an ethos characterized by the local idiom, "doing whatever it takes." In many respects, the pressures of the neoliberal economy of late capitalism (Appadurai 1986, 2001; Harvey 1990; Sassen 1998, 2000, 2001) precipitate extreme forms of gifting by creating dire and dangerous circumstances for children that violate decency and morality and demand moral remedies. Without appropriate schools where kids can be productive and feel they belong, youth spend time on the streets, may get hurt, picked up by the police, land in jail, or become "statistics," the vernacular term for murdered. As working-class people, extreme gifters understand the dire implications of each of these possibilities. Extreme gifting thus emerges as a class phenomenon.

Theoretically, this case is important and unusual because it analyzes a highly informal, personal and local (but largely unrecognized) moral economy of gifting that is nuanced, multilayered, and perpetually changing. From the perspective of gifters, the gifts are "necessities." The gifting processes discussed here do not fit the conventional discussions of gift exchange, peasant moral economies (Scott 1979, 1985; Sivaramakrishnan 2005), commodity-gift continua (Carrier 1995, 1997), and many other well-known conventional frames for understanding gifts and resource flows. Extreme gifting is simultaneously much more complicated and much simpler than other forms. Its complexity resides in the intricate combinations of both market and nonmarket institutions required for the amassing of gifts; its simplicity is in the one-way flow of resources. Among the larger points contributed by the analysis of extreme gifting to the intersection of morality and economics are the following. Gifting represents everyday, continuously practiced moralities that are spontaneous, yet patterned; and extreme gifting is a highly informal, unrecognized (by the power structure and by social scientists) and changing set of everyday economic moralities. Gifting appears to happen idiosyncratically. In fact, if viewed cumulatively over a period of almost ten years (1998–2007), these everyday moral practices are powerful because they involve regular and considerable resource allocations. Extreme gifting is hegemonic *and* counterhegemonic; gifting operates in opposition to the forces of neoliberal capitalism by keeping the school going in the face of market-driven relocation forces. But gifting also equips youth to function as productive adults in a neoliberal capitalist state.

THEORETICAL FRAMES AND PRACTICAL REALITIES

Understanding extreme gifting requires alternative frames and interlocking concepts. First, consider the concept of subjugated, local knowledges from Foucault's 1980 essays, *Power and Knowledge* (see Foucault [1994: 205]).

> By comparison, and in contrast to the various projects that aim to inscribe knowledges in the hierarchical order of power associated with science, a genealogy should be seen as a kind of attempt to emancipate historical knowledges from subjection, to render them, that is, capable of opposition and of struggle against the coercion of a theoretical, unitary, formal, and scientific discourse. It is based on a reactivation of local knowledges—of minor knowledges, as Deleuze might call them—in opposition to the scientific hierarchization of knowledges and the effects intrinsic to their power; this, then, is the project of these disordered and fragmentary genealogies.

Foucault contrasts scientific and local, minor knowledges. Local knowledge is essential for understanding gifting needs and effectiveness. Geertz's essay "Common Sense as Cultural System" in his book *Local Knowledge* (1983) is relevant here. For Geertz, common sense is not biologic, but rather, a culturally shaped set of principles and practices, as he states:

> When we say someone shows common sense we mean to suggest more than that he is just using his eyes and ears, but is, as we say, keeping them open, using them judiciously, intelligently, perceptively, reflectively, or trying to, and that he is capable of coping with everyday problems in an everyday way with some effectiveness. (1983: 76)

Gifters always have their antennae out with constant watchful eyes—taking kids aside to talk, to assess what is going on, what the problem is, and how to solve it. In the vernacular, statements such as, "We haven't got a lot of book smarts, but we sure have a lot of common sense," take on special meaning when we understand the ad hoc but regular patterns of gifting. "Organic intellectuals," in Gramsci's sense (Forgacs 1988: 300, 302, 331), are agents who carry and transmit local knowledge rooted in practical, culturally shaped common sense. Gifting is always ad hoc and spontaneous.

Conceptualizing the moral economy of gifting is challenging. I offer a new formulation—the matrix economy concept—that models agents (extreme gifters) as actors who use multiple and qualitatively different (market and nonmarket) economic processes. That is, gifters use multiple, changing, and fluid institutional arrangements, capitalist and noncapitalist, formal and informal, global and local. These include: the state Department of Education, Wal-Mart and Target, extended family households, community food pantries, and flea markets and garage sales. The concept of hybrid economy (Garcia-Canclini 1995, 1997) might be applied to this urban situation, but the dynamics and structures are more complicated than the concept of hybrid economy would allow. A more appropriate model, I suggest, is the matrix economy—a set of matrices that intersect and overlap one another in space, time, and culture. The matrix economy model accommodates more than two, in fact, an infinite number of power structures and economic formations. Most importantly, it accommodates complex change that is swirling and moving, sometimes in unfathomable, yet rapid, ways. The matrix economy model also incorporates practice, a key element of extreme gifting. Economic anthropology must pay much more attention to practice (Bourdieu 1977). The concept of the matrix economy is more appropriate to refer to the myriad institutional arrangements impacting the school, the community, and especially the children. It is three-dimensional in structure and includes space, time, and culture, here, the changing institutional arrangements and practices required for extreme gifting to work.

To summarize, thus far I have examined economic practices that occur in the context of a public charter school. I refer to these practices as "extreme gifting." Later in this chapter, I analyze, in detail, the nature of gifts and gifters and their rootedness in moral principles of "doing whatever it takes." The significance of this work lies in understanding resistance and accommodation to hegemonic forces that oppress working-class families by attempting to destroy (often in violent ways) institutions such as EECHS that nurture the talents and aspirations of working-class youth. Gifting is essential to the mission of the East End Community Heritage School and to the survival, success, and achievement of working-class kids. The gifts make the difference between a child dropping out or staying in school. Staying connected to the school can be the difference between giving up and going on with a young life.

SITUATING ORGANIC INTELLECTUALS AND LOCAL ECONOMIC KNOWLEDGE

Who are the gifters? Gifters are talented grassroots leaders, community residents, and school founders employed in the school in staff positions: cafeteria workers, the transportation and community-relations organizer, the human resources director, and case managers (lay counselors). In Gramsci's (1971) terms, gifters are organic intellectuals (or, in the case of youth gifters, organic intellectuals in the making) who use subjugated local knowledges to provide appropriate resources to children at risk. Gramsci expanded the definition of intellectuals from formally educated elites to include anyone who organizes and leads subaltern social groups and, in the process, educates others. This concept of organic intellectuals derives from Gramsci's early writings on education. He argued that in order for working class citizens to challenge existing structures (in this case, the conventional class and racist structures of public schools) and become empowered to set appropriate, culturally and economically sensitive agendas, the working-class must create "organic intellectuals" of its own and not rely on intellectuals from higher classes (see Forgacs [1988: 300]).

What special talents render organic intellectuals effective gifters? What form does local knowledge take? Organic intellectuals understand family dynamics and needs such that gifting will not be perceived as charity. Recipients must never feel patronized. The slightest hint of a condescending attitude will cause gifts, gifters, and the school to be shunned. Intimate knowledge of family dynamics is local, based on trust and mutual respect. Organic intellectuals are uncredentialed and hold, at most, a GED or a high school diploma. "Common sense" (local knowledge) includes knowledge of particular families, including their structure, composition, dynamics, and needs.

The complexity of working-class extended families and their dispersion over large areas, including remote rural areas, makes understanding the nuances of working-class families daunting. Organic intellectuals reel off the names and relationships in EECHS families easily, however. An abusive, alcoholic father might "go after" gifters if they attempt to (informally) remove his children from his household. A grandmother is ill and unable to take care of her grandchildren while her daughter works. Someone needs to fill in. The after-school program, staffed by organic intellectuals, seems to accommodate larger numbers of children. More snacks, school supplies, and personnel enable kids to finish homework and go home with full stomachs. Often, kids who live nearby go home and return bringing toddler siblings back to school. One seven-year-old brought a crying toddler to see a case manager. These situations require local knowledge if they are to be handled appropriately. Local economic knowledge is also critical: knowledge of family resources and of the informal and formal economy for purposes of gathering resources at the lowest prices and fitting resources to needs. Following sales at Target, Wal-Mart, and Staples and knowing what can be obtained from the local flea market, where irregular blue jeans, pencils, and socks can be bought in bulk, can ensure clean clothing and school supplies—the matrix economy at work.

For Foucault, knowledge possessed by subaltern social groups is subjugated (read unrecognized, disrespected, illegitimate knowledge). Organic intellectuals are smart and practical; they know how to get things done by using local knowledge in productive ways unrecognized by the power structure—Foucault's main point. Gifting is thus, the ultimate praxis. Gramsci saw the education system as needing reform so that working-class children are not programmed into manual jobs (Willis 1977). In EECHS, the gifters see school success as crucial in this digital age. Manual labor does not produce a viable living. Education itself carries great moral weight because it keeps kids off the streets and out of jail; education provides opportunities for upward mobility and, ultimately, for giving back to the community.

BACKGROUND: THE EAST END COMMUNITY

In 1990 our diverse, University of Cincinnati–based interdisciplinary team of researchers/activists was invited to work in the East End community to help identify strategies for preserving and enhancing community strengths. We helped support the creation of a K–12 school. Before I introduce the ethnographic data supporting the school-based moral economy, I will provide a brief perspective of the East End community.

Historically, East Enders are part of the rural-urban migration streams from the U.S. south (Alabama, Georgia, and Kentucky) and from Europe to cities such as Cincinnati, Chicago, and Detroit. African Americans, people of Scotch-Irish and English heritage, and others from Germany, all migrated seeking work in industrializing northern U.S. cities. East End is unique, however, because it has welcomed all ethnicities and races and remained a diverse neighborhood.

EECHS came about because of a shared recognition among grassroots leaders and the university team of a crisis created by astronomical rates of school dropout. As the former president of the community council put it: "Our kids are marked by no designer clothes, free lunches, and a different dialect of English; they choose to stay home and are falling through the cracks." In the ten years prior to opening EECHS, few, if any youth, graduated from high school; most kids dropped out in the sixth and seventh grades.

The return of the Highlands School building for EECHS was part of a long economic development planning process. The development planning was aided by our team's qualitative, ethnographic methodology and yielded strong positives: charismatic grassroots leadership, strong community networks and identities going back almost a dozen generations, and many other morally driven practices, among them, "gifting the children" (see Halperin [1998, 2002, 2006]). The EECHS was framed with a moral agenda couched in the discourse of social justice, tolerance, and equality. It was initiated, and remains, a grassroots social movement. Almost ten years before the school opened in May 1992, in response to labels of illiteracy and high rates of school dropout, Robbie, a grassroots leader, housing advocate, and community grandmother, wrote a passionate educational prescription for violence avoidance and prevention that included the development of strong identities around children's heritage:

> Along with the need for children to know of their heritage there is still a stronger need for them to know that there is no place in this world that prejudice, intolerance, or violence is acceptable. . . . Right along with the basic education that a school affords you, you will learn who you are and where you come from. The pride in one's heritage should never be dampened. It should always be fostered. You may move from a house but you always take your heritage with you. It is always there but if you are not aware of what your heritage is, there is always a void in history, your own history.

Robbie is speaking of a children's rights agenda based on strong identities grounded in heritage and history. The economic dimensions of this moral agenda are daunting: a state planning grant, property (permission to lease a public school building), hiring of teachers and staff, and budgeting based on per-pupil state allotments, among other items. Textbooks and educational materials, including computers, were borrowed from "wealthier" schools and corporate entities. A neoliberal, global economic environment in which (benefit-bearing) factory jobs have disappeared; wage labor is temporary, low paying, and without benefits; and community children must work while in school did not help. As another school "founding mother," KB, put it:

> The dropout rate in Appalachian communities and in low-income communities all over the city has always been high. The police officer talked about third and fourth graders running the street during school days. . . . It is appalling! Our children are dropping out of school . . . we are losing them. We are just losing hundreds and hundreds of these children. The people here really want to bring their children back to the community and provide them with an education that is meaningful, that speaks to the children, that involves the children . . . and allows them to get the kind of education that they need to compete in this current environment. . . . The school will involve the community, be based in the community.

She continues and talks about gifting (without using the term) as a way of keeping children:

> Helping people pull together the resources that you need to make things happen is gonna take a lot of effort and a lot of money and a lot of time from people who are committed to making a difference. And that effort is going to have to be replicated in other ways across the community so that we don't lose these children. There was a time when you could drop out of school in the seventh grade and get a really good job and support your family and feel good about yourself. Those times are not with us any longer.

The EECHS spent its first six years (2000–2006) in "Highlands," a hallowed historic school building in the East End where two of the founding mothers, Athena and Robbie, gifters mentioned below, attended grade school. In fall 2006, EECHS relocated to another, primarily African American, working-class community in Cincinnati called Bond Hill. Multiple relocations of the school correspond to market forces that caused Highlands to be sold to a developer with a signed codicil preventing the lease of the building to a school. The relocation occurred after Cincinnati Public Schools (CPS), under which the school was originally chartered, in a violent anti–charter school climate, abandoned EECHS as its sponsor and removed ("yanked" in the vernacular) funding in the hundreds of thousands of dollars from the school. The termination of the CPS sponsorship and sale of the building corresponded with the opening of a new CPS public school in the East End, the East End Community School, modeled after EECHS but without the word *Heritage* in the school's name. East Enders refer to this new East End school as "the copycat school." Clearly, CPS did not want a charter school competing for students (and the accompanying per-capita state dollars) in the East End. The EECHS Bond Hill campus lasted only one year. In fall 2007, EECHS moved yet again, this time to its third site in the North Fairmount district, one of seven Cincinnati neighborhoods served by the Urban Appalachian Council, a historically poor white community.

Extreme gifting has, thus far, counteracted the otherwise destabilizing power structures and market development that force such moves. That the forces of economic development/gentrification have created working-class diasporas in many cities is not new; what is new, however, is that local economic moralities, in this case, the practice of "gifting the children," function to sustain the children and the school despite dislocations. These gifting practices certainly undergo change as the school environment changes, but the fundamental pattern of gifting children becomes more elaborate as needs escalate. What will happen to gifting patterns in the long run is difficult to predict. With the shortage of funding and the financial stresses incurred from each relocation of the school, it appears that gifting has intensified in some very important ways.

GIFTING IN AN URBAN COMMUNITY SCHOOL

Intersections of kinwork, paid work, and schoolwork blur distinctions between work, school, community, and family for people connected to EECHS. For EECHS staff, work extends far beyond job descriptions and regular business hours. Organic intellectuals work long days, often spending many hours collecting items to be used in extreme gifting.

Gifting has a long history in the East End, with many precedents and models (Hobsbawm and Ranger 1983). JP ("Grandpa" to community children), a revered elder and head of a large extended family, spent his life provisioning ("gifting") community children, including underwriting the expansion of the city-owned recreation center and opening his house daily to all neighborhood children and youth. His home has always been a children's oasis without cost or obligation. Children filled this hybrid school/recreation center with laughter and good behavior. He modeled gifting in nuanced and generous ways, giving generously to children and adults. At any one time, the amounts given were small, but they were numerous, regular investments in future adults. Gifting was JP's way of brokering the hegemonic system with strong, yet passive resistance—the East End version of a Ghandi-style organic intellectual. He died early in 2005, but his example lives to inspire others, especially children, to become gifters themselves. He never expected anything in return. He knew that timing, materialization, and context were everything. He also knew how to prevent violence.

Extreme gifting began long before school opened in September 2000. Beginning in fall 1998, the founding mothers worked tirelessly and without compensation in collaboration with consulting teachers, professors, and university students to plan the school: acquire the charter; write the curriculum; lease the Highlands building; hire faculty, staff, and administrators; and run the school (Halperin 2006). Some founding mothers abandoned jobs to devote time to planning. Two forms of extreme gifting are detailed below using two models designed for thinking about gifting.

The first model, *intergenerational gifting*, analyzes the most prevalent and most important form of gifting. In this model, the agents, or gifters, are adults who bestow substantial resources on children, either individually, collectively, or both. The gifts and the expectations surrounding them operate outside the regular, ordinary obligations of kinship and friendship in working-class communities. The second model of gifting, *peer gifting*, involves children and youth in the school gifting one another.

Intergenerational Gifting at Highlands (2000–2006)

From the first day of school, intergenerational extreme gifting focused on informal support systems for kids—adults expending considerable resources in time and money on children. These practices grow out of a strong, often ritualized ethos, including secular forms of ritual kinship. To highlight the power of extreme gifting across generations, and across a matrix of economic institutions, I focus on a small set of school staff in two generations: two founding mothers, Robbie and Athena; June, Robbie's partner; Evylyn, close friend of Athena and prominent member of a small African American community within the East End; and Lydia, Athena's daughter. Robbie and Athena are particularly extreme gifters; their dogged commitment and sense of morality is to "heritage" children, broadly conceived as working-class youth. The resources they give include school supplies, food, and housing for homeless children. For the past seven summers, gifters have spent large amounts of time and money buying school supplies on sale at Target, Staples, Wal-Mart, garage sales, and flea markets. They shop carefully to find the best bargains and then stockpile in their garages the hundreds of notebooks, folders, and pencils that they redistribute to students on the opening day of school. They keep careful counts of every item, attending to the different needs of primary, middle, and high school students. Crayons are for younger children, highlighters are for the older ones. Folders with the appropriate designs are carefully selected. Special-needs children require special supplies such as large erasers. Similarly, gifters collect holiday gifts in the "Christmas Store" for children to give to family members. The stockpiling begins right after Christmas when ornaments, wrapping paper, cards, and other items go on sale. Here local knowledge becomes very important: the composition of households by gender and age, the preferences of a child's grandmother or sibling, and the real needs of each household.

Robbie

Robbie gives to children regularly, for weeks and months at a time without compensation. A young high school student moved in with her recently. She delivered a baby and stayed for several months at Robbie's house, which was already housing several other children and youth at that point. The young mother was never asked to leave. In a brief discussion about alternative housing, other school staff volunteered to keep the mother and baby, but since the logistics were so difficult, Robbie decided they should remain with her. Robbie was close to the family since her friend, the grandmother of the baby (the mother's mother) had recently died of cancer; thus Robbie felt she needed to fill in. The gifts, in this case, of housing, food, and childcare are part of Robbie's everyday life (de Certeau 1984). She's a genius at using the matrix economy.

In the school itself Robbie has created "a gifting center" in her office. Robbie's formal titles are: community organizer, transportation director, and volunteer coordinator for the school, but she is so generous and forceful that some parents think she is the vice principal. Many of the younger children call her RuRu, a nickname coined by her own granddaughter who is now in college. Robbie is an extreme gifter because she is constantly providing for children and adults unconditionally. She describes her office as a "home away from home." She would say she provides what is necessary.

Robbie's office looks like a combination living room and small kitchen. It accommodates a couch; comfortable, kid-size beanbag chairs; a desk with a computer; a small refrigerator; a coffee pot and a microwave oven; toys, including a model yellow school bus; and several bowls of candy. Robbie stocks the refrigerator with snacks. Often kids knock on her door crying, upset from a fight with another child, from something a teacher said, or simply from not having enough rest or food. She embraces children, calms them with a quiet, comfortable space, something to eat, and assistance with schoolwork. Her help is always unconditional and extends to her home after school; her resources seem limitless. She manages to find clean clothing for every child who needs it and she spends hours driving children home from school.

Robbie's partner, June, daughter of JP (Grandpa), who works as a case manager (lay counselor) in the school, adds to Robbie's already substantial gifts by accompanying kids to court, visiting their homes, and bringing them homework if they are ill. When the budget could no longer afford a school nurse, June became nurse, psychiatrist, and counselor. She and Robbie have worked in the school since its opening and now have seen the younger children of what are often, large, sibling sets. They know the parents and grandparents well.

Evylyn

Evylyn, the school coordinator, is a lifelong East Ender with a very large extended family. She has an undergraduate degree from the University of Cincinnati and focuses her gifting on transitioning high school students to college. She (with Robbie's help) took one homeless student, Frankie, who lived at Robbie's house, under her wing. She spent hours talking to Frankie, convincing him that he ought to attend college, bolstering his self-esteem, listening to his issues with sexual identity, and providing him with clean clothes. She commented often that he seemed to be much happier when he had clean things to wear. Robbie and Evylyn created a job for Frankie answering the phone for several hours a day and they paid him out of their own pockets. He sounded very professional, and it was difficult to gauge which was the greater gift, the self-esteem he gained or the money he earned.

Evylyn's long history in the East End combines with her tremendous energy to produce many creative forms of extreme gifting. Children and young people congregate in her office just to talk with her. She arranges college classes for high school students through Cincinnati State University, a two-year college with a bridge program to four-year institutions, primarily the University of Cincinnati. One very talented high school student, who wrote a novel in his junior year, could not afford college tuition. Evylyn arranged to delay his graduation, to enable him to continue taking college courses for free. In addition, young staff people spend time with Evylyn, who counsels them about taking graduate courses, special seminars, and general life issues. Rarely does she leave her office before 7 p.m. Evylyn often counsels the older students and young staff people to help the younger ones with homework, family problems, and the like. She also takes children home when need arises. Thus, Evylyn creates a network of intergenerational gifters.

Athena and Lydia

Athena, formally the human resources director, but informally called "MOM" by every child, fashioned a high particle-board wall to provide privacy for students who wanted to talk in confidence. Robbie jokingly called it the "Berlin Wall"; it did separate Athena's office from the public space of the front office. Kids knew they could go back there to talk without anyone seeing them. Athena worked with the kids to solve problems, whether they needed clothes, shoes, family advice, or simply reassurance. As a grandmother in the community, Athena has spent her entire life in the East End. Meals, plates of food to go, transportation, money, a big hug when needed, are only a few of her gifts to children. Athena has a temper, however, especially when she thinks a student has been ill-served or when an injustice has been done. She will "go off" and start yelling and cursing when provoked. People who do not know her say she is irrational, even crude and destructive. People who know her well understand that she is speaking from the heart and that the volume of her voice is directly proportionate to the strength of her feelings. At the same time, she can look a student in the eye and demand they stay in school, regardless of the odds. She backs up the demand with whatever resources are needed.

Athena's daughter, Lydia, is a case manager in the school; her job is to work through problems with high school students, especially girls. She is a role model because of her sense of style and her generosity as basketball coach and beauty specialist. Lydia drives all over the city after a basketball game to be sure that every player arrives home safely. Before each school prom, she provides makeup, nail polish, and a new hairstyle for every high school girl. At times, with Athena's help, dresses and shoes appear as well. She once told me that she always had hot meals growing up in the East End and she would do her best to make sure that all students in the school had hot meals also, whether these were cooked in the school's cafeteria or in her own kitchen.

All of these acts of giving are performed in a casual, almost nonchalant manner such that kids never feel they are receiving anything out of the ordinary. Gifting is regular; not a day passes without adults "gifting the children." Extreme gifting sends resources to dozens of children without anyone ever talking about it. There were times when I suggested opening a dormitory with a cafeteria so that the school would be financially responsible for providing food and housing to the children, but the gifters rejected the idea. Some of the gifters came very close to adopting children, albeit informally. Informal adoptions are, in fact, quite common in the East End, and in many working-class communities.

To summarize, all of the gifting described above occurred within the first six years of the school's life. It is easy to appreciate that extreme gifting—adults going to extraordinary lengths to provide for children—takes many different forms and taps a matrix of economic structures. In the next phase of the school's life, gifting intensifies and becomes even more extreme as resources that are already in short supply diminish further with the relocation of EECHS to Bond Hill.

RELOCATION TO BOND HILL CAMPUS 2006–2007

The transition from the Highlands building in the East End, to a much smaller facility in Bond Hill, was extremely difficult logistically, financially, and culturally. Bond Hill is a predominantly African American neighborhood that is a minimum of a thirty-minute drive north from the East End, within Cincinnati's urban corridor. In rush hours, the trip can take more than one hour. Financially, the costs for the school increased enormously (almost triple the $63,000 annual rent for Highlands), for a much smaller space. Culturally, the Bond Hill community is less stable than the East End, having large boarded-up buildings and empty spaces. Gangs of teenagers seem to control the neighborhood.

Extreme gifting in Bond Hill began with the creation and execution of a summer program in 2006. Fifty-eight children participated, resourced entirely by school staff "out of pocket." This is one particularly strong example of intergenerational gifting that occurred just after the move to Bond Hill. Recreation center memberships, food, supplies, and time were only some of the costs absorbed by EECHS staff. In addition to the monetary costs were the costs for the time to buy food, put lunches together, and run the program.

When the Bond Hill campus of EECHS opened in September of 2006, extreme gifting moved to a higher level than ever before. Gifters felt compelled to compensate not only for what families could not provide (as they had previously in the Highlands building), but also now for what the state had taken away. School staff compensated for the basic deficits in the school's budget, including salaries, copying and supplies, and food, previously provided by the school via the state.

There are several reasons for this escalation and intensification of gifting. Not only did the move to Bond Hill require a lease of $180,000, but the space in Bond Hill was approximately half the size of the space in Highlands. The smaller space limited student enrollment and placed further limitations on a budget based on per-capital income per student. There were other costs: all of the computers had to be moved and networked, a server set up, and new wiring installed. Classrooms had to be reconfigured and equipped with computers, bulletin boards, books, and supplies. To make matters worse, the school lost approximately $300,000 in subsidies provided by CPS because they had severed EECHS's public charter. Fortunately, another sponsor, Educational Resources, Inc., a nonprofit corporation based in Dayton, Ohio, agreed to charter the school. But they did not replace the CPS subsidy and charged for the transfer of sponsorship.

Just before the opening of the 2006 school year, staff paychecks had bounced and were long delayed for the next pay period; the staff of the school continued working regardless. As the principal pointed out: "In no other school would the staff continue to work without pay." A strong, constantly mentioned social justice agenda underlies these alternative economic practices. The principal spent the year lending approximately one-third of her salary to staff to enable them to pay their bills. The goal of this agenda is to provide the resources necessary to "bring kids up to speed" in the face of poor public education and class and race discrimination. "I cannot jeopardize the graduation of our seniors," the principal told me. "They have worked so hard."

To add to the burdens, the school budget did not allow for the costs of paper plates, cups, and flatware for the delivered lunches. Several members of the school staff went to Sam's Club, a national discount chain, and purchased the necessary equipment, along with numerous gallon jugs of milk for the kids' lunches. Since the start-up costs in the new location prohibited paying the milk bill and the staff thought that kids should have it, they gifted milk to the children for the entire fall semester. It is almost impossible to estimate the monetary costs of gifting, much less the time costs. Roughly, though, the principal's total salary was $75,000, so one-third of this salary results in a substantial amount of money.

Peer Gifting

Peer gifters are young adults who are attending high school or middle school or who may be even younger. Peer gifting is the most impressive form of gifting. It requires maturity, judgment, and a substantial amount of time. Children and youth are gifting other young people. While the material resources are not nearly as substantial as they are for adult gifters, the gifts of time and energy are very significant. For adolescents, peer gifting also can be risky; it goes against the pressures to conform so common in youth culture. Peer gifting requires children to exercise self-respect in the face of potential bullying from anyone who does not respect difference or perceived weakness in the recipients. Two examples follow below. One example involves two female cousins from a very large, old East End family. The eldest, AC, is undergoing a liver transplant. Her gifter is Annie. The second example is a twenty-one-year-old male high school student, Lincoln, who has cerebral palsy and who has many student gifters in the high school, both male and female. For youth gifters, after-school, evening, and weekend jobs must be given up to leave time for the uncompensated gifting. There are very real economic costs and sacrifices to the moral economy of peer (youth) gifting.

Annie and AC

A young middle-school girl, Annie, became the primary caregiver for her cousin, an EECHS high school student who is a year older than she and who was undergoing a liver transplant. In addition to bringing AC's homework and notes from teachers and schoolmates, Annie provided unconditional companionship. Annie slept on a cot next to AC's bed most nights, after bringing her special food, books, and videos. Some days Annie came to school looking like she had not slept at all, but she was always very matter of fact about the time she spent with AC, talking about it as an ordinary occurrence, and giving regular updates to school staff and fellow students.

When AC was ready to go home and her weakened immune system prevented her from attending classes, Annie made sure AC kept up with her schoolwork. She worked with volunteers at the school to provide extra tutoring and also made sure AC's room was furnished with an air conditioner. When board members of the school offered to provide other items and did not understand the need for the air conditioner, Annie acted as a culture broker, shaping the gifting to make sure that AC and her family did not feel pitied or patronized. Annie continues to monitor AC. She never took any credit for AC's miraculous recovery.

Lincoln

Lincoln is in a wheelchair with cerebral palsy. Fellow students, most of them quite a few years younger than Lincoln with "attitudes" and some with records, cater to Lincoln's every need. He requires help with all of the basics of daily living, including holding a pencil. Older, able-bodied high school boys rotate taking Lincoln to the bathroom, the cafeteria, and the schoolyard. Initially, his younger sister helped him with his schoolwork, but the demands on her are also great, since she has three children under the age of four. Lincoln stayed in school and graduated in 2005.

In Lincoln's case, help is delicate; he is very sensitive to the fact that his disability separates him from other students just as it makes him dependent on their help. The children come through for him, however, and helping Lincoln becomes a badge of honor. Lincoln's mother gives long speeches about how much she appreciates everything Lincoln has received at EECHS. She champions the school and recruits regularly. Many of her recruits are students with disabilities.

Children with a range of disabilities (ADHD, prominently) regularly receive help from other children, some older, some younger. Older girls teach younger ones how to knit, crochet, read patterns, and estimate stitch gauges. Gifting in the context of hands-on learning through crafts is particularly effective and transfers to many other learning domains, especially math, reading, and writing. I could document many other examples of peer gifting. Suffice it to say that gifting requires time and talent, sensitivity and judgment. Done badly, it could be costly or dangerous.

Whether or not a community of working-class people resides in a single locale, such a community is absolutely essential for gifting to occur and to be maintained for current and future generations of children. EECHS is rapidly becoming an imagined community of working-class families from across the greater Cincinnati area, very much like immigrant families globally (Anderson 1983). The community and the community school are undergoing constant change and redefinition. The children and the grassroots leaders in the school are very flexible and the definition of the community and the school is changing. High school classes are being held in the Heritage Center back in the East End. The school has become multisited. How multiple sites impact gifting practices remains to be seen.

CONCEPTUALIZING THE MORAL ECONOMY

Adults, youth, and children are all important players in the moral economy of EECHS. Extreme gifting is multifaceted in that it is connected to nonprofit organizations as well as to corporate interests and highly bureaucratized government agencies such as city and state governments and school boards. Conceptualizing the moral economy of gifting is thus a challenging task.

The matrix economy models agents as actors who use a variety of institutional arrangements to provision students and the school. Extreme gifting would not be possible without the range of market, nonmarket, and informal institutional arrangements knowledgeably used by organic intellectuals. Knowledge of global, capitalist institutions combines with local knowledge of flea markets as sources of inexpensive necessities. Gifters use global capitalism to their own advantage, including the remnants of capitalism that supply the informal economy. Pencils in flea markets are packaged in packs of twenty-four with logos of companies that are out of business; but these pencils write perfectly. Levi jeans marked "irregular" still fashionably cover subaltern young bodies. The school exists in a complicated institutional matrix. It is a nonprofit corporation currently chartered under another nonprofit organization, as CPS abandoned the school and relinquished it to a nongovernmental organization, as noted earlier. The state (of Ohio) still oversees the institution's operation and must acknowledge that the school's "report card" in 2006 moved up two notches, from a school in "academic emergency" to a school in the category of "continuous improvement." The categories are based on aggregate test scores under the federally mandated No Child Left Behind, an initiative of the Bush administration that requires all public (not private) schools to test children regularly. Thus, the school is nested in federal, state, regional, and local bureaucracies, all with their attendant forms of provisioning and initiatives that simultaneously remove resources. The more we examine such situations, the more we understand the complexity of such matrix economies.

In our postmodern, neoliberal age of late capitalism (Jameson 1991), gifting requires creating good citizens (Ong 1999, 2003). Children must have the skills—intellectual, technical, literacy—to carry on the tradition of "doing whatever it takes" to maintain and enhance the community, conceived as a working-class, imagined community (Anderson 1983). But citizenship and the moral economic practices so essential to it must be understood as constantly contested by the power structure. Working poor Appalachians, blacks and whites, are the "untouchables" of the United States. Members of depressed classes, racialized and not, are often viewed by people in power as undeserving of basic rights, including rights to education. Without extreme gifting, EECHS might have closed after the first year; many children would have been abandoned to the streets. Negotiating the matrix economy by operating in multiple economic spheres is the hallmark of organic intellectuals—here, gifters, and specifically, extreme gifters.

I began this paper talking about subalterns, a social-science term referring to oppressed citizens worldwide. Increasingly, under neoliberal policies, working-class, poor whites and the racialized poor are what experts on subaltern populations in India call "marked citizens" (Pandey 2006: 130). This means, among other things, that legitimizing citizenship rights, such as the rights to education and the resources necessary for educational achievement and success become increasingly difficult. As EECHS moved from one location to another, students experienced greater deprivations, rectified to various degrees by extreme gifts. The sale of the Highlands building in the 2005–2006 academic year was an immoral and, I daresay, violent economic act. Place is central to the mission of the school. The sale is immoral because of its cultural and class insensitivities that deprive poor children of educational resources, its inability to understand the importance of working-class places to working-class children and families, and its failure to understand the importance of translating school (hegemonic school practices) to working-class children. The line between immorality and violence—namely, violence against basic human rights—is thin. The resultant situation of EECHS thus highlights the multiple channels through which "moral" and "immoral" actions are worked out in our complex, everyday economies (Halperin 1994).

SOME CONCLUDING THOUGHTS

What are the critical questions for economic anthropology raised by examining moral economic practices in the urban East End of Cincinnati? Within neoliberal, late capitalism, what kinds of moralities create what kinds of alternative economies? The matrix economy is complex and constantly changing and thus many questions remain. Will a working-class diaspora coalesce in the newly relocated EECHS? Will the various forms of gifting practices continue and intensify as new networks are formed? New forms of gifting and new gifters are definite possibilities. Will the stresses of the borderlands—conflicting and often rigid culture clashes between local and credentialed knowledge, for example—and the associated people become more or less clearly drawn? Will the local knowledge held and passed on by organic intellectuals still be important outside of the East End community context? Will the community leaders employed in the school maintain their roles as counselors, community organizers, founding mothers, and gifters? These are only a few of the many critical questions that have enormous moral and economic implications.

Gifting intensified in the school's first few months in Bond Hill. Will gifting escalate in North Fairmount? Or will this third location entail struggles yet to be anticipated, for children, for teachers, leaders, and for the school as an institution? The transformations and elaborations of gifting have, I think, yet to be realized as more and more stakeholders in the greater Cincinnati community become invested, emotionally and financially, in the moral economy of the school. Ideally, one might imagine the community and the school as a metaphorical *oikos*, writ large. That is, community leaders and school staff see themselves as responsible for provisioning the children and the school as a totality. When resources are scarce, and they almost always are, the adults dig into their own pockets.

In 1944 Karl Polanyi in *The Great Transformation* talked about economies embedded in society and culture. Following Marx (1904, 1964, 1973) but cloaking his Marxism, Polanyi elaborated this idea of embeddedness in his famous 1957 essay, "The Economy as Instituted Process." Moral economies are most certainly embedded economies, and here moral economies are embedded in a matrix of institutional arrangements. Since Polanyi's landmark book, many anthropologists and others have elaborated the idea of embeddedness, including Eric Wolf (1982) in his variously labeled "modes of production" and Pierre Bourdieu (1977) with cumbersome, but powerful concepts such as economic "habitus," which includes everyday class dispositions. All of these writers have provided contexts for understanding how agents, in this case, gifters as organic intellectuals, collect and allocate goods for high moral purposes such as the educational success of children and youth. But context is not everything; the agents analyzed and described above practice their own versions of cultural logic in these contexts. They must use an intricate combination of capitalist and noncapitalist economic structures to carry out extreme gifting, and they must do so in their own ways. Exchange theory has not even begun to accommodate such complexities and combinations of agents and economic processes.

Gifting the children is multifaceted, changing and fluid. It is informal, everyday, and inherently practical. It involves provisioning children in creative and powerfully moral ways. If we recognize that all economic theories and practices require moral positions, implicit and explicit, then thinking about twenty-first-century urban moral economies as localized, situated, and changing practices provides a lens for conceptualizing subaltern economic practices that are often hidden and unrecognized. There are moralities that drive economic practices. These are moralities that are held by contemporary working-class people, for example, who are often perceived if not as less than moral, then as less than respectable—poor white trash, for example, or the racialized poor. How long these moralities can survive in an increasingly conservative political climate in the United States, and globally, remains to be seen.

Acknowledgments. I would like to thank Kate Browne and Lynne Milgram for all of their efforts in organizing the very important Society for Economic Anthropology meeting on "Economics and Morality" and for their insightful comments and editorial suggestions. My thanks also go to the East End leaders and children who welcome me constantly into the community despite my move to New Jersey. Short stints in the school and the Internet and phone keep us connected.

REFERENCES

Anderson, Benedict. 1983. *Imagined Communities: Reflections on the Origin and Spread of Nationalism*. London: Verso Books.

Appadurai, Arjun. 1986. Introduction: Commodities and the Politics of Value. In *The Social Life of Things: Commodities in Cultural Perspective*, ed. A. Appadurai, 3–63. Cambridge: Cambridge University Press.

———. 2001. *Globalization*. Durham, NC: Duke University Press.

Bloch, Maurice, and Jonathan Parry. 1989. *Money and the Morality of Exchange*. Cambridge: Cambridge University Press.

Bourdieu, Pierre. 1977. *Outline of a Theory of Practice*. Cambridge: Cambridge University Press.

Carrier, James G. 1995. *Gifts and Commodities: Exchange and Western Capitalism since 1700*. New York and London: Routledge.

———. 1997. *Meanings of the Market: The Free Market in Western Culture*. Oxford and New York: Berg.

de Certeau, Michel. 1984. *The Practice of Everyday Life*. Berkeley: University of California Press.

Douglas, Mary, and Baron Isherwood. 1979. *The World of Goods*. New York: Basic Books.

Forgacs, David, ed. 1988. *An Antonio Gramsci Reader: Selected Writings, 1916–1935*. New York: Schocken Books.

Foucault, Michel. 1980. *Power/Knowledge: Selected Interviews and Other Writings, 1972–1977*. New York: Pantheon Books.

———. 1994. "Power and Knowledge." In *Culture, Power, History*, ed. N. Dirks, E. Eley, and S. Ortner. Princeton, NJ: Princeton University Press.

García-Canclini, Néstor. 1995. *Hybrid Cultures: Strategies for Entering and Leaving Modernity*. Minneapolis and London: University of Minnesota Press.
———. 1997. Urban Cultures at the End of the Century: The Anthropological Perspective. *International Social Science Journal* 153: 345–56.
Geertz, Clifford. 1983. Common Sense as Cultural System. In *Local Knowledge*, 73–93. New York: Basic Books.
Giddens, Anthony. 1979. *Central Problems in Social Theory*. Berkeley: University of California Press.
Godelier, Maurice. 1999. *The Enigma of the Gift*. Trans. N. Scott. Chicago: University of Chicago Press.
Gramsci, Antonio. 1971. *Selections from the Prison Notebooks of Antonio Gramsci*. Ed. and trans. Quintin Hoare and Geoffrey Nowell. New York: International Publishers.
Halperin, Rhoda H. 1990. *The Livelihood of Kin: Making Ends Meet "The Kentucky Way."* Austin: University of Texas Press.
———. 1994. *Cultural Economies Past and Present*. Austin: University of Texas Press.
———. 1998. *Practicing Community: Class Culture and Power in an Urban Neighborhood*. Austin: University of Texas Press.
———. 2002. The Interstices of Urban Development: An Economic Anthropological Approach to Development in a Midwestern U.S. Community. In *Economic Development: An Anthropological Approach*, ed. Jeffrey H. Cohen and Norbert Dannhaeuser, 69–83. Walnut Creek, CA: AltaMira Press.
———. 2006. *Whose School Is It?: Women, Children, Memory and Practice in the City*. Austin: University of Texas Press.
Harvey, David. 1990. *The Condition of Postmodernity*. London: Blackwell Publishers.
Hobsbawm, Eric, and Terence Ranger, eds. 1983. *The Invention of Tradition*. Cambridge: Cambridge University Press.
Jameson, Fredric. 1991 *Postmodernism or the Cultural Logic of Late Capitalism*. Durham, NC: Duke University Press.
Marx, Karl. 1904. *Capital*, vol. 1. London: Sonnenschein.
———. 1964. *Precapitalist Economic Formations*. Ed. Eric Hobsbawm, trans. Jack Cohen. London: Lawrence and Eishart.
———. 1973. *The Grundrisse*. Trans. Martin Nicolaus. New York: Vintage.
Mauss, Marcel. 1954 [1925]. *The Gift: Forms and Functions of Exchange in Archaic Societies*. Glencoe, IL: Free Press.
Ong, Aiwa. 1999. *Flexible Citizenship: The Cultural Logics of Transnationality*. Durham, NC: Duke University Press.
———. 2003. *Buddha Is Hiding*. Berkeley: University of California Press.
Pandey, Gyanendra. 2006. *Routine Violence: Nations, Fragments, Histories*. Stanford, CA: Stanford University Press.
Polanyi, Karl. 1944. *The Great Transformation*. New York: Holt, Rinehart and Winston.
———. 1957. The Economy as Instituted Process. In *Trade and Market in the Early Empires*, ed. Karl Polanyi, Conrad Arensberg, and Harry W. Pearson, 243–70. Glencoe, IL: Free Press.
Sassen, Saskia. 1998. *Globalization and Its Discontents*. New York: New Press.
———. 2000. "Whose City Is It?" Globalization and the Formation of New Claims. In *The Globalization Reader*, ed. Frank J. Lechner and John Boli, 70–76. Malden, MA: Blackwell Publishers.

——. 2001. *The Global City*. Princeton, NJ: Princeton University Press.

Scott, James. 1979. *Moral Economy of the Peasant: Rebellion and Subsistence in Southeast Asia*. New Haven, CT: Yale University Press.

——. 1985. *Weapons of the Weak: Everyday Forms of Peasant Resistance*. New Haven, CT: Yale University Press.

Sivaramakrishnan, K. 2005. Introduction to "Moral Economies, State Spaces, and Categorical Violence." (Special Feature: In Focus: Moral Economies, State Spaces, and Categorical Violence: Anthropological Engagements with the Work of James Scott). *American Anthropologist* 107(3): 321–30.

Willis, Paul. 1977. *Learning to Labor*. New York and London: Routledge.

Wolf, Eric. 1982. *Europe and the People without History*. Berkeley: University of California Press.

5

"Thiefing a Chance"

Moral Meanings of Theft in a Trinidadian Garment Factory

Rebecca Prentice

It is early morning at Signature Fashions,[1] but work in the factory is already well under way. Throughout the stitching section, workers are busy sewing up the latest line of garments bound for Signature's branded stores in Trinidad, Tobago, and throughout the Caribbean region. Kimberly is quietly at work on the hemming machine, passing T-shirt after T-shirt under its double needles, leaving two, neat rows of stitching on the bottom of each garment. As soon as Cissy, the production manager, leaves the shop floor to enter the cutting room, Kimberly stops working and leans forward in her chair. She hisses at Gita, sitting at the straight-stitch sewing machine in front of her.

"Sssssssst," she says. Gita looks over her shoulder at Kimberly. "If I give you a shirt, you could put a pocket on it and keep your stories straight?"

"Sure," Gita says, turning back to her work.

I do not see Kimberly pass Gita the shirt and pocket, but I suspect that she does so later in the morning, now that Gita has agreed to "thief a chance" for her. For now, the shirt—an exact copy of the brand-name garments that the workers have been laboring over all week—rests in the bottom of a black plastic garbage bag, hanging off the end of Kimberly's machine. By the end of the day, Kimberly—with the help of fellow workers at nearly every stage of the production process—will have completed for herself a precise replica of the shirts that will appear in Signature's stores in time for Easter. She will smuggle it out of the factory either underneath her own clothes, or stashed at the bottom of her handbag, where it will be stitched inside a scrap of cotton cloth, looking to any onlooker like a simple, homemade pincushion.

The purpose of this chapter is to explore a particular variety of shop-floor theft, something that workers in the factory where I conducted fieldwork call "thiefing a chance." Thiefing a chance (or simply, "thiefing") involves producing extra garments on the assembly line that workers covertly distribute among themselves. Because it requires immense coordination and the complicity of workers at nearly every stage in the production process, thiefing a chance provides a rich ethnographic site for analyzing the everyday moralities that support and sustain illicit practices. I have argued elsewhere (Prentice 2007) that thiefing a chance and other illicit shop-floor practices work in the service of capital by skilling-up workers for the quickly changing demands of a "flexible" production regimen. In this chapter, I focus on the intentions and justifications of workers engaged in thiefing activities, to probe how making and taking garments from the assembly line becomes constituted as a moral practice.

This chapter describes thiefing a chance, and examines what thiefing reveals about the social and material world of a Trinidadian garment factory. I ask what moral assessments are involved in thiefing, giving consideration to the interpretive categories that are meaningful to actors themselves. Morality, like ethics, is a slippery concept (Laidlaw 2002) that is best examined ethnographically—not as a fixed system, but as a fluid process of negotiation that makes certain types of action acceptable through the construction of local meanings.

The flexible, quickly changing production regimen of the Signature Fashions factory, coupled with the luxurious enticement of the garments themselves, make thiefing a chance both possible and desirable for workers. I show that despite the intense coordination involved in thiefing a chance, workers conceptualize the practice as a series of individual enterprises, rather than as a collective action. By examining the linkages between workers' formal labor in the factory and their personal enterprises at home, I argue that workers envision the factory as a ready site for pursuing their own projects. These projects need not be ideologically oppositional to the aims of the factory's owners; indeed, thiefing a chance works in the interests of both employers and workers by encouraging workers to skill-up for new tasks and by strengthening networks of mutual aid on the shop floor. Therefore, rather than interpreting thiefing as "everyday resistance" to workplace hegemony (Scott 1985), I show instead that such practices can be located within West Indian cultural mores that celebrate self-reliance, autonomy, and cunning individualism (Browne 2004).

Through thiefing and the unfolding narratives emerging from its practice, workers construct a provisional and shifting morality on the shop floor. I show that even as workers produce copies of brand-name garments in the heart of the factory, they continually force a spatial and symbolic separation between the factory's main production and their own illicit practices. The distinction between these two types of work constitutes the conceptual framework with which workers morally defend thiefing. While workers recognize standard factory production as the legitimate and rightful business of the company for which they work, the making of thiefed garments is commonly understood to be the business of workers themselves. Making, owning, and wearing copies of high-cost garments is perceived as a reward for those workers who are daring enough to take a risk and "thief a chance" in the factory. In the context of Signature Fashions, workers describe thiefing as the *opposite* of stealing, a preeminent example of "doing something for yourself" when the fleeting opportunity arises.

ON THE SHOP FLOOR AT SIGNATURE FASHIONS

Signature Fashions is a small, "high-fashion" garment factory locally owned by a Trinidadian[2] couple of East Indian and Chinese descent. Signature Fashions makes expensive[3] "designer" clothes for its branded stores throughout the Caribbean. The prominent display of the Signature logo on most of its clothes, its admittedly high price, and its association with a famed local designer all imbue the clothing with an allure that has made it a profitable brand since the founding of the company in 1990. Because of its ever-changing product line, the Signature factory is characterized by a flexible production regimen, which requires workers to constantly respond to the quickly changing tastes of elite Caribbean consumers. Signature Fashions imports textiles from abroad—mostly from China—in contemporary patterns and fabrics. Lines of garments are designed in a range of styles based on multiple uses of similar fabrics. These garments are then produced in small, "exclusive" batches, going from design to shop floor to the Signature stores in a matter of days or weeks.

When I first arrived at the factory, its production had only recently moved from a cramped, upstairs workshop in the center of Port of Spain (the capital city) to one of the expansive industrial estates in the suburbs of town. There are about forty people working on the shop floor, including a production manager and two floor supervisors. The owners' offices are located in the upstairs of the factory, which also includes workspace for two designers and a handful of administrators. The Signature Fashions factory contains a cutting room, where fabrics are laid and cut into patterns; a stitching area, where garments are stitched together; and a "back," or "finishing," area where these garments are trimmed of excess thread, pressed, and packaged for sale. Workers are generally assigned to one or two machines on the shop floor and their work is varied based on the demands of production.

The strategy of producing small runs of clothing in fashionable styles has made Signature Fashions a thriving company at a time when the rest of the garment industry in Trinidad is in serious decline. After decades of protecting its garment industry from external competition, in the late 1980s Trinidad and Tobago began relaxing its trade barriers on the importation of ready-made garments from abroad. This, according to one former factory owner, "was the death of the local garment industry. There is no way the local garment industry could compete with goods coming directly out of China." Trinidad's large-scale factories (100–300 workers), which relied on producing high volumes of plain-style clothing, have been most vulnerable to the vagaries of trade liberalization. Such factories are gradually disappearing from the Trinidadian manufacturing sector.

Most of the workers at Signature Fashions are Afro-Trinidadian and Indo-Trinidadian women aged thirty-five to fifty-five. These women usually have been working in the garment industry for more than twenty years, and thus have experienced, firsthand, the changing fortunes of Trinidad's garment industry from its "boom time" in the 1970s, to its subsequent "bust" and recession during the 1980s, followed by the industry's decimation under the competitive pressures of free trade since the 1990s. These workers came of age in the large-scale factories, where they each would be assigned a single task (like sewing pockets onto shirts, or stitching up side-seams), which they would do, repetitively, for months or years at a stretch. At Signature Fashions, owing to its small runs of clothing in a range of elaborate styles, the jobs that workers are allocated change considerably from day to day. A worker may find herself stitching cuffs onto sleeves one morning, and by the afternoon be stitching belt loops or hemming dresses.

The small-scale, flexible production regimen at Signature Fashions sets it apart from most of the other factories in Trinidad, just as its "high-fashion" clothing lines depart from the staple items that most garment factories produce. On the shop floor, these differences manifest themselves in a busy social environment that contrasts sharply to the quieter, more regimented shop floors that I visited elsewhere in Trinidad. Interviews with Signature managers and shop-floor supervisors always evoke a description of the factory as a neat assembly line with each worker conducting her assigned task autonomously. In reality, the shop floor is an active social field in which gaining the aid of fellow workers is always part of the process. Working in a fast-paced company on a constantly changing product means that workers often make mistakes. If a worker on the binding machine stitches up the waistbands on a dozen pairs of shorts before remembering that she was supposed to stitch the care tag into the back of each one, she may turn to a nearby worker operating a straight-stitch sewing machine using the same color thread, and quickly ask for "a stitch just so" to tack the forgotten care tags neatly into place without attracting rebuke from the floor supervisor.

It is within the material space of the Signature factory, where social networks are marshaled in the flexible production of fashionable clothing, that thiefing a chance emerges as an achievable and rewarding practice. While worker theft is a problem at most garment factories—not to mention a regular source of joking discussion among supervisors who marvel at the outrageous ingenuity of their workers in sneaking things out of the factory gate—the prevalence and complexity of making replicas of the company's own products is unique to Signature Fashions. The famed "Signature" logo makes its clothing particularly desirable in Trinidad, where brand-name clothing is a mark of distinction and issues of style and dress have enormous significance in the performance of identity (Miller 1994: 219–26). Even though workers often joke that the high price of Signature garments derives entirely from its logo (making the consumers who pay top price for them the absent subjects of shop-floor mockery), Signature's high-priced garments confer social status on the wearer—of which the workers themselves are well aware.

THIEFING A CHANCE AT SIGNATURE FASHIONS

When I began nine months of participant observation at Signature Fashions,[4] I became quickly aware of a wide range of illicit practices that took place on the shop floor with some regularity. Many of the workers maintain their own home businesses in the evening, designing and stitching clothing for friends and neighbors.[5] Sewing at home helps workers augment the minimum wage that they earn at Signature Fashions[6] and gives them a certain stature in their home communities.[7] Some workers would copy patterns from the factory for their home clients by placing the individual pieces of a garment on which they were working (e.g., a shirt front and shirt back, and a sleeve) onto a sheet of newspaper and then tracing the shape of the fabric with a pen. "Have to keep up with style if you sew for people," a worker named Antoinette once whispered to me as I watched her pilfer the pattern for a designer shirt in this way.

Workers would also sometimes bring such "private jobs" for their home clients into the factory and sneakily hem a dress or serge its inside seams on the factory machines in order to give their homemade garments a more professional look. The managers would sometimes leave, in the lunch area, a box of fabric scraps too small to be used in the factory; workers would use these scraps to furtively stitch up small things for themselves: patchwork aprons and dust masks for use in the factory or cloth bags and doll clothes to take home. Workers might describe *any* of these activities as "thiefing me little chance," which simply means taking advantage of the brief moments when supervisors are distracted or absent from the shop floor to steal a moment's work on other projects. Like *la perruque*, described by Certeau (1984: 25) or the factory-made "homers" described by Anteby (2003), these small acts would redirect hourly paid workers' time and use of factory equipment toward personal projects; nothing material was taken except a trivial amount of thread.

Despite my awareness of everyday acts of copying, pilfering, and mutual aid, workers were reluctant to talk about such activities, usually shrugging off my questions about these practices. All of this changed after I had been working in the factory for six months, when I came to learn a great deal about the complex practice of workers' producing duplicates of the garments for themselves along the assembly line. This type of thiefing didn't become known to me until I became complicit in it, largely by accident, when I asked a worker to thief a chance for me.

That week, we were making camisole tops out of stretch-cotton cloth. Shirley was working on the binding machine attaching straps to each of the garments. One morning while I was helping her cut the straps as they came out of her machine, she said to me casually, "You could ask Kimberly to cut you a camisole and I'll stitch it up for you." Kimberly, it was widely known, was always "cutting." She had the ability to look at a piece of fabric, put a pair of scissors to it, and just by sight, cut out a pattern that would stitch together to make a pair of trousers, a shirt, or a skirt in the correct size.[8] I had noticed Kimberly cutting camisoles that week with what I assumed to be scraps of discarded cloth. A little while later that morning, I approached Kimberly and asked her quietly, "If I get some jersey fabric from Peggy, you could cut a camisole for me?" She nodded slightly. I didn't think much more of it. I had worked with Peggy in the cutting room for a few weeks during the Christmas rush. I would ask her if she had any scraps of cloth, deliver them to Kimberly, and have her cut a camisole shape for me at lunchtime. Shirley had already volunteered to stitch it up for me. It didn't seem like too big a deal. More than really wanting the camisole, I was curious to see if Kimberly would actually cut me one.

After finishing up my work with Shirley, I joined Glenda at a side table to cut and turn collars. A little while later I heard Antoinette hissing to get my attention. I could not see her mouth that was hidden behind her dust mask, but her eyes were smiling. She beckoned me over and I, pretending to cut some threads for her, came and stood next to her machine.

She whispered, "You ask Kimberly to cut you a camisole?" I said yes. She slapped my leg and giggled looking around the room to make sure the production manager was out of sight. "I thought you would *never* ask!" She started laughing again still turning her head left and right every couple of seconds to make sure no one was coming. She said:

> We go make you a whole *closetful* of Signature clothes. You ehnt [ain't] know how *long* I wanted to make something for you. But I didn't know how you would be about it. I didn't know if you would think it was stealing. I wanted to make Michael[9] a jersey; I wanted to make you so many jerseys. And now, girl, we go make you some *real* clothes!

Antoinette's excited chatter about thiefing a chance, and her sudden willingness to describe its material practices and moral logics, marked a deep contrast from her tight-lipped responses to my earlier questions about thiefing. I quickly realized that in simply asking Kimberly to cut me a camisole, I had unwittingly nominated myself as an eager participant in the process. In the time that followed, I came to learn a great deal about thiefing. The first and most obvious thing that I learned was that workers did not just use scraps of cloth to create simple garments for themselves, but instead cut whole cloth that was intended for legitimate production and created precise duplicates of the designer garments that the factory was producing for Signature's stores.

Ethnographic studies of the shop floor provide abundant examples of theft, "poaching," pilfering, and game playing (Anteby 2003; Burawoy 1985; Freeman 2000; Haraszti 1978; Yelvington 1995). Scholars have convincingly demonstrated that workers' illicit practices are neither deviant nor necessarily at odds with the main production processes. Workers' illicit activities on the shop floor may act as a strain on the formal production of the factory, but, as Michael Burawoy (1979) suggests, they may also operate as lubricant to the smooth functioning of production by securing workers' consent to the terms of their exploitation. We cannot know prima facie what illicit acts truly mean in the factory, but instead must examine them in the context of ideological and material struggles. Workers themselves may describe clandestine activities on the shop floor as acts of resistance against the appropriation of their labor value, or they may instead emphasize their attendant pleasures, risks, and feelings of accomplishment. For these reasons, "thiefing" can tell us a great deal about work itself if it is examined in reference to local mores, practices, and interpretations.

At Signature Fashions, thiefing a chance takes place alongside the main production of the factory, but is conceptually and materially separated from it. While the factory's "real work" (a term workers used) comes through official channels, delivered in bundles to the shop floor by first-line supervisors, thiefed work is initiated by individuals who must manage the entire process of completing the garment themselves by asking others to work on it. The negotiations involved in thiefing a chance are enmeshed within the same factory processes that require a constant flow of mutual aid, yet they exist in a parallel plane to the primary work of the factory.

A thiefed garment always began with a worker "begging" Peggy, who worked in the cutting room, for cloth. She could ask either for "cut" cloth, which Peggy would cut into the same patterns as the real work (sometimes by laying an extra length of fabric upon the pile to be cut into patterns, or by hand with a pair of scissors on small scraps of cloth), or plain cloth, which the worker who requested it would have to cut herself. Peggy might furtively pass the extra cloth to workers or attach it to a bundle of real work going to the shop floor. The thiefed cloth was always tied in such a way that it could be distinguished from the real work—forcing a spatial separation between the two even within the same bundle. Peggy was central to the process of thiefing a chance. Though she did not work on a sewing machine, she was known to have in her closet a whole range of clothes—"*all* Signature, and in every color," in the words of one worker—which the other workers had stitched up for her. Workers who thiefed a chance had to be sure to "go down good"[10] with Peggy, and be careful not to demand too much of her.

While almost all workers at Signature Fashions participated in thiefing a chance at some time or another (either in providing stitches or in managing the production of their own garments), those who were most involved in it were workers on specialized machines whose operations were necessary in order to complete most garments. Operators of these machines had the greatest capacity to enlist the aid of others in making their own garments in return. These workers may thief as many as fifteen items in a year; most other workers would thief far fewer.

The production manager and stitching supervisors all participated in thiefing a chance with the workers, expecting them to create duplicates of garments for themselves and their families. Yet even as workers thiefed a chance for their supervisors, thiefing practices had to be scrupulously hidden from view. This concealment upholds the distinction between the public face of garment work and its hidden practices underneath. When one worker, Lata, was discovered with a half-finished shirt on her sewing table, she was harshly reprimanded by the production manager for her carelessness, yet she was not sent home. As far as I could determine, the incident was never reported to the factory owners.[11] While both managers and workers are complicit in thiefing at Signature Fashions, vigorous efforts on all sides make such hidden work disappear from the face of the shop floor in the guise of being work for the factory itself (see also Certeau [1984: 25]).

As thiefed work threads its way through the shop floor, it is stitched up in a materially overlapping but conceptually separate space from the real work of the factory. Both real work and thiefed work are the product of managed negotiations between workers on the shop floor with the occasional intervention of supervisors; both types of work involve social agendas, obligation to others and ideas of reciprocity and trust. Yet, despite these similarities within the spheres of production, real work and thiefed work bear a crucial distinction: thiefed clothes can be justly smuggled out of the factory; legitimate factory work cannot. This distinction forms the basis of moral assessments of thiefing.

"IS WE OWN FACTORY": WHY THIEFING IS NOT STEALING

"I didn't know if you would think it was stealing," Antoinette had said to me, with relief, after I first asked Kimberly to thief a chance for me. Antoinette evoked the possibility of reading thiefing as plain theft. Thiefing is always haunted by its possible interpretation as "stealing," a position that the factory owners would surely take.[12] I was often told by workers not to bring into work any photographs of parties we had attended together in which someone was wearing a thiefed Signature item. When Shirley turned up to work one morning in a shirt she had thiefed from Signature, workers teased her for her "boldness," because if asked about the shirt, she would have to lie and say that she had bought it at one of the stores in town. After growing tired of her fellow workers' poking fun at her during lunch, Shirley announced, "If God say that it wrong, I go say to he, 'I very sorry, I didn't realize,' and that will be *that*." When I asked her if thiefing a chance is stealing, she quipped, "I don't think it stealing because we does do it *quick*."

The association of thiefing and stealing generates a great deal of humorous banter among workers. "All these Christians in here? Check they wardrobes!" Antoinette once said, although I could not be sure if she was using their participation in thiefing as evidence that it was not stealing, or as commentary on the moral laxity of Signature's Christians. Nonetheless, Glenda, the most visible Christian in the factory—owing to her frequent attempts to convert other workers to her newfound faith—commented to me, "Stealing is wrong, eh? But the only reason I don't thief chance here is I wear these long skirts. You could do it, though; you wear them kind of things."

The few workers at Signature who took no part in thiefing seemed to think it not worth the hassle of sneaking stitches and carrying the items out of the factory. These five or six workers tended to sit toward the front of the shop floor, spatially separated from workers who thiefed a chance. These workers rarely relied on any form of mutual aid to complete their work, instead priding themselves on their individual abilities and openly competing with one another (though often in a joking way) for the yearly "best worker" award.[13] While these workers were criticized by others for being "stale" and "boring," they only rarely responded with an outright critique of thiefing. Veena pointedly said during a visit to my home, "[Thiefing] is stealing and I would not take a pin from that factory, not a *pin*."

While such assertions seem to challenge the boundary between thiefing and stealing, all Signature Fashions workers actually draw a sharp distinction between thiefing garments in the factory and stealing them outright. When three completed shirts (real work) went missing from the assembly line during my fieldwork, Annie, a woman who had worked at Signature Fashions for only two months, was dismissed from her job the very next time she was late to work. The official reason for her dismissal was "lateness," but it was well known that management suspected her of having stolen the shirts. Workers assumed that only someone who had been at Signature a short time could have stolen the shirts; any other worker would know simply to thief them. Annie's dismissal saddened those who knew her well and vigorously proclaimed her innocence. Among other workers, the incident gave rise to jokes about Annie's supposed foolishness and arrogance in stealing from the factory.

The fact that stealing is held by all to be a most serious offence demonstrates its conceptual separation from the day-to-day thiefing that is tacitly allowed to flourish. This is an instructive distinction because it goes to the heart of how thiefed clothes are morally interpreted vis-à-vis the legitimate work of the factory. Real work, thiefed work, and stealing are best understood as positions along a continuum. Real work is situated at one end of the spectrum: the work of the factory that people are paid to do. Real work is owned and authored by the factory itself and while workers may rely on social networks of mutual aid to complete this work, they principally labor over it dispassionately, for a wage. Stealing is located at the opposite end of the spectrum and also represents a fixed moral position: to take the real work of the factory from the assembly line is clearly an offence. Stolen items are always seen as the property of the factory and workers say that to steal "just so" is morally wrong.

Yet in-between the fixed points of "real work" and "stealing" lies the gray area in which thiefing is conducted and morally defended. The moral meaning of thiefing essentially hinges on the question of ownership. Veena claims that thiefing is stealing because materials are taken; she declares her refusal to take anything from the shop floor, even something as small as a pin. Most other workers interpret thiefing differently, distinguishing between the materials used in the factory's main production and those used in thiefing. When workers speak of "thiefing a *chance*," they allude, not to the taking of an object, but to the taking of a risk. By begging Peggy to find and cut some cloth for them, they are engaging in social action to claim the items as their own. The rest of the process similarly requires risk taking and social action: each constituent part of the garment must be obtained and stitched together through careful negotiation with other workers. That individual workers entirely manage this process themselves helps them place thiefing in an interpretive category similar to that of their own work—like sewing at home or sneakily stitching in the factory—for which they assume responsibility and ownership.

In the act of thiefing, workers will almost always re-create and wear the exact styles being produced for the stores (and they never sell thiefed garments), not only because copies are easy to produce in the factory, but also because of the singular allure of owning an *actual* Signature Fashions garment. Yet, by pilfering patterns as well, workers can make well-designed outfits for themselves at home in the bright silks and soft satins that they prefer, rather than the linen and brushed-cotton "earth tones" that Signature often produces for sale to Caribbean elites and foreign tourists. In making stylistic choices about the production of quasi-Signature garments at home, even the thiefed factory items come to be seen as initiated and authored by themselves and therefore rightfully theirs.

The workers at Signature Fashions sometimes refer to thiefing a chance as "we own factory." The phrase has a double meaning and it is intended to. In Trinidadian English, the term "we own factory" could be taken to mean two things: "*our* own factory," or "we *own* the factory."[14] The use of the phrase underscores the workers' reconceptualization of the relationship between themselves and the factory. The factory is described as a space in which they can undertake their own projects (*our* own factory), effectively reconfiguring the meaning of the space itself (we *own* [the] factory). The factory thus becomes a resource for workers containing materials, machines, and ideas, all of which the daring person uses for her own purposes.

Thiefing is given individual, not collective, justification. The "wickedness" (miserliness) of the factory bosses was a constant topic of worker discussion, yet workers rarely portray thiefing as a form of retributive justice—a way of recuperating the value that their skill and diligence has infused into garments that are priced far beyond what they can afford. Although workers sometimes said that they deserved "a little jersey or two" because unlike other garment factories, Signature Fashions did not give each worker a T-shirt at Christmas, such compensatory justifications for thiefing were generally muted. Workers never collectively represented their actions as defying management, possibly because their shop-floor supervisors were complicit in thiefing a chance and the factory bosses were so remote.

During my first conversation with Antoinette about thiefing, she told me that she would make me a shirt, adding, "Because I feel you should be getting something, a stipend. You working here everyday and that wicked." The fact of my working at the factory for no pay (a situation the workers found scandalous) was sometimes proffered to me as an explanation for why my thiefed items were well deserved.[15] Still, this rationalization was usually offered in service of worker's personal narratives, as much as my own. Antoinette indicated that by "doing something" for me, she could better the "worthless" factory owners by suitably compensating a foreign guest laboring in her midst.

The formulation of thiefing a chance as individual risk taking rather than collective theft is well demonstrated by the debates that arose from Lata's being caught thiefing. When Cissy discovered the half-finished shirt resting on her sewing table, she immediately demanded to know for whom it was being made. Lata truthfully said that it was for Kimberly. When questioned by Cissy, Kimberly said, "I don't know nothing about that." Lata's naming of Kimberly and Kimberly's subsequent silence in response to Cissy's questions, instantly became a raucous topic of lunchtime gossip among workers.

Workers agreed that Lata had been reckless in leaving the shirt exposed, though they were divided over whether she was wise to identify Kimberly as the owner of the shirt. Some workers argued that she should not have named Kimberly, if only to protect her own interests. Carmela said, "Who go help she [thief a chance] now?" Other workers insisted that because it was Kimberly's shirt, Lata need not risk a scolding or dismissal for illicitly working on an item that was not even hers. Devi said, "If I thiefing for Kimberly and I get caught, I go *say* it for she." Antoinette concurred adding, "At least if I go lose my [job], it go be because I thiefing chance for *myself*," rather than accepting dismissal for participating in someone else's scheme.

Workers universally applauded Kimberly's silence, maintaining that she was not obliged to furnish the truth. As a strategy to avoid punishment, Kimberly's silence succeeded. Cissy scolded Lata and Antoinette (who had obviously serged the garment) and then stormed off with the shirt in hand. In all the debates that circulated around this incident, it was never suggested by workers that they should, on principle, protect one another as a group. Lata's words and Kimberly's silence were assessed as personal, rather than as collective, strategies. Despite the huge coordination involved in thiefing a chance, it is conceptualized as an interconnected series of individual enterprises, which is why Lata was not condemned for identifying Kimberly. While it was deemed too risky to thief a chance with her for a couple of months, Lata was not ostracized by the group.

THIEFING IN EVERYDAY LIFE

Shop-floor moralities are relational; they are also situational and culturally inflected (Anteby 2003). The moralities in play at Signature Fashions are shaped not only by the immediate working context, but also, more generally, by moral values widely discernible in Trinidadian society. Anthropologists have long recognized the existence of multiple value systems at work within West Indian culture. Peter Wilson (1995 [1973]) famously asserted that West Indians are oriented, at different times, to two ideological systems: Euro-centric colonial ideologies which focus on social hierarchy and "respectability," and a locally based "creole" value system characterized by egalitarianism, communitas, and status competitions to build streetwise "reputation" (see also Besson [1993]; Freeman [2000]; Sutton [1974]; Yelvington [1995]). The coexistence of these two frameworks points to dual aspirations among West Indian people: to the "transient" pleasures associated with short-lived status contests and to the "transcendent" moral virtues of stability and domesticity (Miller 1994). Thomas Eriksen (1990: 31–32) suggests that these two value orientations encapsulate different moral valences as in the case of the workers who compete for Signature's "best worker" award and those who pursue instead the material bounty that thiefing provides; people may gravitate to one value orientation or another "based on the rewards a person is seeking" (Browne 2004: 96).

The idiom of thiefing a chance relates to the reputation/transient moral framework in which illicit activities and informal labor are prized inside a "creole" cultural schema that celebrates cunning, resourcefulness, and self-reliance (Browne 2004). Yet, as Katherine Browne (2004) reveals, the values that are embodied in practices like thiefing do not just celebrate cleverness and style; they also extol a past and present ability to survive an uncertain and economically harsh environment. Workers demonstrate the continuities between these culturally valorized modes of autonomy and thiefing a chance in their narratives of gaining entry into and thriving within the garment industry.

While most Trinidadian garment workers are first taught to sew by female kin or a neighborly seamstress, the skills needed in a large-scale factory are different from what one would learn in a strictly home-based trade. Operating a heavy-duty machine and keeping up with fast-paced, piece-rate work cannot be learned until entering the factory. Yet, given the abundance of skilled stitchers in Trinidad and a shrinking industry, factory bosses—including the owners of Signature Fashions—simply refuse to train workers who cannot do work as assigned. As a result, many workers recount acts of duplicity in attaining their first factory job. As Aparna said of her first job in a garment factory, "I had to lie and say that I could work that [industry-grade] machine!" Though her lack of skill was immediately obvious to her supervisors, Aparna was allowed to stay on, learning as she worked. The sweetness in recounting her story derives partly from her boldness in taking a chance.

This narrative exaltation of thiefing as a survival strategy in a tough and unstable industry is best conveyed in the following quotation from Antoinette:

Antoinette: I went [to my first factory] as a trimmer, really.

Rebecca: Did you know how to sew on a machine at that point?

Antoinette: No, I did not. I really worked as a trimmer, just like trimming thread and stuff [by hand], and while I was there now, I used to thief chance and go on the machine, the serger, because I was just, this machine fascinated me when I saw it, nah.

Rebecca: So you would ask people, Can I go on this?

Antoinette: No, well, I would just like, when the boss was to the front, I would run [*claps hands*] on the machine and I would try to learn to thread it and, you know, thief me little chances, and people encourage me, you know? But I learned—there you learned to iron, you learned to cover buttons, you learned to tack—but you wasn't allowed to go on the machine. But I thief chance to go on the machine. And then one day he come out and he saw me, and he start to cuss and, oh, you know, start to

> get on ridiculous, nah? And then, 'bout two or three months after, the person for the machine didn't come to work, and he had a wedding to do. And he didn't have a choice but to put me on that machine! [*Laughs.*] And that's why I will always take chances and I go, yeah, do me little things, nah?

Antoinette's quotation ends with the statement: "And that's why I will always take chances and I go, yeah, do me little things, nah?" By playfully evoking the various meanings of thiefing a chance, Antoinette semantically endorses her copying garments at Signature Fashions by drawing attention to her earlier success in learning how to sew through her acts of personal daring on the shop floor. In an economic sphere where training is not found easily, such skills may be seized by the worker who intends to have them.

Workers' various narratives of thiefing a chance offer suggestive pathways through which to assess their interpretation of *thiefing*'s meaning. Thiefing a chance is part of the life-world of work at Signature Fashions. It is made possible by its flexible labor regimen and busy shop floor where networks of mutual aid are already prominent. Arguably, thiefing practices actually aid the factory by compelling workers to skill-up for new tasks on a constantly changing product and allowing employers to dispense with the obligation of formally training the workforce. Yet, in narrating their experiences, workers find thiefing a chance a useful idiom because the concept so neatly captures their willingness to take chances in order to become the sometime creators of their own destiny.

In assessing the ideological meaning of thiefing practices, we must bear in mind that thiefing a chance materially concerns workers producing high-fashion clothing for themselves (or occasionally for a child, male partner, or sister). It would be a mistake to locate the practice of thiefing a chance within the sphere of working-class survival tactics in a deregulated world (Mollona 2005) as an informal economic activity to generate income (Browne 2004; Freeman 1991) or as "everyday resistance" to workplace hegemony (Scott 1985). Thiefing has much to do with gaining certain symbols of wealth, success, and style in a context where the meanings of these symbols are salient. Daniel Miller (1994: 223) has noted, for example, that in Trinidad the giving of clothing in a romantic relationship is duly expected by many women. By creating and wearing high-status garments themselves, Signature Fashions workers are able to play with the ambiguous signification of their dress in social gatherings outside of work by disguising or leaving open to speculation the exact origin of their clothing.

The garments that are thiefed have use value; they also have symbolic value. Many of the most enthusiastic participants in thiefing a chance at Signature Fashions (Antoinette, Kimberly, Peggy) are single mothers with little disposable income to deal with issues of style for themselves and, importantly, for their daughters. Others (Shirley, Lata, Cissy) have more household income because they are married. Both groups enjoy having access to expensive clothing and the status that thiefing confers on them in the factory. But the performance of thiefing a chance also contains the pleasures of breaking from workplace monotony and the enjoyment of a good ruse. One afternoon, Shirley roared with laughter at Aparna who watched nervously as Shirley quickly hemmed a T-shirt for her calling out, "She frighten, and is *I* taking risk!" Thiefing certainly contains some risk and that risk may be a source of pleasure and excitement.

CONCLUSION

Issues of culture are important in shaping and defining moralities if by "morality" we mean socially sanctioned ways of acting that are meaningful to a particular place and time. For this reason, understanding the shop-floor moralities that sustain thiefing a chance at Signature Fashions requires, not only an intimate look at its practices in the factory, but also an examination of the wider cultural contours of West Indian daily life.

What are the shop-floor moralities that sustain thiefing at Signature Fashions? Unpacking the discourses and practices of thiefing a chance demonstrates that the moral assessments that workers make are, in the first instance, about the *ownership* and *authorship* of the clothing being produced. While all workers recognize the rightful ownership of the "real work" of the factory as belonging to the factory owners—which is why there is a universal injunction against stealing—the relationship between workers and the materials used in thiefing is more nuanced, varied, and individuated.

Workers engage in social action to seize the materials needed to produce their own garments and to get those garments made. This practice is untidy and fraught with social negotiations. Because thiefing requires intense and covert cooperation among workers, it can create a fair amount of conflict as well. In managing all of these elements, workers see themselves as the primary authors of their thiefed garments. Their stylistic selections, their daring in procuring the needed materials and their finesse in managing social networks deeply structure their accounts of what it means to thief a chance.

The relationship between workers and the items they thief is made more complex when we consider the linkages between factory labor and the informal economic activities that workers pursue at home. Workers at Signature Fashions are, on the whole, highly skilled seamstresses who maintain their own home businesses designing and producing clothing for local clients. These activities should not be considered apart from Signature Fashions because they are tightly bound to factory life. Workers copy patterns from the shop floor to give their homemade garments a cutting-edge look; the skills they develop through homeworking similarly prepare them for the dynamic environment of the factory. I have argued in this chapter that the inextricable relationship between factory work and the home trade contributes to workers' seeing the factory not only as a place where they stitch clothing for a wage, but also as "we own factory"—a ready source of both ideas and productive capacity.

The justification for thiefing a chance is rarely pitched as resistance to workplace hegemony. While workers will often talk about their bosses' miserliness, such comments are not often assembled as moral support for thiefing practices. Although I was encouraged by some workers to accept thiefed clothing from them because I was not paid for my factory labor, justifications for thiefing rooted in workplace complaints were more often muted or not expressed at all. Similarly, discourses of thiefing a chance rarely contain descriptions of collective or communal interest. More often—as with Lata's being caught thiefing a shirt—responses to thiefing a chance, like the justifications that uphold it, are individually crafted as strategies of personal action.

While thiefing a chance is a collaborative and coordinated activity, it is fundamentally conceptualized as an act of individual initiative rather than as a collective pursuit. Discourses of thiefing evoke the image of a resourceful, savvy person who takes pleasure in seizing opportunities as they arise. Acts of thiefing are also valorized within West Indian discourses that celebrate cunning, assertiveness, and nerve (Browne 2004). While workers feel ambivalent, at times, about the many similarities between thiefing and stealing, they choose to epitomize the moral meaning of thiefing in the image of the daring individual.

NOTES

Acknowledgments. The doctoral research upon which this chapter is based was supported by the Wenner-Gren Foundation and Universities UK. I am grateful to Geert De Neve, James Fairhead, and Simon Coleman for comments on earlier drafts.

1. "Signature Fashions" and all of the names in this chapter are pseudonyms.
2. Trinidad is one island in the two-island Republic of Trinidad and Tobago. This chapter refers only to Trinidad as this island supports the vast majority of Trinidad and Tobago's garment manufacturing.
3. At the time of fieldwork (2003–2004), a T-shirt with the "Signature" logo would sell for TT$60 (US$10), and a dress would sell for up to TT$350 (US$58). With the minimum wage at TT$8 per hour (US$1.30), Signature clothing, like imported brand-name clothing, was priced far beyond what garment workers could afford.

4. This period extended from October 2003 to June 2004 and November 2004.

5. Such "occupational multiplicity" is well documented in the anthropology of the Caribbean region. Workers often maintain both a primary job and several independent money-making ventures, moving between formal and informal labor arrangements (Browne 2004; Comitas 1973; Freeman 2000; Yelvington 1995).

6. This minimum wage was TT$320 a week. At the time of fieldwork, this was equivalent to US$53 a week.

7. Neighborhood seamstresses maintain continuing importance in Trinidad, particularly for the middle- and low-income individuals seeking fashionable, one-of-a-kind outfits that only local seamstresses and tailors can provide, often based on a client's own selection of fabric and sketched designs (Miller 1994: 222). The cultural centrality of the West Indian seamstress was vividly depicted in the 1997 Jamaican film, *Dancehall Queen* (Elgood and Letts 1997), in which a local dressmaker helps the protagonist design outrageous costumes for her sexy alter-ego, transforming her from a workaday street vendor into the Dancehall Queen. With the increasing availability of ready-made garments from abroad, the role of the neighborhood seamstress seems to be declining; still, many Trinidadians insist that to obtain a special outfit for an important social event (like a graduation or wedding), there is no better choice than to visit a skilled and trusted seamstress.

8. The joke in the factory was that Kimberly cut so much fabric on her lap while sitting at her sewing machine, that her skirts were full of little holes caused by her hurriedly cutting through the fabric on her lap and as well as her own clothes. Donny, my tailoring instructor in Trinidad, once explained to me that "freehand" cutting is valued among working-class women who, in his view, lack confidence in the use of an "inch tape" and in their abilities at arithmetic to construct their own patterns to size. Such a view, while sympathetic to the utility of freehand cutting, underrates the considerable skill required to do it well.

9. Michael is my partner who accompanied me during my fieldwork in Trinidad.

10. To "go down good" is locally understood as, to get along well.

11. While middle management clearly knew about, and participated in, thiefing a chance, I do not believe that the factory owners understood its prevalence and complexity at the time.

12. As Anteby (2003) has demonstrated, illicit shop-floor practices look different from inside the circle of participants than from outside it; what is considered moral depends on where one is located (Anteby 2003: 232).

13. The award presented to the worker chosen for having embodied all of the "best worker" qualities during the previous year was usually a paperweight or clock symbolizing punctuality, efficiency, cheerfulness, and skill.

14. Gayelle Television, a locally owned TV channel promoting Trinidadian arts, culture, and political debate, was launched in February 2004 under the slogan, "At last, we own television!"

15. Reflections on my participation in thiefing a chance have troubled me since leaving the field. My initial justification for accepting thiefed clothing—that as a participant observer, I had license to participate in everything—seems duly problematic. I mostly wonder, in retrospect, whether workers would have got into trouble if they had been caught thiefing a chance for me. The example of Lata getting caught with a thiefed shirt gives me hope that there would have been no penalty. Yet

my plan to take all the blame should someone be caught thiefing a chance for me (even if it meant losing my access to the factory) seems hollow in retrospect. My access to the factory was far less important to me than the workers' access to the factory was to them. It was my fieldsite; it was their workplace. But certainly, for a time, I was caught up in the workers' thrilling assertion that Signature Fashions was "we own factory." Participating in the rhythms of the workplace and being part of its social world, I was taken with the idea that it *was* the workers who, ultimately, "owned" the shop floor; without them, the factory was inconceivable. This view is problematic, but not uncommon. As suggested by Michael Burawoy (1985), such a belief is part of the trick of management upon workers—convincing them, for the most part, that the interests of the property owners are the interests of everyone, meaning that the factory (source of both profit and livelihood) "belongs" to capitalist and worker alike. Burawoy notes that this trick was what Antonio Gramsci meant by hegemony, "the presentation of the interests of the dominant classes as the interests of all" (Burwaoy 1985: 10). Like the workers, I believe that accepting the four shirts that they made for me did not constitute a financial hardship for the factory owners. However, my accepting them did represent a disloyalty to the owners, who so kindly allowed me to conduct fieldwork in their factory.

REFERENCES

Anteby, Michel. 2003. The "Moralities" of Poaching: Manufacturing Personal Artifacts on the Factory Floor. *Ethnography* 4(2): 217–39.

Besson, Jean. 1993. Reputation and Respectability Reconsidered: A New Perspective on Afro-Caribbean Peasant Women. In *Women and Change in the Caribbean*, ed. Janet Momsen, 15–37. Kingston, Jamaica: Ian Randle.

Browne, Katherine E. 2004. *Creole Economics: Caribbean Cunning under the French Flag*. Austin: University of Texas Press.

Burawoy, Michael. 1985. *The Politics of Production: Factory Regimes under Capitalism and Socialism*. New York: Verso.

———. 1979. *Manufacturing Consent: Changes in the Labor Process under Monopoly Capitalism*. Chicago: University of Chicago Press.

Certeau, Michel de. 1984. *The Practice of Everyday Life*. Trans. Steven Rendall. Berkeley: University of California Press.

Comitas, Lambros. 1973. Occupational Multiplicity in Rural Jamaica. In *Work and Family Life: West Indian Perspectives*, ed. Lambros Comitas and David Lowenthal, 157–73. Garden City, NY: Anchor Books.

Elgood, Rick, and Don Letts, directors. 1997. *Dancehall Queen*. (98 min.). New York: Palm Pictures.

Eriksen, Thomas Hylland. 1990. Liming in Trinidad: The Art of Doing Nothing. *Folk* 32(1): 24–43.

Freeman, Carla. 2000. *High Tech and High Heels in the Global Economy: Women, Work, and Pink-Collar Identities in the Caribbean*. Durham, NC: Duke University Press.

———. 1991. Reinventing Higglering in a Transnational Arena: Barbadian Women Juggle the Triple Shift. In *Daughters of Caliban: Caribbean Women in the 20th Century*, ed. Consuelo Lopez Springfield, 68–95. Bloomington: Indiana University Press.

Haraszti, Miklos. 1978. *A Worker in a Worker's State: Piece Rates in Hungary*. Trans. Michael Wright. New York: Universe Books.

Laidlaw, James. 2002. For an Anthropology of Ethics and Freedom. *Journal of the Royal Anthropological Institute* 8(2): 311–32.

Miller, Daniel. 1994. *Modernity, an Ethnographic Approach: Dualism and Mass Consumption in Trinidad*. Oxford: Berg.

Mollona, Massimilliano. 2005. Factory, Family and Neighbourhood: The Political Economy of Informal Labor in Sheffield. *Journal of the Royal Anthropological Institute* 11(3): 527–48.

Prentice, Rebecca. 2007. "'Thiefing a Chance:' Garment Work and the Production of Flexibility in Trinidad." PhD dissertation. University of Sussex, UK.

Scott, James C. 1985. *Weapons of the Weak: Everyday Forms of Peasant Resistance*. New Haven, CT: Yale University Press.

Sutton, Constance. 1974. Cultural Duality in the Caribbean. *Caribbean Studies* 14(2): 96–101.

Wilson, Peter J. 1995 [1973]. *Crab Antics: A Caribbean Study of the Conflict between Reputation and Respectability*. Prospect Heights, IL: Waveland Press.

Yelvington, Kevin A. 1995. *Producing Power: Ethnicity, Gender and Class in a Caribbean Workplace*. Philadelphia: Temple University Press.

6

Patriotism, Profits, and Waste

The Moral Dimensions of Low-Level Radioactive Waste Disposal in Texas

Cynthia Werner

Radioactive waste is an undeniable yet undesired product of modern society. Ironically, in a society where public fears about radiation run high, radioactive waste has the potential to accumulate great economic value for those willing to dispose of it properly. Given that some entities are expected to profit from waste disposal while others are projected to experience a disproportionate share of the risks, the politics of radioactive waste management is fraught with moral implications:

- When there is uncertainty regarding the technological capacity to dispose of waste safely, who has the right to decide where a disposal facility will be located? The government? Scientific "experts"? Private corporations? Or, local communities?
- Is it morally acceptable for a business to profit handsomely from the waste trade?
- Is it acceptable for disadvantaged groups, such as ethnic minorities and the poor, to suffer disproportionately from the transportation and disposal of radioactive waste? If not, how do we determine what counts as "disproportionate" suffering?
- Should a local community that hosts a waste disposal site receive tangible benefits in exchange for accepting the associated risks? If so, what is a fair way to define the boundaries of the affected "community" or "region of interest?" Should communities located along the corridor for the transportation of this toxic waste receive any benefits? What is the best way to determine how and what should be provided in exchange for unknown and uncertain risks?

This chapter examines the ways in which questions of morality such as these are addressed in the political debates about low-level radioactive waste (LLRW) disposal in Texas. The Texas case is unique in that it is not yet characterized by NIMBY (Not-in-My-Backyard) politics. Instead, the proposed host community, Andrews County, is lobbying hard on behalf of a private company that has submitted a license for a disposal facility. This paper considers how both the proponents and the opponents of the proposed facility use moral rhetoric to support their arguments in the political debate over waste disposal.

DEFINING THE PROBLEM OF RADIOACTIVE WASTE

Before turning to the Texas case, it is necessary to provide some background information on the different types of radioactive waste, how new laws have changed the future storage and disposal of radioactive waste, and how the licensing process has played out in other states. Not all radioactive waste is the same. Waste policy makes general distinctions between two sources of radiation (defense and commercial) and between two levels of radioactivity (high-level and low-level). Defense wastes are associated with the nuclear weapons industry. Commercial waste consists of the spent fuel generated by nuclear reactors for electricity production, as well as other radioactive waste from industry, academic research, and medical institutions. By definition, high-level radioactive waste is dangerous to humans and other life forms and will generate significant levels of radiation for over 10,000 years. High-level radioactive waste (HLRW) comes from the use of uranium fuel in nuclear reactors and nuclear weapons processing and requires very special handling. LLRW consists of most other forms of radioactive waste that by definition do not require shielding during handling or transportation. LLRW is generated from hospitals, commercial and academic laboratories, and nuclear power plants and includes papers, rags, tools, soils, and protective clothing and gloves contaminated with radioactive materials. Low-level waste is an umbrella category that includes some items that are not very radioactive and other items that are almost as dangerous as high-level waste. Depending on the level of radioactivity, low-level waste is further subdivided into three different categories (each requiring different handling procedures): Class A, Class B, and Class C. Class A waste will remain radioactive for up to 100 years, Class B for up to 300 years, and Class C for up to 500 years (Envirocare of Utah 2006a). While most wastes can be categorized as either LLRW or HLRW, there are some additional categories: transuranic waste, naturally occurring radioactive materials (NORM), uranium mill tailings, and mixed waste (Murray 2003).

Opponents of nuclear energy highlight the issue of radioactive waste. Although nuclear power plants are known to produce less pollution than conventional power plants that rely on fossil fuels, the problem of radioactive waste has been described as the "Achilles heel" of nuclear power (Song 2003). All of the commercial high-level waste comes from nuclear power plants. There are over one hundred nuclear power plants in the United States, which produce "spent fuel," one of the most radioactive types of waste. In addition to high-level waste, nuclear power plants also generate low-level waste. According to the United States Department of Energy (DOE), nuclear power plants account for 56 percent of low-level waste by volume and 79 percent of low-level waste by radioactivity.[1] The annual volume of low-level waste has increased in recent years due to the cleanup of U.S. DOE sites, and after a temporary decline, the volume is likely to increase in the near future with the decommissioning of nuclear power plants between 2010 and 2030 (English 1992; United States General Accounting Office 2004).

Radioactive waste has been regulated for over fifty years by various government organizations, including the U.S. DOE. However, the U.S. government did not have a comprehensive plan for dealing with the permanent disposal of radioactive waste until new legislation was passed in the early 1980s (English 1992; Flynn and Slovic 1995; King 1995; Murray 2003; Nuclear Energy Institute 2004). Since the 1950s, all of the HLRW from the defense-industry and some of the high-level waste from the commercial sector have been transported to several locations for temporary storage, including Hanford, Washington; Idaho Falls, Idaho; and Savannah River, South Carolina (Murray 2003). The remaining high-level waste from the nuclear power industry, including much of the spent fuel, has been stored on site near the nuclear reactors. Currently, HLRW from the weapons industry and nuclear power plants is temporarily stored at 125 sites in thirty-nine states (United States Department of Energy 2006b). The majority of waste is located east of the Mississippi River (Flynn and Slovic 1995). This is considered a temporary solution and a security problem. In response to this issue, Congress passed the Radioactive Waste Policy Act in 1982. This act gave the DOE a mandate to establish and maintain a national repository for the nation's HLRW. The Yucca Mountain site in Nevada was selected as the national repository site in 1987, yet the licensing process has been stalled by political controversy and legal proceedings (State of Nevada Agency for Nuclear Projects 1998; United States Department of Energy 2006a).

Until the development of nuclear power plants in the 1950s and 1960s, the volume of LLRW waste was relatively low and much of it was dumped in oceans and shallow landfills operated by the U.S. Atomic Energy Commission. Beginning in the 1960s, six different commercial sites were opened to dispose of low-level waste using shallow land burial methods. By the late 1970s, three of these sites (Maxey Flats in Kentucky, West Valley in New York, and Sheffield in Illinois) were closed after it was discovered that radiation leaked into the environment due to a "bathtub effect" during periods of heavy rainfall. Another site (Beatty in Nevada) closed temporarily in 1979 due to violations of waste management procedures, and then closed permanently in 1992 when waste reached full capacity. Only two of these earlier sites are still accepting LLRW: Richland in Washington and Barnwell in South Carolina (English 1992; Kearney and Smith 1994).[2] A new site, Envirocare of Utah, received a license to dispose of mill tailings in 1979 (Bedsworth et al. 2004), and by 2006, Envirocare had expanded its services to include disposal of NORM waste, mixed waste, and Class A LLRW (Envirocare of Utah 2006b).

With LLRW, there have been three general problems: problems with radiation leaking into the environment due to poor technology; high volume of waste and too few sites for disposal; and an unequal burden on a small number of states. New disposal methods have vastly improved the technological issue, but the two other problems have not been resolved. In 1980, the governors of the three host states pressured Congress to pass the Low-Level Radioactive Waste Policy Act. This law essentially transferred responsibility for commercially generated low-level radioactive waste from federal to state governments. The act requires each state to develop its own solution for low-level waste produced within its borders. States may either develop their own waste disposal site, or they may join a compact with other states, one of which serves as the "host" state for LLRW from other compact members. The law was amended in 1985 with deadlines for forming compacts, selecting host states, and licensing sites (English 1992; Murray 2003).

Although it has been over twenty-five years since this law was enacted, the development of new disposal sites has been problematic. As of 2004, forty-three states have entered into one of ten compacts and each compact has selected an initial host state (United States General Accounting Office 2004). Despite spending nearly $600 million collectively in the effort to develop new sites, none of the compacts have succeeded in selecting an acceptable site (United States General Accounting Office 1999). Currently, low-level waste is disposed at two locations that were opened before the law was passed, and one site that developed outside the framework of the compact system: Richland, which now serves as the site for the Northwest Compact and the Rocky Mountain Compact; Barnwell, which plans to limit access to states within the Atlantic Compact beginning in 2008; and Envirocare of Utah, which is limited to the disposal of Class A waste (Murray 2003). Figure 6.1 shows the location of the three active sites. In addition to these disposal sites, much of the

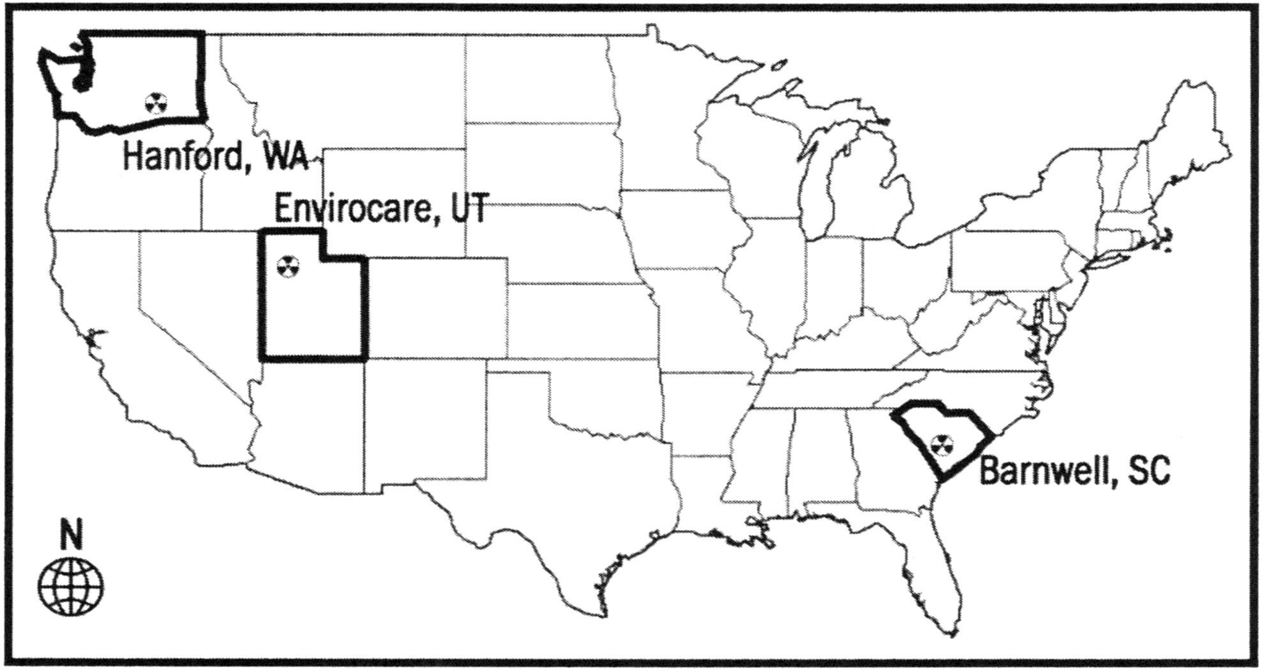

Figure 6.1. Location of Low-Level Radioactive Waste Disposal Sites in the United States

low-level waste produced is temporarily stored where it is generated, that is, at universities, hospitals, and nuclear power plants.

In the United States, the storage and disposal of radioactive waste has been a hotly debated political issue. After new laws were passed in 1980 and 1982, federal and state governments have tried to develop a number of sites to dispose of both HLRW and LLRW. The most notorious case involving radioactive waste is the political stalemate over Yucca Mountain in Nevada. One hundred miles north of Las Vegas, Yucca Mountain is the site selected by the federal government to become the nation's single repository for high-level nuclear waste generated from the defense industry and the nuclear power industry. Experts considered dozens of potential sites, and most of the sites were challenged by local opposition. The list was first narrowed to nine candidates in six states in 1983, and then narrowed to three sites in 1986: Yucca Mountain in Nevada, Hanford in Washington, and Deaf Smith County in Texas (Liebow 1988). In 1987, an amendment to the Nuclear Waste Policy Act cancelled further investigation of all sites other than the Yucca Mountain site (Flynn and Slovic 1995). The DOE favored the Yucca Mountain site for a number of reasons: "the area's dry climate, remote location, stable geology, deep water table and closed water basin" (United States Department of Energy 2006a).

Nevadan politicians and citizen groups, however, do not believe that the site is geologically ideal for radioactive waste and do not want this in their backyard. They resent the fact that the federal government expects Nevadans to accept the bulk of risk associated with radioactive waste disposal. In a recent survey, 76.8 percent of Nevadans oppose the Yucca Mountain project while 19.2 percent support the project (State of Nevada Agency for Nuclear Projects 2004). In 1989, the Nevada Legislature passed a law that made it illegal for any person or government entity to store radioactive waste in Nevada (Flynn and Slovic 1995). By 2002, after $7 billion had been spent on site investigations, the U.S. Secretary of Energy declared that the Yucca Mountain site was suitable as the national repository and that the facility would open in 2017. The governor of Nevada objected, yet this was overruled by the U.S. Congress. In response to continuing political controversy, in March 2006, the DOE announced the formation of a new body of experts to conduct yet another round of independent scientific investigations regarding the technical safety of the proposed facility. The final scene in this political drama is yet to be played out (United States Department of Energy 2006c).

Throughout the public hearings and debates, the opposition has drawn on moral and emotional arguments, as well as on economic and environmental arguments. On the moral side, opponents state that the process is unfair and that the federal waste law (in particular the 1987 amendment) has not adequately considered the will of Nevada's citizens, the majority of whom oppose the project (Flynn and Slovic 1995). Native Americans, many of whom have already been exposed to radiation as "downwinders" from the Nevada Test Site, have objected to the fact that they have not been consulted by the DOE. In a public comment to the DOE, one Native American argues:

> Indian people have already suffered greatly as a result of the US nuclear program. . . . We should not be put at any more risk. If this project is as safe as you claim, there would be no need to build it here far from the sources of nuclear waste. But because you recognize the extreme danger and risk involved in the storage of this waste you choose to ship it far from yourselves, burdening our land and our future generations with it. This is not surprising considering the history of contempt and disregard with which you have treated our lands and people. This is an issue of environmental justice. (Eureka County 2003: 115)

Although the DOE claims that the repository will be "safe," representatives of the State of Nevada as well as citizen organizations question the science behind these studies. In particular, they cite the uncertainty that radioactive substances might leak into the environment, especially if there is an earthquake in the region. One of the greatest concerns is whether or not the transportation of radioactive waste along highways in Nevada will be safe. Another concern is whether or not the development of the waste facility will endanger the tourist industry and other business developments in the region (State of Nevada Agency for Nuclear Projects 1998, 2004).

Although LLRW has not received as much media attention, local debates about low-level radioactive waste mirror the political controversy surrounding Yucca Mountain. Opponents often challenge the validity of scientific studies regarding the safety of sites and criticize the process itself for disregarding local concerns. Since the Low-Level Radioactive Waste Policy Act was passed in 1980, ten compacts have been formed but no new disposal sites have been developed. In dozens of communities, citizens have united against proposals to situate radioactive waste disposal facilities "in their backyard" and have succeeded in preventing or delaying such developments. NIMBY politics and such responses are associated with a decline of public confidence in the ability of government and industry to assess and limit risk from environmental hazards (Kraft and Clary 1991). Proposed sites have failed to receive licenses in a number of states, including Illinois, California, New York, Connecticut, and Texas (English 1992; Kearney and Smith 1994; Rabe et al. 1994).

The academic literature on risk perception can provide useful insights for understanding the problems that plague both high-level and low-level waste management. To begin, studies have shown that laypersons and experts usually do not agree with the risks associated with certain hazards. Laypersons on average have heightened fears of radiation-related hazards, such as nuclear power and radioactive waste. These fears are explained in part by the images of nuclear war and the dread associated with nuclear tragedies such as the accidents at Chernobyl and Three Mile Island (Slovic et al. 1980). Since laypersons do not share the same perception of risk, risk perception analysts have developed more nuanced understandings of variations in risk perception. Building from Mary Douglas and Aaron Wildavsky's (1982) work on the social construction of risk, the "social constructionist" perspective suggests that different subgroups may assign different meanings to events based on their group-based values and beliefs (Albrecht and Amey 1999). In situations of environmental conflict, such as the conflict over the siting of a LLRW facility, different groups assert the "moral superiority" of their own definition of reality. Both sides try to demonstrate that their opponents are "wrongheaded, ill-informed or even evil" (Albrecht and Amey 1999: 742; Bedsworth et al. 2004). Antiwaste activists, in particular, are criticized for being "too emotional" and for "marketing fear" (Rossin 2003).

The existing case studies of low-level nuclear waste politics demonstrate that moral conflicts have played a major role in the failure of most sites. Some studies have pointed out that the siting process has failed in the United States largely because of a top-down approach where a site is first selected by outside "experts," and then during the licensing process, local community members voice opposition and the site is ultimately rejected (Rabe et al. 1994). In the case of New York, for example, the siting process started with "experts" defining criteria to narrow down the list of potential sites, as has been the practice with other forms of hazardous waste. When affected citizens expressed disagreement with the scientific arguments that their backyard was an ideal site for a waste facility, they felt that their views were dismissed as irrelevant and irrational concerns by the Siting Commission. State officials, however, sided with local citizens after a series of nonviolent protests, and the siting process was halted (Freudenberg 2004). Three proposed sites in Connecticut failed for similar reasons after eleven months of hearings and $4 million of research development. In response to cases like this, some authors have recommended a more equitable process where local organizations and local values are considered in the process (Kearney and Smith 1994). Unfortunately, this democratic approach did not work well in California, where the advisory group included representatives from Native American groups and three nongovernmental organizations. Although the process allowed for new voices to enter the process, the advisory group was unable to reach a consensus (Bedsworth et al. 2004). In the context of NIMBY activism, another alternative is to call for towns that meet certain criteria to volunteer to host waste sites in return for a specified set of benefits. This bottom-up approach has been used successfully in Alberta and Manitoba to gain public acceptance from the earliest stage of the licensing process. In both cases, potential host communities had forums to discuss the risks, negotiate compensation packages and to express their preferred method of disposal (Rabe et al. 1994).[3]

In addition to moral issues related to the siting process, there is the moral issue of siting a waste facility near a poor community with higher concentrations of ethnic minorities. Due to greater awareness of the need for environmental justice, the Nuclear Regulatory Commission has added legislative language that prevents the likelihood that a site will have unequal impacts on minorities or the poor. Despite these regulations, accusations of "environmental racism" were a major factor that prevented Texas from developing a LLRW disposal site in Hudspeth County (Amey et al. 1997).

THE DISPOSAL OF LOW-LEVEL RADIOACTIVE WASTE IN TEXAS

Although most communities in the United States have resisted the waste trade, this chapter tells the story of a small Texas town that is rallying behind a company that seeks to dispose of LLRW in their backyard. The leaders of the town argue that the importation of waste will help diversify the local economy, which is dependent on the oil-and-gas industry and that the risks from radioactive waste are not qualitatively different than the risks from oil and gas. Local community leaders have also used patriotic rhetoric to support the further development of the waste facility.

Most of the information regarding LLRW disposal in Texas is of public record. However, my knowledge of this political process has been heavily informed by my participation. For the past two years, I have been employed as a part-time consultant for the Texas Commission on Environmental Quality (TCEQ). TCEQ is the regulatory agency that is currently reviewing the license application from Waste Control Specialists (WCS) for the proposed compact facility in Andrews County, Texas. I have been working with a team of TCEQ employees to review the application at various stages of its development. The other members of the Radioactive Material Licensing Team have scientific expertise in hydrology, geology, health physics, and engineering. I have contributed to the review process by assessing the portions of the application that deal with the social and economic impacts of the proposed facility. The review process consists of multiple steps. At each step, TCEQ provides an official request for further information and then the applicant responds by revising the application. In June 2006, the Radioactive Material Licensing Team finished reviewing the sixth incarnation of the license application. Due to a number of unresolved issues, the Waste Permits Division of TCEQ sent a 146-page "List of Concerns" to WCS and recommended that WCS apply for an extension in order to address these concerns with the application. An extension was granted in August of 2006 and WCS responded to the list of concerns in March 2007 (Texas Commission on Environmental Quality 2006). In addition to reviewing the application documents, I have observed public meetings and public hearings in Andrews and Austin, I have participated in business meetings with executives and consultants working for WCS and I have interviewed about two dozen local community members in and near Andrews County.

Table 6.1 shows a timeline of events that relate to the LLRW licensing process in Texas. The current licensing process represents the second attempt to develop a waste disposal facility in Texas. Shortly after the 1980 legislation was passed, the State of Texas created a new agency, the Low-Level Radioactive Waste Disposal Authority, to develop and manage a waste site for the State of Texas. After investigating several potential sites, the new agency determined that a site known as "Sierra Blanca," about ninety miles southeast of El Paso and about fifteen miles from the Mexican border, had ideal conditions for a disposal site. The Sierra Blanca site had already been used for the disposal of sewage sludge. In 1993, Texas finally formed a compact with two other unaffiliated states, Maine and Vermont, and agreed to become the host state for what is known as the "Texas Compact." Initially, the compact was denied by the U.S. Congress in 1995, but after heavy lobbying by then governor George Bush, Congress accepted a compact bill that even allowed Texas to accept waste from states outside of the compact (Public Employees for Environmental Responsibility 2000). Around the time that a draft permit was issued for the Sierra Blanca site in 1996, public opposition on both sides of the U.S.-Mexico border intensified. The opposition was concerned with the risk of radiation contamination, the geological stability of the site, the issue of environmental racism, the proximity to El Paso and Mexico, and the negative economic impacts (Students for Earth Awareness 2006). Amidst these concerns, the Texas Natural Resources Conservation Commission, the predecessor to TCEQ, decided to deny the permit in 1998 (Texas Environmental Profiles 2006; Tokar and Oliver 1998).

Some political insiders believe that lobbyists for WCS, who were making large campaign donations to Governor Bush and other Texas politicians, helped influence the Sierra Blanca decision, as well as the passing of House Bill 1567 in 2003 (Smith 2003; Texans for Public Justice 2001; Tokar and Oliver 1998). While the Sierra Blanca site would have been a state-controlled site, House Bill 1567 allows private companies the opportunity to acquire a license for radioactive waste disposal in Texas. The law also allows for a private company to dispose of low-level radioactive waste from the DOE's weapons production programs. The compact and federal facilities can be owned by the same company, but the wastes have to be disposed of separately.

Table 6.1. Events Related to Low-Level Radioactive Waste Licensing Process in Texas

Date	*Event*
1980	Passage of Low-Level Radioactive Waste Policy Act
1981	Texas legislature creates the Texas Low-Level Radioactive Waste Disposal Authority (TLLRWDA), which begins a screening process for a LLRW disposal site in Texas
1991	Texas legislature mandates the TLLRWDA to develop the waste disposal site in Hudspeth County, Texas
1993	Texas forms a compact with Maine and Vermont, and agrees to be the host state for the "Texas Compact" (Maine and Vermont agree to pay $25 million each for site construction); Waste Control Specialists begin operations for hazardous waste in Andrews County, Texas
1995	U.S. Congress votes against the formation of the Texas Compact because the states are not contiguous
1996	TNRCC issues draft permit for the Sierra Blanca site in Hudspeth County; Public opposition to the Sierra Blanca site intensifies
1998	U.S. Congress approves of Texas-Maine-Vermont Compact, without a proposed amendment that would limit waste to the compact states; Waste Control Specialists receives license to store low-level radioactive waste; TNRCC decides to deny the permit for the Sierra Blanca site amid public controversy over the safety of the site, and the proximity to El Paso and Mexico
1999	The TLLRWDA is abolished and its charge to find a disposal site is given to TCEQ
2002	The Maine Legislature votes to leave the Texas Compact due to delays in the siting process
2003	Texas House Bill 1567 is passed, allowing private companies the opportunity to apply for a LLRW disposal license
2004	August: WCS submits an application and $500,000 application fee to the Texas Commission for Environmental Quality (TCEQ) for a license to dispose of LLRW disposal; WCS submits an application to the Texas Health and Human Services Commission for a license to dispose of DOE by-product waste
2005	TCEQ completes administrative reviews of the WCS license application
2006	June: TCEQ completes the third technical reviews of the WCS license application, and requests additional information in a "List of Concerns" to WCS August: WCS requests an extension to address these concerns
2007	March: WCS submits a response to the concerns, and TCEQ begins the final review of the application; a draft license was issued in late 2007

The Dallas-based company, WCS, began their operations in Andrews County with a hazardous waste site that opened in 1993. The 16,000-acre site is located about thirty miles west of the small town of Andrews, along the Texas–New Mexico state border. By 1997, WCS expanded its services to include the storage and processing (but not underground disposal) of radioactive waste. Among other sources, the site has received DOE waste from the Rocky Flats site in Colorado and the Fernald site in Ohio. In 2004, after the passing of HB 1567, WCS submitted a license application to the TCEQ to add a low-level radioactive waste disposal facility in Andrews County, Texas. WCS submitted a second license application to dispose of low-level radioactive waste and mixed waste from federal facilities. Both proposed facilities will be built at the WCS site in Andrews County, and both will involve near-surface land disposal. If granted, these licenses are expected to generate billions of dollars for WCS. And, according to state legislation, the State of Texas and Andrews County will each receive 5 percent of the profits from the disposal of the compact waste.

Figure 6.2 shows the proximity of the site to towns in Texas and New Mexico. The majority of residents in Andrews County live in the City of Andrews, thirty miles east of the site. The closest town is actually the city of Eunice in New Mexico, with a population of about 2,600 residents. In all of these towns, Anglos are the dominant ethnic group, but the Hispanic population is approximately 40 percent in both Andrews County in Texas and Lea County in New Mexico (Waste Control Specialists 2006).

Although the site will benefit residents on the Texas side of the border more (due to tax revenue), the border location has not become a big issue, largely in part due to the fact that another company, Louisiana Energy Services (LES), has filed a license application for a uranium enrichment plant on the New Mexico side of the border. The proposed LES site is on a piece of land that is contiguous to the WCS site, or as one Texas state senator put it "a nine iron chip from the Texas border" (Wilder 2005). Rumors suggest that LES is likely to send its waste across the border to WCS (Nuclear Information and Research Service 2005; Sage 2006).

What is fascinating about this case is that the proposed facility is strongly supported by local government officials in Andrews County (who are predominantly white). In their public statements, local officials repeatedly express their trust in WCS as a reliable company that has demonstrated its commitment to the community. This local support can be traced back to community efforts to save the town by creating a new economic niche. Long dependent on the oil-and-gas industry, members of the Andrews Industrial Foundation have actively sought out ways to diversify their local economy. In the early 1980s, Andrews County attempted to bid for an MX nuclear missile base (Lisheron 2005). Being pragmatic about the opportunities for a small, relatively isolated town in an arid region, an economic development study conducted in the late 1980s suggested two other ventures that might be well-suited for Andrews: prisons and waste management (Ingram 1993a). One leader, the late newspaper editor James Roberts, often referred to this economic strategy as "turning liabilities into assets" (Ingram 1993c). Although local leaders failed to secure either a prison or a missile contract,

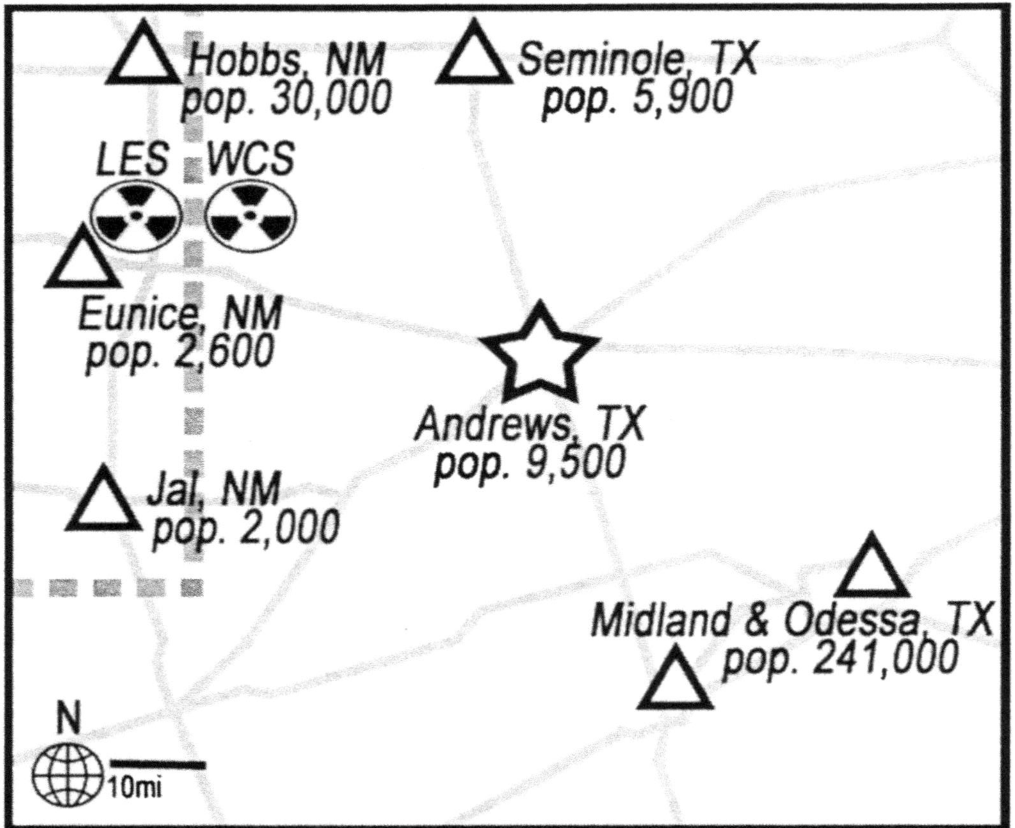

Figure 6.2. Location of Waste Control Specialists Facility in Andrews County, Texas

they succeeded in attracting the attention of Waste Control Specialists, a company that was searching for a site to place a hazardous waste facility in the early 1990s. Although it is unclear who courted whom the most, the match was solidified by 1993 when over 300 local community members showed up to support WCS at a public hearing to discuss their license application for hazardous waste. In 1993, local officials repeatedly stated that the site was not considering radioactive waste (Ingram 1993a; Ingram and Thompson 1993).

Radioactive waste was put on the agenda about five years later, but this did not seem to diminish local support for the company. In a survey of community leaders in the region, 60 percent agreed strongly and 40 percent agreed moderately that the proposed facility would bring economic development to the region (Hicks and Company 2006). They believe that it will create new jobs, create incentives for young people to stay in the town and produce some stability in a region dependent on oil and gas. As Russell Shannon, the vice president of the Andrews Industrial Foundation puts it, "If we thought we could get an NFL franchise or a Riverwalk, we wouldn't have looked at this industry. We just believe it will bring us some jobs, bring people to our community to get involved in an industry, like they did with oil" (*Midland Reporter Telegram* 2005). Local support for WCS is not limited to Andrews County. The company has received letters of endorsement from surrounding towns in Texas and New Mexico (Waste Control Specialists 2006). In light of NIMBY activism in response to most waste sites, the attitudes of local leaders and ordinary citizens in and near Andrews County seem very surprising. As Texas Democratic State Representative Lon Burnham states: "In a way, it's good news for the rest of the country, that Texans are so stupid that they want to take on the risk of becoming a nuclear waste sacrifice zone for the country. This is an after-effect of the Cold War, and nobody—except for Texans—wants it in their home" (Smith 2003).

At the local level, vocal opposition to the proposed facility has been very limited. In a 2005 public hearing in Andrews, thirty-eight people provided positive comments about the proposed facility, and only six local community members expressed concerns with the site. Some worry that the site could contaminate groundwater. A rancher family is concerned that the water used by WCS could affect water supplies for their cattle and that radiation leaks could affect water quality. Another resident is worried that the volume of trucks and rail cars will increase traffic accidents on state highways. Some residents, including one very vocal opponent in Eunice, are also concerned that if WCS receives this license, this might just be the beginning; more dangerous types of radioactive waste might come in the future (Texas Commission on Environmental Quality 2005).

Community leaders and WCS officials regularly make blanket statements about local support for the facility. The mayor of Andrews, for example, has publicly stated that he estimates about 95 percent of the residents do not oppose the site (Gilbert 2005). Further, in the original license application, WCS repeatedly stated that they had "widespread support" from the local community and that there was "no viable opposition" (Waste Control Specialists 2004). With the exception of support letters from local leaders, the application did not provide much evidence to support such strong language. Based on my own interviews in the region, I became convinced that there are probably numerous residents who do not support the site, yet choose not to vocalize their opinions because they feel intimidated and/or powerless. The risk perception literature would suggest that minorities and the poor would be likely to fall into this category. In my capacity as a TCEQ consultant, I have repeatedly made requests for further evidence for statements regarding public support. The first response was to provide qualitative data from a face-to-face survey, using a convenience sample, with twenty-six community leaders and twenty-four residents in the region. The participants were 82 percent white and 71 percent male. While the responses were certainly interesting and informative, the sample size was too small and biased to make any conclusions regarding public acceptance of the site. However, only 8 percent of the Texas sample had "strong concerns" with the facility, and 71 percent had no concerns at all (Hicks and Company 2005). In a subsequent response, WCS has provided quantitative data from a telephone survey with 605 residents in the affected areas, including residents in both Texas and New Mexico (Baselice and Associates 2006).

Figure 6.3 shows the results for one of the questions asked in the larger survey, regarding attitudes toward the disposal of low-level radioactive waste at the WCS site in Andrews County. The data suggests that the majority of community members support the proposal. However, the data also suggests that there is greater support in Andrews County than in surrounding counties, and that there is greater support among non-Hispanics than among Hispanics.

DISCOURSES OF MORALITY IN THE TEXAS DEBATES OVER LLRW

Proponents and opponents of the facility use different discourses of morality in the debates over the proposed facility. To begin, both sides implicitly suggest that "insiders" rather than "outsiders" should be making decisions about the future of the community. However, the two sides do not agree on

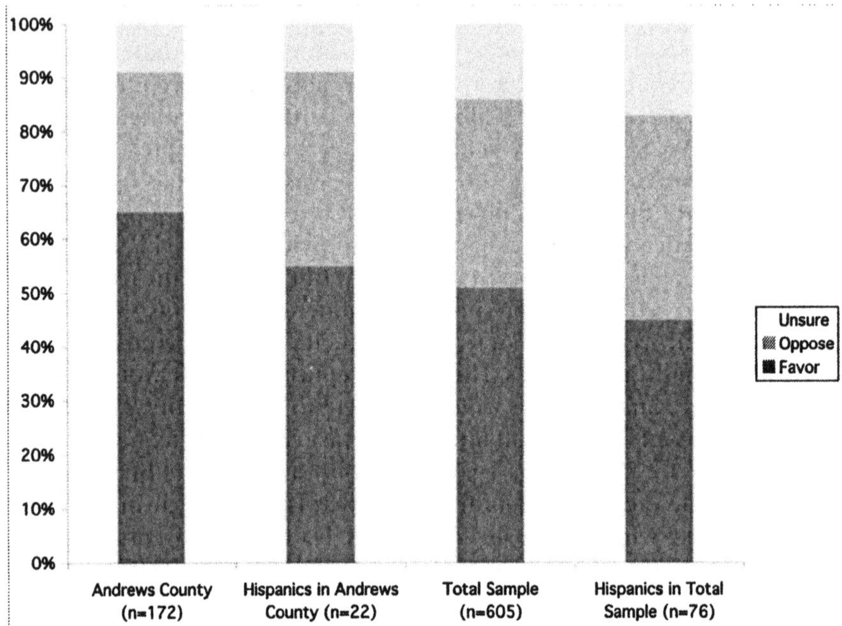

Figure 6.3. Attitudes Toward the Disposal of Low-Level Radioactive Waste by Waste Control Specialists in West Andrews County, Texas

who is an outsider. For the supporters of the site, the image of "outsiders" is used to describe environmental activists representing groups like the Sierra Club and Public Citizen. In 1993, one town leader, for example, predicted that "the majority of opponents of the landfill may come from outside the county" (Ingram 1993b). From the leaders' perspectives, insiders are united in their support for the site. And, now that WCS has been in the area for awhile, WCS is considered a reliable good citizen. In the qualitative survey, one respondent referred to WCS as a "good asset to the community" and a company who donates to community organizations (Hicks and Company 2005). When I was conducting interviews in Andrews last summer, one Hispanic business owner seemed very relieved to hear that I was not with the Sierra Club. He fears that environmental activists might come from the outside to mobilize Hispanics in particular and that this could have negative repercussions for ethnic relations in the town.

Opponents, on the other hand, resent the fact that an "outsider" company is making decisions that might have negative impacts on their local environment. In the public hearing, for example, one opponent pointed out that the WCS executives are constantly referring to her town as a "remote" location. Implicitly referring to WCS as outsiders, she asked: "From whose perspective is Andrews County a remote location?"

A second moral dimension to the debates is the issue of profit. Throughout the process, the company has never publicly stated how much profit they expect to make from the facility and local officials have never stated how the 5 percent tax revenues will be spent by county officials. In response to my requests for a rough estimate of expected revenues, WCS has repeatedly stated that this information is "indeterminate" (Waste Control Specialists 2006). While there are surely legal reasons for this declaration, I question whether the company's executives want to downplay the fact that they are likely to profit immensely from this deal. In an interview, Harold Simmons, the owner of WCS stated: "I don't think it's going to be any real fast gold mine. But it could be very productive and big business over a period of years" (Oppel 1996). Instead of discussing profits to the company, WCS and local officials continually promise that the facility will bring new jobs and indirect economic benefits to the community.

In contrast, opponents at the local and state level have discussed the profit issue in moral terms. To begin, in the media and on environmentally oriented websites, critics villainize the owner Harold Simmons as an immoral person.[4] He is described as a billionaire who has personally donated over $400,000 to political campaigns and who has been charged with exceeding federal contributions limits and making illegal campaign contributions in his daughters' names. The same source notes that the two companies that he controls have donated an additional $825,000 in unregulated corporate soft money to GOP candidates in the past two election cycles (Texans for Public Justice 2001). He is also cited as the top donor to Tom DeLay's defense fund (Wheat 2005) and the former owner of a lead smelting facility that is now listed as a Superfund site (Toxic Texas 2006). Critics have been more willing to discuss the expected profits, and they do so in moral terms. According to the Public Employees for Environmental Responsibility, the compact's waste will generate "hundreds of millions in disposal fees" for the State of Texas and WCS (Public Employees for Environmental Responsibility 2006; Toxic Texas 2006). An article in *Mother Jones* suggests that the federal waste is likely to generate more profits than the compact waste because the DOE has generated so much waste and there is nowhere to send it (Smith 2003).[5] Erin Rogers of the Sierra Club has discussed the ethical problem of profiting from the waste business: "We don't think private companies should be entrusted with something this serious and potentially dangerous. The state is publicly accountable, and they're not driven by a profit motive" (Smith 2003).

While NIMBY politicians would argue that it is immoral to site a waste facility near a community, the leaders of Andrews County have made it seem like it is immoral to question the licensing of the WCS facility. Some leaders have even made a link between supporting the site and being patriotic. In other words, hosting a waste site is discussed as a sacrifice for the nation comparable to military service. Andrew city manager Glen Hackler, for example, has stated: "As hokey and idealistic as it sounds, this community has a feeling that we have provided a solution to a true state and national problem" (Lisheron 2005). According to one political analyst, "Waste Control has hitched its campaign to growing fears of terrorism. . . . Since the Sept. 11 attacks, dump proponents have been warning that terrorists might steal radioactive material from Texas hospitals to make 'dirty bombs'" (Smith 2003). Given the strong support in the community, it is not surprising that opponents feel pressured to stay quiet. One vocal critic said that friends and family support her in spirit, but they are afraid to join her activism against the company. People worry about how this might affect their jobs, their economic well-being, and their social life.

Finally, I want to say a few words about environmental racism. Race and class are clearly issues in this case, but this concept has not yet surfaced in public discourse about the site. Although there is a high percentage of Hispanic residents in the region, the numbers do not exceed the criteria established by law, which would occur if "either the minority or low-income population percentage exceeds 50 percent within the Region of Interest, or if the percent of minority or low-income populations is 20 percent greater than the state average." In the required section about environmental justice, WCS insists that this is not an issue because all groups would be equally disadvantaged by the facility. They state that transportation routes, for example, will not be limited to poorest areas of the nearby counties (Waste Control Specialists 2006). An interesting moral dilemma is whether or not regulations for environmental justice should be limited to existing demographic patterns, or whether they should consider population projections. If the latter were to be the case, environmental justice would be a stumbling block in the licensing process.

CONCLUSION

The case of LLRW disposal shows how moral issues are tied to economic issues, especially when new commodities such as toxic waste are concerned. This case also demonstrates once again that what is moral and what is immoral is defined differently by individual actors.

It has been over twenty-five years since the Low-Level Radioactive Waste Policy Act was passed in Congress, yet not a single new waste facility has been developed. Technical issues always play into the political discussions, but most proposed sites have failed largely due to moral concerns about waste in general and the siting process in particular. In other locations where waste facilities have been proposed, local community members who feel excluded from the siting process have raised moral concerns. The Andrews County case is fascinating because the vast majority of community leaders are in favor of the facility and there are few vocal opponents. One of the major differences in the Texas case is the fact that Texas law has allowed a private company to apply for a waste disposal license. In all of the other cases in the United States, a government agency at the state level has established criteria to narrow down a site, using a "top-down" approach that emphasizes technical, not social issues. In case after case, moral concerns have been raised about the nature of the siting process and public opposition has halted the process. While these approaches have consistently failed, the Andrews County site still stands a chance to be the first facility to receive a license for waste disposal since the Low-Level Radioactive Waste Policy Act was passed. Rather than surveying Texas for the "best" geological site, WCS started with a community that was relatively enthusiastic about hosting a radioactive waste disposal facility, and now representatives from the company (and the community) are trying to make a case for why this location is ideal for this facility. It is yet to be seen whether this case demonstrates that a private approach is more likely to succeed than a public approach. At the moment, this site is unlikely to fail due to public opposition. If the company does fail to gain a license, it will be primarily due to technical issues related to the geological suitability of the facility.[6]

In most other cases of LLRW, profit is not an issue because waste is handled by a state agency. In the Texas case, however, a private company is planning to profit from the disposal of radioactive waste. On the one hand, local community leaders who support the facility have not expressed concerns about the profits that WCS is likely to gain from the waste trade. Rather, the leaders of Andrews County appear to be satisfied with the additional tax revenue (e.g., 5 percent of profits) that Andrews County will receive, and they are not lobbying for any additional compensation. On the other hand, opponents have questioned the morality of the company owner and company lobbyists who have been involved in corruption scandals. And, they have also rightfully questioned whether a private company will be *more* interested in making profits than ensuring the safety of local citizens. This concern implicitly fails to recognize the role that state regulatory agencies, such as the TCEQ, play in the process. So far, opponents have directed their moral concerns at the company and its owner, not the regulatory agency. If the TCEQ commissioner decides to grant the license, opponents may shift their focus and begin to publicly question their trust in the regulatory agency, as has been the case with the Yucca Mountain site.

By regulating the risks associated with radioactive waste and ensuring that disadvantaged groups are not burdened with a disproportionate share of risks, the state has become a site where morality is institutionalized. Morality has been institutionalized at several different levels of the state. At the federal level, the Nuclear Regulatory Commission provides guidelines for the siting of radioactive waste facilities, including guidelines that address the potential problem of environmental racism. At the state level, the Texas Legislature voted to allow private companies to submit bids for a low-level radioactive waste facility, yet ensured that a percentage of the profits would return to the local community. And, finally, state regulatory agencies, such as the TCEQ are responsible for reviewing the safety and socioeconomic impacts of the low-level radioactive waste disposal facility. Although the state of Texas has opened up the waste trade to market conditions, all of these state agencies are acting collectively to limit the potential harm to society that might result from the free market trade of toxic waste.

NOTES

Acknowledgments. I would like to thank Margie Serrato-Sparks for her assistance during a research trip to Andrews County and Lea County in June 2005, and Chris Sparks for his assistance with the preparation of the maps for this paper. I would also like to thank George Fitzgerald at TCEQ for his patience in explaining information about radioactive waste and waste politics in Texas.

1. Figures regarding the relative volume of low-level waste from nuclear power plants vary widely for political reasons. Proponents of particular waste sites use data that emphasizes other more "benign" sources of waste material, while opponents (who often oppose nuclear power as well) tend to exaggerate the amount of waste generated by power plants (Albrecht and Amey 1999).
2. In the literature on nuclear waste, the Washington site is referred to as either the "Richland" or the "Hanford" site. I have chosen to refer to the site as the "Richland" site to distinguish it from the nearby high-level waste storage site, also known as "Hanford." Richland is the town closest to the Department of Energy's Hanford site, which produced plutonium and enriched uranium for nuclear weapons. The high-level and low-level waste sites are located in separate areas within the Hanford Reservation. The Richland LLRW facility is operated by U.S. Ecology, a company that leases land from the DOE. The Barnwell LLRW facility is operated by a company called Chem-Nuclear Systems LLC.
3. Using the case of Ontario, Hunold (2002) argues that voluntary siting processes that use the municipality as the unit of participation do not truly achieve the goal of participatory democracy.
4. Harold Simmons is currently listed as number 278 on *Forbes* magazine's list of the world's billionaires, with $2.6 billion dollars in assets.
5. Although the State of Texas and Andrews County will each receive 5 percent of the profits from compact waste, this is not true for federal waste. One Republican Texas senator, Robert Duncan, unsuccessfully attempted to require financial benefits to the state of Texas for all federal waste. According to Duncan, South Carolina receives about $24 million per year from the Barnwell site (Gilbert 2005).

6. A number of problems have been cited in the "List of Concerns" prepared by the TCEQ Radioactive Waste Materials Licensing Team. Some of the technical concerns include the depth of the water table, the possible impact of erosion, and radiological protection methods.

REFERENCES

Albrecht, Stan L., and Robert G. Amey. 1999. Myth-Making, Moral Communities, and Policy Failure in Solving the Radioactive Waste Problem. *Society & Natural Resources* 12: 741–61.

Amey, R. G., S. L. Albrecht, and S. Amir. 1997. Low-Level Radioactive Waste: Policy Failure, Regional Failure? *Regional Studies* 31(6): 620–31.

Baselice and Associates. 2006. *A Tabulation of Survey Results among Adults in West Texas and East New Mexico*. Report Submitted as Part of WCS License Application. January 21–23, 2006.

Bedsworth, Louise Wells, Micah D. Lowenthal, and William E. Kastenberg. 2004. Uncertainty and Regulation: The Rhetoric of Risk in the California Low-Level Radioactive Waste Debate. *Science, Technology, & Human Values* 29(3): 406–27.

Douglas, Mary, and Aaran Wildavsky. 1982. *Risk and Culture: An Essay on the Selection of Environmental and Technological Dangers*. Berkeley: University of California Press.

English, Mary. 1992. *Siting Low-Level Radioactive Waste Disposal Facilities: The Public Policy Dilemma*. New York: Quorom Books.

Envirocare of Utah. 2006a. Low-Level Radioactive Waste. Electronic document, www.envirocareutah.com/pdf/LowLevel.pdf (accessed April 14, 2006).

———. 2006b. History of Envirocare. Electronic document, www.envirocareutah.com/pdf/History.pdf (accessed July 31, 2006).

Eureka County. 2003. *Eureka County Summary of DOE's Yucca Mountain's Final EIS Comment-Response Document*. Report prepared for the Board of Eureka County Commissioners and the Eureka County Yucca Mountain Information Office. September 2003. Eureka County, Nevada.

Flynn, James, and Paul Slovic. 1995. Yucca Mountain, a Crisis for Policy: Prospects for America's High-Level Nuclear Waste Program. *Annual Review of Energy and Environment* 20: 83–118.

Freudenberg, William R. 2004. Can We Learn from Failure? Examining U.S. Experiences with Nuclear Repository Siting. *Journal of Risk Research* 7(2): 153–69.

Gilbert, Jeffrey. 2005. State Wants Its Share in Nuclear Waste Deal. *Houston Chronicle*, February 14.

Hicks and Company. 2005. *Socioeconomic Impacts of the Waste Control Specialists Proposed Low-Level Radioactive Waste Disposal Facility, Andrews County, Texas*. Environmental Report. Submitted as part of WCS license application. Original version.

———. 2006. *Socioeconomic Impacts of the Waste Control Specialists Proposed Low-Level Radioactive Waste Disposal Facility, Andrews County, Texas*. Environmental Report submitted as part of WCS license application. March 2006 version.

Hunold, C. 2002. Canada's Low-Level Radioactive Waste Disposal Problem: Voluntarism Reconsidered. *Environmental Politics* 11(2): 49–72.

Ingram, Don. 1993a. Waste Facility Slated for Andrews: Landfill Project Would Cost $12 Million, Employ 130 People. *Andrews County News*, March 11.

——. 1993b. County Approves Resolution for Waste Facility. *Andrews County News*, March 11.

——. 1993c. Three Hundred Residents Attend Public Hearing. *Andrews County News*, October 3.

Ingram, Don, and Judy Thompson. 1993. Groups Hear Waste Officials Tuesday. *Andrews County News*, March 18.

Kearney, Richard C., and Ande A. Smith. 1994. The Low-Level Radioactive Waste Siting Process in Connecticut: Anatomy of a Failure. *Policy Studies Journal* 22(4): 617–30.

King, Ginger P. 1995. Science, Society, and U.S. Nuclear Waste. In *Radiation and Public Perception: Benefits and Risks*, ed. Jack P. Young and Rosalyn S. Yalow, 283–314. Washington, DC: American Chemical Society.

Kraft, Michael E., and Bruce B. Clary. 1991. Citizenship Participation and the Nimby Syndrome: Public Response to Radioactive Waste Disposal. *The Western Political Quarterly* 44(2): 299–328.

Liebow, Edward. 1988. Permanent Storage for Nuclear Power Plant Wastes: Comparing Risk Judgments and Their Social Effects. *Practicing Anthropology* 10(3–4): 10–12.

Lisheron, Mark. 2005. One Town's Nuclear Option. *Austin American-Statesmen*, July 4.

Midland Reporter Telegram. 2005. Town Embraces Radioactive Waste Industry. *Midland Reporter Telegram*, May 2.

Murray, Raymond L. 2003. *Understanding Radioactive Waste*, 5th edition. Columbus, OH: Battelle Press.

Nuclear Energy Institute. 2004. Disposal of Low-Level Radioactive Waste. Electronic document, www.nei.org/resourcesandstats/documentlibrary/nuclearwastedisposal/factsheet/disposallowlevelradioactivewaste/ (accessed April 13, 2006).

Nuclear Information and Research Service. 2005. Citizens' Groups Expose Critically Flawed LES Radioactive Waste Disposal Plan. Electronic document, www.nirs.org/press/08-03-2005/1 (accessed August 2, 2006).

Oppel, Richard. 1996. West Texas Nuclear Waste Dump Plan Back on Drawing Board. *Dallas Morning News*, June 25.

Public Employees for Environmental Responsibility. 2000. Nuclear Dump Sprouts in West Texas. June 20. Electronic document, www.peer.org/news/news_id.php?row_id=36 (accessed April 14, 2006).

——. 2006. Bush Romances the Atom in Texas. Electronic document, www.txpeer.org/press/76.html (accessed April 13, 2006).

Rabe, Barry G., William Gunderson, Hilary Frazer, and John Gillroy. 1994. NIMBY and Maybe: Conflict and Cooperation in the Siting of Low-Level Radioactive Waste Disposal Facilities in the United States and Canada. *Environmental Law* 24: 67–122.

Rossin, A. David. 2003. Marketing Fear: Nuclear Issues in Public Policy. *American Behavioral Science* 46(6): 812–21.

Sage, Fran. 2006. Welcome to the Neighborhood! The Neighborhood Nuclear Industrial Complex. *Lone Star Sierran* 42(2): 8–9.

Slovic, Paul, Baruch Fischhoff, and Sarah Lictenstein. 1980. Facts and Fears: Understanding Perceived Risk. In *Societal Risk Assessment: How Safe Is Safe Enough?* ed. R. C. Scwing and W. A. Albers, Jr., 181–216. New York: Plenum Press.

Smith, Chris. 2003. A Radioactive Recipe for Profit. *Mother Jones*. Electronic document, www.motherjones.com/news/update/2003/05/we_421_01.html (accessed April 10, May 22, 2003).

Song, Francis. 2003. Currently Indisposed: Managing Radioactive Waste. *Harvard International Review* 25(2): 8–9.

State of Nevada Agency for Nuclear Projects. 1998. Why Does the State Oppose Yucca Mountain. Electronic document, www.state.nv.us/nucwaste/yucca/state01.htm (accessed April 14, 2006).

———. 2004. State of Nevada Yucca Mountain Survey Summary Report. Electronic document, www.state.nv.us/nucwaste/news2004/pdf/nv0410survey.pdf (accessed July 26, 2006).

Students for Earth Awareness. 2006. Proposed Sierra Blanca Radioactive Waste Dump Fact Sheet. Electronic document, http://studentorgs.utexas.edu/aware/blanca-fact-sheet.pdf (accessed July 26, 2006).

Texans for Public Justice. 2001. Corporate Raider Targets Lege: Simmons Would Make Billions, Sticking Texas with Nuke Liability. Electronic document, www.tpj.org/Lobby_Watch/simmons.html (accessed April 13, 2006).

Texas Commission on Environmental Quality. 2006. Response to Public Meeting. Interoffice Memo. April 26.

Texas Environmental Profiles. 2006. Radioactive Wastes. Electronic document, www.texasep.org/html/wst/wst_6ird.html (accessed April 13, 2006).

Tokar, Brian, and Gary Oliver. 1998. The Texas-Vermont-Maine Nuclear Dump: Bringing Environmental Racism Home. *Z-Magazine*. Electronic document, www.zmag.org/zmag/articles/nov98tokar.htm (accessed August 2, 2006).

Toxic Texas. 2006. WCS and Bush. Electronic document, www.txpeer.org/toxic-tour/wcs.html (accessed April 14, 2006).

United States Department of Energy. 2006a. Why Yucca Mountain? Electronic document, www.ocrwm.doe.gov/ym_repository/about_project/why/index.shtml (accessed April 14, 2006).

———. 2006b. What Are Spent Fuel and High-Level Nuclear Waste? Electronic document, www.ocrwm.doe.gov/factsheets/doeymp0338.shtml (accessed April 14, 2006).

———. 2006c. DOE Awards $3 Million Contract to Oak Ridge Associated Universities for Expert Review of Yucca Mountain Work. Electronic document, www.energy.gov/print/3418.htm (accessed August 30, 2007).

United States General Accounting Office. 1999. *Low-Level Radioactive Wastes: States Are Not Developing Disposal Facilities*. Report to the Chairman, Committee on Energy and Natural Resources, U.S. Senate. GAO/RCED-99-238. Washington, DC: U.S. GAO.

———. 2004. Low-Level Radioactive Waste: Future Waste Volumes and Disposal Options are Uncertain. Testimony before the Committee on Energy and Natural Resources, U.S. Senate. GAO 04-10097T. Washington, DC: U.S. GAO.

Waste Control Specialists. 2004. Application for License to Authorize Near-Surface Land Disposal of Low-Level Radioactive Waste (initial application). August 4, 2004.

——. 2006. Application for License to Authorize Near-Surface Land Disposal of Low-Level Radioactive Waste (Response to Technical Notice of Deficiency-2). March 31, 2006.

Wheat, Andrew. 2005. DeLay's Corporate Defenders. *Texas Observer*, November 18.

Wilder, Forest. 2005. Going Nuclear in West Texas. *Texas Observer*, February 18.

7

Virtue at the Checkout Till

Salvation Economics in Kenyan Flower Fields

Catherine S. Dolan

As you fly out of Nairobi headed west over the Great Rift Valley, it is not long before the papyrus-fringed shores of Lake Navaisha come into view. Once the home of Masaii pastoralists, the lake is now dominated by a labyrinth of modern greenhouses that comprise some of the largest flower farms in the world. This is the site of Kenya's cut flower industry, an oft-considered economic success story that has brought thousands of employment opportunities to poor rural women. Yet accompanying the fresh tracks of global capital on Kenyan fields is the familiar paradox of the neoliberal model—booming economic growth lying side by side with human suffering. In recent years this juxtaposition has spawned a new moral discourse surrounding Kenya's integration into the global economy, with images of toxic flower fields and lurid working conditions broadcast into the living rooms of suburban London homes. These sorts of images are part of a new morality of consumption where consumers, nongovernmental organizations (NGOs), trade unions, and global supermarkets aspire to "save" the African worker from the downside of globalization. It is through the consumption of Kenyan fair-trade flowers, for example, that the British public encounter the African "other," not only through an imagined voyage to an eternal summer but, increasingly, as a way to extend an "ethics of care" to the distant "poor" through everyday purchasing practices (Cook and Crang 1996; Smith 2000).

In this chapter, I explore how Kenya's cut-flower trade has become a site upon which UK consumers articulate and actualize notions of justice, economic rights, and moral personhood. Although fair trade brings many actual (and potential) benefits to Southern producers and workers, here I concentrate on the ideological assumptions that underlie fair-trade consumption, using the cut-flower industry as a heuristic device to explore the co-construction of the social and the material in economic exchange. Drawing on two qualitative research projects on ethical trade in African agriculture conducted between 2000 and 2004, and a series of in-depth interviews conducted with British consumers and UK NGOs in 2004, I explore three main lines of inquiry. First, I suggest that ethical consumption forms an important aspect of self-formation in a context of neoliberal globalization, as increasing numbers of consumers articulate moral principles and ethical sensibilities through fair trade. For example, by purchasing a fair-trade flower (the object of moral practice), individuals are not only expressing their ideals and values, but also translating them into a "mode of being," an embodied practice that mediates competing tensions of greed and generosity, vice and virtue, luxury and necessity and the sacred and profane (Foucault 1985). Consumers, in Aristotelian terms, "become just by *doing* just acts, temperate by *doing* temperate acts, brave by *doing* brave acts" (Mahmood 2003: 851, emphasis added).

Second, I argue that like the charity business and the international development industry, fair trade constitutes a practice that is at once sacred and secular, as shoppers convey moral dispositions and humanitarian sentiments through the medium of the market. Consumers, thus, not only signal their ethical capacities through the purchase of a fair-trade flower, but often strive to redraft moral relations between "self" and "other," rich and poor, and savior and sufferer. These market moralities, I add, not only aim to produce an African farmer fully safeguarded by modern rights and protections, but are also part of a global landscape that employs liberal ethics as a mode of governmentality over the African "other." Third, I argue that the consumption of fair-trade products inhabits the borderlands of altruism and self-interest, thus blurring the canonical anthropological distinction between the price-driven spheres of commodity circulation and the spirit of sociability associated with gift exchange. At times the sociability of the gift is impelled by the moral injunctions of Christian theology; other times it is grounded in a sympathy-based humanism of secular morality. In both cases, although British consumers are embedded in a transnational economy where self-interested calculation, profit maximization, and impersonal ties predominate, they cast their purchases of fair-trade products as a socially engaged act of duty and obligation, one that is resonant with moral evaluations of past and present.

Thus by imputing charitable sentiments to otherwise abstract exchange relations, today's consumers are redefining capitalist consumption as economic altruism. But they are also engaging in a form of ethical practice (consumption) that functions as both the source and palliative of their moral concerns. In other words, while individuals constitute ethical selfhood through fair-trade purchases, they do so through a practice that simultaneously perverts and sustains the architecture of global capitalism and the ethos of a liberal democratic tradition. As the chapter explores, this paradox complicates the meanings and functions of ethical action (e.g., is it sacred or secular, gift or commodity, right or duty?) and renders fair trade a particularly rich site for exploring emergent moralities in a neoliberal world.

CAMPAIGNING ETHICS IN THE KENYAN CUT-FLOWER INDUSTRY

Each evening, British Airways carries thousands of flowers from the fields of Kenya to European capitals, where within twenty-four hours they adorn the shelves of supermarkets and florists. To many observers, these flowers are a fulfillment of globalization's promise. Fuelled by IMF and World Bank policies for export diversification, Kenya has recently surpassed Israel and Columbia as the largest cut-flower exporter to the European Union (EU), accounting for 58 percent of all ACP cut-flower exports to the EU (COLEACP 2002; Hennock 2002). The flower industry is now the fastest growing sector in the Kenyan economy, with year-round, ready-made bouquets outpacing the nation's traditional hard currency earners of coffee and tea. In a context of persistent poverty, the industry is also a boom for unskilled labor; an estimated 40,000 to 50,000 workers are now directly employed on flower farms, with a further half million Kenyans and their dependents reliant on the income generated by the industry (HCDA [1999] statistics cited in KFC [2002]).

Yet while the flower industry has flourished through market liberalization, it also bears the familiar social imprimatur of economic neoliberalism. Like its kin the *maquiladora*, for example, the flower industry depends on migrant women who face low wages, excessive working hours, job insecurity, and embedded gender discrimination (Dolan et al. 2003). During the 1990s these conditions became the focus of a well-orchestrated attack on global retailers who fell under the media spotlight when BBC One's *Real Story* trekked to Kenya to "expose the cheap labor, health risks, and environmental damage at farms that supply supermarket flowers to the UK."[1] At the same time, Kenyan producers quickly found themselves on the firing line of several well-publicized NGO campaigns when a confidential report from the Kenya Women Workers' Organization to the UK-based Ethical Trading Initiative (ETI) cataloged allegations of pesticide poisoning, sexual harassment, and rape on flower farms exporting to the UK (Dolan and Opondo 2005). Within months, Kenya's cut flowers became the symbol for globalization gone awry, bringing the African worker and the British consumer into a highly moralized conversation on the injustices of global trade.

Such concerns are, of course, neither new nor unique to Kenya. The morality of consumption was a key issue among early free-market economists such as Smith and Ricardo (Wilk 2001), and unease with sybaritic tastes underlined a rich history of consumer politics in Britain in the eighteenth and nineteenth centuries (Hilton 2003; Taylor 1996; Thompson 1971; Thompson 2001; Winch 2004). This time, however, the spiraling of public anxiety and the media sensationalism threatened to destabilize the market segment (fresh produce) in which UK supermarkets enjoyed unrivalled power. One consumer captured the threat such labor rights abuses posed to corporate profitability, stating: "I think that companies overseas should be aware of the backlash, adverse publicity, if they're not providing fair working agreements with their producers." This portent was echoed by the UK's *Guardian* (2004) newspaper.

> If the major food retailers are not willing to change on their own account, they will find themselves dangerously vulnerable to customer backlash. They need only ask their counterparts in the clothing sector, such as Nike and Gap, about the consequences of losing the public's trust over suppliers and sources, a situation that can take many years and millions of pounds to reverse.

The supermarkets, aware that poor labor and environmental conditions among their suppliers could lead to regulatory sanctions and sabotage their market position, embarked on a campaign to refurbish their image. At one level, this entailed issuing public statements touting their involvement in the ETI and their commitment toward educating their wayward suppliers. At another level, retailers responded to the public's ethical concerns by broadening their product portfolio to include a range of ethically produced wares, including fair-trade flowers.

FAIR TRADE AND GEOGRAPHIES OF NEED

The fair-trade movement seeks to move disadvantaged small producers out of poverty by providing them a fair return for their work and decent working and living conditions (Nicholls and Opal 2005). The movement, whose origins lie in the charity and humanitarian activities of religious communities and development agencies in the mid-twentieth century, is founded on a practical expression of Christian faith. In the United States, Mennonite and Brethren missions of the 1940s and 1950s assisted poverty-stricken communities in the South by selling their handicrafts to Northern markets (Grimes and Milgram 2000). Similarly, in the UK and Europe, aid organizations engaged in handicrafts importation as a way to support marginalized producers and workers (Barratt-Brown 1993). By the 1960s, myriad church and development organizations had emulated this model, establishing alternative trade links with groups and cooperatives across a range of developing countries. Within the last few decades, alternative trade organizations such as Equal Exchange, Bridgehead, Twin Trading, Traidcraft, and Ten Thousand Villages have mushroomed on both sides of the Atlantic (Barrientos and Dolan 2006).

As growing numbers of consumers raise moralizing questions about who gets what at whose expense, several large food companies that shunned fair trade in the past (e.g., Cadburys, Starbucks, Kraft, and Nestlés) are beginning to take on its mantle by adopting fair-trade lines (Barrientos and Dolan 2006; Teather 2006). As a result, sales of fair-trade products have expanded rapidly, particularly in the UK, where sales reached £195m in 2005, a 40 percent increase over 2004, and a figure largely attributable to the expansion of fair-trade goods in UK supermarkets. The UK's first fair-trade flowers, launched by Britain's largest supermarket, Tesco in 2004, came from Kenya, where according to Tesco they are "grown on farms that have been specially selected for their high standards of worker welfare, community support and environmental awareness."[2]

Much of the popularity of fair trade, and its kinship to contemporary development orthodoxies, stems from its ethos as market-friendly, "bottom-up" poverty-reducing growth. Adopting an approach of "trade not aid," fair trade operates within rather than against the market, casting the marketplace rather than Northern charity as a way to rehabilitate producers caught in the throes of declining commodity prices.[3] As Charlie, a young fair-trade consumer, explained:

> It's not charity, it's not about giving them loads of rice, or giving them loads of money. It's about continuing to earn. . . . With fair trade the idea is that you pay the sensible amount for how much it costs to grow it and allow them to take control of their own destiny, if you like. Because they also get a social premium which they decide themselves what to do with. So you don't just go and build a clinic and then run off again. . . . They decide what they need most, which is a kind of more sustainable, more respectable form of help.

Yet while fair trade is premised on helping people to help themselves, it nevertheless evokes a powerful moral injunction, one that is abetted by the marketing campaigns of organizations and corporations. New branded goods such as fair-trade flowers, for example, represent the skillfulness with which supermarkets have commodified ethics in response to (and in anticipation of) the concerns of monied consumers. This is most visible in the traffic of morally charged messages featured on press releases and corporate websites that seek to convert emotional capital into a concern for Third World poverty, competing for what Applbaum (1998: 334) terms a "share of mind." Like the techniques of governmentality employed by charities to shape the conduct of giving subjects (Allahyari 2000), website testimonials of "saved" fair-trade producers transform African farmers into a commodity sign while branding retailers as forward thinking, beneficent global citizens. But the strategy of moral entrepreneurship also refigures the meanings of exchange, converting both the commodity and the relations that it enjoins from the abstract sphere of economic relations to what Carrier (1990: 583) terms "the symbolism of possession." By implanting images of distant cultural worlds on website vignettes, retailers evoke a sense of global kinship, replacing the sterility and anonymity of our digital age with an experience of affinity and authenticity (Carrier 1990). As Paul, a fair-trade consumer, noted:

> You know, cultural identity is tied up with all of this. . . . In every country you go to there is a McDonald's, there's whatever, then that is such a loss. . . . So there is a cultural aspect to it as well. I want the small farmer to be able to stay at home, stay on his land, help his family to become educated and to go out into the wider community. You know, it's about family life as well. . . . It's not just about the product. It's about the culture.

Thus in the same way that catalogs market the "exotic" to create the illusion of a gift economy, cloaking wares in the rhetoric of global villages and fraternal affinities allows retailers to personalize exchange, reregistering consumption as a moral (and cultural) rather than self-interested act. This choreography was explained by one marketing guru: "These days, retail is about so much more than merchandise. It's about casting customers in a story," a story, in this case, that bestows the consuming public with both the obligation and the power to save the "African poor" (Gester n.d.).

Retailers may expose the lives of Third World producers to public consumption in order to rouse the sympathies of "imaginatively active" consumers, but fair trade is not simply a discursive strategy (Watson 2007: 265; Wright 2004). Rather, it is a figurative instrument for the production of the consuming self and the distant other, drawing the two together in a socially embedded form of exchange (see also Mauss 1969: 31). For example, for some interviewees, consuming fair-trade products forms part of their extended sense of self (Belk 1988), that is, a way they convey ideas about the kind of person they are and "the sort of person they would like to be seen as by others" (Baudrillard 1988; Moore 1994: 66). Hence, by externalizing their virtue through the purchase of a fair-trade flower, individuals are signaling a public persona as a socially aware consumer who is "prepared to sacrifice personal pleasure to communal well-being" in an expanding spatial dynamic of concern (Gabriel and Lang 1995: 175–76; Watson 1997).

Although the consumption of fair-trade products may be motivated by the promise of social recognition (Wright 2004), it is also a means through which ethical character is cultivated, as consumers instantiate their moral subjectivity through the labor of shopping. In the same way that the moral codes of respectability and virtuosity inspired socially productive consumption in the eighteenth and nineteenth centuries (Bushman 1992; Hilton 2003; Smith 2002), constituting oneself as a more virtuous being through contemporary ethical consumption forges a connection between purchasing commodities and "thinking and acting appropriately." This process of "moral selving"[4] was expressed to me by Paula, an eighty-three-year-old retired school teacher who said that many people were buying fair trade "because it is mainly politically a good thing to do, morally, ethically a good thing to do." Importantly, this moral enactment is premised on a dialectic of self and other, drawn from stories people tell themselves about others that move them to extend benevolence and compassion to distant communities through fair trade.[5] Indeed, for many consumers, fair trade both depends on and reifies distinctions between self and others through long-standing discourses that cast the "African poor" as victims in need of salvation, albeit salvation of an often secular nature (Nandy 1987). One interviewee described her impression of Africa as: "a huge amount of interior which seems to be . . . chaotic and anarchic . . . dark, corrupt." Another reflected:

> We went to Nigeria many, many years ago and, uhm, I went back to Kenya on holiday a couple years ago and the conditions there were exactly the same sort of conditions that I had seen [in Nigeria] . . . shanty towns, open sores, women carrying water on their heads. All these things, children with no clothes playing . . . exactly the same as it had looked like in Nigeria forty years ago. And you just can't believe that, uh, some small advance hasn't taken place. In Africa, everything seems to stand still.

That Africa is invoked as a metonymy for poverty is unsurprising, yet such tropes form a discursive frame in which many narratives of fair trade are cast.[6] The images of impoverished African workers commodified by supermarkets, for instance, regulate cultural alterity to draw attention to the differences between the fortunate "us" and downtrodden "them." As one consumer responded when asked how he envisioned African producers, "[The] people are living in a situation where they can't even cope properly with the basics, where they can't afford food, drink and shelter. . . . Or even whatever we consider to be the absolute necessities . . . they can't even stretch to that." By portraying Kenyan produce as the product of a benighted landscape, fair trade taps into the familiar place Africa occupies in British memory and imagination, a place, according to one woman "so bad that you can't quite imagine people *being* able to produce things."

Historical imaginings of Africa continue to inform the moral sentiments conveyed through fair trade—sentiments embedded within the broader historical and political processes that define Britain's position in the world and its obligations to citizens near and far. For instance, images of a poverty-riddled

Africa, informed by a checkered history of colonialism, missionization and charity work, not only define what other nations are, but also remind consumers of what the UK is not—parochial, self-serving, and xenophobic—an observation well understood by fair-trade marketers.[7] Fair trade thus not only forges new (albeit imagined) relationships between cosmopolitan consumers and the have-nots of the Global South, but also recuperates an enduring connection between Britain and its African subjects, subjects once deemed ripe for imperial salvation. The purchase of a fair-trade flower recalls "rather than inaugurates or consummates" this relationship as consumers seek to renew the social welfare ideals of the late colonial state through the medium of fair trade (Dolan 2005; Goddard 2000: 147).

This spirit of relationality denotes the way in which fair trade is as much about the "subject" as the "object" of exchange. Indeed, it is only by exercising their responsibility to "those who live 'there,'" what Augé terms a "sense for the other" (Augé, cited in Rutherford [2004: 143]), that consumers can realize the material and the moral intents of fair trade and thereby render the "other" a "non-other" through exchange (Russ 2005: 149).

THE SACRED AND THE SECULAR

Although the obligations consumers espouse are expressed through a secular market economy, the moral discourse they bear is often informed by Christian principles of compassion, justice, and mercy. For example, when I asked seventy-eight-year-old Amanda what role religious values played in her decision to purchase fair-trade products she said:

> I think it's because I have a faith that I feel there ought to be more justice for everybody. I belong to what's called the Anglican Church, Church of England. . . . If you translate the message of Jesus about the poor and about justice for everyone, if you translate that into modern terms then [you see that] . . . the Christian religion seems to have inspired a lot of people over many years to try to help others who aren't as well off as themselves in whatever land it might be.

Her neighbor Charlie agreed: "I can see how it's religious. . . . It links in with religion for a lot of people. I mean, well, the thing is, Christian values are more about charity . . . but also for other religions, too, I mean, you know, the idea of helping people who are less fortunate than you in some way. It can be a very religious value." These intimations convey how some individuals interpret fair trade as a form of sacred consumption, a spiritual response to economic injustice that is theologically informed by Christian virtues of love, honor, integrity, and social ethics (see also Featherstone 1991: 122). Such conceptions also underlie the adoption of fair trade among many NGOs, for whom a fair-trade purchase is an act of witness, a form of discipleship expressed through solidarity with the poor (Masson 2001). As

Richard Adams, founder of UK-based Traidcraft noted, "Jesus gives us a personal mission statement which demands a total realignment of ourselves . . . where material values are discarded and where service, not excellence, is the final criterion for judgement" (cited in Raistrick 2001: 119).

Yet despite the fact that fair trade is seen by many as part of "a long tradition of religions . . . going overseas and helping people," and part of a "duty to conduct yourself in a way which is not detrimental to other people,"[8] it is not always freighted with Christian sentiments. Indeed, many people I spoke with did not connect religion per se to the fair-trade ethos. As Imogen, a TV producer, said,

> I hope it's not a religious effort, is it?! I would not want to put fair trade and religion in the same sentence. . . . Religion to me, at the moment, means following a dogma that could lead you into war and could encourage you to hate somebody. . . . [Fair trade is] much more a humanitarian philosophy. I think fair trade does appeal to our human morality. But I don't think fair trade and religion to me can ever be in the same sentence.

Indeed, for the most part consumers described the moral values espoused through fair trade in the liberal democratic discourse of rights and responsibilities, a language that appears much closer to notions of a modern rational subjectivity than to Christian caritas (Cloke et al. [2005]; see also Comaroff and Comaroff [1999]). For example, Nicole, a thirty-something British woman, claimed that her support of fair trade in "underdeveloped" countries was "about people's rights to be . . . respected and recognized" and treated fairly by companies and governments. In some measure this can be explained by the historical precedent of secular humanism in the UK, including the important Cooperative Movement, which resisted religious influence but nevertheless drove forward social and community reform, and many nineteenth-century philanthropic charities, which derived their inspiration from secular altruism rather than evangelism (Cloke et al. 2005). It also, however, points to the salience that liberalism plays in framing the decision to purchase fair-trade commodities, with several consumers casting their consumption as a way to ensure that all humans could enjoy the same rights and protections as they did. As Belinda, a twenty-two-year-old student and fair-trade volunteer, explained:

> Yeah, it's more about my morals, it's more about I think it's unfair and I think there's a lot of shit going on in the world, I want to do something about it. And in my personal case it's nothing to do with being a member of this religion or that religion, or being a member of religion at all. . . . I think it's a good way of at least trying to say to, you know, big businesses and companies, "wait a minute. We're not going to just let you go and do whatever you want to developing countries and people in developing countries." You know, they've been screwed over enough to do something about it.

Belinda's conception of inviolable human dignity is indicative of the assumptions that fair-trade adherents often carry about the nature of the social world and the place universal dignity plays within that world. These convictions, which harken back to a Ruskinian ideal of social justice (Hilton 2003), suggest that consumers experience an obligation to conduct themselves in accordance with a rights-based notion that all peoples be treated justly (Watson 1997). These intimations of justice are not, however, actually very far from Christian conceptions of pastoral care. Indeed, several consumers aligned fair trade with international aid and development, a "modern Christian concept" of charity. Claiming that development workers, like missionaries, "also believe that they are making progress and helping people and alleviating poverty," self-described conscious consumer Alvin said:

> Well, the issue for me is really a moral one, or an ethical one. . . . And I think that most of us should have, I would hope, a strong sense of doing what we think is ethically and morally right. So I think help individuals, and make sure you don't buy products that have been the result of exploitation or environmental disruption. . . . It's a matter of conscience, and, . . . in a wide sense, we're also helping to maintain a proper stewardship of the world we're in by the products we buy, and who's making them, and how.

Hence, in the same way that eighteenth-century abstention movements emphasized the moral and spiritual responsibility of individual consumers (Sussman 2000), fair-trade adherents often embed a pastoral ethics of care within a vernacular of liberal democracy. As Foucault (1982: 215) presaged, in a neoliberal context salvation rests no longer on redemption in the next world, but rather on a secular and worldly deliverance from insecurity and ill-being in this one. Indeed, the Christian-inspired testimonials conveyed on fair-trade websites challenge the boundaries between the sacred and profane, as the salvation narratives are directly tied to the benefits that secular universal rights (e.g., ILO labor standards) bestow to small producers.[9]

COMPETING ETHICAL VISIONS

Consumers may express duty and obligation as personal guiding philosophies, but these convictions are also part of a broader moral landscape that employs universal rights as a mode of "governmentality"[10] over the African "other." This governmentality is visible in the practices and discourses that retailers and fair-trade labeling organizations exercise to shape a certain type of African subject, and particularly in the standards and auditing practices that discipline producers to comply with the demands of fair-trade markets. Thus in the same way that Goldman (2005) describes the "ecogovernmentality" extended through World Bank environmental conservation programs, fair-trade organizations employ ethics as a form of governance, marshalling a set of technologies that produce an African worker fully safeguarded by modern rights and protections. As Freeden (1991: 94) notes however, the notion of human rights is a "prioritizing concept" in the sense that certain rights are privileged at the expense of others. Studies show, for example, how civil society organizations such as fair-trade organizations often embody Northern notions of society, governance, and citizenship at odds with the communities they are slated to serve.[11] In this case the grammar of rights extended through fair trade—ILO Conventions and the Universal Declaration of Human Rights—is derived from a liberal conception, which positions the individual rather than the social, and the right to dignity rather than autonomy, as central in the ethical framework. These rights, derived from Euro-American philosophical and legal traditions, not only exclude African (or otherwise "local") constructions of social organization (Blowfield 2004), but also reflect the moral certainties and ethical absolutism of nineteenth-century imperialists who assumed stewardship over African welfare (Comaroff and Comaroff 1999: 16). Several individuals like Nicole, who explained that it was their "duty to make it a more just world," embraced this welfarist conception of rights, which defines African producers not by their capacity for choice and self-determination, but by their right to dignity. While this ethical frame interprets Kenyan flower workers as rights-bearers, it also positions them as too "powerless" to attain these rights without the external intervention of a moral agent, rendering the moral claims exercised by fair trade redolent of colonial beneficence. Indeed, imperial constructions of duty and moral obligation, ingrained in a civilizing mission that reified the distinction between the virtuous self and the needy other, are often incarnate in the moral imperatives of today's consumers (Dolan 2005). This genealogy does not necessarily undermine the rights that consumers, NGOs, and corporations wish to extend, but rather points to the tensions between the universal ethics of fair trade and the competing ethical visions of a human plurality (Ricoeur 1992/1990: 305). This fraught relationship was expressed by Kathy when I asked her how fair trade was related to other social justice issues:

> I think there is possibly a common background . . . of universal rights . . . and with freedoms [that are] universally recognized by society because of historical development that has taken place in most of societies. But then you go into, I think, a risky situation that is because of history we have different kinds of developments in different parts of the world. And I think it's completely wrong to say that one value should dominate over all the values. So I think it's important to recognize the universality of some of the rights and then, in a way, some level of . . . reason or some other values.

This antonymous positioning between ethical absolutism and cultural particularism is no more easily resolved in fair trade than in other morally charged issues. There are, for example, no criteria within fair-trade standards that specify how competing notions of rights and well-being are to be reconciled (Blowfield 2004); to the contrary, fair trade is often promoted as a universal rights ethos (see for example, PURE n.d.). Herein lies a paradox of fair trade: while moral action is founded on a liberal recognition of cultural integrity and freedom of choice, its consequence is the erasure of difference through a lexicon of international rights and covenants.

THE GIFT OF REDEMPTION

As the previous discussion suggests, fair trade operates at the interstices of two different economies, straddling the border between rational, individualist market relations and the ideals of obligation associated with the gift (Mauss 1969; Russ 2005). Unlike the fungible, abstract utilities of conventional market exchange, fair-trade flowers are commodities of regard whose value is tethered to social investment and bonds of moral obligation. These social affinities confound the unfettered exchange of goods embraced by the liberal market, compelling and reinforcing its antithesis: duty, obligation, and need. One way this is apparent is in the hierarchy between consumer (donor) and producer (recipient) which significantly compromises the latter's access to alternatives that are materially feasible and renders their autonomy and capacity to choose otherwise open to question.[12] In essence, the economic options of flower producers are so often constrained (e.g., by poverty, food insecurity, climatic factors) that it is difficult to read their engagement in fair trade as a calculated and impersonal transaction between free subjects.

Like the Maussian gift, fair-trade exchange is often less an economic than a social contract grounded in webs of attachment and emotional exchange antipathetic to the logic of our postindustrial market. This complicates the clear-cut boundary between things and persons in exchange, as it is sociality, "the personal relationships that the exchange of gifts [e.g., flowers] creates" rather than materiality that drives the demand for goods (Gregory 1982: 19). As one consumer explained, "With fair-trade products . . . I like the idea of it going straight to people that have actually worked on it, and just to bypass this fucking multi-global blah blah, you know, just letting the rich get richer and the poor get poorer type thing. . . . I'd rather it go to real people rather than people that are just scraping off the world." The social intentions underlying fair trade are most explicit in the fact that many consumers buy fair-trade products despite their dissatisfaction with the taste and/or quality. Indeed, several individuals described their purchases as an act of benevolence, since lower-priced and better-quality products were available. As one middle-age man said, "You've got to be fairly altruistic to want to pay more to help people who you don't know." Hence, what is trafficked is not fresh flowers but rather the moralities, values, and affective ties their consumption enacts, a reality acknowledged by NGOs and consumers who typically represent fair trade as a virtuous practice rather than, for example, as a low-cost, high-quality or convenient product (see also Russ [2005]).

This virtuous intent blurs the neoliberal prescriptions of "trade not aid" and instead suggests certain ideological continuities with charity and international development industries, both of which gloss economic imperative as moral injunction. In fact, many consumers viewed fair trade as an expression of charity since as thirty-year-old Judith commented, "we can survive without fair trade. . . . It's giving them something that we don't really need. You know, you're helping out people that you don't really have to help." This comment suggests an act of beneficence, an observation shared by several Kenyan producers who perceived fair trade as a charitable act extended by a munificent "fair-trade Mzungu," (white man), who keeps on "giving, giving, giving." Thus, much like Miller's discussion of thrift as a practice that signals a higher purpose beyond immediate gratification, the value of the fair-trade commodity is not what it costs but who it saves (Miller 1998: 100). This renders the commensurability of exchange less clear and the proximity to the gift more apparent, as what the consumer desires are the possibilities for redemption, intimacy, and moral expression the exchange engenders, and not solely the things themselves (Gregory 1982: 19).

Finally, in contrast to conventional market exchange, where "paying ends the obligation and dissolves the relationship," the fair-trade purchase erases neither the perpetuity of obligation assumed by the British consumer nor the debt incurred by the African producer (Carrier 1991: 124). Like the donor of charitable assistance, the fair-trade consumer hails from a "superior" social, geographical, and economic position, a difference in material means that vastly privileges them in the transaction (Wright 2004). This distance is not a contingent, but a determinative aspect of fair-trade exchange. In contrast to Hume's (1988 [1740]) position that moral affections and sympathies fade as the object of our concern becomes increasingly distant—what Forman-Barzilai (2005: 189) describes as "sentimental nearsightedness"—distance is conducive to the sympathetic sentiments expressed through fair trade (Watson 2007). Indeed, fair-trade advertising is explicitly designed to accentuate the material hierarchy dividing privileged consumers from less fortunate producers, cultivating an emotive connection that both motivates and is euphemized through ethical practice. Yet despite the desire to alleviate this difference through intimate exchange, the economic dissymmetry remains tenacious, thereby sustaining the architecture of giving and the sense of obligation that underwrites it.

In the same vein, the moral authority and material generosity consumers enact through fair trade affirms the dependency of the African producer and reinforces their ongoing debt to their Northern benefactors, a process writ large in the debt bondage experienced by African states (Offer 1997). As the Alaskan Inuit claims, "With gifts you make slaves" or at the very least perpetuate enduring relations of patronage and dependence (cited in Bourdieu [1997]; cited in Offer [1997: 455]).[13]

Yet like all social practice, ethical consumption is a process that expresses and reflects varying motivations and consequences. Indeed, whether reflexive consumers perceive the moral basis of their intentions as an act of charity or an act of justice, whether they are moved by altruism or self-interest, or guided by spiritual or secular reasoning, may have little bearing on the everyday experiences of Southern producers and workers. As Watson (2007: 449) notes, "(f)rom a consequentialist standpoint, all consumption is ethical if it leads to reduced human suffering in the most disadvantaged parts of the world." Hence, even if the transnational commonweal consumers imagine is produced through paternalism rather than partnership, this *may* be irrelevant to the on-the-ground outcome of fair trade, an outcome that has undoubtedly engendered real benefits for Kenyan flower workers. In terms of redressing the international trading system, therefore, what our intentions are may matter less than understanding the particular ways that our ethical consumption reworks the economics of exchange.

CONCLUSION

This chapter has explored how Kenya's cut flower industry has become a site upon which narratives of duty, obligation, and justice are articulated, as a consuming UK public aspires to "save" the African worker from the ills of globalization. One way that these moral convictions are actualized is through the social and economic practice of fair trade, which fosters alternative forms of economic exchange between Northern consumers and Southern producers. Yet while fair trade is enacted through the market, it is a practice governed by sociability, as individuals seek moral expression and economies of affection through ethical consumption. For instance, at its most mundane, fair-trade consumption can be read as a vehicle through which individuals cultivate and express the ideas they have (or wish to have) about themselves as ethical subjects (Geertz 1973). However, fair trade also reveals the ways that consumers engage with the world beyond them, both as individuals and as members of perceived national communities through an imaginative act of moral sympathy (Watson 2007). This engagement with distant others is pivotal to the discourse and practice of fair trade, as consumers seek to minimize the effects of transnational accumulation on the world's poor cross-national relations of solidarity. Yet while consumers describe fair trade as a way to shrink the distance that divides the privileged North from the wanting South, fair trade actually naturalizes the separation and, by extension, the asymmetrical access to resources that motivates consumers to give in the first instance (Hattori 2003). Thus, at the same time that the act of buying a fair-trade flower (coded as "giving") confirms the piety, prestige, and moral rectitude of the consumer, it also reproduces the consumer's power in the relationship, a power both inculcated within and disguised by the act of giving (Bourdieu 1990).

Ultimately, the mutuality of relations remains largely metaphorical. The affective ties (transnational kinship) consumers secure by purchasing a fair-trade flower, for example, are not, in fact, with a "real" African producer, but with a paradigmatic African "everyman" whose face evokes the archetypal African condition (Barthes 1980; Malkki 1996). This "anonymous corporeality" (Malkki 1996: 388) is central to the moral valence of fair trade, as the social relations aspired to through exchange are not about recognizing localized differences and particular moralities, but rather about constructing an international community that is ethically aligned. That the Global North exercises the power to define this vision of ethics and moral rights means that fair-trade exchange, irrespective of its benevolence, produces an ethical economy with a paternalist cast, one in which the virtue of the consumer rather than the rights of producers are affirmed. While consumers may believe that they are dispensing their obligation to the "African poor" by purchasing a fair-trade flower, they may, in fact, re-create the obligation by reaffirming the relationship of which it is a part, a relationship based on enduring inequalities and social hierarchies (Carrier 1991: 124).

NOTES

1. BBC, *Real Story*, 2003.
2. See www.tesco.com/flowers/product.asp?leftNav=31&product=050369864.
3. It is important to note, however, that most consumers (myself included), operate under the assumption that producers are aware that they are producing for fair-trade markets, and that the production systems underwriting fair-trade consumption are more ethical than those of conventional markets. However, the flowers produced in Kenya for fair-trade markets are typically cultivated on exactly the same farm and in the same manner as those supplied to mainstream markets.
4. This term is derived from the work of the sociologist Rebecca Anne Allahyari (2000: 4) who describes moral selving as the process of moral self-improvement associated with charity.
5. As anthropologists have shown, such notions of intimacy and estrangement can often determine the nature of exchange as much as the quality of the commodity itself (Gregory 1982; Mauss 1969; Valeri 1994).

6. While these narratives only reflect a partial view, similar images permeate fair trade literature.

7. See Breen (1988) and Sussman (2000) for a discussion on the links between consumption and discourses of national identity.

8. This reflects Smith's moral theory, which posited that individuals have special duties to the poor who represent "the greatly unfortunate" members of society (Smith 1982 [1759]).

9. As Mauss (1969) and Belk et al. (1989) show, commodities often confound the boundaries between the sacred and the profane as individuals engage in practices that both sacralize and desacrilize goods.

10. Foucault coined the term governmentality to denote "the totality of practices, by which one can constitute, define, organize, instrumentalize the strategies which individuals in their liberty can have in regard to each other" (Foucault 1988: 20).

11. See Comaroff and Comaroff (1999), Garland (1999), Karlstrom (1999), Fisher (1997), Ferguson and Gupta (2002), Edwards and Hulme (1996), and Moore (1993).

12. There are, for example, far more growers who wish to enter fair-trade markets than there are opportunities to supply them, and those producers fortunate enough to secure a spot in fair-trade networks must meet a set of exacting technical and social standards to remain.

13. Bourdieu (1997) argues that the unreciprocated gift is a form of symbolic violence, converting the powerful into the generous benefactors and the weak into grateful recipients.

REFERENCES

Allahyari, Rebecca. 2000. *Visions of Charity: Volunteer Workers and Moral Community*. Berkeley: University of California Press.

Applbaum, Kalman. 1998. The Sweetness of Salvation: Consumer Marketing and the Liberal Bourgeois Theory of Needs. *Current Anthropology* 39(3): 323–49.

Augé, Marc. 1998. *A Sense for the Other*. Stanford, CA: Stanford University Press.

Barratt-Brown, Michael. 1993. *Fair Trade: Reform and Realities in the International Trading System*. London: Zed Press.

Barrientos, Stephanie, and Catherine Dolan, eds. 2006. *Ethical Sourcing in the Global Food System*. London: Earthscan.

Barthes, Roland. 1980. *Mythologies*. New York: Hill and Wang.

Baudrillard, Jean. 1988. *Selected Writings*. Oxford: Polity Press.

Belk, Russell. 1988. Possessions and the Extended Self. *Journal of Consumer Research* 13: 139–68.

Belk, Russell, Melanie Wallendorf, and John Sherry. 1989. The Sacred and Profane in Consumer Behavior: Theodicy on the Odyssey. *Journal of Consumer Research* 16 (June): 1–38.

Blowfield, Michael. 2004. CSR and Development: Is Business Appropriating Global Justice? *Development* 47(3): 61–68.

Bourdieu, Pierre. 1990. *The Logic of Practice*. Trans. T. R. Nice. Stanford, CA: Stanford University Press.

——. 1997. Marginalia—Some Additional Notes on the Gift. In *The Logic of the Gift: Toward an Ethic of Generosity*, ed. Alan Schrift, 231–41. New York and London: Routledge.

Breen, Timothy. 1988. Baubles of Britain: The American and Consumer Revolutions of the Eighteenth Century. *Past and Present* 119: 73–105.

Bushman, Richard. 1992. *The Refinement of America*. New York: Knopf.

Carrier, James. 1990. Reconciling Commodities and Personal Relations in Industrial Society. *Theory and Society* 19: 579–98.

——. 1991. Gifts, Commodities, and Social Relations: A Maussian View of Exchange. *Sociological Forum* 6(1): 119–36.

Cloke, Paul, Sarah Johnsen, and Jon May. 2005. Exploring Ethos? Discourses of "Charity" in the Provision of Emergency Services for Homeless People. *Environment and Planning A* 37: 385–402.

COLEACP. 2002. *European Imports of Flowers and Ornamental Plants, 1994–2000*. Rungis Cedex, France: COLEACP.

Comaroff, John, and Jean Comaroff. 1999. Introduction. In *Civil Society and the Political Imagination in Africa: Critical Perspectives*, ed. John Comaroff and Jean Comaroff, 1–43. Chicago: University of Chicago Press.

Cook, Ian, and Philip Crang. 1996. The World on a Plate: Culinary Culture, Displacement and Geographical Knowledges. *Journal of Material Culture* 1: 131–53.

Dolan, Catherine. 2005. Fields of Obligation: Rooting Ethical Consumption in Kenyan Horticulture. *Journal of Consumer Culture* 5(3): 365–89.

Dolan, Catherine, and Maggie Opondo. 2005. Seeking Common Ground: Multi-stakeholder Initiatives in Kenya's Cut Flower Industry. *Journal of Corporate Citizenship* 18: 87–98.

Dolan, Catherine, Maggie Opondo, and Sally Smith. 2003. *Gender, Rights and Participation in the Kenya Cut Flower Industry*. NRI report no. 2768, Natural Resources Institute, University of Greenwich, www.nri.org/NRET/kenyareportfinal2.pdf (accessed February 7, 2007).

Edwards, Michael, and David Hulme. 1996. *Beyond the Magic Bullet: NGO Performance and Accountability in the Post–Cold War World*. West Hartford, CT: Kumarian Press.

Featherstone, Mike. 1991. *Consumer Culture and Postmodernism*. London: Sage Publications.

Ferguson, James, and Akhil Gupta. 2002. Spatializing States: Toward an Ethnography of Neoliberal Governmentality. *American Ethnologist* 29(4): 981–1102.

Fisher, William. 1997. Doing Good? The Politics and Antipolitics of NGO Practices. *Annual Review of Anthropology* 26: 439–64.

Forman-Barzilai, Fonna. 2005. Sympathy in Space(s): Adam Smith on Proximity. *Political Theory* 33(2): 189–217.

Foucault, Michel. 1982. Afterword: The Subject and Power. In *Michel Foucault: Beyond Structuralism and Hermeneutics*, ed. Hubert Dreyfus and Paul Rabinow, 208–26. Chicago: University of Chicago Press.

——. 1985. The Use of Pleasure. In *The History of Sexuality*, Vol. 2. New York: Random House.

——. 1988. The Care of the Self as a Practice of Freedom. In *The Final Foucault*, eds. James Berbauer and David Rasmussen, 1–20. London: MIT Press.

Freeden, Michael. 1991. *Rights*. Buckingham, UK: Open University Press.

Gabriel, Yiannis, and Tim Lang. 1995. *The Unmanageable Consumer: Contemporary Consumption and Its Fragmentation*. London: Sage Publications.
Garland, Elizabeth. 1999. Developing Bushmen: Building Civil(ized) Society in the Kalahari and Beyond. In *Civil Society and the Critical Imagination in Africa: Critical Perspectives*, ed. John Comaroff and Jean Comaroff, 72–103. Chicago: University of Chicago Press.
Geertz, Clifford. 1973. *The Interpretation of Cultures*. New York: Basic Books.
Gester, David. n.d. Retail Experience: How to Capture the Imaginations of Today's Smart Shoppers—and Keep Them Coming Back Again and Again, www.rtkl.com/docs/retail_experience.pdf (accessed February 7, 2007).
Goddard, Michael. 2000. Of Cabbages and Kin: The Value of an Analytic Distinction between Gifts and Commodities. *Critique of Anthropology* 20(2): 137–51.
Goldman, Michael. 2005. *Imperial Nature: The World Bank and Struggles for Social Justice in the Age of Globalization*. New Haven, CT: Yale University Press.
Gregory, Chris. 1982. *Gifts and Commodities*. London: Academic Press.
Grimes, Kimberly, and B. Lynne Milgram, eds. 2000. *Artisans and Co-operatives: Developing Alternative Trade for the Global Economy*. Tucson: University of Arizona Press.
Guardian, The. 2004. Leaving a Bad Taste. *Guardian*, March 30, www.guardian.co.uk/politics/2004/mar/30/economy.supermarkets (accessed February 7, 2007).
Hattori, Tomohisa. 2003. The Moral Politics of Foreign Aid. *Review of International Studies* 29: 229–47.
Hennock, Mary. 2002. Kenya's Flower Farms Flourish. BBC News February. http://news.bbc.co.uk/1/hi/business/1820515.stm (accessed February 7, 2007).
Hilton, Matthew. 2003. *Consumerism in Twentieth-Century Britain: The Search for a Historical Movement*. Cambridge: Cambridge University Press.
Hume, David. 1988 [1740]. *A Treatise of Human Nature*. Oxford: Oxford University Press.
Karlstrom, Mikael. 1999. Civil Society and Its Presuppositions: Lessons from Uganda. In *Civil Society and the Political Imagination in Africa: Critical Perspectives*, ed. John Comaroff and Jean Comaroff, 104–23. Chicago: University of Chicago Press.
KFC. 2002. A Growing Responsibility. Nairobi: Kenya Flower Council, www.kenyaflowers.co.ke/page4.html.
Mahmood, Saba. 2003. Ethical Formation and Politics of Individual Autonomy in Contemporary Egypt. *Social Research* 70(3): 1501–30.
Malkki, Liisa. 1996. Speechless Emissaries: Refugees, Humanitarianism, and Dehistoricization. *Cultural Anthropology* 11(3): 377–404.
Masson, Margaret. 2001. Traidcraft and the Churches. In *Markets, Fair Trade and the Kingdom of God*, ed. Paul Johnson and Christopher Sugden, 130–40. Oxford: Penguin.
Mauss, Marcel. 1969. *The Gift*. London: Routledge & Kegan Paul.
Miller, Daniel. 1998. *A Theory of Shopping*. Cambridge: Polity Press.
Moore, Henrietta. 1994. *A Passion for Difference*. Bloomington: Indiana University Press.
Moore, Mick. 1993. Good Government? Introduction. *IDS Bulletin* 24(1): 1–6.
Nandy, Ashis. 1987. *Traditions, Tyranny, and Utopia*. Delhi: Oxford University Press.
Nicholls, Alex, and Charlotte Opal. 2005. *Fair Trade: Market-Driven Ethical Consumption*. London: Sage Publications.

Offer, Avner. 1997. Between the Gift and the Economy of Regard. *Economic History Review* 3: 450–70.
PURE. n.d. PURE Ethos and Values. http://soton.pureuk.org/uk/View/Page/pureethos (accessed February 7, 2007).
Raistrick, Stuart. 2001. Traidcraft's Christian Basis and the Secular Marketplace. In *Markets, Fair Trade and the Kingdom of God*, ed. Paul Johnson and Chris Sugden, 117–29. Oxford: Penguin.
Ricoeur, Paul. 1992/1990. *Oneself as Another*. Chicago: University of Chicago Press.
Russ, Ann Julienne. 2005. Love's Labor Paid For: Gift and Commodity at the Threshold of Death. *Cultural Anthropology* 20(1): 128–55.
Rutherford, Blair. 2004. Settlers and Zimbabwe: Politics, Memory, and the Anthropology of Commercial Farms during a Time of Crisis. *Identities: Global Studies in Culture and Power* 11(4): 543–62.
Smith, Adam. (1982 [1759]). *The Theory of Moral Sentiments*. The Glasgow Edition of the Works and Correspondence of Adam Smith, ed. D. D. Raphael and A. L. Macfie. Indianapolis, IN: Liberty Fund.
Smith, David. 2000. *Moral Geographies in a World of Difference*. Edinburgh: Edinburgh University Press.
Smith, Woodruff D. 2002. *Consumption and the Making of Respectability, 1600–1800*. New York: Routledge.
Sussman, Charlotte. 2000. *Consuming Anxieties: Consumer Protest, Gender and British Slavery, 1713–1833*. Stanford, CA: Stanford University Press.
Taylor, Lynne. 1996. Food Riots Revisited: Public Protests in the Seventeenth to the Nineteenth Century. *Journal of Social History* 30(2): 483–96.
Teather, David. 2006. Big Retailers Help Raise Fairtrade Sales by Third. *Guardian*, June 28, www.guardian.co.uk/business/2006/jun/28/fairtrade.ethicalliving (accessed February 7, 2007).
Thompson E. P. 1971. The Moral Economy of the English Crowd in the Eighteenth Century. *Past and Present* 50: 76–136.
Thompson, Noel. 2001. Social Opulence. Private Asceticism: Ideas of Consumption in Early Socialist Thought. In *The Politics of Consumption: Material Culture and Citizenship in Europe and America*, ed. Martin Daunton and Matthew Hilton, 51–68. Oxford: Berg.
Valeri, Valerio. 1994. Buying Women but Not Selling Them: Gift and Commodity Exchange in Huaulu Alliance. *Man* 29(1): 1–26.
Watson, Matthew. 2007. Trade Justice and Individual Consumption Choices: Adam Smith's Spectator Theory and the Moral Constitution of the Fairtrade Consumer. *European Journal of International Relations* 13(2): 263–88.
Wilk, Richard. 2001. Consuming Morality. *Journal of Consumer Culture* 1: 245–60.
Winch, Donald. 2004. Thinking Green. Nineteenth-Century Style: John Stuart Mill and John Ruskin. In *Markets in Historical Contexts: Ideas and Politics in the Modern World*, ed. Mark Bevir and Frank Trentmann, 105–28. Cambridge: Cambridge University Press.
Wright, Caroline. 2004. Consuming Lives. Consuming Landscapes: Interpreting Advertisements for Cafédirect Coffees. *Journal of International Development* 16(5): 665–80.

3

FRONTIERS OF SOCIAL RESPONSIBILITY

8

Beyond CSR

Dilemmas and Paradoxes of Ethical Conduct in Transnational Organizations

Christina Garsten and Tor Hernes

FROM (IR)RESPONSIBILITY TO "ACCOUNTABILITY"

Corporations are powerful actors. With economic globalization, the power of corporations has increased tremendously over the last decades. The contemporary, large corporation has emerged as one the most dominant institutions in society, influencing not only the distribution of financial resources around the world, but also our social and personal lives.

Until recently, corporations could go about their dealings with little concern for wider social responsibilities. Big businesses could be content simply to earn money and capture large markets shares. Seldom were questions asked about whether their operations were harmful in any way or if they served dubious political agendas. Being big, powerful, and appealing to the consumers seemed an end in itself, and company strategies could be formed with the exclusive aim to be more effective. "What is good for General Motors is good for America."

The 1970s witnessed a rising concern with civil rights, a growing focus on the environment, and an increasing awareness of human rights and equality. This is also the decade when questions began to be raised about the role of big business in politics and about the darker side of corporate activities. The International Telephone and Telegraph Corporation (ITT) under Harold Geneen was allegedly involved in the military coup and overthrow of the democratically elected Chilean president Salvador Allende in 1972 and subsequently came under sharp criticism (Sampson 1972). Geneen, famous for his ruthless management style, fell perhaps from sticking to his dictum: "The only unforgivable sin in business is to run out of cash." In other spheres of society, people began to ask if there were not other sins of which businesses might be guilty. Media coverage of public damage and corporate involvement in dubious affairs intensified. In Europe in the 1970s, banks came under attack for their investments and operations linked to the apartheid regime in South Africa (see, e. g., Bond [1998]).

A decade later, the responsibility of big business in preserving the environment became an actuality with the Bhopal disaster in India in 1984 (Dunér 2002). Thousands of local residents were killed or mutilated when gas leaked out from the Union Carbide plant. Due to falling profits, the safety measures at the plant had become increasingly lax. The Bhopal disaster served to raise the issue of the legal accountability of corporate actors in society and not just their social responsibility. Responsibility in the Bhopal case became subject to court rulings. However, legal sanctions could not be induced due to failures of the international legal regime to handle issues of accountability in a globalized business corporation such as Union Carbide. The nation-state-based system of legal accountability failed to deal with the damages caused by a transnational corporation.

Court rulings about misconduct are potentially more harmful to a company's image than any other event, and thus such decisions have decisive negative effects on the company's economic viability. The costs of not appearing as a responsible company are just too important in a mediatized, brand-conscious society. Companies cannot afford to have their brand and logotype associated with a violation of human rights or workers' rights. They cannot afford the risk of being seen as causing environmental damage. Reputation management has become all the more important for the globalized corporation (Hutton et al. 2001).

Not surprisingly, during the last decade companies have increasingly created or adopted rules or codes of conduct intended to reduce risks of wrongdoing. Such developments do not belong to the corporate world alone. To be sure, parallel developments in society have forced different kinds of organizations and their actors to become more open to their constituents. The call for accountability applies to politicians, private organizations, and public agencies such as schools and universities, as much as it applies to corporations. It is all part of a trend that is referred to as the "audit society" (Power 1997) or "audit culture" (Strathern 2000). An audit society implies the growth of new administrative-style control systems that play an important public role. As part of this development, organizational performance becomes increasingly formalized, rule-governed, and amenable to formal auditing. Currently, there are a wide variety of experiments and attempts with the aim to make companies auditable and thereby accountable to the broader public. Standards for corporate social responsibility, codes of conduct, and other policy texts are part and parcel of the audit culture of the corporate world.

The extent to which measures actually enhance corporate accountability is, however, an open question. Corporate actors still make decisions and choices that have harmful effects. Why do some companies act in ways that harm people in their neighborhood, their employees, or their competitors? Why do company leaders sometimes choose not to act responsibly? How is it that people in corporations can become greedy automatons when placed in powerful positions?

Part of the answer to these questions may be found in the broader socio-economic changes in society. In his work on postmodernity and morality, sociologist Zygmunt Bauman (1995) sketches a world of individuals afloat in society; they have lost their bearings and are no longer investing in other individuals, only in themselves. When the organization of society moves from community logics to market logics, there is a loss of morality and an irretrievable loss of conscience, in Bauman's view. Formal organizations may simply "suspend" moral responsibility, pretending it is not an issue. In so doing, they do what the Church did with certain issues in the Middle Ages, declaring them not related to faith, neither sinful nor virtuous (Bauman 1989). Company leaders may declare that they go about their business—earn money—and leave it to others to decide what is wrong or right. Jérôme Bindé (2001: 91) has argued that, "By giving precedence to the logic of 'just-in-time' at the expense of any forward-looking deliberation, within a context of faster technological transformation and exchange, our era is opening the way for the tyranny of emergency"; under such a "tyranny of emergency," people are left with short-term perspectives and gains.

Although Bauman (1995: 37) is critical of the moral standards to be achieved by modern organizations, he also talks with some optimism about our age as "the age of morality." He argues that as the risks of society take on global proportions and force people to deal with them in new ways, then critical reflection and social responsibility will increase. Conscience and morality will again be reconstructed because people recognize that there are other values than bottom-line results. In a similar vein of thought, Bindé (2001: 109) posits an "ethics of the future" as a conceivable potentiality in which the political and moral deficiency of contemporary societies can be confronted.

Corporate social responsibility may be highly visible and apparent today, but it is not entirely new. Throughout modern history, morality has been handled in various ways in the economy. Some early founders of business operations were more than just corporate owners; they took paternal interest in the welfare of their workers and their families. Although this was the exception rather than the rule, in many societies their activities substituted for a nonexistent public welfare system. Another measure of achieving some degree of morality or responsibility in business was the formation of various types of cooperative movements in the second half of the nineteenth century in Europe. Cooperatives were formed to support the interests of consumers, farmers, fishermen, and workers, for example, in order to provide them with some protection from exploitation by industrialists, traders, and finance institutions (see, e.g., Evers and Laville [2004]).

The role of corporations in society is thus a question of long standing, and one that has become ever more pertinent today, with increasing globalization and emerging governance gaps in the system of international jurisdiction. In this chapter, we argue that increasing pressures for accountability and the attempt to achieve a degree of moral legitimacy in the corporate world give rise to discursive strategies and ways of repositioning the corporation as a "conscientious organization." In so doing, corporate leaders make use of audit technologies that function as "lightning rods" in that they serve to direct attention to particular issues, hence allowing for other, perhaps equally pressing, issues to be overshadowed. We argue that beyond policy statements and audit technologies, such as corporate codes of conduct and standards for corporate social responsibility (CSR), more fundamental questions are waiting to be addressed. These include the role of the corporation in a globalizing world, the degree to which corporations are to be socially responsible and accountable, and the conditions for ethical reflexivity in a market context.

CSR STANDARDS AND STRATEGIES

A significant feature of the audit society is the proliferation of voluntary rules or standards of all sorts. The institutionalization of standards has become increasingly dominant in social life (Brunsson and Jacobsson 2000). Standards seem to guide the lives of individuals as well as the lives of companies to an ever-greater extent. Standards developed by governments and the European Union (EU) as well as agencies such as the International Labor Organization (ILO) and World Trade Organization (WTO), for example, serve to protect rights, to facilitate coordination, and to assure fair play among market actors. Standards are, Collier and Ong (2005: 11–12) argue, "global forms," that contribute to the articulation of "global assemblages" in which new material, collective, and discursive relations are defined. They invite a variety of actors into a common problem space in which the role of the corporation in society, boundaries of corporate activity, and the allocation of rights and duties between individual and collective are problematized and negotiated. They encourage a particular kind of "reflexive practice" in Stark's terms (quoted in Collier and Ong [2005: 7]), relating to questions of value and morality, and offer technologized solutions to these problems. Standards exist in different varieties. As such, standards are voluntary in nature, and may compliment systems of binding rules when these are not sufficient. Standards for moral conduct and social responsibility of corporations belong to this category. Over time, standards may become compulsory. Standards on emissions and pollution, for example, are enforced through international standards and subsequently through national legislation, which means that they become compulsory rules. Some standards are produced by national or international organizations such as the International Standards Organization (ISO) and are then offered to, or imposed on, other organizations to follow. They are what we would call exogenous standards; they are imposed by external bodies such as regulatory agencies. Others are what we might call endogenous standards, developed in-house by companies that choose to apply them to their own operations. They are self-imposed for a variety of reasons, oftentimes to allow for organizational particularities to be recognized while still recognizing the generalized normative content of exogenous standards.

One important reason for the imposition of standards is to promote the image of a responsible company to the public and to consumers. In an increasingly globalized marketplace, it has been recognized that large corporate actors as well as governments may escape national and regional regulations. At the same time, large brand-based actors, such as Nike, H&M, IKEA, and others, depend upon being perceived by the public as morally responsible actors in order to prosper in their respective markets. Hence a number of organizations have enrolled into the CSR movement that, in turn, has created more opportunities for consultants as well as for the research agendas of academics and teaching curricula in business schools. CSR has been hailed as a major means by which corporate actors develop their internal capacity for auditing their impact on targeted areas (environment, labor relations, human rights). It was thought, until the Enron/Andersen scandal erupted, that there was a correlation between a corporation's commitment to CSR and its "real" commitment to being morally responsible (Sims and Brinkman 2003).

CSR standards (as well as other regularized standards) are based on the idea that problems are avoided by imposing rules. An important trend in past years has been to leave it to standards to ensure moral conduct. To be sure, standards may be effective means of ensuring some degree of moral conduct. But although enforcement through standards may improve the overall level of moral conduct, they may, by the same token, allow for more perverse breaches of moral conduct to emerge. Standards are double-edged swords. One edge is explicit. It sets the minimum lower limits for conduct. Not falling below this level means basically that the company is "OK," and it will normally keep it out of trouble. An advantage of the explicit minimum standard is that people inside the company and people outside it are able to assess its performance. It means that the very existence of the standard helps create awareness of the importance of moral conduct. The other edge of the sword, however, is more problematic. This is about the implicit effects of standards of conduct. It basically implies that as long as the company apparently performs well enough and attention is focused on those operations where it does well enough, operations may be performed that are morally irresponsible. This is not just because actors in the company willfully perform deceptive operations. It may just as well be because organizational operations are simply very complex, and it is, more often than not, difficult to know what is really morally defensible.

But let us deal with intentional misconduct first. In the pre-Enron scandal era, for example, CSR was seen by many writers and practitioners as a way to infuse corporations and public organizations with a sense of morality and ethics. Paradoxically (or maybe not so paradoxically, after all), Enron scored very high CSR indicators and was seen as an example worth following in terms of exercising their social responsibility (Sims and Brinkman 2003). We know the story. The consequences were disastrous for thousands of employees and small investors. Authorities, institutions, and individuals were tricked into believing the good intentions of Enron. What was at play behind the sincere façade was a remarkable deftness with which select individuals could lure huge numbers of people around the world. Their CSR was bogus. But we could turn the phrase and say that CSR allowed their practices to be bogus. The example suggests how CSR standards, along with many other standards, may sometimes serve as smokescreens. Enron stuck to the explicit standards that they could—and would—measure. As smokescreens, such standards may detract attention from practices that are condemnable. At the same time, as smokescreens, they serve a different function, which is to make people in the companies believe that the company conscience is pure (more or less). What is at stake is not so much Enron, however. Rather, it is how Enron could trick the world with the help of CSR technologies when CSR is intended to prevent exactly such an occurrence. We would argue that it is the conceptualization of CSR that is at stake—more precisely the foundations from which CSR is developed.

We are not arguing that CSR is a mistake. What we are arguing is that CSR has its limits and it is at its limits that the consequences of mischief are potentially most disastrous. The Enron story shows us that with some deftness and ingenuity corporations may actually use instruments such as CSR in order to circumvent the responsibilities that CSR is meant to help. Part of the explanation is to be found in the functionalist logic of CSR, which demands that corporations put into place a certain number of functions whose role it is to ensure that codes of ethics are adhered to. One example is "environmental accounting," which demands that the corporation monitors its effects on the natural environment. Such measures have their obvious strengths. It is not easy for management to ignore data that are produced through institutionalized structures instigated by themselves. There are in fact many arguments why such structures are a good idea. They do not just perform regulatory functions internally, but they are also educational in the sense that they serve to sensitize organizational members to issues of global concern.

On the whole, corporations and public agencies have a long history of applying a good dose of "discretion" when it comes to their functions. For example, a strategy that is becoming increasingly common in the globalized economy is to outsource activities that could prove to be harmful to the image of the corporation. Outsourcing, or decoupling, effectively moves the responsibility for questionable practices to another corporate actor and hence outside the reach of the corporation's own monitoring responsibility. A common practice is to move production to companies operating in countries where public disapproval does not engender sanctions. Heightened attention to one particular issue or activity may bring about a decoupling of other activities.

Another common practice is for a company to highlight "best practice" in terms of adherence to standards of social responsibility in one location and to create showcases of responsible action, while at the same time, shadowing violation of CSR standards at a different location. In order to channel media attention to their advantage and respond to public pressure, corporate leaders innovatively steer their ways around the burning issues with the CSR standards as lightning rods. Thus, as long as CSR remains functional in nature, it may be subject to manipulation. Manipulation of CSR functions is more likely to take place when there is strong pressure from external stakeholders, such as shareholders or owners.

BEYOND CSR: THE HETEROGENEITY OF MORAL VALUES

So far, we have assumed that misconduct is a result of willful actions and that CSR at times cannot prevent such occurrences. On the contrary, CSR practices may sometimes make it worse by serving as lighting rods that direct attention away from operations that might be condemnable. But beyond standards, beyond the mere application of CSR, emerges the complexity of doing right. Beyond applying standards, companies are forever facing the challenge of actually distinguishing right from wrong. The fact is that companies operate in a world of multiple standards with regard to what is right and wrong. To be sure, protecting nature through reduction of emissions is a laudable thing. This is also true for ensuring a secure and healthy work environment.

We believe that rather than suggest definite answers or rules of thumb about what is, and what is not, responsible corporate conduct, a more informed approach is to study real, on-the-ground cases in organizations, to explore moral and ethical issues confronted by organizational actors and to explore how actors deal with such issues. We need to explore how actions and structures of organizations may emerge, cause dilemmas, and find solutions, or how they may be "organized away" through formal organizational functions and technologies of responsibility (Garsten and Hernes, in press).

As emphasized by Pardo (2000), what constitutes a legitimate (or desirable or tolerable) rule and behavior may, and often does, differ between individual and collective levels of action. What may seem a legitimate way of reasoning at collective or systemic levels may appear as wrongful and illegitimate at the individual level, or the other way around. It is often in the interplay between the moralities of different levels that the quality of the relation between grassroots and state representatives, or between individual consumers and managers of supplying companies, become most evident and can be put to the test. Given the heterogeneity of morality, moral values cannot be assumed to be rigidly normative; they are, instead, negotiable and changing (Pardo 2000: 9).

The CSR business literature, however, does not pay much attention to the heterogeneity of moral values, ethical perspectives, or the multiplicities of interests at stake. In general, such literature focuses on the Western corporate actor, namely, the manager. It tends to be premised on the idea that it is possible to separate right from wrong and that the proper management tools, or functions, may successfully take care of organizational problems (see, e.g., Bennett and James, [1999]; Grayson and Hodges [2002]). In general, the CSR business literature takes a structural, functional view of organizations. In our view, however, ethical dilemmas and paradoxes are perhaps best revealed by taking a process view of organization. By studying "organization as process" (Hernes [2007]; see also Weick [1979]), as a continuous unfolding of events and actions, the real complexity of organizing, with its multiple stakeholders, interests, and resources, reveals itself. A process view on organizing allows us to go beyond the traditional focus on top management decision making toward a more interactive and multiplex view of organizational action—to look at how "right" and "wrong" are defined and articulated in practice rather than as given opposites, and to inquire into the challenges and dilemmas that emerge in the wake of the choices and decisions made rather than simply evaluate effects. By this more ethnographic approach, tracking corporate activities down, as it were, we may see how the choice of responsible behavior, of sorting "right" from "wrong" and "good" from "bad," is not a straightforward one. Rather, it involves balancing the many tenets in the assemblage that together make up the "ethical problem" at hand.

STRATEGIZING AND REPOSITIONING: "THE CONSCIENTIOUS CORPORATION"

In our studies of corporations and ways of organizing in the global economy, we have seen how organizing is not so much about setting up and adhering to plans, recipes, or rules as it is about processes of meaning making, negotiating interests, reducing equivocality, and assembling ongoing interdependent actions into sequences that appear sensible. The case we report, outlined below, highlights how corporate actors continuously negotiate the world of meaning around them by acting strategically in handling ethical dilemmas as they arise between the corporation and external stakeholders. Rather than illustrate how dilemmas are handled through fixed rules and structures, our case study illustrates how organizing involves continuous processes of "muddling through" (Lindblom 1959) and inventing ways of coping with ambiguity and dilemmas. Absolute moralities sit uneasily with the ways in which people relate to what is good and bad in particular situations and circumstances. Organizational actors experience these often diverging and ambiguous relationships between official rules and the ways in which they receive and relate to such rules. The job of organizational leaders is partly to invent ways of navigating through this field and to engage in "ethical reflexive practices" that position the organization in relation to different moral claims and demands.

In Garsten's (2004) studies of how organizational leaders engage in CSR, she identified four metaphoric structures, representing different ways in which corporate actors position themselves in society and rework their organizational boundaries. These were, in brief, "the entrepreneurial corporation," "the collaborative corporation," "the cosmopolitan corporation," and "the conscientious corporation." While these images or metaphoric constructs are based on interviews and participant observation, they are not entirely emic in character, but rather represent the researcher's own interpretations and extrapolations of the empirical material.[1] These constructs may serve the purpose of illustrating different voices and strategies in the process of engaging with CSR and to create a degree of moral legitimacy in relation to stakeholders. Thus, while all corporations, to some extent, were seen to respond to calls for social responsibility and enhanced transparency, in order to allow for and encourage ethical reflexivity in the organization, the extent to which they actually engaged in CSR, as well as the ways in which they did this, varied.

The fourth metaphor for the repositioning of the corporation in the wider society—that of "the conscientious corporation"—is of particular relevance here. This is where the call for ethics and morality is strongest, where morality testing of employees is seen as legitimate and where "transparency" and "accountability" are endorsed as ways of "flushing through" and "cleansing." Managers of conscientious corporations tend to take the issue of CSR seriously, and in their enthusiasm, they take on the role of "missionaries" or "evangelists" of what they see as ways of contributing to a new and better world order. At the same time, they are self-critical and endorse ethical reflexivity as an ongoing element in the conduct of business. At a conference devoted to corporate social responsibility held in London in the spring of 2006, a representative of a large bank expressed such views in the following manner during his plenary talk:

> Stakeholders' expectations are rising. We need to be self-critical and self-aware. Stakeholders expect that from us. We need to be serious about it, to engage in responsible banking. . . . You see the choices that we made as we try to be a socially responsible corporation. That's also why we try to take our business very seriously.

The speaker continued his presentation by stating that: "We're on a journey in the area of CSR. We have made some progress and we are motivated by that progress. The role of leaders is to serve as missionaries on this journey." The dairy corporation that we report on below, highlights nevertheless how, even in the case where "cleansing" is a most appropriate term (milk being associated with purity), a corporation may still invent strategies in order to deal with ethical dilemmas. In a complex world with a wide range of often conflicting ethical demands, corporations have no choice but to employ strategies on a case-by-case basis. As the following case illustrates, this applies also to corporations who base their activities on clearly defined ethical values.

The metaphoric construct of the conscientious corporation may be said to work as a model, not only *of* the world (Fernandez 1974; Geertz 1973), but more importantly, *for* the world. For organizational actors they serve as tools for ordering the world and the role of corporations within it, and as a device for the structuring of their own thoughts and actions (Garsten 2004). Through their accounts, corporate leaders define challenges and problems, direct attention to particular issues for reflection and give direction for thought and action. Such accounts serve to position and reposition the corporation in a desirable context of values and actions. While initiatives pressing for enhanced moral reflexivity and social accountability may well be worthwhile tools in scrutinizing corporate behavior, they also set into motion new kinds of discursive strategies to direct attention to particular issues thereby diverting attention away from other issues, as noted earlier.

WHITE MILK: A CONSCIENTIOUS DAIRY PRODUCER

TINE[2] was founded in 1881 as a dairy cooperative in Norway, and today it is the country's major producer of dairy products, with an annual turnover of approximately US$1.6 billion and providing work for approximately 4,400 employees. It dominates, by far, the Norwegian domestic market in terms of dairy products. Such a position is not unique to TINE and Norway. In 2001 approximately 93 percent of the world's production of milk was consumed in the country of production (Pritchard 2001). TINE is also a major exporter of cheese (e.g., Jarlsberg cheese) to other countries, primarily the United States (Jarlsberg is currently the most sold foreign cheese on the U.S. and Australian markets), Great Britain, and Japan.[3]

When the corporation was established, its activities were merely based on a collective logistical necessity for local farmers to get their milk to consumers. Over time, the corporation and its activities have become woven into national, as well as transnational, questions of nutrition and politics to the extent that today it has to maneuver in a complex discursive space in addition to its functional operations.

From the middle of the nineteenth century, Europe experienced a sharp increase in the focus on hygiene, which derived, in part, from Pasteur's work on germ theories in France in the 1860s (Latour 1988). "Pasteurization," the killing of pathogenic bacteria in fluids such as milk, was adopted as an important way of protecting the public from diseases. On the other hand, there was a concurrent, although not entirely unrelated, focus on health. As Latour (1988) explains, industrialization took its toll on the health of workers through the demands of hard work under harsh conditions. Amid rapidly rising industrial activity, the general health of men and women was degenerating, and medical journals in Europe began to focus on the "regeneration" of populations. At the same time, a demand emerged in industry for "healthy men" in order to sustain production outputs (Latour 1988: 18).

A concurrent increase in focus on nutrition, health, and hygiene prepared the groundwork for the mass consumption of milk. Milk production, however, demands close attention and control to prevent lactic bacteria cultures from developing. But milk was often extracted and processed in environments that were far from clean. Hence, the logistics of milk production have from early on been subjected to constant refinement of methods of extraction, tapping, storage, and transport in order to ensure that the milk is safe for human consumption. Dairy corporations such as TINE have, since their inception, not only ensured such logistics, but have also provided advice, training, and controls to ensure that standards of hygiene were kept. This is alluded to throughout their annual reports. In fact, much of the rationale of dairy corporations lies in facilitating the logistics imposed by the combined challenge of the high volume and organic fragility of milk. Similarly, in her study of the American dairy industry, DuPuis (2002: 35) observes that milk, as the perfect source of nutrition, led to tight links between industry, technology, and science. The focus on technology and science has also made its mark on the organizational culture. One director explains in an interview; "Listen, this has traditionally been a culture of straight pipes." Another informant was amused when he recalled that less than twenty years ago, staff at the TINE corporate headquarters in Oslo actually wore white technician coats.

Milk is simultaneously a symbol of life, a source of nutrition, and a food product. This makes it a particularly interesting object of study in relation to ethics. The essence of milk is that it has strong connotations of health and hygiene. Much of the Norwegian national diet in the post–World War II years was based on dairy products. In fact, the diet proved to be far more than just a diet. It also connected to national culture and perceptions of "Man" and nature. TINE has been the main corporate carrier of this strong symbolism in Norway. Values related to milk and its several symbolic qualities have also underpinned TINE's organizational culture.

So, what happens then, when milk is perceived to be a health hazard rather than being "the source of life itself"? After World War II, the belief was that the more milk and dairy products one consumed, the better. People's main concerns were related to logistics, costs, prices, and hygiene of the products that they purchased and consumed. With recent research suggesting that milk fat causes heart disease and arteriosclerosis, corporations such as TINE have had to review the content of their products as well as the discourse around their products. In the case of TINE, the image of the cooperative shifted from being primarily a provider of health to being seen as a potential producer of risk. We found that TINE has gone from being a functional organization, whose main concerns were how to best serve their owners' (dairy producers) economic and political needs, to a market orientation, and with this new orientation some ethical dilemmas have emerged (Hernes et al., in press).

Traditionally, milk has been closely connected to cleanness. Allusions to its white color are pervasive in the TINE discourse, suggesting a number of associations. Cleanness relates to high ethical standards. Mary Douglas (2002 [1966]) suggests that rituals serve to separate what is considered clean from what is considered dirt, and this distinction, in turn, serves as a mechanism of social cohesion. Social cohesion and institutional rules are created and maintained by reminding members of a society about what is considered proper and clean in that particular society. She quotes Lord Chesterfield, who defined dirt "as being matter out of place" (Douglas 2002 [1966]: 26). Consistent with this definition, Douglas sees dirt as that which upsets the sense of coherence in a society and hence threatens to upset the social order. For example, monks of various orders, if they are in touch with women, need to cleanse themselves through praying and repentance. Hence cleansing is a central element in being brought back into the fold of "the coherent." Cleansing is a logical remedy to having become dirty, because dirt, according to Douglas, is associated with that which is found at the edges or margins of society. Getting dirty should induce bad conscience while staying clean should guarantee good conscience (or at least avoiding bad conscience).

In Western society, cleanness tends to be associated with bright colors whereas dirt tends to be associated with dark colors. For example, myths and fairy tales have traditionally shown white color and brightness as representing the good as opposed to black color and darkness as representing evil. Witches, for example, are often imagined with dark hair and dressed in black, whereas princesses are imagined to have fair hair. Angels are white whereas the devil is dark. Hell is dark whereas heaven is bright. Thus we see that TINE has successfully made use of a preestablished cultural dichotomy between white (good/clean) and dark (evil/dirty).

Milk, as it is presented in the TINE discourse, symbolizes cleanness. Cleanness because it is white, but also because milk is seen to represent health and nature, which, in the Norwegian context, connects to snow, which of course is also white. The annual report from 1986, for example, shows a link between milk and health by featuring a photograph of the Norwegian female cross-country skiing team drinking milk. Milk is nature's own perfect food, to borrow from DuPuis's (2002) study of the role of milk in American society.

The connection between milk, cleanness, and ethics is particularly acute to corporations such as TINE. Cleanness is positioned as being synonymous to health, and to that which is good. Health is good for the nation, so the corporation that produces milk, and thus contributes to good health, is good for the nation. The connections between health, cleanness, nation, and corporation thus become interwoven and nested. The nesting takes place in the form of positive loops, where a positive value attached to one element triggers a positive value in another element. In this way a positive mutual reinforcement circulates among the discursive elements.

TINE's Strategies for Handling Ethical Dilemmas

TINE has employed several strategies over the last thirty-seven years in order to adapt to changing market orientations. It has been under pressure for several reasons. We have mentioned above the concerns regarding milk fat and heart disease that create ethical dilemmas for dairy corporations. We now describe how TINE has preformed four strategies to address these concerns. We also propose a fifth strategy that we did not find in TINE's repertoire, but that we have identified in other business cases.

Differentiation

Companies whose identity is built around a core product may seek to differentiate its activities so that its fate is not exclusively linked to this product. This is a strategy that seeks to avoid putting all one's eggs in one basket, so to speak, and is particularly relevant when the main product or service puts the organization in a particularly vulnerable light. Differentiation diverts attention to a broader range of products and activities and detracts some of the negative attention toward the main product line.

The market orientation at TINE has involved a distinct differentiation of the product range in order to cater to more diverse needs and customer groups.

Forty years ago, there were basically two versions of milk produced: whole milk and fermented milk. Today the range includes more than a dozen options, such as low-lactose milk for people with lactose intolerance. It is clear that the corporation talks and acts in a wider range of domains than it did previously. Its areas of expansion and differentiation have, over time, altered its discursive structure. Examples of market expansion include: (1) targeting new consumer groups such as the toddler market, in which TINE launched a number of products in 1999; (2) introducing functional foods and fresh instant dinners through the joint acquisition of Fjordland in 1994; (3) developing new tastes and products such as exotically flavored yogurts in the 1980s and fruit juices in 1990; and (4) expanding production into foreign markets such as setting up a Jarlsberg cheese plant in the United States in 2002 (TINE 2002).

These initiatives reflect a diversification of TINE's products that, in turn, expands its discursive structure in the way that the company handles new elements with regard to product research and consumer concerns. One effect of differentiation is to diminish the risk of being seriously hit by ethical ambiguities associated with whole milk–based products. It means, for example, that when stakeholders focus on the harmful effects of milk, the criticism does not have to be absorbed by the entire range of products.

Countering

Countering may be seen as a means to defend one's actions based on evidence about one's actions. Countering is largely a defensive strategy, attempting to thwart attacks on the organization from, for example, pressure groups and competitors. This may occur when outside research institutes are contracted to carry out research. Countering usually involves building capacity to provide validated evidence. As mentioned earlier, this commonly means mounting scientific counterevidence to show that products, seen from another angle, are less harmful than what critics allege. Countering may be done through a number of different communicative means including publicity, conferences, and publications.

In the case of TINE, we identified several ways of countering. We have mentioned that the largest organizational crises that TINE has faced occurred in the late 1990s when prominent health spokespersons, practitioners, and researchers emerged in the public with warnings for drinking too much milk, arguing that this practice was highly correlated to arteriosclerosis. A reactive discursive strategic change was witnessed in the annual reports. This initially resulted in TINE first denouncing these charges (TINE 1998: 11–12) as unscientific. "The Board is worried about the effect of the biased presentation some of our central nutrition experts give of milk and dairy products. . . . The Board has a hard time understanding the negative critique that occurs from time to time and hopes for a better cooperative climate in the time to come" (TINE 1998: 11–12). Later reports indicate that the board members subsequently realized the gravity of the situation, arousing their organizational conscience, so to speak. To this end, the TINE annual reports began to devote more coverage to this issue in order to demonstrate to the public and to its owners that board members were willing to work with the national health authorities to find solutions to reducing the risk of osteoporoses; this is clearly indicated in the Annual Report in 1999:

> TINE's research projects within the field of nutrition are often conducted in collaboration with other research bodies, either within the agricultural cooperative or externally. Two examples of research projects carried out during 1999 are the significance of milk in the diet in connection with diabetes and osteoporoses respectively.
>
> TINE aims to increase the degree of nutritional expertise involved in product development and to promote TINE's nutrition strategies vis-à-vis the authorities and the trade. In order to safeguard milk's market status, it is essential that we increase our knowledge about the consequences for nutrition and health derived from the consumption of milk and milk products. (TINE 1999: 12)

A Web-based information service on dairy products cofinanced by TINE, was established in 2003. The information service provides data on a number of issues related to dairy products. Rather than touch upon the question of heart disease, it offers a range of other research and consumer data on dairy products to reassure consumers of the safety of the product. For example, the information provided may highlight an internationally published article on how milk facilitates weight loss. Such information serves as a structural discursive strategy for TINE, as the organization has cofinanced an external agency to act as the former's voice on this issue. At the same time, the outside agency appears, in this case, as an autonomous entity, and this, in turn, lends credibility to the information the agency presents, in its role as a countering device. Such negotiations of marketing public image emerge as a communicative strategy that aims to defend the legitimacy of milk as a source of nutrition.

Repackaging

Repackaging entails redefining practices—putting them into a context in which if particular practices are criticized, the case against them will be more difficult to sustain. For example, companies who outsource activities to countries of the Global South may come under attack for "selling out" employment from under local residents, in what is currently a global business practice. These companies may then repackage their intentions as a means of ensuring the consumers that the trademark remains associated with national ownership. Repackaging is primarily a means of diverting attention from practices that consumers may not consider to be socially responsible on the part of the company.

That milk was a nutritious substance was an a priori factor that was rarely questioned in the early stages of the history of the TINE corporation. As mentioned above, much of the Norwegian national diet in the post–World War II years was based on dairy products. This gave TINE a central national role as a provider of health during the reconstruction of the economy at this time.

After approximately 1986, however, the nutritious qualities of milk came under increasing attack. To counter this criticism, TINE began to market the cow as a symbol closely linked to nature and also to national identity. Although there was still strong emphasis on the nutritional aspects of milk, the annual reports shifted significantly toward marketing a romantic image of milk and cows. This occurred at the time when milk was slowly starting to lose ground in the market as the premium source of nutrition. Criticism forced TINE to shift their discursive strategy to focus strongly on the national importance as well as the historical importance of milk for the building of a healthy society. For example, in 1994, when Norway hosted the winter Olympics, TINE was very keen on tying its product and logo to these high-profile events to further enhance the perception of the strong ties of nationality and their importance in the national project. To this end, the corporation ran ads in which the leading Norwegian athletes were pictured with milk moustaches, and these were later included in the company's annual reports.

In this strategic action, the corporation repackaged its main product, and thus significantly attributed a different image to this particular product than what had been done previously. The main product (milk) being a core discursive element, the repackaging of the product thus represented an alteration of TINE's overall discursive structure.

Structural Decoupling

Structural decoupling occurs when the organization dissociates itself from practices that are potentially harmful to the image of the organization. It may entail firing a person employed by the organization because (s)he may have harmed or sullied the reputation of the organization. It may also occur in situations where the organization wishes to distance itself from subcontracting activities in which it has engaged and with which it does not want to be associated. This is the tactic that Nike employs, for example, when outsourcing the production of their sneakers to poorly paid workers in Southeast Asia (see, e.g., Lim and Phillips [2007]). After researchers and social justice advocates uncovered that Nike and other similar companies were paying minimum wages to workers in Southern countries, Nike repositioned itself to declare that production in these factories had been largely subcontracted and thus these workers were not actually employed by Nike. Instead, the subcontracted workers were on the payrolls of local and national subcontractors whose practices Nike claimed they were not able to control. With continued criticism from activist groups and research institutes, Nike realized that their strategy of merely decoupling—distancing themselves from such subcontracting arrangements—was not enough to protect their image; Nike, thus, began to demand that their subcontractors must adhere to basic labor laws as well as accept human rights. As Nike successfully began to impose their demands, they were able to counter criticism by developing and then controlling the dissemination of the information documenting their practices (see, e.g., Cushman [1998]; Greenhouse [2000]).

Like Nike, in 2005, TINE experienced a similar crisis of business ethics, which led to a decision to decouple core business values from senior management, although in a different way than at Nike. Having enjoyed an almost monopolistic position in the Norwegian market, TINE became increasingly threatened by competitor Synnøve Finden, a privately owned dairy company. Competition focused on the efforts of these companies to obtain exclusive access to food chain stores. In one case, reports indicate that TINE had paid—or offered to pay—the ICA food store chain if it removed Synnøve Finden's cheese from its retail stores.[4] Removing Synnøve Finden's cheese from store shelves would make TINE cheese the only brand available. When this story became public, it set off anger among consumers as well as among farmers and other stakeholders (*Aftenposten* 2005).

After repeated attempts to cover up the real story, TINE finally admitted to unethical behavior. In order to retain its legitimacy with its stakeholders, TINE fired its CEO. In this way, TINE decoupled structurally in the form of a discursive strategy—it sent a clear message to the public that the CEO was responsible for the unethical behavior. In effect, the CEO was an element of the corporation that could be easily disposed, such that the corporation could make a fresh start with its customers and society at large. In a discursive sense, the incident was all the more acute because the CEO had repeatedly claimed that TINE welcomed new players in their market niches. Under the title "Faith is a fresh produce" we hear TINE through its new CEO voice the organizational crisis: "In the spotlight of the media, politicians, consumers and our owners, the dairy producers, we in TINE have been through our roughest ordeal, maybe ever. . . . We still want to be represented in most refrigerators, and we will get there through healthy competition" (TINE 2004: 4). At the start of this crisis, according to the Synovate MMI[5] list of most important companies, TINE firmly occupied the number two position. Subsequently, TINE dropped to number twenty-five in 2005, but had worked its way up to number eleven by 2006; by August 2007,

TINE had managed to climb up to the number nine position. The magnitude of this crisis is mirrored by the fact that in this company listing, as well as in others, TINE has for the past ten years been among the three most popular businesses in Norway.

Cover-Up

Lastly, we propose a fifth discursive strategy; cover-up. This activity entails purposely hiding certain corporate practices or internal values from the wider public as well from most of the people in the organization. One famous example is the forty-five-year cover-up by the American tobacco industry of its knowledge of the link between cigarettes and cancer. This is outlined in their confidential research reported in 1953 that tobacco was harmful to health (Stauber and Rampton 1995). Upon this fact becoming public knowledge, members of the American tobacco industry acted promptly to counter such claims by declaring that there was no proof that smoking causes lung cancer. They were not taken to task before the late 1990s.

Cover-up becomes possible when a few centrally placed actors control information that deceives not just the public, but also many of those working in the organization. Apart from the incident where TINE tried to cover up in relation to the ICA/Ahold crisis, we have not been able to find signs of cover-up in our investigations at TINE. However, it is a strategy potentially used by corporations.

The case of TINE illustrates how corporations invent strategies to deal with moral issues and dilemmas—how they attempt to highlight some issues and to conceal others. In a sense, their discursive strategies and repositionings function as lightning rods that direct attention to particular issues, hence allowing for other, perhaps equally pressing, issues to be shadowed. The case of TINE bears out the main argument of our paper—that rules and guidelines, such as those laid down by CSR, cannot guarantee ethical conduct by a corporation. On the contrary, because several demands arise among stakeholders, corporations employ successive strategies of a discursive nature to mitigate dilemmas as they appear. In a situation in which the corporation holds a central symbolic, cultural, and financial position in the society in question, as is the case with TINE in Norway, it becomes all the more pressing to develop ways of handling ethical concerns among its stakeholders.

TINE's dilemmas were acute, given the symbolic features of milk and its interwoven connotations with health at the national level. We argue, in addition, that this creates moral dilemmas, since an organization will have to respond, not only to the moralities of its investors and shareholders, but also to the moralities of the people who staff them as well as to those of consumers and other stakeholders. Organizational leaders will have to work out an ethical reflexive practice that is both flexible enough to respond to divergent interests and claims, yet coherent enough to provide a point of direction for organizational thought and action. The case of TINE suggests that, although a corporation may have "cleanness" at the basis of its activities, it is far from certain what the ethically correct actions should be at any time, and that the corporation will still employ strategies in a "muddling through" type of way.

CONCLUSION: THE MORAL TRANSFORMATION OF DILEMMAS

To some extent, the CSR turn in business is a case of "moral transformation." In this process, already existing dilemmas and concerns are transformed and come to exist in a new moral field with its own particular configuration of values. One might say that ethical standards, codes of conduct, and principles, aimed at providing a degree of legitimacy for global business, are to some extent in the business of creating a particular moral order (Harper 2000: 47). In this moral field, the standards and codes of conduct that companies develop and embrace are given a status beyond political contestation, as morally and ethically sound, and hence, difficult to question in principle. Oftentimes, the measures and tools by which a socially responsible organization is to be fashioned also work to organize the dilemmas away. Difficult questions are, so to speak, taken care of by the audit technologies in use. Standards may at times neutralize what are essentially contested issues, or direct attention away from them.

We thus agree with Harper (2000: 51) who argues that such moral transformations are likely to be salient in all organizations and institutional contexts subject to audit. Wherever this audit is, there are also ways around it, behind it, or out of it. This suggests that "audit society" is much less rational in the Weberian sense than we may think. Rather, the moral transformations linked to audit practices reflect the continuous negotiation of meanings, moralities, and interests that take place within organizations, and the ongoing transformation of economies.

In this chapter, drawing upon some of our experiences of qualitative studies in organizations, we have suggested that the rise in pressures for accountability and the attempt to achieve a degree of moral legitimacy in the corporate world give rise to discursive strategies and ways of repositioning of the corporation as a "conscientious organization." In doing so, corporate leaders make use of audit technologies as lightning rods, serving to direct attention to particular issues, hence allowing for other, perhaps equally pressing, issues to be shadowed.

NOTES

1. Fieldwork for Garsten's study was undertaken as part of the projects Fashioning Markets: Accountability and Transparency in the Global Marketplace, and Social Affairs: Governance for a Normative Economy, during the years 2000–2006. The fieldwork is multilocal and mobile in character, involving participant observation at corporate meetings, conferences on corporate social responsibility, and other public events organized around the theme. These meetings and conferences took place mostly in Europe (mainly Sweden), but also in the United States. Part of the study also involved a series of interviews (around fifty) with corporate leaders and representatives of nongovernmental organizations and consultancies in Sweden. Thanks to the Swedish Research Council and the Bank of Sweden Tercentenary Foundation for funding this research.

2. The company has had several names from its origin, but TINE was the official new name for the company in 2002.

3. From www.jarlsberg.com (accessed December 28, 2007).

4. ICA AB was formerly ICA Ahold AB. ICA has a strong hold on the Nordic grocery market. Its ICA Norge unit is one of Norway's leading food retailers (www.ica.se, accessed December 28, 2007).

5. MMI, one of the leading market research companies in Norway, merged in 2006 with the international market research corporation Synovate, and changed its name accordingly (www.synnovate.no, accessed December 28, 2007).

REFERENCES

Aftenposten. 2005. TINE Raided by Competition Authority. *Aftenposten*, February 17, www.aftenposten.no/english/local/article971593.ece (accessed December 28, 2007).

Bauman, Zygmunt. 1989. *Modernity and the Holocaust*. Cambridge: Polity.

——. 1995. *Life in Fragments*. Oxford: Blackwell.

Bennett, Martin, and Peter James. 1999. *Sustainable Measures: Evaluation and Reporting of Environmental and Social Performance*. Midsomer Norton, UK: Greenleaf Publishing.

Bindé, Jérôme. 2001. Toward an Ethics of the Future. In *Globalization*, ed. Arjun Appadurai, 90–113. Durham, NC: Duke University Press.

Bond, Patrick. 1998. *Elite Transition: From Apartheid to Neoliberalism in South Africa*. London: Pluto.

Brunsson, Nils, and Bengt Jacobsson, eds. 2000. *A World of Standards*. Oxford: Oxford University Press.

Collier, Stephen J., and Aihwa Ong. 2005. *Global Assemblages: Technology, Politics, and Ethics as Anthropological Problems*. Oxford: Blackwell.

Cushman, John Jr. 1998. Nike Pledges to End Child Labor and Apply U.S. Rules Abroad. *New York Times*, May 13.

Douglas, Mary. 2002 [1966]. *Purity and Danger*. London: Routledge.

Dunér, Bertil. 2002. *The Global Human Rights Regime*. Lund: Studentlitteratur.

DuPuis, Melanie. 2002. *Nature's Perfect Food—How Milk Became America's Drink.* New York: New York University Press.
Evers, Adalbert, and Jean-Louis Laville. 2004. *The Third Sector in Europe.* London: Edward Elgar Publishing.
Fernandez, James. 1974. Persuasions and Performances: Of the Beast in Every Body and the Metaphors in Everyman. In *Myth, Symbol and Culture,* ed. Clifford Geertz, 39–60. New York: Norton.
Garsten, Christina. 2004. Market Missions: Negotiating Bottom Line and Social Responsibility. In *Market Matters: Exploring Cultural Processes in the Global Marketplace,* ed. Christina Garsten and Monica Lindh de Montoya, 69–90. Basingstoke, UK: Palgrave Macmillan.
Garsten, Christina, and Tor Hernes. In Press. Introduction. In *Ethical Dilemmas in Management,* ed. Christina Garsten and Tor Hernes. London: Routledge.
Geertz, Clifford. 1973. *The Interpretation of Cultures.* New York: Basic Books.
Grayson, David, and Adrian Hodges. 2002. *Everybody's Business: Managing Risks and Opportunities in Today's Global Society.* New York: DK Publishing, Inc.
Greenhouse, Steven. 2000. Anti-Sweatshop Movement Is Achieving Gains Overseas. *New York Times,* January 26.
Hernes, Tor. 2007. *Understanding Organization as Process: Organization Theory for a Tangled World.* London: Routledge.
Hernes, Tor, Gerhard Schelderup, and Anne-Live Vaagaasar. In Press. White as Snow or Milk? Strategies for Handling Ethical Dilemmas in a Dairy Corporation. In *Ethical Dilemmas in Management,* ed. Christina Garsten and Tor Hernes. London: Routledge.
Harper, Richard. 2000. The Social Organization of the IMF's Mission Work: An Examination of International Auditing. In *Audit Cultures,* ed. Marilyn Strathern, 21–53. London: Routledge.
Hutton, James G., Michael B. Goodman, Jill B. Alexander, and Christina M. Genest. 2001. Reputation Management: The New Face of Corporate Public Relations. *Public Relations Review* 27: 247–61.
Latour, Bruno. 1988. *The Pasteurization of France.* Cambridge, MA: Harvard University Press.
Lim, Suk-Jun, and Joe Phillips. 2007. Embedding CSR Values: The Global Footwear Industry's Evolving Governance Structure. *Journal of Business Ethics.* Published online 21 July 2007, www.spingerlink.com.
Lindblom, Charles. 1959. The Science of Muddling Through. *Public Administration Review* 19: 79–88.
Pardo, Italo. 2000. Introduction—Morals of Legitimacy: Interplay between Responsibility, Authority, and Trust. In *Morals of Legitimacy: Between Agency and Structure,* ed. Italo Pardo, 1–26. Oxford: Berghahn Books.
Power, Michael. 1997. *The Audit Society: Rituals of Verification.* Oxford: Oxford University Press.
Pritchard, Bill. 2001. Current Global Trends in the Dairy Industry. Unpublished manuscript, University of Sydney.
Sampson, Anthony. 1972. *The Sovereign State: The Secret History of ITT.* London: Hodder and Stoughton.

Sims, Ronald R., and Johannes Brinkman. 2003. Enron Ethics (or: Culture Matters More Than Codes). *Journal of Business Ethics* 45(3): 243–56.

Stauber, John, and Sheldon Rampton. 1995. How the American Tobacco Industry Employs PR Scum to Continue Its Murderous Assault on Human Lives. *Tucson Weekly*, November 22–29, www.tucsonweekly.com/tw/11-22-95/cover.htm (accessed December 28, 2007).

Strathern, Marilyn. 2000. *Audit Cultures: Anthropological Studies in Accountability, Ethics and the Academy*. New York: Routledge.

TINE. 1998. Annual Report, www.tine.no (accessed September 15, 2007).

——. 1999. Annual Report, www.tine.no (accessed September 15, 2007).

——. 2002. Annual Report, www.tine.no (accessed September 15, 2007).

——. 2004. Annual Report, www.tine.no (accessed September 15, 2007).

Weick, Karl E. 1979. *The Social Psychology of Organizing*, 2nd edition. New York: Random House.

9

"I Am the Conscience of the Company"

Responsibility and the Gift in a Transnational Mining Corporation

Dinah Rajak

In August 2002, when Johannesburg was playing host to the World Summit on Sustainable Development, a cartoon by the renowned South African satirist Zapiro appeared in the *Mail and Guardian*. The cartoon, entitled "A Gift from the Corporate World!" shows the doors of the summit opened wide to embrace a Trojan Horse. On the outside of the horse the inscription, "sustainable development," is clearly written. On the inside, Zapiro shows us cigar-smoking corporate fat cats holding a banner of "profit, self-regulation and unfair trade" (Shapiro 2002: 147). The Trojan Horse of Homeric myth remains a potent image for the potential danger of the gift. The metaphor suggests that, like the Trojans, in receiving gifts we can unwittingly be embracing our own enslavement. The veiled power of the gift to empower the donor while oppressing the recipient is summed up most poignantly in the words of a community worker from South Africa's platinum mines: "As long as we're dependant on handouts from the mining companies, we'll be their slaves."

This chapter is based on thirteen months of multisited ethnographic research during which I tracked the "translocal aspects"[1] of a transnational mining corporation in my pursuit to understand the slippery and shifting notion of *corporate social responsibility* (CSR). This pursuit took me from the corporate boardrooms of the company's headquarters in London to their offices in Johannesburg and ultimately to the town of Rustenburg, the metropolitan hub of South Africa's Platinum Belt.

Across these sites, this chapter examines how corporate responsibility is dispensed and deployed in the so-called community around the company's mining operations. It considers how the practices of partnership and "community engagement" in Rustenburg generate relations of patronage and clientelism that recall the paternalistic and personalized bonds created by the corporate *gift*. As Crewe and Harrison (1998: 74) state: "As in a relationship between landlord and tenant, at the centre of the donor-recipient relationship is an exchange of deference and compliance by the client in return for the patron's provision." By drawing on the elusive yet persistent concept of the gift, I examine how the discursive practice of CSR, as it is deployed by a transnational mining company, creates categories of benefactor and recipient on which structures of control and dependency are built. In so doing, I explore how the practices of CSR create geographies of incorporation and exclusion that not only serve to demarcate the company's responsibility, but also to consolidate its authority.

CSR IN A TRANSNATIONAL MINING CORPORATION

It is not until you are right inside 20 Carlton House Terrace, London, that you will see a small sign informing you that you are inside the London headquarters of Anglo American Plc (Public Limited Company), the third-largest mining company in the world. The impeccably designed lobby is a multistory glass atrium decorated with a fountain; pieces of mineral ores in glass cases; a plaque to Sir Ernest Oppenheimer, who founded the company in 1917; and beaded decorations, sourced and imported from Kwazulu-Natal by the décor consultant. Books of African art sit on the table alongside copies of the *Financial Times*, and on the reception desk there is a picture of two small children outside a village school in South Africa; scrawled in children's handwriting at the bottom of the image are the words, "Thank you Anglo."

In Johannesburg, the Anglo complex is well known. The buildings at 44 and 45 Main Street, with their huge stained glass windows and sandstone eagles guarding the forbidding façade, were built by Ernest Oppenheimer himself. It is said that he told his architect that he wanted something between a cathedral and a bank. Around the corner, Anglo American's subsidiary, Anglo Platinum Ltd[2] (the world's largest platinum producer), is housed in a fifteen-story, 1980s glass office block—another globalized high-tech corporate temple. It is hard not to feel the visceral contrast of moving from these sites to the barren landscape of the Platinum Belt in South Africa's North West Province.

The single lane highway from Pretoria to Rustenburg—"The Bakwena Platinum Highway"—takes you past the Magaliesburg mountains. The clouds of smoke billowing up on the horizon and the huge slow trucks signal the platinum mines and refineries that encircle Rustenburg. On first entering the town, the stillness, slowness and flatness of this one-mall, fifteen-church town is striking. In time, the groundswell below the quietened surface becomes evident. Almost as if the mines are physically pushing up through the ground, the pressure from their expansion and the resultant commercial boom is stretching Rustenburg at its seams. In 2005, the SABC national news even made the claim that Rustenburg was the second-fastest-growing city in Africa, second only to Cairo.[3] In certain places, at about 4:00 or 5:00 every afternoon the ground shakes slightly accompanied by distant bangs similar to the sound of distant fireworks. This is the sound of blasting somewhere in the miles of mines underground. This is a landscape scarred by imposing mine dumps, towering mine shafts, smelters, refineries, crushers, chimney stacks, barracks-style hostels, and mountainous slag heaps. It is here that a large portion of the world's platinum is produced—blasted from the rock, transported to the surface, processed, and refined by Anglo Platinum's 25,000 or so employees until it is ready to be flown to the coast from where it makes its way across the globe to be molded into autocatalysts for cars or jewellery for those who can afford it. Rustenburg is the global center of platinum production, where Anglo Platinum is the dominant player among five multinational mining houses. It is here that I went looking for the tangible products of the phenomenon known as CSR.

In recent years CSR within the South African mining industry has been subsumed under the all-embracing mission of sustainable development (SD). The redefinition of CSR as SD suggests a radical shift in paradigm from corporate philanthropy, or as it is sometimes called "enlightened corporate giving," to a progressive focus on "empowerment," "transformation," and "participatory development" aligned with the political agenda of the postapartheid government.[4] Where mining companies once expressed their social responsibility through "*ad hoc* charitable donations to good causes motivated by the sense that it was 'the right thing to do'" (Hamann 2004: 6), companies now have teams of dedicated CSR and SD managers, socioeconomic development budgets, finely worded policies, and annual CSR or sustainability reports.

However, I question whether the lines between CSR and philanthropy are not, in fact, blurred—whether the notion of corporate responsibility is not profoundly bound up with the politics of the gift. In adopting the language of responsibility, are corporations speaking what James Ferguson (1998: 11) describes as the "language of economic correctness" according to which international development agencies hide the power they exert over states behind the guise of benefactor or even partner? The question arises: is development a gift or an obligation? Equally, as Eyben and León (2003: 1) ask, to whom does development belong, who should give it, and who should receive it?

Conventional models of modern capitalist economics claim that the market is independent from other forms of social life and from the concerns of morality. Yet, the *Economist* tells us that: "Greed is out. Corporate virtue, or the appearance of it, is in" (*Economist* 2004: 59). My concern here is with what might be called the moral underpinning of CSR practice. How can the CSR movement and its claims to "compassionate capitalism" (*Economist* 2004: 59) be reconciled with this conventional representation of the modern market economy? The much-extolled ideal of "corporate virtue" seems to summon up visions of Victorian philanthropic industrialists. The image of "corporate virtue" is juxtaposed with that of "corporate greed"—an image that seems reminiscent of the unbridled corporate greed of the 1980s depicted in Tom Wolfe's *The Bonfire of the Vanities* (1990) or the notorious Gordon Gekko in the film *Wall Street* (Stone 1987). CSR seems, at times, to be held up to represent the triumph of selfless good over the selfish pursuit of profit. The widely used phrase "compassionate capitalism" even seems suggestive of a merciful and beneficent ruler. Ultimately we must ask: does the advent of CSR signify the reconnection of the market economy with the realm of morality?

CSR: BETWEEN POLICY AND PRACTICE

In recent years, significant resources and attention have been devoted to developing effective, efficient, and comprehensive CSR policy both within companies and in the national and international arenas concerned with the role of corporations as vehicles of sustainable development.[5] Most companies that are mining in South Africa now have a package of policies covering various areas that fall under the broad spectrum of CSR; which, within the South African mining industry, has become almost synonymous with socioeconomic development (SED). Such agendas commonly include HIV/AIDS awareness and treatment, community engagement, education, and infrastructure development. These policies are supported by detailed management, implementation, and reporting mechanisms, a formal corporate social investment (CSI) budget, often set at around 1 percent of pretax profits (Hamann 2004: 6), and teams of CSR or SED officers charged with the job of implementation. Anglo Platinum Ltd., for example, established a department dedicated to SED in 2002 (Hamann 2004: 6) and in 2005 created the post of SD manager at the corporate level to sit alongside the already established positions of SED advisor and HIV/AIDS manager.

However, the emphasis on creating perfect policy has led to the neglect of the relationship between these frameworks and the actions, interactions, and practices that they are assumed to drive and legitimize (Mosse 2003). Such documents are all too often taken as statements, not only of intentions, but also of activity. My research findings challenge the prevailing belief that the practice of CSR is driven by policy rather than by an intricate web of social relations, power dynamics, and organizational culture interacting within constantly changing, and oftentimes, unpredictable socioeconomic realities. As Mosse (2003: 1) suggests, "the things that make for 'good policy'—policy which legitimizes and mobilizes political support—in reality make it rather unimplementable within its chosen institutions and regions." This is reflected in recent criticism of global CSR strategy and reporting mechanisms developed in the North and exported to the South, often with little regard for the historical, socioeconomic, and political specificities of the regions in which they are to be implemented (see for example Fox [2004]; Hamann et al. [2005]).

Policy claims to be, and is seen to be, concerned with apolitical and pragmatic goals such as efficiency, productivity, and economic development. The formal framework of policy has the effect of isolating and institutionalizing a particular belief, position, or idea as a collective good. CSR policy-making is thus framed in terms of an objectively identifiable societal or collective need, denying the moral impetus behind a policy or decision. As Bauman (1989: 170) states, policies are the product of supposedly "non-moral institutions which lend them their binding force." In this way, the mechanistic tools of policy-making and planning are used to mask political processes under a veil of "scientistic rationalism" (Apthorpe 1997:55). The effectiveness of power is seen to rest on this ability to "hide its own mechanisms" (Foucault 1978: 86). Policy can thus be seen as part of the political technology used to remove the highly political issue of social responsibility from the realm of political and moral discourse (Dreyfus and Rabinow 1982). The notion of responsibility is therefore stripped of its subjective nature and the discursive framework from which it derives.

Yet, a disjuncture exists. On the one hand, we have the ritualized frameworks of policy, social impact assessments, and codes of conduct in which CSR is represented as technical and rooted in efficient business practice, cleansed of awkward notions of morality, and reformulated as the latest orthodoxy of sustainable development. On the other hand, a contradictory impulse seems to exist in the reconnection of the realm of business with notions of virtue—an impulse that enshrouds CSR with the language of moral and, at times almost, spiritual duty. This disjuncture was cynically captured in the words of the longtime resident anthropologist of one of Anglo's rival mining companies: "We used to say, God bless you," he remarked, "now we say, let's have sustainable development!" His witticism seemed to imply that sustainable development, with all its technocratic sophistication, is simply "old-world" faith dressed up as science. However, a far more explicit sense of spiritual duty is manifest in the words and actions of individuals charged with conducting the "ethical" work of the company—the front-line CSR agents, so to speak. As one CSR manager put it: "I am the conscience of the company; my job is to raise the conscience of the company." Thus, as

Garsten and Hernes (this volume) argue, CSR comes to represent a process of cleansing or transformation within the company, and the CSR manager appears in the figure of a missionary within the company, bringing the sacred realm of morality into the profane realm of business.

CSR managers around the mines in Rustenburg often present a deeply personalized vision of CSR in which it is tightly bound up with a sense of personal morality. The sense of a moral mission is powerfully evoked in the words of one of the CSI managers working at the mining operations in Rustenburg:

> My passion is nutrition, I'm reading up a lot about nutrition and I've become very passionate about feeding and this new hydroponic system. . . . I have visions of being a Mother Theresa in khaki pants and white shirt. . . . I have visions of going and doing my thing, taking hydroponics up and down Africa.

At the same time, internal corporate management systems, along with external frameworks such as the Global Reporting Initiative, demand that the actors involved must strive to "maintain a coherent representation of their actions as instances of authorized policy, because it is always in their interest to do so" (Mosse 2003: 7). Such narratives play to the broader institutional need to represent the company as unified and its activities as coherent and systematic. For, maintaining order, or the image of order, is vital in order to preserve the implicit moral authority of the organization as an agent of progress and development.

The emotiveness and zeal of CSR rhetoric, like that of the broader development movement, endows it with the sense of a moral mission, projecting images of "liberation," "human fulfillment," and "human flourishing" (Gasper 1996: 643), as epitomized in the words of the CSI manager quoted above. Such statements express the mission of a grand modernizing paradigm of development. The language of CSR can therefore be viewed as part of the modernizing discourse of development, as it espouses a universal vision of social improvement and elevates the corporation as both architect and agent of this vision. Thus an SD manager at Anglo states: "We've come up with a post-closure vision for Rustenburg, for when the mine closes—we must now take that vision to the municipality because it must become a societal vision."

As an ethical agenda, CSR implies "an agenda of care of the other in a hegemonic manner where what is good for the other has already been defined by the benevolent self" (Giri and van Ufford 2003: 254). The company's vision of sustainable development thus becomes a hegemonic vehicle through which its authority over the social, environmental, and economic order is authenticated. The appeal to the concept of responsibility—and the agenda of care it implies—supports the role of transnational corporations as dominant institutions of governmentality, for as Ferguson (1998) points out, claims to moral purpose have enormous power in their ability to naturalize authority. In this way, the beneficiaries of this ethical agenda, those commonly referred to as "partners in development," come under the authority of the company as they become subject to its notions of responsibility and recipients of its paternalistic concerns. The company becomes the primary local supplier of sustainable development, a *gift* from the company to the communities in which it operates. The roles of donor and recipient generated by the discourse of CSR form the basis of relationships of power, patronage, and subordination.

CSR AS A GIFT

> All gifts have an inevitable tendency to pauperise the recipients.
>
> —Dickens (1958 [1854]: 106)

In recent years, mining corporations have moved away from the rhetoric of philanthropy toward that of capacity building, social investment, and empowerment programs, allowing them, as Stirrat and Henkel (1997: 73) comment with respect to nongovernmental organizations (NGOs), "to avoid the charge that they are patrons." Nevertheless, CSR as practiced by transnational mining companies takes on many of the forms of the gift. Both personal and organizational relationships between the company and the community are expressed and transformed by the process of giving. Behind the rhetoric of partnership and the economistic language of "social investment" used by transnational corporations (TNCs), the politics of the gift prevail, undermining Mauss's (1967 [1925]: 73) representation of the gift as the antithesis to the amorality of the modern market economy and "the cold reasoning of the businessman, banker or capitalist."

In his seminal essay of 1925, Mauss identifies reciprocity as one of the key distinguishing characteristics of the gift economy in so-called primitiveor premodern societies. The elusive power of the gift to demand reciprocity, contained in the act of giving, was for Mauss (1967 [1925]: 8) and his followers "the spirit of the gift." The bonds created through the exchange of gift and counter-gift provided Mauss with a model of the social contract. The gift therefore stood for the perceived solidarity and cohesion of so-called primitive societies, which he juxtaposes with commodity exchange, upon which, according to Mauss, modern societies are based. I argue, however, that the Maussian dichotomy between primitive and modern forms of exchange—between gift exchange and the market economy—is disrupted by the phenomenon of CSR, which overtly reconnects the apparently modern and depersonalized world of commerce with the moral discourse and social politics of giving.[6]

According to Mauss (1967 [1925]), the interplay of gift and counter-gift creates and maintains a strong social bond between the donor and the recipient and therefore acts as an essential method of forging diplomatic alliances and avoiding conflict between autonomous units. Similarly, CSR can at first, act as a form of consensus building in the communities around the mines. For example, bursaries awarded by mining companies as part of their education initiatives to disadvantaged students from mining areas create permeating ripples of loyalty to the mine. The obligation of reciprocity implicit in a gift is crucial for ensuring the continuation of these ties. The gift therefore acts as a powerful mechanism for the company to co-opt support. This is clear in the case of CSR as it is seen to perform a vital function of mitigating and lubricating the harsh realities of the mining business. Thus one CSR coordinator states:

> You know, we think CSR is just giving out a few things, but then you realize how crucial it is. A few years ago CSR was just a "nice-to-have," but now . . . we had a meeting with the mine manager the other day and he said to us that, "in a rugby match the guy with the ball is being protected by all the other players from being attacked," and he sees CSR as protecting the guy with the ball, as a buffer, keeping the community happy.

This relationship, however, is a precarious one. Mauss's preoccupation with reciprocity seems to have led him to neglect what happens when a gift is not, or cannot be, reciprocated. He (1967 [1925]: 63) hints briefly at this, commenting, "the unreciprocated gift debases the recipient." Yet, he takes it no further. If the gift carries an inherent expectation of reciprocity, what happens to the recipient who cannot reciprocate or repay the gift? If the reciprocity of gift giving stands for social cohesion and stability, a denial of reciprocity, presumably, signals instability, fragility, and profound inequality. Or as Parry (1986: 458) puts it, the unreciprocated gift, "denies obligation and replaces the reciprocal interdependence on which society is founded with an asymmetrical dependence."

The expectation of reciprocity inherent in the gift leaves the receiver in a position of indebtedness and vulnerable to the whims of the donor, thus empowering the giver, while weakening the recipient and making the pursuit of accountability virtually impossible. Speaking about the company's black empowerment education initiative, an education coordinator at one of the Rustenburg mines remarks that:

> People around the mines feel an entitlement over and above the level of productivity they are willing to put in. Even my school children—who we've been giving a 40,000 rand bursary . . . more than their parents will be able to earn

> in a life time, . . . you know those are the kids who phone me the first night they're on the programme and tell me they don't like the food.

The recipients of the company's 40,000 rand bursaries are placed in a position of indebtedness in which they are expected to receive the bursary with gratitude and not complain. The sense of reciprocity—or lack of it—is implied as the CSR coordinator criticizes people for expecting more than they can give back in terms of productivity. Crucially, the "gift" is juxtaposed with "entitlement," thus asserting the dominance of the company as a paternalistic institution. The gift appears as the antithesis to entitlement, which is "alienable," defined in terms of the impersonal rather than the personal—"once passed over to the other person, the original owner no longer has any claims on it" (Eyben with León 2003: 10). In contrast, ownership and control of social responsibility or community investment projects around the mines tends to remain with the donor, the company. Thus the CSR coordinator above claims personal responsibility as she refers to the participants of the bursary scheme as "*my* school children." As Eyben and León (2003: 10 emphasis added) state, "while *giving*, the owner is also *keeping* . . . if the donor maintains most of the decision-making powers he remains the owner although the recipient is in possession of the money."

Through investment in community development, the corporation extends the hand of ownership over the community itself, which in turn, often becomes "*our* community" in company discourse. The claims to "our community" express a sense of a personal relationship between corporation and community reflecting the way in which gift relationships are often described in terms of the personal rather than the professional (Eyben with León 2003: 8). Gifts wrapped up as corporate social investment or responsibility projects around mining operations contain inescapable elements of power and morality that create a social bond between giver and receiver. Ultimately, the gift becomes "the currency of systems of patronage," while the act of receiving, as Stirrat and Henkel (1997:74) argue, "is hedged with conditionality at best, while at worst the gift may become . . . a means of control"—a form of control that can be seen in the delivery of community development projects by mining companies and that can be identified with the coercive powers of the gift (Mauss 1967 [1925]: 58).

Nevertheless, the power of social giving to project the moral claims of the company is clear. A high level of ritualization and public drama often attend the giving of gifts—there is usually "nothing secret about them" (Douglas 1990: xviii). This is epitomized in the grand ceremony held to mark the opening of the senior school addition to one of Rustenburg's few English-speaking primary schools, funded by substantial donations from the two major platinum producers in the area. According to Anglo Platinum's *Let's Talk* magazine, the ceremony, commemorated with a plaque memorializing the donors, was attended by "distinguished guests and dignitaries representing the mining houses, the Department of Education, parents and educators of the school." The event was highly ceremonious: "Three choirs entertained the crowd with beautiful songs such as 'praise the lord' and 'catch a falling star'"; the headmistress, we are told, thanked the donors for their "belief attitude in making this dream come true," referring to it as an "everlasting gift" (Anglo Platinum 2004: 5).

Recently a paradigm shift is emerging as the CSR activities of mining companies are increasingly responding to a state-driven national agenda for Black Economic Empowerment (BEE) and sustainable development. Thus, the South African government's legislative transformation agenda, as articulated in the BEE Scorecard, which rates corporate performance according to a set of CSR-related and BEE criteria,[7] has gone some way toward translating responsibility into obligation. As stipulated by the Mineral and Petroleum Resources Development Act, companies are now required to convert their "old order" mining rights into "new order rights"; in order to do so, and in competing with other companies for new exploration and mining rights, they must meet a number of social and labor targets (Hamann 2004: 8–9; Hamann and Kapelus 2004: 89). As one CSR coordinator explains: "the mining charter means that . . . the company can't try to be father Christmas anymore."

While the imperatives of BEE represent the role of the state in the provision of corporate social investment, the emphasis on *economic empowerment* (as opposed to a redistributive form of social justice) simultaneously highlights the extent to which the postapartheid state has embraced business as a vehicle for social improvement. Implicit within this vision of development is an ideal citizen who can respond to the moral exhortation to "help oneself" by embracing the opportunities provided by expanding business and, in so doing, will be uplifted out of poverty and brought into "the market." This dominant ideology thus fits perfectly with the discourse of corporate social responsibility, authenticating the position of TNCs such as Anglo American in the new South Africa as central agents of social improvement. The state thus becomes the advocate of a market- or business-led vision of development rather than the guardian of society against the potential perils of the market.

The goal of empowerment has itself been elevated as a spiritual duty infused with a faith in the power of conversion and transformation. Such a vision is fervently projected in an article advertising *The Business* (an NGO contracted to provide entrepreneurship training to members of the community around the mines) entitled "The Ultimate Entrepreneur," in Anglo Platinum's monthly mine newsletter:

> Surely we are the generation to bring liberty to our children from the disaster that befell our ancestors. . . . I believe that in the next generation in South

> Africa, we will see the *rise of a new breed of entrepreneur, a society not dominated by counterproductive bureaucrats and paper pushers!* A society where parents will teach their kids "dream yourself a radical new business idea, develop it into a financially successful enterprise and retire before you are 40."

For, "it is time," the article implores, "to . . . [develop] an *entrepreneurial mindset* and [learn] to become your own boss" (Zwennis 2003: 16).

Participation in the market comes to stand for the promise of individual autonomy and empowerment denied black South Africans under apartheid. However, in order to attain the emancipatory and transformative power of the market, a conversion is required. The particular vision of development pursued through the practice of CSR preaches conversion to market virtues and values (Rajak, in press). Anna-Clare Bezuidenhout,[8] director of *The Business,* described the process that those selected for the program must undergo:

> It's a mammoth task—transforming someone into a different animal. We do six months entrepreneurial training and we call it "the army," not training, because it's really toughening up. We call it "self-mastering people"—so that people who go through it can say "I am the master of my own destiny."

Bezuidenhout's remark highlights that implicit within this model of empowerment through enterprise is the creation of a new class of empowered and entrepreneurial citizens who are not only the "ideal" beneficiaries of CSR, but embody the core values of the new South Africa—citizenship, enterprise, and transformation—thus claiming the convergence of business values with those of the community, and indeed the nation. Yet, as I will go on to discuss in the next section, while the company's "beneficiaries," or "partners in development," as they are often dubbed, are apparently converted to the emancipatory promise of business, empowered through CSR programs, they are simultaneously subjected to the coercive powers of the gift, which serve to reassert the hierarchy of the company's power over the community.

PARTNERSHIP OR PATRONAGE?

The concept of partnership has been invoked as a central strategy in the pursuit of corporate citizenship, linking together TNCs with governments, NGOs, and local communities. The language of partnership has become ubiquitous. Partnership is seen to embrace a wide spectrum of relationships—from the collaboration between a national government and a transnational mining corporation, to the legal agreement between two corporations, to the relationship between a TNC and a Kenyan tobacco farmer. Where once TNCs spoke loudly of their philanthropic gifts to society, they now speak in terms of partnerships with local communities, NGOs, or community-based organizations in pursuit of the mutual goal of sustainable development. This shift is encapsulated in the words of the former chairman of one of the world's biggest mining companies:

> This isn't a grand philanthropic gesture, I don't see it as my responsibility to spend shareholder money on grand philanthropic gestures, it's actually how we build security for long-term business investment. It makes the company a much more attractive *partner* to a host government or host community.

Under this new rhetoric, "donor" and "recipient" have been recategorized as "partners." This change seems to mirror similar shifts in the development industry from the language of charity and gifts to that of sustainable development, capacity building, and empowerment (Stirrat and Henkel 1997: 73). However, while donors might use the language of *partnership* in an attempt to deny inequality and claim affinity with the poor recipient, in practice, a gift "reinforces or even reinvents these differences" (Stirrat and Henkel 1997: 69).

Partnership is a particularly slippery concept. Partnerships claim a common cause, namely, that business interests can be pursued in parallel with those of other stakeholders, bringing government, business, and civil society together in what has become the new orthodoxy of the CSR world: tri-sector partnerships. Yet, partnerships are as much a site of struggle and competition as they are a site of solidarity in a common cause. Anthropologists have long been concerned with the discursive power of partnership and the way in which dramatic inequalities and conflicting interests are masked behind the veneer of equal collaboration (see, for example, Crewe and Harrison [1998]; Baaz [2005]; Brinkerhoff [2002]; Mosse et al. [1998]). Following Stirrat and Henkel's (1997: 75) analysis of the relationship between donors and NGOs in the delivery of development aid, I argue that, for corporations, the great benefit of the partnership paradigm, and particularly the emphasis on partnership with Southern and local NGOs, is legitimization: "it allows them to claim a certain authenticity, 'we are of and for the people.'" This generates competition between companies operating in the same area to publicly claim partnership with the "community" around the mines. From newspaper advertisements promoting a company's investment of millions of rand in the "community" of South Africa over the past decade, to billboards announcing "investment" in a particular school or social enterprise, the company can effectively claim social development as a commodity and themselves as the "primary local supplier" (Mosse 2003: 13). In this way they co-opt local and national political support and "reap the rewards of high-profile visibility and reputation" (Mosse 2003:13). Thus the director of Rustenburg's Community Foundation describes how one of the mining companies gave them money to set up the foundation:

> They wanted us to put up a big billboard with their name on it. But we knew if we did, then none of the other mines would touch us. So they put it up and we took it down. It's crazy how they want to claim their fame and exclude others—the whole thing's supposed to be about partnerships with the community, but when it comes down to it they just want their name on it and to say it's theirs. They get petty about not putting their name on a board or verbal thanks at a ceremony, but they can't give 40–50,000 rand of technical support and hope to get the world's approval.

Such relationships between corporations and civil society are at best precarious, and at worst, they serve to increase the power of corporations to pursue their own interests at the expense of the communities they claim to serve while blurring the lines of accountability between the company and the NGOs with whom they work. For, no matter how fervently the parties assert a collaborative venture for a collective goal, the asymmetry between giver and receiver cannot be completely eliminated. After all, "he who pays the piper not only calls the tune but attempts to make sure that it is performed" (Stirrat and Henkel 1997: 75–76). The asymmetry of power and expectation of reciprocity inherent in the relationship between donor and recipient is exemplified in the account given by Anna-Clare Bezuidenhout, director of *The Business*:

> When the mine opened about four years ago there was a lot of demonstrations—a lot of people toyi-toying around looking for work and with expectations of the mine—so we were part of (the company's) attempt to please the community because they couldn't give jobs to everyone—so others could have training. . . . They make use of us when they have to brag about their CSR; when they have important people, they bring them to see us. . . . Whenever the mine wants to bring people there . . . whether it's from Joburg or America we must give up whatever we've planned, so they can have their photos taken in front of everything and put it in the magazine. They like to talk about us when they're talking about community development. . . . Maybe our view of partnership is different from theirs. . . . They don't listen to our financial realities. We're constantly getting feedback from their top management that our statistics aren't good enough, but their expectations are unrealistic. . . . They expect people to be in business the minute they leave our training. . . . They don't realize economic empowerment is a process, that transformation is a process. They just want tangible results. They put in 500,000 rand and want to see a major miracle. . . . *But they're giving it to us for free so what can we do?*

The funding provided by the company is bound by conditionality and brings with it the coercive powers of the gift. The company demands, in return, the implementation of projects that accord with its particular vision of development. This asymmetry of power is not only neglected but veiled by the elevation of the partnership paradigm. In this case, the NGO is trapped between the impossible demands of the company and the inability to voice their discomfort due to a fear that their funding will be taken away and that, in the end, they are indebted to the company for this "free gift."

Mining companies commonly describe their relationship with so-called service providers in terms of a partnership in which organizations are contracted by the company to provide a specific service—whether it is to provide catering, mining equipment, or training courses for teachers in local schools as part of the company's CSR initiatives. In these cases, despite the claims to collaboration through joint planning workshops, the agenda has already been set by the company. Arguably, in South Africa the weakness of the NGO sector in the postapartheid period (Habib and Taylor 1999) has contributed further to the dominance of the privatized, corporate model of company and service provider. By extending the hand of patronage to civil society organizations—giving and taking away social investment where it sees fit—the practice of CSI further weakens the NGO sector as it strips NGOs of autonomy under the banner of empowerment. Anna-Clare Bezuidenhout forcefully evokes this sense of impotence:

> We had a very negative experience with the previous CSI manager, as he gave us nothing. But the new one has been wonderful; . . . he's really interested in what we do. One of the big problems people have with the mines is that if you get to know one person and then they leave. . . . You never know whether the next person is going to support your project or whether they'll just cut you off. They throw a bit of money at you, but they'll never make a contract over six months.

Thus, front-line CSR practitioners often found themselves acting as local patrons and benefactors—a role that at times inspired a sense of personal honor and achievement, and at others, discomfort. In this way, responsibility is personalized and shifted from the corporation as a whole to an individual. The sense of personal honor derived from this role as patron is evident in the description of a recent project given by a CSR coordinator at another mine:

> You see this is how we empower the community—we needed some land clearing—so I got young people from around here who were unemployed to form a company and I contracted them to do the job and then they have something to take home and they were so happy and now in the village they'll shout, "Hey, Mr. Enele." This is the thing that Daniel has done. This is what motivates me—to see myself doing these things and see them happening—I can feel proud of that.

Conversely, the coordinator of the mining company's education programs within the SED unit, when honored at a function for one of the outside school programs, stated: "I don't like it when people give me things like this—because it's not me it's [the company]—I'm just a vehicle for [the company] to work through—so you must thank them—it's they who gave you all this, it's their money."

The sense of personal achievement expressed by local-level company CSR and SD employees was commonly balanced by a contrasting sense of failure and impotence resulting from this individualization of corporate responsibility. While on the one hand they had become individual patrons driven by personal commitment, they remained, on the other hand, trapped under the weight of the company's rigid hierarchy and opaque bureaucracy. Many CSR officers spoke of their budgets being suddenly cut or projects prematurely curtailed and having to creatively negotiate ways to fulfill commitments to their beneficiaries and sustain relationships they had personally built up:

> At first these people were demanding and threatening, always demanding—they came to a meeting carrying guns. But now the chairman of the informal settlement and myself—we're the best of friends. . . . I go out of the office . . . go to his place and I sit and have tea with him in his shack. . . . People say, "what are you doing going from the office to the shack?" . . . But you have to be flexible. . . . You see we never have enough money, and there is such high unemployment, so you have to be flexible. These pipes needed painting, so I went to the community and found some people to do it, but there was no more money in the CSI budget, so I had to get the money from the operating budget, not my CSI budget—so you have to be clever to find ways to empower people through business.

In the Municipality of Rustenburg, as in all municipalities in South Africa, there is a sophisticated Integrated Development Plan (IDP),[9] a strategy for multistakeholder partnerships to which all parties claim to subscribe. While CSR managers within the mining companies commonly referred to the IDP as "the motherboard" or "template" guiding the companies' SED activities and stated their commitment to not only working with local government but being guided by them on CSI planning, a different picture emerges from the accounts of local government officers. It is a picture in which decision making within the company appears to outsiders as opaque rather than transparent, and planning seems arbitrary and driven by company interests rather than local needs. As one local government officer stated:

> People just manoeuvre their way in and then the mine just hands them the money; there is no identification of need. If they followed the IDP as they say they do, they would come to us to ask where is the need that we have identified through our community consultation process—but instead most companies

send a junior manager with no power to the meetings. They send the photocopy boy who knows nothing and can't make any decisions.

While the company argues that chronic incapacity and lack of resources within local government has forced them into a position of taking on this responsibility, by adopting a role as guardian of the social as well as economic order, they are arguably complicit in the weakening of local government as they undermine it through the network of patronage and the webs of power that such giving produces. This in turn "reinforces the perception that the company, rather than the . . . government, is responsible for decision-making, benefits and change" (Sillitoe and Wilson 2003: 248). Ultimately, the accounts from the Platinum District in South Africa's North West Province, seem to contest, rather than affirm, the myth of partnership.

The systems of patronage generated by the practice of CSR thus create categories of "beneficiaries" or "recipients." But where there are beneficiaries or recipients there are also those who are excluded from the educational, medical, or infrastructural benefits provided by CSR initiatives. These are often the poorest of the poor, who become further marginalized as they are excluded from the systems of patronage created through the processes of CSR. The marginalized become further marginalized. This is epitomized in the experience of informal settlers around Rustenburg. The rapid expansion and industrialization of the city has created enormous developmental pressures. Rustenburg's IDP states that:

> This is a stark reality, in that the municipality now continues to see an influx of migrant and seasonal workers, imported crime activities, over burdening of existing resources, shrinking land availability, widening gap between "haves" and "have-nots." (Rustenburg Local Municipality 2005: 4)

The informal settlements (IFs) occupy a liminal position on the edge or outside what is defined as "mainstream society." Consequently, they remain outside the supposedly "integrated" development processes of both local government and the mining houses. Migrants, or "nonmembers" of existing structures aimed at recruiting stakeholder participation, inhabitants of the IFs (which account for somewhere between 10 and 20 percent of the total population of the municipality), are often absent or simply vanish completely from the institutional perspective and planning processes, becoming, in effect, nonstakeholders, as their stake is denied. The IDP even goes so far as to refer to "*formal* and *informal* stakeholders" (Rustenburg Local Municipality 2005: 25, emphasis added) thus implying that the inhabitants of the IFs do not constitute full-fledged stakeholders in the development process with the same interests and rights as "formal" stakeholders.

In debates around planning in Rustenburg, the inhabitants of IFs are often the subjects of talk yet rarely function as participants in these conversations. The IFs have become a categorized problem of their own, isolated from the list of core development issues identified in planning processes, which commonly reads as education, healthcare services, water provision, SME development, and IFs. As such, they have become an unclaimed responsibility displaced between the uncomfortable relationship among local government, corporate, and civil society institutions. Through this construction of the IFs as "outside" society, they sit outside the webs of patronage and donor support provided through CSR initiatives to other sections of society, which thus serve to further alienate the most vulnerable. This situation was summed up by the manager of one of the company's mine-workers hostels:

> You see the informal settlements there, just over the railway track. We'd like to do something for them, give them water or sanitation, but the Local Authority would accuse us of formalizing an illegal settlement on their land—so they get nothing from them and nothing from us.

CONCLUSION

The theory of the gift is, as Mary Douglas (1990: xiii) states, a theory of "human solidarity." As such, the gift, as Eyben and León (2003) note, has both a bright and a shady side: on the one hand, personal commitment, passion, and warmth, and on the other, paternalism, patronage, and control. The latent power of the gift to oppress the recipient is poignantly expressed in the words of one of Anglo's CSR managers:

> Many times we kill people with kindness, and it's an insult. That's why with the education program we said that any student who is accepted must pay 600 rand towards it—it's not much, but it's important because it makes people feel that they've earned it, they've paid for it, it's not just given.

This chapter has argued that the practice of CSR is, in fact, profoundly bound up with the politics of the gift. The quest for responsibility brings together the self and the other as it generates categories of donor and recipient, patron and beneficiary, binding people in relationships of power and dependency. The precarious and personalized relationships created by the quest for responsibility unsettle the confidence placed in the scientific rationality of policy and the increasingly sophisticated management models it generates.

In pursuit of the slippery notion of responsibility, mining corporations operating in South Africa, and the individuals within them, are demonstrating significant commitment to the national goals of transformation and empowerment. Yet, I have argued that the concept of *responsibility* itself is problematic.

As a moral discourse, responsibility can be seen to inspire a paternalistic duty of care on the part of the corporation while placing the "beneficiary" in a position of deference and subordination, vulnerable to the whims and will of the corporate donor. In this way, CSR can serve to empower the corporation rather than the supposed subjects of their empowerment initiatives.

The words of Ernest Oppenheimer, founder of Anglo American, continue to be invoked by the mining executives of today almost as if harking back to a golden age of the company: "The aim of the company is to make profits, but profits in such a way as to benefit the people and communities in which we operate." In this way, claims to moral probity are subtly entwined within economic imperatives. On the one hand, the moral authority of the company is asserted—an agent of progress and instrument of governmentality. On the other, commitment to a global economic order that is represented as secular, rational, and driven by profit-maximization is maintained. In the words of an Anglo executive of today:

> The market is a completely neutral mechanism—there's no right or wrong about it. . . . It's like gravity—you can erect tall buildings and fly in an aeroplane, but one thing you can't do is dance around on a tightrope. There's nothing moral about gravity, but if you don't pay attention to it, it will grind you up.

Yet, the certainty that resounds from this absolutist representation of business is challenged by the practice of CSR. For, as we have seen, behind the rhetoric of partnership and the economistic language of "social investment" or "sustainable business" used by TNCs, the politics of the gift prevail, exposing the hegemonic myth that business is politically and morally neutral.

NOTES

Acknowledgments. The research on which this chapter is based was funded by a grant from the Economics and Social Research Council of the UK. I am grateful to Simon Coleman, James Fairhead, Elizabeth Harrison, Samuel Knafo, Geert de Neve, and Roderick Stirrat, for their comments and advice at various stages of this paper.

1. The world of CSR is a new area for anthropological enquiry. Gupta and Ferguson ask: "Why . . . has there been so little anthropological work on the translocal aspects of transnational corporations?" (Gupta and Ferguson 1997: 15).
2. While officially under separate management, Anglo American has increased their shareholding of Anglo Platinum to around 75 percent. The presence of the parent company is strong, especially in the fields of CSR and socioeconomic development.
3. The Rustenburg Integrated Development Plan (2005) goes even further, claiming that Rustenburg is "viewed as the fastest growing city in Africa" (Rustenburg Local Municipality 2005:18).

4. It should be noted here that, as Hamann points out, CSR within the mining industry, is "a special case" owing to the "transitory nature of mining" and the inevitable social and environmental footprint left behind. Furthermore, "in South Africa, such concerns are aggravated by mining companies' implication in South Africa's tortuous history" (Hamann 2004: 5).

5. Examples of such international initiatives include the UN Global Compact, the International Council on Mining and Minerals (ICMM), and the World Business Council for Sustainable Development (WBCSD), to name but a few.

6. Within consumer-driven industries CSR has become closely bound up with the fair-trade movement. In her study of fair trade within the cut-flower industry in this volume, Catherine Dolan reveals a similar blurring of the conventional anthropological boundaries between the profit-driven realm of commodity exchange and the socially embedded nature of gift-exchange.

7. These include criteria such as "community development, improved employee housing, affirmative procurement" (Hamann 2004: 5), as well as targets for HDSA (historically disadvantaged South Africans) quotas in management positions, the identification of a talent pool and women in mining (Department of Minerals and Energy 2004).

8. For the purposes of anonymity real names have been substituted with fictitious names.

9. The government of South Africa demands that each municipality produce a comprehensive IDP every five years, which is reviewed annually in consultation with all local stakeholders from representatives of the corporate sector to local ward councillors.

REFERENCES

Anglo Platinum. 2004. Best in the Northwest. *Let's Talk Magazine* 3: 4–5. Johannesburg: Anglo Platinum.

Apthorpe, Raymond. 1997. Writing Development Policy and Policy Analysis Plain or Clear: On Language, Genre and Power. In *Anthropology of Policy: Critical Perspectives on Governance and Power*, ed. Cris Shore and Susan Wright, 43–59. London and New York: Routledge.

Baaz, Maria Eriksson. 2005. *The Paternalism of Development*. London: Zed Books.

Bauman, Zygmunt. 1989. *Modernity and the Holocaust*. Cambridge: Polity Press.

Brinkerhoff, Jennifer M. 2002. *Partnership for International Development: Rhetoric or Results?* Boulder, CO: Lynne Reinner Publishers.

Crewe, Emma, and Elizabeth Harrison. 1998. *Whose Development? An Ethnography of Aid*. London and New York: Zed Books.

Department of Minerals and Energy. 2004. *Scorecard for the Broad Based Socio-Economic Empowerment Charter for the South African Mining Industry*. Electronic document, www.dme.gov.za/minerals/pdf/scorecard.pdf (accessed March 2, 2006).

Dickens, Charles. 1958 [1854]. *Hard Times*. New York and Toronto: Rinehart and Company Incorporated.

Douglas, Mary. 1990. Foreword. In *The Gift*, by Marcel Mauss, ix–xxiii. London: Routledge.

Dreyfus, Hubert L., and Paul Rabinow. 1982. *Michael Foucault: Beyond Structuralism and Hermeneutics.* Brighton, UK: Harvester Press.

Economist (staff). 2004. Business: Two-faced Capitalism, Corporate Social Responsibility. *Economist* (January 24) (370): 59.

Eyben, Rosalind, with Rosario León. 2003. Who Owns the Gift? Donor-Recipient Relations and the National Elections in Bolivia. Paper presented at the EIDOS Workshop on "Order and Disjuncture: The Organisation of Aid and Development," SOAS, London, September 26.

Ferguson, James. 1998. Transnational Topographies of Power: Beyond "the State" and "Civil Society" in the Study of African Politics. In *Concepts and Metaphors: Ideologies, Narratives and Myths in Development Discourse,* ed. Henrik Secher Marcussen and Signe Arnfred, 45–71. Roskilde: Roskilde University, International Development Series Occasional Paper 19.

Foucault, Michel. 1978. *The History of Sexuality.* Harmondsworth, UK: Penguin.

Fox, Tom. 2004. Corporate Social Responsibility and Development: In Quest of an Agenda. *Development* 47(3): 29–36.

Gasper, Des. 1996. Culture and Development Ethics: Needs, Women's Rights and Western Theories. *Development and Change* 27(4): 627–61.

Giri, Ananta Kumar, and Philip Quarles van Ufford. 2003. Reconstituting Development as a Shared Responsibility: Ethics, Aesthetics and a Creative Shaping of Human Possibilities. In *A Moral Critique of Development,* ed. Philip Quarles van Ufford and Ananta Kumar Giri, 253–79. London and New York: Routledge.

Gupta, Akhil, and James Ferguson. 1997. Discipline and Practice: "The Field" as Site, Method, and Location in Anthropology. In *Anthropological Locations: Boundaries and Grounds of a Field Science,* ed. Akhil Gupta and James Ferguson, 1–47. Berkley: University of California Press.

Habib, Adam, and Rupert Taylor. 1999. Anti-Apartheid NGOs in Transition. *Voluntas* 10(1): 73–82.

Hamann, Ralph. 2004. Corporate Social Responsibility, Partnerships, and Institutional Change: The Case of Mining Companies in South Africa. *Natural Resources Forum* 28: 1–13.

Hamann, Ralph, and Paul Kapelus. 2004. Corporate Social Responsibility in Mining in Southern Africa: Fair Accountability or just Greenwash? *Development* 47(3): 85–92.

Hamann, Ralph, Tagbo Agbazue, Paul Kapelus, and Anders Hein. 2005. Universalising Corporate Social Responsibility? South African Challenges to the International Organisation for Standardization's New Social Responsibility Standard. *Business and Society Review* 110(1): 1–19.

Mauss, Marcel. 1967 [1925]. *The Gift.* Trans. Ian Cunnison. London: Cohen and West Ltd. and New York: W. W. Norton and Company.

Mosse, David. 2003. "Good Policy Is Unimplementable? Reflections on the Ethnography of Aid Policy and Practice." Paper presented at the EIDOS Workshop on "Order and Disjuncture: the Organisation of Aid and Development," SOAS, London, September 26.

Mosse, David, John Farrington, and Alan Rew. 1998. *Development as Process: Concepts and Methods for Working with Complexity.* London: Routledge.

Parry, Jonathan. 1986. The Gift, the Indian Gift and the "Indian Gift." *Man* [New Series] 21(3): 453–73.
Rajak, Dinah. In Press. "Uplift and Empower": The Market, Morality and Corporate Responsibility on South Africa's Platinum Belt. *Research in Economic Anthropology* 27 (2008).
Rustenburg Local Municipality. 2005. *Draft Integrated Development Plan 2005/2006*. Technical report. Rustenburg: Rustenburg Local Municipality.
Shapiro, Jonathan. 2002. *Zapiro Bushwhacked*. Cape Town: Double Storey Books in Association with Zaprock Productions.
Sillitoe, Paul, and Robin A. Wilson. 2003. Playing on the Pacific Ring of Fire: Negotiation and Knowledge in Mining in Papua New Guinea. In *Negotiating Local Knowledge: Power and Identity in Development*, ed. Johan Pottier, Alan Bicker, and Paul Sillitoe, 241–73. London: Pluto Press.
Stirrat, R. L., and Heiko Henkel. 1997. The Development Gift: The Problem of Reciprocity in the NGO World. *Annals of the American Academy of Political and Social Science* 554: 66–80.
Stone, Oliver. 1987. *Wall Street*, 125 min. Hollywood, CA: 20th Century Fox.
Wolfe, Tom. 1990. *The Bonfire of the Vanities*. London: Picador.
Zwennis, Vivienne. 2003. The Ultimate Entrepreneur? *Lebone*. (October).

10

Moral Behavior in Stock Markets

Islamic Finance and Socially Responsible Investment

Aaron Z. Pitluck

Would you feel uncomfortable financially supporting and profiting from a corporation that used sweatshop labor, produced products that were harmful to consumers, paid excessive compensation to its executives, or had recently violated environmental regulations in order to make a profit? Many people would feel uncomfortable. In a U.S. poll of households with investments in the stock market, one-third would like to incorporate moral criteria in their investment decisions and an additional third would consider it (MMA 2003: 11).[1] The above social concerns were the top four of significance to U.S. investors in 2003 (MMA 2003).[2] We could consider these "harmful business practices" since they include a corporation's behavior vis-à-vis its employees, consumers, and our environment (see Dolan and Werner, this volume).

Money management subject to moral, ethical, religious, or some other nonfinancial constraint is known as socially responsible investing (SRI). Yet in contrast to the one-third of investors who wish to incorporate ethical concerns in their investment behavior, the size of funds invested in the United States in SRI account for only $7 in every $100 invested with professional money managers, approximately $171 billion (Social Investment Forum 2006). Even more interestingly, in contrast to the "harmful business practices" of concern to American investors, the top four prohibited investments of actually invested SRI dollars were (in declining size of funds) tobacco, alcohol, gambling, and defense/weapons—sin stocks and war (Social Investment Forum 2006).[3] Thus we can observe a gap between individuals' beliefs on moral investment behavior and the menu of ethical investment vehicles presently available and purchased in the market.[4] Moreover with the weak exception of occasional shareholder resolutions, this sizable minority of SRI funds does not appear to have much of an influence over corporate behavior of U.S. listed corporations.[5]

In contrast to socially responsible investing in the United States, in the Malaysian stock market there is a coherent and unified vision of ethical investment. As of December 2005, I estimate that the size of funds invested in "Islamic" or "ethical" investment accounts is approximately $15 in every $100 invested with professional money managers.[6] Even more importantly, this investment behavior systematically influences Malaysian corporations' behavior.

The organization of the article is as follows. I begin by briefly describing popular social movements in both the United States and Malaysia that partially shaped peoples' preferences to extend ethical or religious criteria to their investment behavior. I also distinguish "Islamic finance" from "conventional" finance and introduce a Malaysia-specific concept of "ethical finance." I then make two arguments to explain the more powerful influence of morality on investment behavior (and by extension, on corporate behavior) in Malaysia as compared to the United States. The first is a bottom-up argument that focuses on professional money managers' behavior. I argue that clients' preferences and their "mandates" (to use the native term) in both the United States and Malaysia are relatively weak external constraints on fund managers' behavior because they are socially constructed by the interaction between powerful money managers and their relatively less powerful clients. As a consequence, SRI in the United States has a weak influence because it relies on mandates. I then make a top-down argument that the Islamic capital market in Malaysia has been shaped by a powerful social movement with a coherent ideology and backed by powerful actors, namely the Malaysian government, that has altered the market's structure by institutionalizing Islamic finance. When this institutionalization is combined with bottom-up social pressure on asset management firms to invest in conformance to Islamic principles, the combined social forces create a potentially powerful influence over corporations in Malaysia, regardless of the religion (if any) of their leadership. This article draws on over 125 tape-recorded semistructured ethnographic interviews with financial workers in Malaysia in 2001–2002 (Pitluck 2005) and in 2006, particularly a subset of 22 interviews with current and 6 interviews with former money managers (whom I also refer to as fund managers), 3 members of the Syariah[7] Advisory Council and 3 regulators at the Securities Commission.

Note that this argument need not assume or claim that Malaysia's stock market is unproblematic (see Gomez and Jomo [1999] for a sophisticated catalog of problems). Rather, this article seeks to explain the relatively greater prevalence of explicitly moral, nonfinancial investment behavior by professional money managers in the Malaysian stock exchange relative to that in the U.S. equities market.

U.S. AND MALAYSIAN ETHICAL INVESTMENT SOCIAL MOVEMENTS

Drawing on two decades of data from the World Values Survey, Inglehart and Welzel (2005) describe a global, uneven, and potentially reversible temporal shift in cultural values toward postmaterial values in countries with pervasive existential security. This shift in cultural values provides an opportunity for social movements and market entrepreneurs to promote the incorporation of nonfinancial criteria in financial markets (see Dolan, chapter 7 and Garsten and Hernes, this volume).

Before describing how social movements have created a market for Islamic finance and socially responsible investing, it may be helpful to define three forms of finance: "Islamic," "conventional," and a Malaysia-specific "ethical" finance. Islamic finance, like other Islamic entrepreneurship, is largely (but not entirely) self-defined (Henry and Wilson 2004: 1–2) and differs from conventional financial institutions insofar as its objectives and operations are based on Islam (Warde 2000: 5). There are two important characteristics distinguishing Islamic finance from conventional finance. The first is that Islamic finance emphasizes a "risk-sharing philosophy" in which fixed, predetermined interest rates are inferior to a profit-and-loss sharing agreement. The second is "the promotion of economic and social development through specific business practices and through *zakat* (almsgiving)" (Warde 2000: 5). However, as a leading scholar of Islamic finance acknowledges, "no definition of Islamic finance is entirely satisfactory" (Warde 2000: 5; see also Maurer [2002]).

With a few exceptions, every country in the world with an Islamic Capital Market has in parallel a "conventional" capital market, and therefore there are few "Islamic" stock exchanges.[8] Instead, there is a subset of corporations on each country's stock exchange that could be considered ethical (*Shariah*-compliant) insofar as the corporations conform to Islamic principles. At present, whether a firm is considered ethical by Islamic criteria in global stock exchanges (including Malaysia and the United States) rests on four principles of corporate behavior (IOSCO 2004: 5–9; Iqbal and Molyneux 2005: 4–17; Securities Commission 2005; Usmani 2002; Warde 2000: 55–72):

1. Prohibition of *riba*. One may not profit from "fixed, predetermined aspects of interest-based lending" which is perceived as an unfair advantage lenders impose on borrowers (Warde 2004: 40).
2. Prohibition of *gharar*. Contracts should be transparent, minimize risk, and not seek to profit from uncertainty.
3. Prohibition of *maysir*. Related to *gharar*, one may not profit from gambling and games of chance, including pure speculation.

4. Corporations' activities must be productive and must not primarily engage in "*haram*" activities forbidden by the religion such as producing liquor and gambling. The precise list of such activities may vary, reflecting the global reach and adaptability of the religion (see also Warde [2000: 41–42]).

Of course there is a great deal of potential interpretation of these principles in practice. Corporations are complex organizations frequently engaged in multiple activities. Like Domini (2001: 54) and other SRI advocates, Islamic finance seeks to set a "percentage limit of acceptable involvement in an unacceptable industry."

In Malaysia, in addition to "Islamic" or "Syariah-compliant" investing, a second type of social investing called "ethical" investing has been adopted by government bodies and agencies such as the Employee Provident Fund. This simpler investment philosophy only prohibits investment in companies that are involved in alcohol or gambling. Some entities additionally prohibit investments in tobacco.

The operationalization of Islamic finance in Malaysia is a product of global and national social movements. Advocacy of contemporary Islamic finance originated in the mid-1970s when there was firstly, a shift in political economic power from the global North to the Organization of Petroleum Exporting Countries (OPEC) and secondly, the rise of pan-Islamism (Kahf 2004; Warde 2000: 73–112, 2004). Nongovernmental Islamic banks were founded throughout the world in the 1970s as a consequence of social movement activism by Saudi Arabian leaders (principally King Faisal, Prince Mohammad Al-Faisal, and Sheikh Saleh Kamel), social networks (the Dar al-Maal al-Islami Group and the Dallah al-Baraka Group), and Organization of the Islamic Conference (OIC) governments (IOSCO 2004: 19–20; Warde 2000: 73–112, 2004; Kahf 2004).

In Malaysia, the Islamic revival movement (popularly known as *dakwah*, literally "to summon or call") dates from the same years of Middle Eastern pan-Islamism and increased piety but originates with older, local concerns of Malay nationalism, religious-ethnic identities, and postindependence ethnic politics (see Chandra Muzaffar [1987]; Shamsul [1997]; Zainah Anwar [1987]). As documented by Shamsul (1997), the dakwah movement flourished first in the domestic universities, radicalized in overseas universities, and in the 1980s entered into government with the retrospective milestone of ex-deputy prime minister Anwar Ibrahim joining the government in 1982. As a continuation of the above domestic concerns, as well as a frequently pan-Islamic foreign policy dating from the 1970s, the Malaysian government promoted Islamic finance as well as numerous other Muslim institutions associated with economic development and cultural modernization (see Bank Negara [1999: 243–60]; Securities Commission [2002: 7]).

An additional motivation for promoting Islamic finance is that the Malaysian government estimates that $800 billion is owned by Muslims worldwide and that this may be potentially invested in global Islamic capital markets, including Malaysia (Securities Commission 2001: 181–82).[9] A symbol of the Malaysian government's commitment to becoming a global "Islamic capital market centre" is that it was one of six "strategic initiatives" enshrined in the government's touchstone, *Malaysian Capital Market Masterplan* (Securities Commission 2001: 173–97). This goal was reiterated in the economy-wide *Ninth Malaysia Plan, 2006–2010* (Economic Planning Unit 2006: 184).

The market for socially responsible investing in the United States has also arisen from social movements. Beginning in the 1960s, antiapartheid, civil rights, and consumer social movements targeted corporations and their investors to promote social justice and to improve consumer and environmental protection. In 1969, the Council on Economic Priorities began rating corporations on their social and environmental performance. In the 1970s the Investor Responsibility Research Center and Interfaith Center on Corporate Responsibility was founded. In the 1980s, U.S. antiapartheid social movements focused their energies on persuading universities, churches, and charitable endowments to disinvest from South Africa. As a product of these diverse social movements, in the early 1980s, entrepreneurs and activists created several religiously based and politically based SRI funds (Domini 2001). This financial services industry niche market has grown such that in 2006 the SRI sector comprised approximately $171 billion, with over 7 percent of funds invested with professional money managers (Social Investment Forum 2006).

THE SOCIAL CONSTRUCTION OF MANDATES

To begin a bottom-up argument that examines how money managers incorporate moral decision making in their investment and disinvestment decisions, and particularly how these choices are structured by social forces, including their clients, we must first address the generic question of how money managers make their speculative decisions. In this section I will argue that the social construction of "mandates" as practiced in both the United States and in Malaysia offers one explanation why socially responsible investing in the United States—including religiously based criteria—is so infrequently conducted and so poorly mapped to investors' stated preferences.

Money managers are like positivistic social scientists; they systematically gather information, create simplified descriptions of a dynamic and complex reality, and then seek to make predictions based on this representation.

These predictions are then operationalized into investment and disinvestment decisions (see also Brügger [2000]). Figure 10.1 illustrates four social forces influencing money managers' cognition and behavior. In the illustration, pictured on the left is the influence of the money managers' clients and the client preferences in the form of a *mandate.* On the right is *market structure,* that is, the formal and informal regulations—as well as the degree of enforcement—of the stock exchange. Below is the very important structuring influence of the *asset management firm* that employs the money manager (e.g., Clark and Thrift [2005]). And finally, above is the money manager's *social cognitive network*—his or her community of cothinkers and codoers in the industry, composed of market analysts, brokers, and other fund managers. Within the context of the discussion in this chapter, the most relevant social forces are those on the left and right; I have documented elsewhere the independent effects of the money managers' asset management firm and social networks (Pitluck 2005). The second section of this article focuses on market structure.

Typically the preeminent criterion by which a client gauges a money manager's performance is how much money he or she makes for every dollar invested. When clients have additional constraints that they wish to place on the fund managers, the native term for this in the international asset management industry is a *mandate.* The typical mandate describes the riskiness of the fund's investments and/or the investment strategy that the money manager should pursue. As a product of the shifting cultural values and of campaigning by the ethical investment social movements described earlier, an increasingly popular mandate is a "social" or "religious" mandate

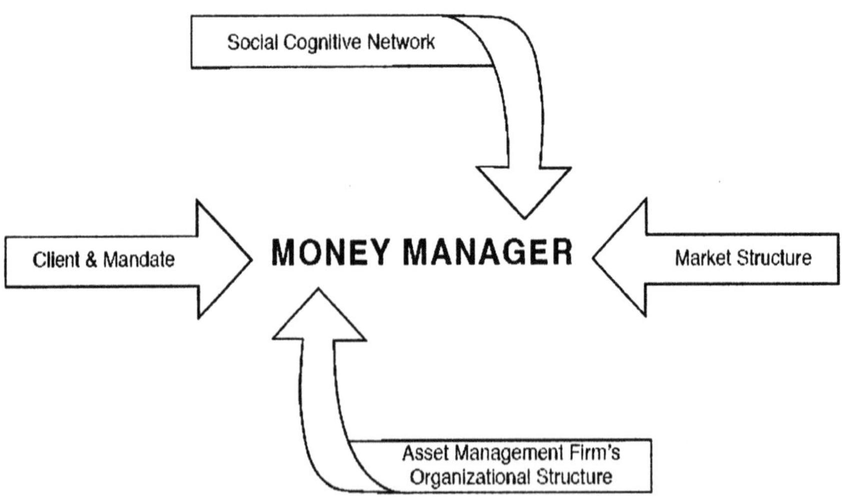

Figure 10.1. Social Forces Shaping Money Managers' Decision Making

that prohibits investments in specific lines of business. In the case of these ethical funds, the mandate specifies nonfinancial criteria that the client imposes on the money manager. Mandates are created and defined in each asset management firm and may be customized for particular clients.

Drawing on my interviews in Malaysia, as well as on the international financial press, I have identified three perspectives with which we can understand mandates, both financial and social: the economics, marketing, and cultural-tool perspectives. The first is the *economics perspective*, which is closest to the dictionary definition of *mandate*: a mandate is an "authoritative command," "a formal order from a superior to an inferior," and "an authorization to act" given to an agent (*American Heritage Dictionary* 2004). In principal-agent theory (Jensen and Meckling 1976) and in the rational choice literature, a mandate could be viewed as a social contract between a principal (the client investor) and the agent (money manager) he or she hires. According to this perspective, since client investors have diverse goals for investment, investment philosophies, and tolerances for risk, these "mandate" terms are intended to match appropriate fund types with particular types of investors. For example, risk-loving younger or wealthy individuals may prefer a fund with a risky aggressive investment strategy. Alternatively, a hospital's pension fund may take an ethical stance by not investing in corporations that profit from alcohol or tobacco. In sum, in the economics perspective, a mandate is a constraining social contract binding the behavior of the money manager to the preference structure of the hiring principal. A client agrees to a mandate as an imposition of will on the behavior of the hired money manager. In interviews with financial workers, this is the most frequently voiced interpretation of mandates by fund managers: "When you sell is up to you, although some funds have guidelines. [For example] one fund has a maximum of 20 percent gain. If the fund mandates that you sell, you sell."

If a mandate is a social contract, as the economics perspective suggests, it is in practice a weak social contract. The mandates that U.S. clients are aware of—namely the names of the funds and their descriptions—have little correlation with the types of stocks that the funds in practice purchase. Consider the observations of a director of fund analysis and two financial journalists who observed mutual fund companies changing their fund's names to reflect a "value" orientation following the end of the U.S. technology bubble in 2000:

> The portfolios remain much the same, but the names are changing at a rapid rate. Hundreds of U.S. mutual funds have altered their names this year to reflect the sober mood of the markets—"New Economy" and "Growth" are out, and "Value" is definitely in. "Investment companies are ripping names from the headlines and slapping them on funds that haven't changed a bit," said Russ Kinnel, director of fund analysis at Morningstar, which tracks the performance of mutual funds. (cited in Cooper et al. [2003: 2])

The U.S. Securities and Exchange Commission (SEC) requires that merely 80 percent of a fund's assets need to be invested "in the type of investment suggested by its name," (O'Brian 2001; Securities and Exchange Commission 2004). Such a standard is rather weak; consider the effect on a risk-averse fund if up to 20 percent of its assets are invested in extremely risky investments. For example, in July 2001, Alliance Capital North American Government Income Trust, whose nominal mandate was investing in nearly risk-free U.S. debt, held 17.4 percent of its portfolio in extremely risky Argentine government debt (O'Brian 2001). In December, such risk was tragically transformed into certainty when Argentina's economy collapsed and the government announced it would not pay its foreign creditors. A further illustrative example can be seen in the prospectus of the American Century Heritage Fund (2006), which claims to constrain itself "to invest the fund's assets primarily in U.S. stocks." At the beginning of 2005, it held 93 percent of its funds in U.S. stocks. During 2005, the American Century Heritage Fund began investing overseas, and by early 2006 it held only 76 percent of its funds in American stocks. This shift to a strategy contrary to their mandate was not mentioned in shareholder reports. These are not atypical cases. According to Morningstar, Inc., an independent market research corporation, over 100 mutual funds that were classified by Morningstar as "U.S. stock funds" held over 20 percent of their portfolios in non-U.S. securities in February 2006 (Lauricella 2006). Given the discrepancy between mandates and the actual investments U.S. money managers make, it appears that mandates act as only a weak constraint on shaping fund managers' behavior. While I do not have similar statistical evidence from Malaysia, anecdotal comments by Malaysian interviewees suggest that mandates can be a similarly weak constraint on Malaysian money managers' behavior. Two interviewees with mandates for investing in small and medium-size corporations explained that in practice they do not invest substantially in such corporations. Similarly, a large and diverse number of interviewees participated in or witnessed out-of-mandate investments during the "Super Bull Run" prior to the Asian Financial Crisis of 1997–1998.

In both the United States and Malaysia, mandates are only strong constraints on professional fund managers' behavior if they are carefully defined by the stock market's regulatory authority or are strictly defined and monitored by the asset management firm itself. In both countries, few mandate terms are defined by the national regulator. In the United States, the SEC has no official definition of most mandate terms, including such self-evident adjectives relating to a corporation's size such as "small cap," "mid-cap," and "large cap." More ambiguous terms like "ethical," "green," "Christian," "value," and "growth"—terms that reflect broad and contested ethical values or investment strategies—are similarly not defined by the SEC regulation (Cooper et al. 2003; O'Brian 2001). As long as an asset management firm does not define these terms in its prospectus, a "value" fund can legally invest entirely in "growth" corporations.

An alternative perspective of mandates is the *marketing perspective*; mandates are a brand, or marketing exercise, or story. Asset management firms design mandates in order to attract investors who associate with the brand. Likewise, clients choose money managers not only for their expertise, but also based on a social relationship of trust. This trust is facilitated when mandates mirror the clients' identity or affinities or tells a story that the client can literally buy into by placing money in the fund. In the same way that laundry soap brands seek to market themselves as unique, despite selling nearly identical products, asset management firms may advertise themselves as an "Islamic fund," "ethical fund," "technology fund," "small-company growth fund," or another niche identity. Such clustering of small numbers of firms into partially monopolized niche markets based on identity is pervasive in economic markets (White 2002), and in the asset management market, where "quality" is so elusive and uncertainty so high (O'Barr and Conley 1992a; Podolny 1993), niche market names may be particularly useful symbolic signals of quality and identity (Lounsbury and Rao 2004). Ethnographies (O'Barr and Conley 1992a, 1992b), interviews, and analyses of university endowment funds and public pension funds' trading behavior (Lakonishok et al. 1992; Shefrin 2000: 213–24), as well as one of my interviews with a director on a Malaysian investment committee, all suggest that a niche identity can contribute to attracting and retaining investors' money. These studies suggest that clients are attracted to asset-management funds that market themselves as active traders with a distinctive niche mandate. Asset-management firms can gain clients and therefore revenue by marketing multiple mandate niches independent of their actual investment behavior. In sum, according to the marketing perspective, a mandate is like a "brand" such as Coca-Cola; the ingredients of Coca-Cola no longer contain coca leaf or perhaps even kola nut (Pendergrast 1993) but the inaccurate brand name remains and continues to serve as a useful marketing tool.

Client Management and the Social Construction of Mandates and Benchmarks

In my perspective, a mandate is a more complex and flexible tool than either the economic or marketing perspectives suggest. A mandate is a *cultural tool* that assists a fund manager with interpreting her or his speculations of the future and arriving at a decision. Mandates also provide meaning to fund managers, since they can assist these players in justifying their behavior to their boss or their client by referring to their mandate. The mandate is therefore also a means of communication between the fund manager and those with whom she or he needs to communicate, including clients and coworkers. As a result, a mandate is like a code or a blueprint that provides fund managers with a template for how to invest (Griswold 1987).

Even financially sophisticated clients have a single, preeminent, implicit mandate, which is to receive high rates of return for their investment; they want to make money. More specifically, they want their fund's performance to outperform benchmarks associated with that fund's mandate. Money managers prefer a narrower mandate and therefore shape their clients' preferences. I argue that money managers' clients' preferences are endogenous and are predominantly constructed in their social interactions with money managers. This includes the operationalization of clients' ethical preferences into guidelines for ethical investment. In these interactions, money managers are in a more powerful position vis-à-vis their clients and shape their clients' preferences and perceptions to their advantage. As a consequence, money managers and asset management firms shape mandates to fit their professional and organizational needs, except insofar as the mandate is a credible marketing exercise.

I had previously described that mandate terms' precise definitions vary between the asset-management firms within which money managers work. In addition to this firm-level variance, however, there is also considerable leeway for the interpretation of the mandate, and it is part of the money managers' job to perform this task. For example, in the interview below, Puan Aysha,[10] a Malaysian fund manager of Islamic and ethical funds, explains that "[m]andates are broad, but you make them specific." In the following excerpt, Puan Aysha provides a stylized example of an interaction she would have with a client while opening a new account.

Aysha: Mandates are kind of broad, but you make it specific. Usually [the client gives] you a broad mandate, like, okay, "We are a government agency retirement fund." Maybe "we want stable income" or something like that. So when you draft up the agreement, you try to be specific. Because you don't want [the mandate] to be very broad because it will be difficult for you to manage. So you put in some kind of suggestion. "Do you want it to be ethical?" or something like that. And they say, "Okay, yeah, fine." So you just take that one. "Will you allow us to invest overseas?" . . . So you have to put in those guidelines and ask them. "Do you allow us to buy Second Board stocks?" "Do you allow us to buy non-trustee stocks?"

Pitluck: When you say "non-trustee" ones, what do you mean by that?

Aysha: We classify trustee . . . [*voice trailing*] I think that is a gray area, also, how you define trustee status. There's no such proper definition for that. But the most commonly used is that the stock must declare dividends for five years after listing. Of course there are exceptions to

> that. But that's the most widely used one. So if you have clients with very long-term objectives, I'm sure they would want companies that can declare dividends for them. So most—I'm not saying all—but most of the clients with long-term objectives require you to have either 100 percent, or a certain percentage in trustee stocks. They would give you maybe 70 percent or 50 percent or 100 percent.

In this narrative, note that the fund manager sought to narrow a broad investment objective—"stable income"—with specific categories of stocks allowable on the buy list (e.g., "Do you allow us to buy non-trustee stocks?") in her ideal-typical conversation with her client. And yet the terminology—for example "trustee stocks"—is not specific enough to actually constrain a fund manager's strategies (with exceptions detailed in the next section). A 70 percent threshold may be specific, and may in practice be a strict bright-line regulation for the asset-management firm's employees. But this "hard" constraint is "soft" if the definition of whether the corporation is a "trustee stock" is malleable and is partly a function of changing contextual factors such as its behavior relative to other corporations.

In Malaysian (Securities Commission 2005) and U.S. securities legislation (Langevoort 1996) such a conversation between Puan Aysha and her clients is legally necessary and the fund manager is legally bound to know the financial circumstances and objectives of the client. Because such client preferences are simultaneously created and shaped by the fund manager's conversation with the client, I refer to these preferences as "endogenous," that is, they are shaped by the process that reveals them.

The need for interpreting investment objectives for clients is particularly important when the broad mandate is not specified when the account is first opened. Another fund manager of Islamic funds, Hassan, described how this was rarely done for public sector client investors in the recent past:

> If you look at the fund management agreements, only now do you see objectives being stated, time horizons, benchmarks, etcetera. Previously there was no agreement. They just give you the money, and they expect you to make more money for them. . . . So when I took over [the account two years ago], the first thing I had to do was to actually try and figure out who are these people. Who are these institutions. What should be their required returns. Their risk tolerances. So that was the first thing. The second thing, then, would be, to restructure their portfolios to meet these objectives.

This was particularly true for the recent past when Malaysian federal and state government ministries were first beginning to invest their funds in the stock market. As Hassan described it, "It was like the blind leading the blind," since the early fund managers were typically accountants teaching themselves how to be fund managers.

Even a client's interpretation of the monthly, quarterly, and annual reports of their fund's performance (and that of their fund manager) is shaped by interactions with their fund manager.[11] This is because, firstly, even professional clients require money managers to interpret performance relative to a benchmark given the shifting macroeconomic context in which these investments are made (O'Barr and Conley 1992a: 172; Sheffrin 2000: 217). In addition, a fund's observable performance can be reinterpreted by referring to the unobservable risk absorbed or avoided (see also Beck 1992).[12] Secondly, fund performance is interpreted relative to a benchmark, and money managers typically have a great deal of power in suggesting these benchmarks and in interpreting them, thereby allowing "obfuscation games" to the fund manager's true performance (Sheffrin 2000: 159–74). Thirdly, there are high transaction costs involved in firing and replacing an external money manager (O'Barr and Conley 1992a) and often insufficient incentives to do so in mutual fund industries due to conflicts of interest (Bogle 2005: 139–214). Finally, the problems of interpreting a money manager's performance and the choice of a performance benchmark is exacerbated when funds have nonfinancial goals and/or constraints, as is the case in Islamic finance and SRI.

When performance is below expectations, the conversation continues in operationalizing the client's wishes into an investment strategy. As Hassan explained, "They [his clients] don't really understand, they don't really know what they themselves want. So basically it is up to me to impose it on them." Half an hour later in the interview, he stresses that without such cognitive management of his clients, they have "unrealistic expectations" of what is financially possible, and what risks are involved. Thus, not only are clients' preferences endogenous, but their ongoing expectations and interpretations of the funds' performance are as well.

Multiple studies in the United States have made similar observations regarding the asymmetrical relationship between money managers and bureaucratic clients, including civil servants, corporate treasury departments, and even financial corporations' investment committees (Sheffrin 2000: 213–24; see also Langevoort [1996]; Lakonishok et al. [1992]; O'Barr and Conley [1992a, 1992b]). In sum, money managers have considerable power to shape even sophisticated and powerful client investors' endogenous preferences.

What becomes evident in this section is that the social construction of mandates as practiced in both the United States and Malaysia offers one explanation for why socially responsible investing in the United States is so infrequently conducted and so poorly mapped to investors' stated preferences. I argue that mandates are a particularly weak constraint on money managers' behavior relative to the other social forces listed in figure 10.1, and therefore clients' preferences are not translated into their money managers' behavior. Mandates are socially constructed as a credible marketing exercise and by an unequal interaction between money managers and their clients. As a consequence, money managers and asset management firms use mandates as communication tools to lightly coordinate their investment strategies with the (malleable) endogenous preferences of clients.

In Malaysia, as in the United States, financial mandates appear to be a weak constraint on money managers' behavior. However, ethical investing in Malaysia, particularly Islamic finance, is treated as a strong constraint on money managers' actions. In the following section, I argue that the success of Islamic finance as a powerful influence on money managers' and corporations' behavior is not because of the proliferation of Islamic mandates, but rather because the Islamic finance social movement altered the nation's market structure.

THE POLITICAL ECONOMY OF MARKET STRUCTURE IN THE ISLAMIC CAPITAL MARKET

In Malaysia, Islamic finance's morality has been operationalized in a constellation of social forces I categorize as "market structure," a far stronger influence on money managers' behavior than firm-level and interaction-level mandates (recall figure 10.1). Market structure includes self-enforcing regulations within the stock exchange, national financial regulation by national political bodies on all exchanges within their jurisdictions (e.g., the Securities Commission, the Central Bank, and the Ministry of Finance), and finally the degree of enforcement of such written regulations. Market structure also includes informal regulations and local market cultures (Abolafia 1996; Pitluck 2005). I argue here that the uniform interpretation and enforcement of Islamic investing in Malaysia is created by a transformation of the market's structure, specifically the institutionalized role of the Syariah Advisory Council as a quasi-governmental body in concert with the Securities Commission. This has resulted in an unambiguous bifurcation of listed corporations as either "Syariah-compliant" or "noncompliant," accompanied by unambiguous rules to determine the investment universe for money managers with Islamic mandates. As a consequence, Islamic principles influence the behavior of listed corporations in Malaysia, at present narrowly, with the potential for wider influence in the future.

Like the socially responsible investment movement in the United States, in Islamic finance there is no universal ethical thresholds or uniform operationalization of Shariah principles. Fragmentation of Shariah interpretation exists not only at the level of differing traditions in Islamic jurisprudence (Warde 2000: 15–17, 32–37) and competing applied and academic standard-setting organizations,[13] but also at the level of individual financial firms with each having its own board of Shariah advisors (see also IOSCO

[2004: 64–65]). This has produced fragmentation of interpretation and operationalization of Shariah principles and periodic public distrust of Shariah advisors' independence from their paymasters as well as accusations of leniency of interpretation in favor of their paymasters (Iqbal and Molyneux 2005: 105–6, 109; Kahf 2004; Warde 2000: 226–30).

In contrast to SRI and nonfinancial mandates, all of which are primarily defined, operationalized, and audited by individual asset-management firms, the Malaysian government has created a national Syariah Advisory Council (SAC) to advise the Central Bank (Bank Negara) and the regulatory authority of the stock exchange (the Securities Commission, *Suruhanjaya Sekuriti*). Twice per year the SAC produces a list of Syariah-compliant securities in the Malaysian capital market, highlighting corporations added or removed from the previous list. As an institution, the SAC is unique among large Islamic capital markets (IOSCO 2004: 64–65) and enjoys support by its national government and legitimacy from the public.[14] This is a significant difference in market structure between Malaysia and other centers of Islamic finance in that, (1) the potential universe of ethical corporations is centrally determined and listed by a national body, and (2) this body is aligned with the national regulatory authority and is therefore able to require corporations to provide uniform documentation of whether they meet ethical criteria.

As a consequence, in contrast to financial mandates in Malaysia or to financial and SRI mandates in the United States, the definition of which corporations are Syariah-compliant is uniform across Malaysian asset-management firms and is operationalized within the firms as a bright-line constraint, as a true mandate in the economic perspective and as a social contract that strictly constrains the behavior of money managers. For example, in Malaysia, to be Syariah-compliant, the SAC requires that a corporation have a positive public image and engage in core activities that are beneficial to both the Muslim community and to the country (Securities Commission 2005). Like SRI, percentage limits of acceptable involvement are set in unacceptable industries. For example, such corporations may also generate up to 5 percent of their turnover and profit in clearly prohibited activities such as earning interest, gambling, liquor, or pork. There are also 10 percent thresholds for prohibited activities that Malaysian society finds difficult to avoid, such as tobacco. Finally, there is a 25 percent threshold for lines of business that involve activities that are deemed nonpermissible. For example, hotel and resort operations often involve nonpermissive activities, such as mixed-sex massage or swimming pools, such that a Syariah-compliant corporation can only generate up to a quarter of its profit or turnover by owning or operating a hotel or resort (Securities Commission 2005).

Thus in Malaysia, in contrast to mandate terms like "growth" or "income," and in contrast to Shariah-compliance in most other countries in the world, including in the United States, money managers in Malaysia work with a uniform definition of "Syariah-compliance" and a uniform list of corporations in their universe of strategic decision making. In 2006, Syariah-compliant corporations constituted approximately 63 percent of total market capitalization. As of May 2006 this universe of 871 securities constituted 85 percent of listings on the Malaysian stock market (Securities Commission 2006b: 18). The pragmatic standards of Syariah-compliance are therefore, in practice, not too distant from current corporate economic practices in Malaysia. Nevertheless, due to Malaysia's historic legacy of Chinese capitalists and its current multiethnic and multireligious population, a large percentage of these Syariah-compliant corporations are run by non-Muslims and without any religious corporate identity or mission.

The potential power of the Islamic capital market on corporate behavior in Malaysia can be understood by examining the SAC's recommendations for firms that lose their Syariah-compliance status. The SAC (Securities Commission 2006a: 10), like any investment manager, uses boilerplate language such as: "This document does not constitute a recommendation to buy or sell the listed Syariah-compliant securities by the Securities Commission's Syariah Advisory Council." Nevertheless, in the same document five pages later, they unequivocally state that in the case of the fourteen Syariah-compliant corporations that were recategorized as "Syariah-non compliant securities," "[t]he SAC advises investors who invest based on Syariah principles to dispose of any Syariah-noncompliant securities which they presently hold, within a month of knowing the status of the securities" (Securities Commission 2006a: 15). Every fund manager I interviewed with an Islamic portfolio is required by his or her firm to completely disinvest in any corporation that loses its Syariah-compliant status.

What influence, if any, does this coherent and uniform vision of Islamic investing have on corporate behavior in Malaysia? Islamic principles influence the behavior of corporations listed in Malaysia, at present narrowly, but with the potential for wider influence in the future.

In 2006, regulators and Islamic fund managers did not believe that there was an "Islamic premium" for corporations that behave according to Islamic principles, nor that there was a "penalty" for non-Syariah-compliant corporations. This is because, at present, the size of funds invested in the Malaysian stock market under an Islamic mandate is small relative to the size of the entire market. When a corporation loses its Syariah-compliant status, Islamic funds are required to wholly sell their corporate shares, but there are sufficient investors to purchase it, so share prices are not affected in the medium term.

One important influence on corporate behavior, however, was noted by regulators in the Securities Commission and by members of the Syariah Advisory Council. Syariah-compliant corporations are required to earn no more than 5 percent of turnover or profits before tax from interest income. Corporations with funds stored in the conventional banking system can easily find themselves in violation of this single criterion for maintaining their Syariah-compliant status. The solution is logistically simple and potentially profitable—to move funds from the conventional banking system to the Islamic banking system. As a consequence, at present the single notable influence on corporate behavior of the Syariah Advisory Council's uniform definition of Syariah-compliance appears to be a steady pressure for Malaysian corporations to withdraw savings from the conventional banking system and to increase savings in the Islamic banking system.

Two potentially reversible trends suggest that Islamic finance may have a larger influence on Malaysian corporations' behavior in the future. Firstly, as the size of the Islamic banking system grows relative to the conventional banking system, the pool of funds invested under an Islamic mandate will also grow. This will make stock market prices increasingly sensitive to whether corporations' behavior meets Islamic criteria. Secondly, the federal government, the largest investor in the Malaysian capital market, is under pressure to increasingly invest using Islamic criteria. The federal government is either directly or indirectly responsible for the investment of funds under a forced savings scheme for all workers (the Employee Provident Fund) as well as the management of optional savings and pension schemes designed to redress racial inequalities in economic growth (e.g., *Permodalan Nasional Berhad*). At present, with the exception of a few state governments, these funds can be invested in any corporation with the exception of those involved in alcohol, gambling, and (sometimes) tobacco. Malaysian money managers of these funds describe this mandate as "ethical" rather than Islamic—a weaker set of nonfinancial constraints on their decision making disconnected from the Syariah Advisory Council. There are conflicting political pressures on the government both to maximize its returns for its citizen-investors as well as to invest according to a wide range of political criteria. Although Malaysia is a multiethnic and multireligious country, the state is under some pressure by Malay nationalism, the *dakwah* movement, and pan-Islamism, to increasingly invest according to Islamic criteria, as operationalized by the SAC (see also Abdul Razak Baginda and Schier [2002]; Gomez and Jomo [1999]).

In the future, if government and government-linked funds are increasingly invested under an Islamic mandate, and/or as the Islamic banking system grows relative to the size of the conventional banking system, stock market prices will grow increasingly sensitive to whether a corporation's behavior meets Syariah compliance. The stock market prices of Syariah-compliant corporations may increasingly have an "Islamic premium" while noncompliant corporations may absorb a "penalty." For noncompliant corporations, there are numerous potential consequences of this. These include a decline in the "paper" wealth of managers holding stock, a decline in the corporation's capacity to acquire loans by using its stock as collateral, a decrease in investors' and/or consumers' confidence in the corporation and an increase in the corporation's cost of future financing (Demirgüç-Kunt and Levine 2001). Corporate boards of directors therefore have numerous personal and professional interests in sustaining their corporations' stock market prices. In the future, Malaysian corporations that are listed as Syariah-compliant, regardless of the religious makeup of the corporation's board of directors or management, may have an increasing material interest in maintaining their corporation's categorization as Syariah-compliant by avoiding corporate behavior that the SAC may regard as contrary to Islamic principles.

CONCLUSION

In this chapter, I have argued that the investment mandates to which clients subscribe in order to constrain money managers' behavior are, at best, a weak constraint. Because clients have an "implicit mandate" of making money and due to clients' reliance on money managers to interpret whether this is achieved, what the mandate is, and whether the mandate is being enacted, I prefer to view mandates as a marketing exercise to attract funds, as well as a social construction coproduced by money managers and their clients in an asymmetrical relationship to ease the cognitive and organizational tasks of the former. The weakness of mandates as a guide to money managers' investment and disinvestment behavior is a partial explanation for the failure of socially responsible investing in the United States to reflect investors' interest in ethical constraints, as well as to reflect their ethical criteria. In the United States, in 2006, approximately only $7 in every $100 was invested according to "ethical criteria," and these ethical criteria were diverse and often contradictory, thereby decreasing any potential for this small segment of investors to influence corporate behavior.

In most of the world's stock markets with an Islamic capital market (including the United States), money managed using Islamic criteria is treated like any other mandate; the specifications and the day-to-day operationalization of the mandate's principles vary by asset-management firm. In Malaysia, in contrast, due to global and national Islamic-finance social movements, there has been a single quasi-governmental body (the Syariah Advisory Council) associated with the national stock market regulators that twice per year updates a list of which corporations are Syariah-compliant (that is, not violating Islamic criteria of ethical investment) and non-Syariah-compliant. This nationwide coordinating mechanism has created a bifurcation of the stock market into a large Syariah-compliant segment and a relatively smaller non-Syariah-compliant segment with fewer potential investors. If a Malaysian corporation is recategorized by the Syariah Advisory Council from Syariah-compliant to non-Syariah-compliant, fund managers with Islamic mandates are required to sell the corporation. At this point in time, the size of Islamic funds is not sufficiently large to create material incentives for corporate management, regardless of their religious affiliation, to maintain their Syariah-compliant status by avoiding corporate behaviors at odds with Islamic principles. The one significant exception to this is a pressure on Syariah-compliant corporations to move their surplus funds to the Islamic banking system from the conventional banking system. In the future, if Malaysia's Islamic banking system continues to grow as a percentage of the finance industry, and/or if popular or political pressure requires the federal government to invest its substantial funds under an Islamic mandate, Malaysian corporations will grow under increasing pressure to behave according to Islamic criteria, as written and judged by the Syariah Advisory Council.

In conclusion, ethical investing has a potentially large influence on corporate behavior. Drawing on ethnographic interview evidence of the ways that money managers make their investment and disinvestment decisions, as well as the academic literature on money managers' behavior in the United States, I suggest that a social movement promoting ethical investment is insufficient to alter corporate behavior. However, as observed in Malaysia, if the social movement puts pressure on the government to alter the market structure of the stock exchange so that a common ethical standard and common interpretation of that standard is provided to the capital market (in Malaysia, this is the Syariah Advisory Council), stock market prices can be socially constructed to be sensitive to corporations' ethical behavior. In Malaysia, this acts as a guide to corporate behavior in compliance with the ethical criteria set out and interpreted by the Syariah Advisory Council. In other countries' stock markets, the ethical regulations could be nonreligious and shaped by the national regulatory authority, just as current financial regulations are designed to shape corporate behavior.

NOTES

Acknowledgments. This research would have been impossible without the generosity of time and insight from my Malaysian interviewees in the finance industry. This paper is stronger due to the feedback I've received at the University of Chicago's Workshop on Money, Markets and Consumption, the Society for Economic Anthropology's Annual Meeting, the American Anthropological Association Annual Meeting, the European Business Ethics Network Research Conference, and the SASE Annual meeting. This research was originally formulated under a Fellowship of the Center for Southeast Asian Studies (University of Wisconsin–Madison). This research has been generously funded by a Fulbright (IIE) Research Grant, an Illinois State University New Faculty Initiative Grant, College of Arts and Sciences Travel Grant, and the American Sociological Association's Travel Award Grant (SES-0548370) supported by the National Science Foundation. I received valuable detailed feedback from John Boatright, Kate Browne, Julie Hogeland, Karin Knorr-Cetina, Lynne Milgram, Paul Rivera, Shann Turnbull, and Neeraj Vedwan.

1. MMA, a financial services company, was formerly known as Mennonite Mutual Aid. Note that in contrast to MMA's 2003 title, the report's data is a random sample that includes respondents that do not self-identify as religious or spiritual.

2. In the MMA survey of investors' concerns, on a five-point scale in which 5 is "very likely to avoid investing" and 1 is "not likely to avoid investing," sweatshops, product safety, high executive compensation, and environment respectively received 4.0, 3.9, 3.8, and 3.6.

3. This ranking is based on the total net assets of funds *without* a mandate to invest in one or more social criteria. For example, the two highest-ranked social screens were tobacco and alcohol, suggesting that these are the most common social constraints on investment (used singly or in combination with other criteria) in SRI funds.

4. Note that the one-third figure and the 7 percent figure are not strictly comparable because not all investors have equal wealth or make equally large investments in the stock market. Nevertheless, this comparison does provide an indication of a significant gap between investors' preferences and existing investment behavior.

5. I suggest that this influence is "weak" because shareholders have very little influence over U.S. corporate behavior in annual general meetings. Arguably the influence is larger for large investors who capture a seat on the board of directors—although to gain a seat also requires extra-democratic persuasion (Bogle 2005; Sobering 1981). Were we to include shareholder activism in our definition of SRI, the number of dollars invested would rise to almost $10 in every $100 under professional management (Social Investment Forum 2006).

6. The 15.3 percent back-of-the-envelope calculations are based on Malaysian data (e.g., Bank Negara [2006] and Securities Commission [2006b]) and the Social Investment Forum's (2006: 2, 38–39) definition of social investment. Specifically, since 8 percent of all unit trust (pension) funds are Syariah-compliant (Securities Commission 2006b), and RM98,484.89 million is held in unit trusts, then approximately RM7878.79 million is managed in Syariah-based unit trusts. An additional RM7,790.47 million is managed by the Employee Provident Fund, which my interviewees report is managed using "ethical criteria" (see main text for a Malaysia-specific definition distinct from Islamic finance). An additional RM3,341.97 million is managed by diverse government agencies and government bodies that my interviewees report is managed according to clients' criteria, which is typically Islamic or ethical criteria. This totals to RM19,011.33 million total funds managed using Islamic or ethical criteria out of RM124,162.65 million total funds managed under licensed fund managers (Bank Negara 2006), and therefore 15.3 percent. To the degree that this estimate based on aggregate data is accurate, it is comparable to the survey-based Social Investment Forum (2006) estimate.

7. This is the correct spelling in Malaysia. This article also uses *Shariah*, a common transliteration in English.

8. The exceptions are governments that by fiat have required that their entire banking system conform to Islamic criteria. In 2004 these are Sudan, Iran, and contestably Pakistan (Kahf 2004: 30–32; Iqbal and Molyneux 2005: 36–71).

9. Moody's Investors Service, a credit-rating agency, estimates that $300 billion is invested in Islamic mutual funds and an additional $250 billion in Islamic banks (IOSCO 2004: 35; Prystay 2006; Warde 2000: 6). As Warde (2000: 6–9) outlines, such figures are point estimates with wide margins of error since a census of Islamic financial institutions is nonexistent and the reporting standards in many emerging markets are poor.

10. Aysha is a pseudonym, like all interviewees' names in this article.

11. I wish to thank Julie Hogeland for debating my original formulation.

12. For example, consider the aforementioned American Century Heritage Fund that invested outside of its mandate in risky Argentine debt. The risk of the Argentine government choosing in the future not to repay its creditors is real but unobservable unless it occurs. Prior to the default in 2001, the American Century Heritage Fund didn't need to explain to its investors that its high returns were in part a function of their decision to purchase such risky debt. After the default, the fund lost investors' money and the fund could interpret this poor performance as a consequence of a rare and risky event.

13. The two primary standard-setting bodies are the Islamic Fiqh Academy and the International Association of Islamic Banks (Henry and Wilson 2004: 5; Iqbal and Molyneux 2005: 108; Warde 2000: 229). Arguably such standard setting has increasingly fragmented in recent years as academic Islamic finance research institutes create new interpretations of Shariah principles outside of the "new power alliance" (Kahf 2004) of Shariah religious scholars and financial industry economists.

14. In 2004 the only other countries with Shariah certification conducted by national regulators were Indonesia, Sudan, and Pakistan (IOSCO 2004: 64–65). None of these countries in 2004 had an economically significant stock market relative to the size of their respective national economies.

REFERENCES

Abdul Razak Baginda and Peter Schier. 2002. *Is Malaysia an Islamic State? Secularism and Theocracy: A Study of the Malaysian Constitution*. Kuala Lumpur: Malaysian Strategic Research Centre.

Abolafia, Mitchel Y. 1996. *Making Markets: Opportunism and Restraint on Wall Street*. Cambridge, MA: Harvard University Press.

American Century Investment Services. 2006. *American Century Investments Prospectus. Heritage Fund*. March 1, 2006.

American Heritage. 2000. *American Heritage Dictionary of the English Language*, 4th edition. Boston: Houghton Mifflin.

Bank Negara. 1999. *The Central Bank and the Financial System in Malaysia: A Decade of Change, 1989–1999*. Kuala Lumpur: Bank Negara Malaysia.

———. 2006. Statement of Assets. Kula Lumpur: Bank Negara Malaysia. www.bnm.gov.my/files/ib_statistic/2006/pdf/asset1.pdf (accessed January 15, 2007).

Beck, Ulrich. 1992. *Risk Society: Towards a New Modernity*. London: Sage.

Bogle, John C. 2005. *The Battle for the Soul of Capitalism*. New Haven, CT: Yale University Press.

Brügger, Urs. 2000. Speculating: Work in Financial Markets. Theme issue, "Facts and Figures: Economic Representations and Practices," *Ökonomie und Gesellschasft Jahrbuch* 16: 229–55.

Chandra Muzaffar. 1987. *Islamic Resurgence in Malaysia*. Petaling Jaya, Malaysia: Fajar Bakti.

Clark, Gordon L., and Nigel Thrift. 2005. The Return of Bureaucracy: Managing Dispersed Knowledge in Global Finance. In *The Sociology of Financial Markets*, ed. Karin Knorr Cetina and Alex Preda, 229–49. Oxford and New York: Oxford University Press.

Cooper, Michael J., Huseyin Gulen, and P. Raghavendra Rau. 2003. Changing Names with Style: Mutual Fund Name Changes and Their Effects on Fund Flows. Unpublished MS.

Demirgüç-Kunt, Asli, and Ross Levine. 2001. *Financial Structure and Economic Growth: A Cross-Country Comparison of Banks, Markets, and Development*. Cambridge, MA: MIT Press.

Domini, Amy. 2001. *Socially Responsible Investing: Making a Difference and Making Money*. Chicago: Dearborn Trade.

Economic Planning Unit (Malaysia). 2006. *Ninth Malaysia Plan, 2006–2010*. Putrajaya, Malaysia: Economic Planning Unit, Prime Minister's Department.

Gomez, Edmund, and K. S. Jomo. 1999. *Malaysia's Political Economy: Politics, Patronage and Profits*. Cambridge and New York: Cambridge University Press.

Griswold, Wendy. 1987. A Methodological Framework for the Sociology of Culture. *Sociologica Methodology* 17: 1–35.

Henry, Clement, and Rodney Wilson. 2004. Introduction. In *The Politics of Islamic Finance*, ed. Clement M. Henry and Rodney Wilson, 1–14. Edinburgh: Edinburgh University Press.

Inglehart, Ronald, and Christian Welzel. 2005. *Modernization, Cultural Change, and Democracy: The Human Development Sequence*. Cambridge and New York: Cambridge University Press.

Iqbal, Munawar, and Philip Molyneux. 2005. *Thirty Years of Islamic Banking: History, Performance and Prospects*. Houndmills, UK: Palgrave Macmillan.

IOSCO (International Organization of Securities Commissions). 2004. *Islamic Capital Market Fact Finding Report*. Report of the Islamic Capital Market Task Force of the IOSCO.

Jensen, Michael C., and William H. Meckling. 1976. Theory of the Firm: Managerial Behavior, Agency Costs and Ownership Structure. *Journal of Financial Economics* 3: 305–60.

Kahf, Monzer. 2004. Islamic Banks: The Rise of a New Power Alliance of Wealth and *Shari'a* Scholarship. In *The Politics of Islamic Finance*, ed. Clement M. Henry and Rodney Wilson, 17–36. Edinburgh: Edinburgh University Press.

Lakonishok, Josef, with Andrei Shleifer and Robert Vishny. 1992. The Structure and Performance of the Money Management Industry. *Brookings Papers on Economic Activity*, 331–39. Washington, DC: Brookings Institution.

Langevoort, Donald C. 1996. Selling Hope, Selling Risk: Some Lessons for Law from Behavioral Economics about Stockbrokers and Sophisticated Customers. *California Law Review* 84: 627–701.

Lauricella, Tom. 2006. U.S. Stock Funds Need a Map. *Wall Street Journal*, February 24.

Lounsbury, Michael, and Hayagreeva Rao. 2004. Sources of Durability and Change in Market Classifications: A Study of the Reconstitution of Product Categories in the American Mutual Fund Industry, 1944–1985. *Social Forces* 82(3): 969–99.

Maurer, Bill. 2002. Anthropological and Accounting Knowledge in Islamic Banking and Finance: Rethinking Critical Accounts. *Journal of the Royal Anthropological Institute* 8: 645–67.

MMA. 2003. *The Ethical Issues Report: What Matters to Religious Investors: MMA's National Survey of Religious Americans and How Business Ethics Affect Their Attitudes about Investing*. Goshen, IN: MMA, www.mma-online.org/pdf/2030459_investing_survey.pdf (accessed August 11, 2006).

O'Barr, William M., and John M. Conley. 1992a. *Fortune and Folly: The Wealth and Power of Institutional Investing*. Homewood, IL: Business One Irwin.

———. 1992b. Managing Relationships: The Culture of Institutional Investing. *Financial Analysts Journal* (Sept–Oct): 21–27.

O'Brian, Bridget. 2001. Quarterly Mutual Funds Review: What's in a Name? To the SEC, 80% of a Fund—Agency's Revised Rule Leads to Change in Appellations and Revisions in Focus. *Wall Street Journal*, July 9.

Pendergrast, Mark. 1993. *For God, Country, and Coca-Cola: The Unauthorized History of the Great American Soft Drink and the Company That Makes It*. New York: Scribner's.

Pitluck, Aaron Z. 2005. "Social Cognitive Networks in an Emerging Market: A Sociology of Speculation in the Malaysian Stock Market." PhD dissertation, University of Wisconsin–Madison.

Podolny, Joel M. 1993. A Status-Based Model of Market Competition. *American Journal of Sociology* 98: 829–72.

Prystay, Cris. 2006. Malaysia Seeks Role as Global Player after Nurturing Islamic Bond Market. *Wall Street Journal*, August 9: C1.

Securities and Exchange Commission (United States). 2004. Invest Wisely: An Introduction to Mutual Funds, www.sec.gov/investor/pubs/inwsmf.htm (accessed November 2, 2004).

Securities Commission (Malaysia). 2001. *Capital Market Masterplan Malaysia*. Kuala Lumpur: Securities Commission.

———. 2002. *SIDC: The Quarterly Bulletin of the Securities Industry Development Centre*, Various Issues. Kuala Lumpur: Securities Industry Development Centre.

———. 2005. *Guidelines on Compliance Function for Fund Managers*. Kuala Lumpur: Suruhanjaya Sekuriti. Date Issued/Effective 15 March 2005.

———. 2006a. *Senarai Sekuriti Patuh Syariah oleh Majlis Penasihat Syariah Suruhanjaya Sekuriti/List of Syariah-Compliant Securities by the Syariah Advisory Council of the Securities Commission*. Kuala Lumpur: Suruhanjaya Sekuriti, April 27.

———. 2006b. *Malaysian ICM: Quarterly Bulletin of Malaysian Islamic Capital Market by the Securities Commission*. Various issues.

Shamsul A. B. 1997. Identity Construction, Nation Formation, and Islamic Revivalism in Malaysia. In *Islam in an Era of Nation-States: Politics and Religious Renewal in*

Muslim Southeast Asia, ed. Robert W. Hefner and Patricia Horvatich, 207–27. Honolulu: University of Hawaii Press.

Sheffrin, Hersh. 2000. *Beyond Greed and Fear: Understanding Behavioral Finance and the Psychology of Investing*. Boston: Harvard Business School Press.

Sobering, Barry James. 1981. Comment: Shareholder Democracy: A Description and Critical Analysis of the Proxy System. *North Carolina Law Review* 146(60): 145–69.

Social Investment Forum. 2006. *2005 Report on Socially Responsible Investing Trends in the United States: 10-Year Review*. Washington, DC: Social Investment Forum, Industry Research Program.

Usmani, Muhammad Taqi. 2002. *An Introduction to Islamic Finance*. Arab and Islamic Laws Series. The Hague: Kluwer Law International.

Warde, Ibrahim. 2000. *Islamic Finance in the Global Economy*. Edinburgh: Edinburgh University Press.

———. 2004. Global Politics, Islamic Finance and Islamist Politics Before and After 11 September 2001. In *The Politics of Islamic Finance*, ed. Clement M. Henry and Rodney Wilson, 37–62. Edinburgh: Edinburgh University Press.

White, Harrison. 2002. *Markets from Networks: Socioeconomic Models of Production*. Princeton, NJ: Princeton University Press.

Zainah Anwar. 1987. *Islamic Revivalism in Malaysia: Dakwah among the Students*. Petaling Jaya, Malaysia: Pelanduk.

Afterword

Moral Economies, Economic Moralities

Consider the Possibilities!

Bill Maurer

> If to die you invite me, do not ask me for pardon; smiling I accept gladly a gift so glorious.
>
> —Seneca, in Monteverdi's *L'incoronazione di Poppea* (c. 1642)

> I'm still optimistic, and intend to keep trying.
>
> —George M. Foster (1966)

In a recent review essay, Gerda Roelvink (2007) helpfully identifies two tendencies in new literature on the market. One, represented by David Harvey (2003), seeks to describe and document the ongoing dispossession of the peoples of the world by capitalist relations of production. The other, represented by Michel Callon (1998), stands opposed to this documentary project, because, it is argued, the critical analysis of capitalism is part and parcel of its consolidation and helps to perform it. Callon seeks an approach to economics and markets that interrupts tales of capitalism's dominance and triumph with accounts of its messiness. Indeed, Callon captures a certain analytical exhaustion with the old paradigms of Marxist-inspired critique. One might add in this regard J. K. Gibson-Graham's (2006) politics of "economic possibility," which unsettles capitalism's totality by drawing attention to alternative "economic" relationships and the linguistic practices that subsume them under capitalism. Nigel Thrift (2000) has been attempting to produce a "nonrepresentational" account of economies, since like Callon and Gibson-Graham he sees in the very representation of capitalism, whether critical or not, a performative affirmation of capitalism's unquestioned power that conjures what it critiques.

The chapters collected in this volume sit uneasily between these two tendencies. On the one hand, they could be read as descriptions of proliferating and diverse relationships that do and do not constitute "economies" as conventionally understood.[1] By drawing attention to gifting taking place within, alongside, or in defiance of conventional capitalist economic relationships, the authors provide evidence for Gibson-Graham's claim that there is much more to "the" economy that can be captured in the standard or critical narratives (see Halperin, this volume). On the other hand, they show the dual nature of these gifts—for a gift always leaves one indebted, and, in capitalism, those debts are generally owed the rich and powerful (see Walsh, Robbins, and Halperin, this volume). Gifts pauperize, Rajak reminds us in this volume, borrowing from Charles Dickens. They can also serve as an ideological cover for exploitation or expropriation, or, in other words, business as usual, but with a friendlier face. Efforts to ensure "accountability" along with "participation" (see Werner, this volume) and discourses of "responsibility" (see Garsten, and Hernes and Rajak among others, this volume) depoliticize corporate decisions and denature critical perspectives on them. It's hard to be against "social responsibility," after all. And it's hard not to accept the gift.

In this concluding chapter, I would like to reflect on the juxtaposition of the terms *morality* and *economy* that animates this book. I have two broad points to make. The first is that we should pause to consider how we are part of the broader movement we seek to analyze. It is not just within anthropology that people are once again fascinated with the relationship between morality and economy. The chapters collected here show that the same excitement is spreading throughout the business and investment communities (see Pitluck, Dolan, Rajak, Garsten, and Hernes, this volume). They also show reactions ranging from acceptance to ambivalence to hostility toward moral dilemmas posed by newly commoditized crises, like radioactive waste (see Werner, this volume) or global warming (witness the now near universal acceptance of market mechanisms like carbon trading schemes to address fossil fuel emissions). The use of market mechanisms—and participatory ones at that—to deal with such crises is increasingly common. Behavioral economics in the academy and a spate of recent popular books by economists demonstrate the wide dispersion of the idea that economies can be, should be, are already infused with moral values or virtues. Some of these are on the order of Voltaire's Dr. Pangloss: with the apparent global demise of state socialism and the spread of market ideologies and practices worldwide and in seemingly every domain of life, perhaps the capitalist market offers—or could offer—the best of all possible worlds after all (e.g., Bragdon [2006]; McCloskey [2006]; Young [2003]).

The second broad point I hope to make in this concluding chapter is that we should be wary of the juxtaposition of morality and economy itself and that we should allow it to continue to trouble us. There is a danger in resting comfortably once we have discovered the moral foundations of capitalist economies or the moral economies that lie alongside and present alternatives to them. The danger is that making such discovery our analytical or political objective might lie in the way of opening ourselves up to other possibilities we cannot imagine in the present. It bears remembering the crucial place of unintended consequences in Weber's (1992 [1930]) argument in *The Protestant Ethic and the Spirit of Capitalism.* If one effect of Protestant asceticism was the funneling of accumulated wealth into enterprises rather than its expenditure on luxuries, which in turn propelled capital formation, we have to be open to the possibility that there may be effects of apparently unfettered commodification and marketization that we cannot discern at the present time and that may not square with our current imagination of the ends of those processes.

First, I explore our own implication in the relationship between morality and economy. This brings me to the epigraphs to this chapter. In Monteverdi's opera, *L'incoronazione di Poppea,* the stoic philosopher Seneca dispassionately faces Roman Emperor Nerone's order that he commit suicide and thereby enacts one of the chief virtues he has tried to instill in his followers: principled, willing indifference toward all that surrounds him. For Seneca, death is a glorious gift because it flies in the face of worldly attachments, themselves apparitions lying in the way of true knowledge. Love is one such attachment. Commentators on the opera have argued that it can be read as a stoic reflection on the transitory and false nature of love, false because a mere surface appearance distracting humanity from deeper virtues. Indeed, to a modern audience the opera is disturbing: the plot concerns the despotic emperor's desire to marry his mistress, his true love, Poppea, and dispatch his wife, Ottavia. The moral of the story is explicit: love conquers all. That conquest is not necessarily a just one. The opera concludes with a beautiful duet by Nerone and Poppea, in which they affirm their love for one another after having been crowned by Amore:

Amore

> The consuls and tribunes, Poppea, have crowned thee empress,
> Reigning o'er all Rome's dominions,
> Now thou art crowned by Love,
> O thou happiest of women, over all of earth's beauties,
> Of beauties thou art the empress . . .

Nerone and Poppea

> I adore you, I desire you, I embrace you, I enchain you,
> No more grieving, no more sorrow
> O my dearest, o my beloved [Act III, scene 8; Jacobs translation; in Curtis 1989].

Yet Love has indeed conquered: in the course of the play, Seneca is forced to kill himself because he stands in the way of Poppea and Nerone's wishes, and the empress Ottavia is banished, along with the young lovers Drusilla and Ottone, who had gotten caught up in Nerone's plot to kill her (the latter having cross-dressed as the former in a thwarted attempt to steal upon and murder Poppea while she was sleeping; this, too, done in the name of love). Poppea ascends to the throne. Her nurse, Arnalta, reflects ambivalently at the end of the play about the change that has taken place in her own station in life. Those of high status regret the end of their days, she muses, while those born to serve welcome it. She wonders whether it wouldn't have been better to have been born a lady and die a servant, rather than to have been born a servant and die on "the steps of greatness" where "all conspire to praise" her, even though, as she says, "I know I'm only a bag of wrinkles like some pre-Roman ruin" (Act III, Scene 7). Although drawn to the pleasures of the good life that awaits her, the nurse, like Seneca, is quite aware of the insincerity of surface appearances. Given the fate of the historical Poppea—Nerone eventually killed her—a contemporary of Monteverdi's would have seen in the opera a repudiation of love because it trucks in appearance, flattery, and inconstancy, and an exaltation of the virtues exemplified in Seneca and perhaps Poppea's nurse.[2]

The second epigraph is from George M. Foster's (1965) rebuttal to criticisms of his classic article, "Peasant Society and the Image of Limited Good." In a series of numbered paragraphs, David Kaplan and Benson Saler, in 1966, pulled apart some of the methodological and epistemological problems they found in Foster's essay. Foster responded in turn. Foster's essay today is remembered for its essentially conservative take on peasants. Since, according to Foster, they operate as if in a world of limited good, such that one person's gain is always another person's loss, peasants' shared cognitive orientation (his term) has the effect of promoting equality rather than status competition. Everyone knows the game is zero sum and resources can neither be created anew nor augmented, so everyone knows that if one gets ahead it is at the expense of another. The result is a steady-state equilibrium.

The discussion in the pages of *American Anthropologist* over Foster's thesis had to do with whether peasant societies were closed systems or not, whether one could ascribe to them a shared cognitive orientation after all, and whether they did in fact achieve equilibrium. But the debate also had to do with the nature of the reality that is accessible to the anthropologist. For Foster, the cognitive orientation of peasants was something "psychologically real" (1965: 294). Yet how does one arrive at such "reality"? How is it observable, accessible, and commensurable with the anthropologist's ways of knowing and perceiving? With the benefit of hindsight, we can see the lineaments of a by now tired discussion in American anthropology over the limits of cognitive anthropology and its emphasis on culture in the mind rather than culture in the intersubjective space between minds, as it were. We can also hear echoes of long-standing debates in anthropology over the existence and possibility of translating incommensurable difference. There are also elements of an even broader discussion in the human sciences and the Western philosophical tradition over empiricism: how can one observe a psychological reality, anyway, and what kinds of claims about it can one make given all the prior work necessary to render that reality the object of empirical investigation?

In one way or another, these were all questions leveled against Foster. I am struck by his response: one paragraph consisting of exactly one sentence, affirming that optimistic standpoint of universalistic humanism, *homo sum, humani nihil a me alienum puto* (I am human; nothing human is alien to me). It also affirms a continuous, never-ending quest for knowledge, emphasizing the effort—I will keep trying—over the result.

Though I had never really cared much for Foster's analysis of peasant society, I was reminded of it by a series of questions suggested by the ethnographically rich and theoretically compelling chapters in this volume and, going back to it, I was captivated by that one-sentence paragraph. First, I was led back to Foster by the chapters' consideration of the possibility of a moral economy. As Katherine Browne's introduction reminds us, and as Joel Robbins discusses in his chapter, from Foster to James Scott's (1977) moral economy of the peasant, to Michael Taussig's (1980) *Devil and Commodity Fetishism*, and indeed throughout the anthropological canon there are numerous examples of peasant peoples and those newly incorporated into the capitalist world system either evidencing their own moral critique of capitalist relations of production or being enlisted as part of such a critique by anthropologists and other social scientists (see also chapters by Little and Prentice, this volume). Second, I was interested in how the debate over access to the "reality" of other ways of being resonated with the suggestion presented by these chapters that there is more to capitalism than meets the eye. Both anthropology and Marxism, for different reasons, have struggled with the possibility of grasping an outside, an other, an alternative, or a critique in spite of the presumed totality of culture or capitalism. For Marx, it was capitalism itself that presented the conditions of possibility for its own critique—Marxism as capitalism's internal critique *required* capitalism, just as the working class required its constitution as a class in itself by capitalist relations of production in order to become a class conscious of itself that would then have revolutionary potential. Similarly, the very idea that one can stand "outside" one's culture is itself a product of the principle that we are all enmeshed in webs of significance not of our making or choosing, to paraphrase Geertz (1973). And we have been continuously reminded, from Althusser (1974) to Zizek (1989) to Haraway (1997) and even beyond the critical tradition, that the very moment we think we have achieved a point "outside" is the moment we are most "inside" our own lifeworld with its deep investment in the idea of enlightened reason surmounting mere tradition and worldly commitments.

One might explore the unexpected homology between Monteverdi's Seneca and George Foster on the question of the real and its constancy, versus the falsity of surface appearances. This would lead us to wonder why anthropologists and others, including those we often study, seem both fascinated and horrified at the supposedly increasingly abstract "economy of appearances" (Tsing 2000) that some argue characterizes the global economy. The "violence of abstraction" (Comaroff and Comaroff 1999) entailed in contemporary economy has spurred a new generation of moral critique couched in terms of hidden or occult forces beyond the grasp of mere mortals. Monteverdi's Seneca might join anthropologists Edward LiPuma and Benjamin Lee (2004) in decrying financial derivatives, for example, for objectifying and abstracting "risk" itself as a tradable commodity, and displacing the presumably more "real" economy of production with the speculative and fictional economy of circulation.

As may be evident, I am skeptical of the implicit (and sometimes explicit) quest to discover a real economy behind the surface fictions of the contemporary economy. As I have argued elsewhere, grain (for example) is just as "abstract" as grain futures (Maurer 2005a). The former depends on practices of purification and stabilization of discrete tiny objects as "grains," and then, subsequently, their being made fungible with one another such that they can be understood "in bulk." Money operates similarly—the dollar I deposit into the bank does not need to be the same material object as the one I take out of the automatic teller machine. Fungibility and the abstraction that enables it are at once material and discursive practices. They are no more fictional and no less real than anything else to which humans turn their activity. The understanding of abstraction as a "fiction" and of fictions as masking realities is itself part of the Western folk theory of money and economy (Bloch and Parry [1989]; see also Maurer [2006]).

All of this is to say that the emphasis on the real for Monteverdi's Seneca and for George Foster is interesting, not for its explanatory potential, but for being exemplary of analytical *and* cultural preoccupations with "reality" in the face of the apparently fictional, whether fictions of love or fictions of speculation of the intellectual (Foster 1965) or economic (Marx 1977; LiPuma and Lee 2004) kind.

Monteverdi's Seneca warns us that love is not moral—introducing a third term alongside reality and fiction. This is why the opera is discordant for a contemporary observer. We want to root for love, and we are confused at the end of the opera when we consider all that has happened to allow these two lovers to finally come together (not to mention our confusion if we know that the historical version of the tale ends with Poppea's death at Nerone's hand!). This is a classic case of incommensurability (although I realize that my parsing of it is itself a paradox, since the truly incommensurable would be untranslatable in this text; see Davidson [1973–1974]). It bears on our understanding of morality and economy. For us, love—true love, real love—is good; its ends are just; it is a moral force. For Monteverdi's Seneca, if not for Monteverdi himself, love is passion that gets in the way of what's really important, the true virtues. Similarly, for us, at least most of us anthropologists and many others who have lived through the world historic rise and dominance of that system we call capitalism, economy tends to be without morals, knowing only the law of supply and demand and leaving all values besides monetary value in the dust. It is because we tend to presume that the economy is amoral (the more positive reading) or immoral (the more critical one; either immoral because it is amoral, or immoral in actuality, the economist's pretence of its amorality itself is an ideological justification for it) that we find something compelling about the conjunction of "morality" and "economy," as Browne discusses in her introduction. Hence, "socially responsible" investment—or manufacturing or export agriculture or whatever—takes special salience because it is presumed that the unmarked, "normal" investment or manufacturing or agricultural production is *not* socially responsible. The idea of the moral here serves as a critique, and as an alternative to the dominant formation—both for analysts like anthropologists and for everyone else.

This brings me to my second major point, about the dichotomy presumed between economy and morality. Julia Elyachar (2005) reminds us that Adam Smith's conception of the invisible hand was his solution to a very specific problem of moral philosophy, namely, the problem of reconciling inequalities of wealth with a divinely ordained world in which God gave everything to everyone in common. Browne's introduction to this volume reminds us that the dichotomy between morality and economy has a historical provenience and that its current manifestations are contingent and arbitrary. Yet the discovery of a morality behind the economy, or of moral critiques to the economy, or of alternative "moral economies," all continue to fascinate and surprise. Why is this so? It may be because these articulations of morality to economy bring us up against the limits of that arbitrariness, and specifically, the arbitrary nature of value and values in a postfoundationalist world, a world no longer subtended by one universal standard of value, whether Godly or monetary. The lack of universal standards compels moral or ethical stances—themselves revisable, tentative, and often "for now" rather than forever—toward the pragmatic resolution of specific problems of value. And those stances reflexively loop around to catch those who seek to analyze them, who are often left with a moral critique of moral regimes of value. This may be an increasingly common condition of knowledge, or, at least, a condition some scholars are increasingly contending (if not always exactly comfortable) with.

By way of example, allow me briefly to relate an example of the moral/economic nexus from my own recent research on efforts to regulate offshore financial services in the Caribbean. These efforts were articulated in explicitly moral terms, and the techniques developed to attempt to curtail offshore finance were forms of ethical practice, ranging from "soft law" standards, agreements, and nonbinding commitments, to due diligence procedures for evaluating the "quality" of people and corporations seeking to place their money offshore (Maurer 2005b). Their formation does not fit the standard tale about the role of markets and economic principles in the so-called neoliberal moment, and their effects were unexpected. At the end of the day, these efforts appear to have had no impact on the amount of money held offshore (Vlcek 2006). They did, however, propel a whole new set of discourses about offshore finance and tax competition, as well as new networks of "trust and estate practitioners"—newly constituted as such—that linked them up with anthropologists and others studying efforts to "morally" regulate offshore finance (see Sharman and Rawlings [2005]), whose commentaries became part of the phenomenon they were studying.

In the late 1990s, international standard-setting bodies, multilateral institutions and nongovernmental organizations (NGOs) began to worry that, in a world of the free movement of money, governments would lose tax revenue to those states that competitively lowered their rates to attract foreign investment. "Tax competition," it was feared, would erode the ability of states to provide needed social services to their citizens. Although market promoters around the world had been extolling the virtues of liberalization, even those institutions most associated with the promulgation of neoliberal reforms like the World Bank and the Organization for Economic Cooperation and Development (OECD) began to express alarm about the effect of those reforms on revenue collection as well as financial crime and money laundering interdiction. The OECD and the World Bank adopted the moral argument that unfettered capitalism and, in particular, a market in sovereignties that allows wealthy people to shop for the lowest-tax jurisdiction causes harm and must be curtailed. Indeed, tax competition was labeled "*harmful* tax competition," yoking a medical metaphor of harm reduction to a core feature of capitalist economy to create a new moral valence for offshore finance.

The OECD (OECD [1998]), the Financial Action Task Force of the G7 (e.g., FATF 2001), the Financial Stability Forum (FSF) and NGOs like Oxfam sought to "name and shame" tax havens like the British Virgin Islands (my fieldsite) into compliance with international financial norms.[3] In the process, they created those norms, but not as they might have pleased. The impetus behind the actions of each was slightly different. For the OECD, the issue was tax competition. For the FATF, the issue was money laundering. For the FSF, the issue was stability in the wake of the Asian financial crisis. Countries on the receiving end of these efforts experienced them as of a piece, however. And nearly all countries initially named on so-called blacklists of noncompliant or noncooperating jurisdictions—including almost all of the world's tax havens—complied, often rather quickly. In some cases, compliance came even before the blacklists were issued, preempting international "shaming" through "advance commitments."

Tax competition itself is a product of an imagined future inspired by economic theory (Webb 2004: 795), and thus a fine example of the way economic theory performs, rather than describes or predicts, the economy (after Callon [1998: 22]). Rather than describing an actually existing condition whereby the lowering of tax rates in one jurisdiction in fact spurs a race to the bottom in revenue regimes elsewhere, tax competition is the logical, not empirically observable, outcome of a particular economic theory.[4] In calling for an end to tax competition, NGOs like Oxfam (2000) argued that tax competition saps revenue from poor countries when their wealthy elites squirrel their money offshore. That phenomenon, however, is not necessarily linked to tax *competition*, a process of competitive lowering of rates internationally, so much as the mere presence of lower-tax jurisdictions. It would occur regardless of whether the race to the bottom predicted by economic theory took place. That "tax competition" names a phenomenon of dubious ontological status makes the debate about it an interesting object for anthropological investigation—like Evans-Pritchard's (1937) ensorcelled granaries, or the divine—as well as an object that intertwines the moral and the economic in a tangled web of discourses, relationships, and practices.

I will not go into the specifics of the harmful tax competition initiative (but see Maurer [2005b]; Rawlings [2005]; Sharman [2006]). But if we understand neoliberalism to be the "infiltration of market-driven truths and calculations into the domain of politics" (Ong 2006: 4), and we consider the OECD, World Bank, IMF, and other such bodies as the agents of neoliberalism, as most anthropologists and left critics do, we have no way to grasp it. Neoliberal institutions have been understood as eroding the sovereignty of the state, at least in its fiscal functions, and structural adjustment programs have generally entailed the lowering of tax rates and customs duties in favor of market mechanisms for generating revenue. The very idea of curbing harmful tax competition, however, depended on a vision of the maintenance of the fiscal state's integrity, not its evaporation. Furthermore, the initiative was trying to promote a *nonmarket*-based system of payments in the form of revenue collection (and the nonmarket nature of state revenue collection is what often makes neoliberals seek to curtail it). The initiative was also trying to preclude or close off the formation of a market in sovereignty (see Palan [2003]). Yet it did so in terms of the logical extension of a theory about that market in sovereignty and then articulated that theory to a moral discourse of harm reduction. One analytical lesson, then, is that evidence of the infiltration of market logic does not always guarantee "marketization" as an outcome. There are other things going on besides markets, calculation, equivalence, and so on, *even when—indeed, I would argue, especially when*—we *see* markets, calculation, equivalence going on.

We often focus on presumed ends of things, however: here, that the extension of the market must result in certain foreordained outcomes, ones we are all too familiar with, ones that pose continual dilemmas for our scholarship and our actions as moral agents. I am arguing, however, that this focus on the ends disables that key insight of Weber (1992 [1930]) about unintended consequences. If we are hoping for a different world, then that different world in the future will contain different versions of the "ourselves" who are currently imagining that future. We will not, should not, be the "same" in that unpredictable future as we are now (Wiegman 2000). What is needed, instead, is an openness to the possibilities without any necessarily predictive attitude toward them, a hope in the means, as Hirokazu Miyazaki puts it (2005), that allows us to "keep trying" as Foster did, without foreclosing any of the analytical, political, or moral/economic possibilities that such hope affords us.

Every apparently capitalist formation seems to generate its own accompanying forms of the gift. The continual rediscovery of the gift often becomes an end in itself, as if to say, capitalism is not total, or there are still alternatives: that we are still optimistic, and we intend to keep trying, whether to forge new imaginings and instantiations of morality/economy or merely to call them forth in the act of critically documenting them. This is our hope for anthropology, of course: that it will offer something beneficial, that it will do something (good) in the world. Recognizing that we cannot know the ends of our work in advance, however, may be the only moral approach to the unrealized possibilities that lie within our own gifts of life, love, and hope.

NOTES

Acknowledgments. I would like to thank Kate Browne and Lynne Milgram for inviting me to contribute this afterword, the authors of the chapters for writing such inspiring pieces, and an anonymous review for an important reference. I would also like to thank Jane and George Collier, for introducing me to Poppea, as well as Tom Boellstorff and Susan Greenhalgh, for their support and comments. Research on Caribbean offshore financial services and the OECD initiative has been supported by the National Science Foundation (SES-0516861). Any opinions, findings, and conclusions or recommendations expressed in this chapter are those of the author and do not necessarily reflect the views of the National Science Foundation.

1. On the invention of the very idea of "the economy" as a separate domain see Mitchell (2002) and Poovey (1998).

2. I have greatly benefited from the interpretations of *Poppea* offered in Carter (1997), Fenlon and Miller (1992), Lewis (2005), Rosand (1985).

3. Although not all of the jurisdictions targeted by these efforts are politically independent nation-states (many are dependent territories, like the British Virgin Islands), I will use the term *country* here for convenience. And although the term *tax haven* is a highly charged one for those counties so labeled, I will employ it here in place of more convoluted locutions (like "countries or territories deemed not in compliance with the FATF's 40 recommendations" or some such), also for convenience. See Sharman (2006).

4. Webb (2004) makes the most sustained argument that the OECD's harmful tax competition initiative was based on and shaped by norms rather than actual revenue crises or rational policy decisions independent of the predictions of liberal economic theory. On the question of whether competition among states to attract investment leads to a taxation race to the bottom, the evidence is contradictory at best. As Webb (2004: 788) puts it, "governments certainly behave as if tax competition has increased," but the empirical evidence does not always support the contention (see Webb [2004]; Weiss [1999]).

REFERENCES

Althusser, Louis. 1974. *Essays on Ideology*. London: Verso.

Bloch, Maurice, and Jonathan Parry. 1989. Introduction: Money and the Morality of Exchange. In *Money and the Morality of Exchange*, ed. J. Parry and M. Bloch, 1–32. Cambridge: Cambridge University Press.

Bragdon, Joseph. 2006. *Profit for Life: How Capitalism Excels*. Cambridge, MA: Society for Organizational Learning.

Callon, Michel. 1998. The Embeddedness of Economic Markets in Economics. In *The Laws of the Markets*, ed. M. Callon, 1–57. Oxford: Blackwell.

Carter, Tim. 1997. Re-Reading *Poppea*: Some Thoughts on Music and Meaning in Monteverdi's Last Opera. *Journal of the Royal Musical Association* 122(2): 173–204.

Comaroff, Jean, and John Comaroff. 1999. Occult Economies and the Violence of Abstraction: Notes from the South African Postcolony. *American Ethnologist* 26(2): 279–303.

Curtis, Alan, ed. 1989. *Claudio Monteverdi: L'incoronazione de Poppea*. London: Novello and Co., Ltd.

Davidson, Donald. 1973–1974. On the Very Idea of a Conceptual Scheme. *Proceedings and Addresses of the American Philosophical Association* 47: 5–20.

Elyachar, Julia. 2005. *Markets of Dispossession: NGOs, Economic Development, and the State in Cairo*. Durham, NC: Duke University Press.

Evans-Pritchard, E. E. 1937. *Witchcraft, Oracles and Magic among the Azande*. Oxford: Oxford University Press.

FATF (Financial Action Task Force). 2001. *Financial Action Task Force Annual Report on Money Laundering, 2000–2001*. Paris: FATF Secretariat.

Fenlon, Iain, and Peter N. Miller. 1992. *The Song of the Soul: Understanding Poppea.* London: Royal Musical Association.

Foster, George. 1965. Peasant Society and the Image of Limited Good. *American Anthropologist* 67: 293–315.

——. 1966. Foster's Reply to Kaplan, Saler, and Bennett. *American Anthropologist* 68: 210–14.

Geertz, Clifford. 1973. *The Interpretation of Cultures.* New York: Basic Books.

Gibson-Graham, J. K. 2006. *A Post-Capitalist Politics.* Minneapolis: University of Minnesota Press.

Haraway, Donna. 1997. *Modest Witness@Second Millenium. FemaleMan Meets OncoMouse: Feminism and Technoscience.* New York: Routledge.

Harvey, David. 2003. *The New Imperialism.* Oxford: Oxford University Press.

Kaplan, David, and Benson Saler. 1966. Foster's Image of Limited Good: An Example of Anthropological Explanation. *American Anthropologist* 68(1): 202–6.

Lewis, Rachel A. 2005. Love as Persuasion in Monteverdi's 'L'incoronazione di Poppea': New Thoughts on the Authorship Question. *Music and Letters* 86(1): 16–41.

LiPuma, Edward, and Ben Lee. 2004. *Financial Derivatives and the Globalization of Risk.* Durham, NC: Duke University Press.

Marx, Karl. 1977. *Capital.* New York: Vintage Books.

Maurer, Bill 2005a. "Does Money Matter? Abstraction and Substitution in Alternative Financial Forms." In *Materiality*, ed. Daniel Miller, 140–63. Durham, NC: Duke University Press.

——. 2005b. Due Diligence and "Reasonable Man," Offshore. *Cultural Anthropology* 20(4): 474–505.

——. 2006. The Anthropology of Money. *Annual Reviews in Anthropology* 35(2): 15–36.

McCloskey, Deirdre. 2006. *The Bourgeois Virtues: Ethics for an Age of Commerce.* Chicago: University of Chicago Press.

Mitchell, Timothy. 2002. *Rule of Experts: Egypt, Techno-politics, Modernity.* Berkeley: University of California Press.

Miyazaki, Hirokazu. 2005. From Sugar Cane to "Swords": Hope and the Extensibility of the Gift in Fiji. *Journal of the Royal Anthropological Institute* (n.s.) 11: 277–95.

OECD (Organization for Economic Cooperation and Development). 1998. *Harmful Tax Competition: An Emerging Global Issue.* Paris: OECD.

Ong, Aihwa. 2006. *Neoliberalism as Exception: Mutations in Citizenship and Sovereignty.* Durham, NC: Duke University Press.

Oxfam. 2000. *Tax Havens: Releasing the Hidden Billions for Poverty Eradication.* London: Oxfam.

Palan, Ronen. 2003. *The Offshore World: Sovereign Markets, Virtual Places and Nomad Millionaires.* Ithaca, NY: Cornell University Press.

Poovey, Mary. 1998. *A History of the Modern Fact.* Chicago: University of Chicago Press.

Rawlings Gregory. 2005. Mobile People, Mobile Capital and Tax Neutrality: Sustaining a Market for Offshore Finance Centers. *Accounting Forum* 29: 289–310.

Roelvink, Gerda. 2007. Review Article: Performing the Market. *Social Identities* 13(1): 125–33.

Rosand, Ellen. 1985. Seneca and the Interpretation of *L'incoronazione di Poppea. American Musicological Society Journal* 38(1): 34–71.

Scott, James. 1977. *The Moral Economy of the Peasant*. New Haven, CT: Yale University Press.
Sharman, Jason. 2006. *Havens in a Storm: The Struggle for Global Tax Regulation*. Ithaca, NY: Cornell University Press.
Sharman, Jason, and Gregory Rawlings. 2005. *Deconstructing National Tax Blacklists: Removing Obstacles to Cross-Border Trade in Financial Services*. London: Society of Trust and Estate Practitioners.
Taussig, Michael. 1980. *The Devil and Commodity Fetishism in South America*. Chapel Hill, NC: University North Carolina Press.
Thrift, Nigel. 2000. Afterwords: Environment and Planning D: *Society and Space* 18(3): 213–55.
Tsing Anna. 2000. Inside the Economy of Appearances. *Public Culture* 12(1): 115–44.
Vlcek, William. 2006. "Offshore Finance, Harmful Tax Competition, and Global Capital Flows." Ms., cited with the author's permission.
Webb, Michael C. 2004. Defining the Boundaries of Legitimate State Practice: Norms, Transnational Actors and the OECD's Project on Harmful Tax Competition. *Review of International Political Economy* 11(4): 787–827.
Weber, Max. 1992 [1930]. *The Protestant Ethic and the Spirit of Capitalism*. Trans. Talcott Parsons. London: Routledge.
Weiss, Linda. 1999. Globalization and National Governance: Antinomy or Interdependence? *Review of International Studies* 25: 59–88.
Wiegman, Robyn. 2000. Feminism's Apocalyptic Futures. *New Literary History* 31(4): 805–25.
Young, Stephen. 2003. *Moral Capitalism: Reconciling Private Interest with the Public Good*. San Francisco, CA: Berrett-Koehler Publishers.
Zizek, Slavoj. 1989. *The Sublime Object of Ideology*. London: Verso.

Index

About the Contributors

Katherine E. Browne is professor of anthropology at Colorado State University. Her long-term ethnographic research in French Afro-Caribbean societies and more recent work in post-Katrina New Orleans has focused on culture, economics, gender, and morality. She is author of *Creole Economics: Caribbean Cunning under the French Flag* (2004) and has produced two ethnographic films in partnership with filmmaker Ginny Martin. The first, *Au Tournant de l'Histoire (Lifting the Weight of History)*, based on research with female entrepreneurs in Martinique, was broadcast internationally on French TV in summer 2008. The second, *Still Waiting: Life after Katrina* aired on PBS stations in the United States in 2007 and 2008. Browne's research and film work is funded in large part by National Science Foundation.

Catherine Dolan teaches in the Culture, Marketing and Society Programme, Said Business School, University of Oxford. She is concerned with the social and development dimensions of global commodity chains, with an emphasis on how global consumption practices affect gender and labor processes in East Africa. Her research has been published in a range of journals including *Journal of Development Studies* (2000), *World Development* (2003), *Rural Sociology* (2004), *Environment and Planning A* (2004), *Journal of Consumer Culture* (2005), *Ethnos* (2007), *Globalizations* (2008), *Development and Change* (2008) and in a recent coedited volume, *Ethical Sourcing in the Global Food Chain* (2006) (with S. Barrientos). She is presently examining the linkages between the trade of manufactured cosmetics, poverty reduction, and gender empowerment in South Africa.

Christina Garsten is professor and chair in the Department of Social Anthropology, Stockholm University; and research director at Score, Stockholm University and Stockholm School of Economics. Her research interests lie in the anthropology of organizations and markets, with a current focus on new forms of regulation and accountability in the labor market and in transnational trade. Her particular research concentrations are the varieties of cultural articulation at the interface of market and community, organization, and sociality. She has published in the areas of organizational culture, the flexibilization of employment, and corporate social responsibility. Her most recent books are *Workplace Vagabonds: Career and Community in Changing Worlds of Work* (2008) and *Transparency in a New Global Order: Unveiling Organizational Visions* (coedited with M. L. de Montoya 2008).

Rhoda Halperin is professor emerita in the Department of Anthropology, University of Cincinnati. In 2004 she became professor of anthropology at Montclair State University. Her recent publications include: *Whose School Is It? Women, Children, Memory and Practice in the City* (2006); "Introduction: Youth Engage the City and Global Culture" (*City and Society* 19, no. 2, 2008); and in process: *Istanbul: Orhan Pamuk as Urban Anthropologist.* She is currently working on a set of essays entitled, *Reflections on Fieldwork in the City.*

Tor Hernes is professor of organization studies at the Copenhagen Business School and previously was professor and head of the Department of Innovation and Economic Organization at the Norwegian School of Management, Oslo. His research applies forms of process perspectives to the study of organizations. This work is published in the following books: *Managing Boundaries in Organizations* (coedited with N. Paulsen [2003]); *The Spatial Construction of Organization: Autopoietic Organization Theory* (coedited with T. Bakken [2004]); *Actor-Network Theory and Organizing* (coedited with B. Czarniawska-Joerges [2005]); and *Understanding Organization as Process: Theory for a Tangled World* (2007).

Walter E. Little is a sociocultural anthropologist whose research on Guatemalan Mayas has focused on the interrelationships among political economy, cultural identity, and language. He is the author of *Mayas in the Marketplace: Tourism, Globalization, and Cultural Identity* (2004) and coauthor of *La ütz awäch? Introduction to the Kaqchikel Maya Language* (with R. McKenna Brown and J. M. Maxwell [2006]). He has published in *American Ethnologist, Ethnology, Latin American Perspectives, Research in Economic Anthropology* and *Signs*. He is an associate professor at the University at Albany, SUNY.

Bill Maurer is professor and chair of the Department of Anthropology at University of California–Irvine. His research spans the anthropology of law, finance, and money, and he has published widely on offshore finance in the Caribbean, alternatives to financial globalization, and Islamic banking and mortgage financing. He is the author and editor of several books, including *Recharting the Caribbean: Land, Law and Citizenship in the British Virgin Islands* (1997); *Pious Property: Islamic Mortgages in the United States* (2006); and *Mutual Life Limited: Islamic Banking, Alternative Currencies, Lateral Reason* (2005). The latter received the Victor Turner Prize in 2005.

B. Lynne Milgram is professor of anthropology, Faculty of Liberal Studies at the Ontario College of Art & Design. Her research on gender and development in the Philippines analyzes the cultural politics of social change with regard to fair trade, microfinance, and women's work in crafts, street vending, and the secondhand clothing trade. This research is published in edited volumes and in journals including *Human Organization* (2001), *Anthropologica* (2004), *Asian Studies Review* (2005), and *Urban Anthropology* (2005, 2008). She has coedited (with K. Grimes) *Artisans and Cooperatives: Developing Alternative Trade for the Global Economy* (2000) and (with R. Hamilton) *Material Choices: Refashioning Bast and Leaf Fibers in Asia and the Pacific* (2007).

Aaron Z. Pitluck is an assistant professor in the Department of Sociology and Anthropology at Illinois State University. His fields of expertise include Economic Sociology, Development Studies, and Southeast Asian Studies. He is currently working on two projects: (1) an ethnographic comparison of professional investor behavior in the U.S. and Malaysian stock exchanges and (2) a series of articles on the sociological foundations of financial markets.

Rebecca Prentice teaches social anthropology at the University of Sussex in Brighton, England. Her doctoral research examined informal and illicit labor among Trinidadian garment workers within a context of trade liberalization and industry collapse. She has taught social anthropology and gender studies at the University of Sussex, the Brighton and Sussex Medical School, and the University of the West Indies (St. Augustine).

Dinah Rajak is a lecturer in anthropology at the University of Sussex, UK. Her doctoral research examined discourses of corporate social responsibility (CSR) and ethics in a transnational mining company, and the role of multinational enterprise as a vehicle of development. Her wider interests lie in the anthropology of development policy making and practice. Some of her publications include (with R. L. Stirrat) *Parochial Cosmopolitanism and the Power of Nostalgia* (2007) and "The Romance of the Field" in H. L. Seniveratne (ed.) *The Anthropologist and the Native* (2007).

Joel Robbins is professor and chair of the Anthropology Department at the University of California, San Diego. His work has focused on cultural change, the anthropology of Christianity, morality, and the anthropology of exchange. He is author of *Becoming Sinners: Christianity and Moral Torment in a Papua New Guinea Society* (2004). He is also coeditor of the book *Money and Modernity: State and Local Currencies in Contemporary Melanesia* (with D. Akin, 1999) and of the journal *Anthropological Theory*.

Andrew Walsh is an assistant professor of anthropology at the University of Western Ontario. Articles emanating from research concerning northern Madagascar's sapphire and ecotourist trades can be found in recent issues of *Journal of the Royal Anthropological Institute* 8 (2002), *American Ethnologist* 30 (2003), *American Anthropologist* 106 and 107 (2004, 2005); and *Anthropology Today* 22 (2006).

Cynthia Werner is an associate professor of anthropology at Texas A&M University. Most of her ethnographic research has been conducted in Kazakhstan. Her publications examine gift exchange, bride kidnapping, small-scale merchants, and international tourism development including *Human Organization* (2000) and *Ethnology* (2003). She coedited (with D. Bell), *Values and Valuables: From the Sacred to the Symbolic* (2004). In recent years, she has been doing research on the politics of risk after decades of nuclear testing in northern Kazakhstan (*Central Asian Survey* 2006; *Risk Analysis* 2007). Due to her expertise on radiation and risk perception, she was hired as a consultant for the Texas Commission on Environmental Quality to evaluate the socioeconomic portion of a license application for a low-level radioactive waste disposal facility in west Texas.

www.ingramcontent.com/pod-product-compliance
Ingram Content Group UK Ltd.
Pitfield, Milton Keynes, MK11 3LW, UK
UKHW021909150926
475560UK00003B/271

9 780759 112018